FOOLING AMERICA

How Washington Insiders Twist the Truth
and Manufacture the Conventional Wisdom

Robert Parry

WILLIAM MORROW AND COMPANY, INC.
New York

Library of Congress Cataloging-in-Publication Data

Parry, Robert.
    Fooling America: how Washington insiders twist the truth and manufacture the conventional wisdom.
        p.   cm.
    ISBN 0-688-10927-6
    1. Public opinion—United States.   2. Elite (Social sciences)—United States.
    3. Political leadership—United States   4. Press and propaganda—United States
    I. Title.
    HN90.P8P37   1992
    303.3'75—dc20   91-36496
                                                                                CIP

Printed in the United States of America

First Edition

1   2   3   4   5   6   7   8   9   10

BOOK DESIGN BY LISA STOKES

In memory of my mother

Dedicated to my father; to my four great children: Samuel, Nathaniel, Elizabeth and Jeffrey; and to my gorgeous wife, Diane

Contents

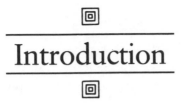

Introduction

Each New Year's Day, Washingtonians, many still recovering from the previous night's revelries, stumble out their front doors to retrieve the year's first copy of *The Washington Post*. Unlike most days, when busy professionals peruse the world and national news over a quick cup of coffee, the slower pace of the holiday leads many readers to turn first to the *Post*'s bright and sassy, appropriately named "Style" section. There, dominating the front page, is an annual feature entitled simply "The List."

The List is a clever rendering of what will be "in and out" for the new year, which makes it "must" reading for the government-connected residents of the nation's most conformist city. The List covers a wide range of personalities and events, from the frothiest of pop art to weighty matters of war and peace.

For 1992, for instance, "chaos" was in; "order" was out. The Moscow Circus in; the Soviet Union, most definitely, out. "A good insult" was in, while well-meaning "political correctness" was out.

In rock 'n' roll, Nirvana was in; Guns N' Roses out. Among offbeat fictional families, the ghostly Addams Family was in; the Simpsons out. For dead media magnates, Robert Maxwell (whose mysterious death at sea sent a tidal wave of financial scandal through London and New York) was in, but Malcolm Forbes (whose death was far less controversial) was out. In the age of AIDS, autoeroticism had made it among the ins, but car sex, a very different concept, was parked among the outs.

Among oddly named "pirates," Long Dong Silver (the porno star made famous by the Supreme Court confirmation of Clarence

Thomas) was in, while Hook (Peter Pan's famous rival) was out. In another reference to the Thomas hearings and their raucous allegations of sexual harassment, Alan Simpson (the senator) and Nina Tottenberg (the National Public Radio reporter) were both dumped among the outs. The pair argued loudly and publicly after Simpson, a Thomas defender, tongue-lashed Tottenberg for divulging the sex harassment affidavit of Thomas's former assistant, Anita Hill. On the "in" side of the ledger, balancing out outcasts Simpson and Tottenberg, was a classic TV couple, Ralph and Alice Kramden, "The Honeymooners," known for their high-volume bickering.

Recognizing 1992 as a presidential election year, The List could not ignore politics. But teammates, Vice-President Dan Quayle and President George Bush, ended up in opposite columns. Quayle, presumably because he would be the subject of a flattering week-long series in the *Post*, was an in; Bush, whose lofty polls from the Persian Gulf War had sunk into a deep recession, was an out. But an even worse insult was in store for a well-known Democrat who announced that he would not run for president. Mario Cuomo, the New York governor, was shoved onto the out list to make room for Perry Como, the crooner, among the ins.

Two hot topics from the Kennedy clan won The List's attention, too. Washington's ambivalence toward the innocent verdict in the rape trial of William Kennedy Smith plunked "Willie Smith" into both columns, as an in and an out. Court TV, which broadcast the trial proceedings endlessly, was gaveled onto the in category, while the music video channel, MTV, got rapped and rocked among the outs. Even Au Bar, where Smith met the woman in question, was an in, but "au pairs," live-in baby-sitters for yuppies, were on the outs.

The List also registered official Washington's sputtering rage over Oliver Stone's movie *JFK,* which postulated that the capital's military-intelligence establishment had a hand in John F. Kennedy's assassination. The List judged that the "trashing of Kevin Costner," who played *JFK* conspiracy prosecutor Jim Garrison, was now in, while the "trashing of Warren Beatty," who played gangster Bugsy Siegel in the critically acclaimed movie *Bugsy,* was now out. But even despised conspiracy theories ranked higher than tending the grass: Dallas's famous "grassy knoll," where Garrison believed a second gunman lurked, rose onto the in column, while "Chem-Lawn" sank down roots among the outs.

While in many cities a pretentious feature like The List might deserve no more than a chuckle or an annoyed look before a reader heads on to the sports or local news, in Washington it is a fitting start to the new year. After all, for the next twelve months, charting who's in and who's out, what's up and what's down, will be a primary occupation for the TV pundits, political consultants, the major newspapers, the newsmagazines and the cocktail-party set.

Amid the careerism and conformity of the 1980's and early 1990's, this preoccupation with power status, always an annoyance in Washington, had come to be an end in itself. Ideas, principles, history took a back seat. What counted was knowing what was in and what was out, who was hot and who was not. Lucrative careers were built by otherwise undistinguished thinkers who landed spots on television punditry shows where they got to expound on their "insider" insights. The compilation of these pedestrian thoughts, these thumbs up and thumbs down, these ranking of issues on scales of one to ten, came to be known as "the conventional wisdom," or CW for short.

But the conventional wisdom had another role as well. After all, the flip side of the Washington passion for insiderdom was a deathly fear of slipping outside the framework of the city's acceptable debate, and landing among the outs. In that broader sense, the CW came to define the boundaries of permissible thinking within the journalistic and government communities of Washington. The CW was what everybody simply knew to be true. It was the enforcement mechanism for the city's passion for conformity.

A politician or a journalist who ventured too far past the CW borders might quickly find himself marginalized by Washington political society. Not only would he not get a plum seat on a weekend talk show or prominent place on a big paper's op-ed page, he would find himself ridiculed as an outsider, a maverick—and nothing in Washington is worse than that.

Sadly, for the United States, this rise of the trivial conventional wisdom came at a crossroads moment in American history. Ronald Reagan, a politician affably detached from reality, had come to power just as foreign economic challengers were mounting an assault on the American business supremacy that had reigned since World War II. Since the conventional wisdom dutifully follows the power of the moment, it offered the country no protection from the costly flights of fancy that soared to remarkable heights during the Reagan years.

Guided by the CW's judgment on what is news, the Washington press corps managed to miss nearly every major scandal of the 1980's—and the American people will be paying for many of those oversights for decades. "Every taxpayer deserves an answer to the question," declared former *Wall Street Journal* reporter Ellen Hume, "Why did the well-paid, well-educated and constitutionally protected press corps miss the savings and loan scandal, which is the most expensive public finance debacle in U.S. history?"[1] Among her possible answers, she noted that "serious investigative journalism has fallen on hard times. It is considered too wasteful for today's bottom-line oriented journalism corporation managers."

But Hume, now executive director of Harvard University's Shorenstein Barone Center on the Press, Politics and Public Policy, saw the broader problem as Washington's social/political circles. "The press has become more the keeper of the status quo than the challenger from outside, partly because reporters tend to be much better paid than they used to be, and they hobnob with the policy makers they're allegedly monitoring," she noted. "Our inability to unravel and explain the importance of the Iran-contra abuses, the Housing and Urban Development influence-buying schemes and the savings and loan excesses is a scandal in itself."

Polite Washington, for instance, had long snubbed the nasty rumors floating around an unsavory Middle Eastern bank, the Bank of Credit and Commerce International. After all, the bank's Washington affiliate, First American Bank Shares, was represented by many of the city's most respected and best-heeled figures. The legendary Democratic wise man Clark Clifford was the bank's chairman. New Age power broker Robert Altman, chum to potent Republicans and media bigwigs, was president. And the bipartisanly powerful Hill and Knowlton public-relations firm burnished the bank's image.

As William von Raab, former Customs director, told a Senate investigating panel, an earlier federal probe into BCCI had simply disappeared into a "bad plea-bargain" on the bank's role in laundering drug money. After that, von Raab witnessed a "general softening of resolve on the part of senior U.S. officials," which he blamed on the "incredible pounding" from seasoned Washington "influence peddlers," like Clifford and Altman. The "general softening" was helped along, von Raab said, by Hill and Knowlton's potent public-relations team.

"There wasn't a single influence peddler who wasn't being used to work this case," the conservative von Raab complained. "The result is that senior U.S. policy-level officials were constantly under the impression that BCCI was probably not that bad, because all these good guys that they play golf with all the time were representing them."[2]

Von Raab, who left as Customs commissioner in 1989, had never made it as a CW insider. Among the in-the-know journalists at *Newsweek*, where I worked, he was privately scoffed at as a "wild man" or a "loose cannon," not compliments at the dinner parties of Washington. Long before he left office, von Raab had been marginalized as someone who was marching to a different drummer.

On the other side, through their endless A Lists of connections, Clifford and Altman had placed an invisible shield around the BCCI scam. The occasional public allegation or private suspicion harmlessly bounced off and stayed safely outside the CW in Washington. Clifford schmoozed and soothed inquiring Democrats, while Altman feted Republicans and his press pals at lavish parties.

In September 1990, Altman and his wife Lynda Carter, TV's Wonder Woman, hosted the surprise forty-fifth birthday party for President Bush's economic adviser Michael Boskin. As Boskin walked through the grand entranceway of Altman's luxurious home in Potomac, Maryland, he was greeted by his friends and associates all wearing Groucho Marx nose-and-glasses masks. The gag was to mimic Boskin's facial appearance: his prominent nose, moustache and plastic-frame glasses. As white-gloved waiters served hors d'oeuvres and drinks, the celebrants chuckled and chatted. Besides guest-of-honor Boskin and the host Altmans, the luminaries included Cabinet secretaries Clayton Yeutter, Jack Kemp and Samuel Skinner; White House chief of staff John Sununu; Senators John Heinz and Robert Kasten; and *Wall Street Journal* bureau chief and *Capital Gang* pundit Al Hunt,* with his wife, *MacNeil/Lehrer*'s Judy Woodruff.[3]

Only when the BCCI scandal came crashing down in July 1991

---

*In an interview, Hunt agreed that too much socializing between the press and government officials was "a constant danger" in Washington journalism. But he said his social acquaintance with Boskin and Altman had not influenced the *Journal*'s news coverage. "No one's been tougher on the Boskin-Altman link than the *Wall Street Journal*," Hunt told me. "If you can't socialize with politicians and still kick the shit out of them, you shouldn't socialize with them."

did the Bush Justice Department energize its long-dormant criminal investigation of the bank and the press suddenly discover a hot story. In the meantime, both Clifford and Altman, who insisted they had been ignorant of BCCI's secret control of First American, had made millions for their efforts. But one could argue that for the Middle East operators behind BCCI, who made billions, the purchase of Clifford's and Altman's respectability—and the CW that had come with it—had been a bargain.

The conventional wisdom is established in as many ways as Washington works. It can emerge from polite conversation over delicately appointed dinner parties or from the all-business talk of salad-and-mineral-water lunches. Because of the continuing importance of New York financial and media circles, phone calls, faxes and shuttle flights between the two East Coast power cities further influence this shaping of acceptable thought.

The CW is the collective judgment of that community of insiders—what the Washington–New York elites in government, journalism, academia and business think or at least say they think is true about any number of hot topics. The CW is neither Republican nor Democrat, neither liberal nor conservative; rather, it enforces the dominant Washington attitudes of the moment. It anoints some stolid politicians as substantial and thoughtful, while others with fresh or unusual ideas are dismissed as light and flaky. No points for courage or foresight. To stake out an unpopular position, even one that is later proven to be right, marks a politician as an oddball or gadfly, not a statesman.

For good reason, this insular Washington thinking has gone a long way toward alienating the broader American public, which feels excluded by the capital's vacuous debate. A 1991 report sponsored by the Kettering Foundation concluded that many citizens "feel locked out" of the Washington political process; they sense that their democratic institutions have been the target of a "hostile takeover."

"In the end, citizens believe that they do not—cannot—have a say in this system," the Kettering study said. It cited a public disgusted with negative political campaigns and with the tight connections between politicians and monied interests. "Americans . . . believe that public officials are out of touch with citizens and their concerns." The citizens, interviewed in ten cities across the country, attacked the news media for joining this elite political class. News coverage of political campaigns, the citizens complained, was obsessed with triviality, negativism and a lack of comprehensible explanations of the nation's choices.[4]

As this government/business/media political class has grown in power, its collective judgment—the CW—has turned into a Washington version of "politically correct" thinking. "Politically correct," known by the initials PC, is a derisive term applied by many in the Washington power circles to attempts by colleges to indoctrinate students against race or sex bias. A hot topic of the early 1990's, PC became a scourge for editorial writers and columnists who recoiled at the notion of "thought control" on campus. But just as the PC tries to smother "antisocial" attitudes among students, so does the CW restrict the range of free expression in Washington, by creating subtle and not-so-subtle taboos against unapproved points of view.

In journalism these days, CW-challenging stories rarely get written at all. Washington editors, who absorb the CW from both the executive level above and the cocktail-party circuit all around, blue-pencil many entries off the story list because they clash with what-everybody-knows-to-be-true. This mind set helps explain why in the mid-1980's so few of the thousands of crack Washington journalists picked up on the workings of an obscure Marine lieutenant colonel, named Oliver North, in the White House basement. North and his activities were not unknown, but the CW just didn't take the story seriously.

A positive CW can protect a favored politician, even to the point that he won't be asked tough quesitons. In August 1990, after Iraqi dictator Saddam Hussein's army invaded Kuwait, questions were in order about the White House bungling that had flashed to Saddam what he regarded as a green light. Instead, the CW quickly acclaimed President Bush's brilliance for organizing international condemnation of the invasion. Bush was thus spared any grilling about his policies that may have paved the way to the crisis.

"It's difficult to play devil's advocate, especially against such a popular president as George Bush," said *ABC News*'s feisty Sam Donaldson, explaining but not forgiving. "I was surprised and dismayed by the jingoistic tone of some of my colleagues. . . . I don't think the media have been as skeptical as they could be."[5]

As modern-day political image-masters came to understand the power of the CW, they devoted greater and greater resources to molding and shaping it. In campaigns, that can be called "raising your opponent's negatives." On day-to-day issues, particularly foreign policy disputes, the goal has been to depict a critic as irresponsible, disloyal or simply laughable.

When President Reagan and his advertising geniuses took the White House in 1981, they turned their skills toward eradicating one particularly nettlesome CW that they felt hampered the use of American military power abroad. The CW which so bothered the Reagan team was known as the Vietnam Syndrome, an American reflex against committing troops to far-off conflicts. Fearing a replay of the painful Vietnam War, the public shied away from any proposed military intervention, and the Reagan administration considered that timidity a serious threat to the national security.

So, in the early 1980's, the White House quietly established a domestic "public diplomacy" apparatus to shake the nation out of its post–Vietnam War funk and to create a new prointerventionist CW. Guided by CIA director William J. Casey and staffed, in part, by CIA propaganda and military psychological-warfare experts, this domestic campaign went to unprecedented lengths to discourage any conflicting views on President Reagan's pet foreign-policy programs. The administration not only applied modern advertising techniques to promote these presidential causes, it constructed a propaganda apparatus which harassed opposition groups, targeted antiwar politicians, punished out-of-step journalists and lied whenever necessary (see Part 2).

Like Oliver North's Iran-contra operations, the "public diplomacy" campaign was run out of the National Security Council offices. Its director at the NSC was Walter Raymond, Jr., a career CIA covert-operations specialist who systematically brought to the national debate the same CIA tactics that would normally be reserved for hostile foreign states. In defining the U.S. debate, Raymond advocated a strategy of "gluing black hats" on Reagan's foreign enemies and "white hats" on the president's friends. For those journalists and politicians who would reject the stark coloring, one of Raymond's top enforcers promised that their criticism would no longer be "cost-free." The White House plan was to shape a favorable CW on foreign controversies and punish those who refused to go along.

Although parts of Reagan's "public diplomacy" apparatus were dismantled after funding abuses surfaced during the Iran-contra scandal, Raymond's "gluing black hats" strategy is still in place. Foreign conflicts are still sold to the public as clashes between good guys and bad guys with little room for "gray hats." Meanwhile, the Reagan administration's assault on the Vietnam Syndrome continued under President Bush, who rallied the nation to large-scale military interventions in Panama and the Persian Gulf in his first two years in office.

After U.S. forces crushed the Iraqi military in Kuwait in 1991, President Bush's first public comment about the victory was a heartfelt satisfaction in winning this other victory over America's reluctance to go to war. "By God, we've kicked the Vietnam Syndrome once and for all," he exulted. For Bush and others who had served in the trenches of the Reagan administration, this war over the annoying Vietnam Syndrome CW had taken a full decade.

In maintaining strong news-media support for the conflicts in Panama and the Persian Gulf, Bush also benefited from Reagan's nasty disciplining of the Washington press corps. It was much easier for Bush to shape favorable CWs to support his foreign policy because the American press and Congress had been so thoroughly housebroken by Reagan.

This CW preeminence is, of course, not what our civics textbooks taught us about democracy. We learned about the "marketplace of ideas" that permitted a free and open debate to flourish, affording the best ideas a fighting chance to emerge for the benefit of the nation. Instead, today's Washington has become home to a kind of information cartel, where only CW-approved ideas and information reach the general public with any frequency.

Pushing this trend are economic changes in the news industry that have made the press less and less likely to challenge the powers-that-be. Over the past two decades, media megacompanies have consolidated the industry and look more and more to quarterly profits and the bottom line than to advancing the cause of a well-informed public. Investigative journalism, as Ellen Hume noted, is not seen as cost-effective and can lead to enormous expenses from libel suits, even those filed frivolously as harassment to aggressive reporting.

But simultaneously, the nation's need for straightforward and comprehensive information has never been greater. The United States—its lead industries struggling, its banks collapsing, its educational system failing, its economic infrastructure crumbling—is facing relentless challenges from foreign competitors. In many ways, the threats are unparalleled in American history. Never before has the United States been as dependent on foreign money for the functioning of its economic system. The nation's huge deficits are, in effect, loans held by the same foreign competitors who are grabbing U.S. markets and grinding down American industries. These competitors, especially the gigantic Japanese banks, can now throw America into a financial panic simply by not showing up at the next Treasury auction. In short, despite its military might, the United States is losing control of its own destiny. Its future national economy seems likely to be summed up as: "I'll flip hamburgers for you and you flip hamburgers for me."

To bolster their own favorable CWs, America's foreign competitors are investing heavily in Washington, hiring some of the city's most respected names as lawyers and lobbyists. Japan, alone, has spent tens of millions—on salaries to ex–U.S. government officials, on pro-Japan propaganda and on "grass roots" political campaigns—to assure that the Washington CW favors "free trade" and trusts in the promises that a post–nation-state world economy will make national competition irrelevant. Under these reassuring banners, Japan has ravaged American industry through predatory trade practices, from dumping of low-priced products to the buying out and shutting down of U.S. companies.

As Japan and other foreign competitors have plundered the U.S. economy, they have quieted public alarm by spreading money among Washington's CW elite. That money has created a dual loyalty for members of this American political class, though these CW leaders bristle at the suggestion. On the one side are their high-salaried careers and on the other, their countrymen. It is not surprising that the money often wins out.

In *Agents of Influence*, author Pat Choate notes that "hundreds of Washington's power elite now work to advance Japan's political and economic interests in America. Nothing comparable is found in the capital of any other nation. Any of the elites in Japan, Korea, France, Germany or Britain who did the same would be considered, and treated as, social lepers."[6] But in CW-drunk Washington, these influence peddlers give the best parties, and the CW is firmly set against "protectionism."

Yet, even as America's economic wealth is drained, the smashing military victory of the U.S.-led coalition forces in the Persian Gulf established the United States as the undisputed military power in the post–Cold War era. High-tech American weaponry crushed Saddam Hussein's army, inflicting tens of thousands of dead while holding U.S. casualties to a bare minimum.

With the impressive American military victory, the war marked a historic widening in the relative power between the First and Third worlds. The qualitative difference between the American arsenal of "force multiplier" weapons (designed to counter a massive Soviet invasion of Europe) and what is available to Third World countries was now comparable to a fight between one army using machine guns and another using bows and arrows. No Third World nation, not even one as heavily militarized as Iraq, could think it stands any chance against American might, whatever the merits of the cause at stake.

The military power that President Bush unsheathed in the Arabian desert was an awesome warning to poorer nations that, as Bush put it, "what we say goes." The president envisioned the crushing, bloody defeat of Iraq as the first policing action of a "new world order," which would place international law at the center of relations between nations.

But amid the CW-silly American political debate, there is no guarantee that the United States will use its terrifying military power wisely or even within the tenets of the United Nations Charter. A trivialized absorption with the latest CW, mixed with the cynical application of advertising skills, could make America a dangerous home for these massively destructive weapons. They could be brought to bear to prop up pro-U.S. dictators facing domestic unrest or to overthrow troublesome enemies who somehow angered the protectors of this ill-defined new world order.

The only meaningful check on possible abuse of America's awesome military might in this "unipolar world" is the sophistication and vibrancy of the nation's democratic institutions. Issues as grave as war and peace demand a thorough debate by a population given as much relevant information as possible, not a country governed by a tyranny of the conventional wisdom, not an opinion elite satisfied with viewing enemies as comic-book villains.

Without a recommitment to its own democratic values and an appreciation of other people's history, the United States could flick on its unprecedented killing machine casually. It could grind up some geopolitical nuisance who simply found himself on the wrong side of the Washington CW, a punching-bag enemy of the talk-show pundits. The nation could awake with blood-covered hands, realizing too late that it has slaughtered the wrong people.

PART 1

The CW Runs
for President

Newsweek's Mickey Kaus chomped into a greasy hamburger at the incongruously named Burger Heaven restaurant on Forty-ninth Street in midtown Manhattan. The two-level coffee shop with fake brown wood and slow-moving waiters may have seemed an odd place to divine what Washington insiders were thinking about the down-and-dirty 1988 presidential campaign. But on many Friday afternoons, a day before *Newsweek* goes to press, Kaus and his collaborator, Jonathan Alter, would take a break from the magazine's office across the street, order some burgers at Burger Heaven and muse about the campaign's conventional wisdom.

Starting in early 1988, the pair had written a weekly tongue-in-cheek chart for *Newsweek*'s *Periscope* page that, with arrows up, down, or sideways, kept track of what the insiders were thinking about the campaign. Although partly a spoof showing how often the pundits ended up with egg on their faces, the *CW Watch* was the first systematic endeavor to follow the periodic twists and turns of Washington's influential conventional wisdom.

By 1988, the conventional wisdom had emerged as arguably the dominant institution in the nation's capital, even though it lacked a building, had no roster of deputy assistant secretaries and never convened an 8:30 A.M. intelligence briefing. Through its power to legitimate and delegitimate, the CW exercised enormous influence over the direction of the nation's public debate—and especially the presidential race. The CW's disdain guaranteed that a candidate had little hope of getting his message to a national audience and could hasten his departure from the campaign.

Yet while munching hamburgers at Burger Heaven and mulling the latest CW on the 1988 campaign, Kaus and Alter would readily agree that the conventional wisdom they tracked had been a "reign of errors," the title of a CW wrap-up piece they wrote on the election. "For years there has been an informal but discernible universe of reporters, consultants and commentators who reach the same predictable conclusions about the same political events at roughly the same time," Kaus and Alter wrote in *Newsweek*. "After a few days, of course, these political creatures often change direction (and analysis) completely, en masse and without apology, like a school of fish. . . . Cursed by its need to constantly find something new to say, by its slavish devotion to polls, its insular reliance on the Washington–New York gossip axis, the CW has compiled a track record this year that is even more abysmal than usual. Week after week, what seemed obvious to every respected analyst on Monday morning looked ludicrous by Tuesday night."[1]

Nevertheless, each week of the presidential campaign, Kaus and Alter, with the help of political correspondent Howard Fineman, charted the CW. They gave arrows up and down to candidates, staffers, strategies, hot issues, even occasionally other journalists. A typical construction would be Old CW–New CW, showing how last week's brilliant insight would be this week's campaign refuse. In the April 18, 1988, issue, for instance, Democratic front-runner Michael Dukakis got an arrow up, "Old CW: Attempt at humanization pathetic. New CW: Attempt at humanization brilliant." George Bush, meanwhile, got an arrow down, with the comment: "If he's such a shoo-in, why is Dukakis beating him in the polls?" Sadly for Dukakis, it would be his Old CW that would prevail in the November elections, as Bush rolled to a landslide victory as the "shoo-in" that the CW had mocked. With CW, the trend's the thing, not long-term accuracy.*

Newsweek's CW chart was born from the frustration Alter and Kaus felt about the magazine's constant temperature taking of the political campaigns. "One week in 1987," Alter said, *Newsweek*'s

---

*A good example of the CW's long-range unreliability came in a "special *glasnost* edition" of the June 6, 1988, *CW Watch*, which tried its punditry hand on Soviet political rivalries. Boris Yeltsin was "x'd" off the list altogether with the clever remark "Forget those comeback rumors. If the party confab drafts him, it's for the army." Three years later as the elected president of Russia and the man who faced down a hard-line-communist coup, Yeltsin stood as a major international figure and the man who forced Mikhail Gorbachev into retirement.

editors "wanted some kind of political piece that had all the hackneyed political handicapping in it. I thought why not do it as a chart. . . . The main motivation behind it [was as] a way of freeing up the 'Nation' section [of *Newsweek*] for doing something more interesting. Very quickly, it took on a life of its own." Before long, the chart was the most talked-about feature in the magazine, and its "findings" were even promoted in news releases touting *Newsweek*'s top stories.

The magazine was on to something with the *Conventional Wisdom Watch*. The chart hit an immediate and responsive chord with many readers, especially the younger ones. Its clever, often snotty tone captured the public's new cynicism toward government. The *Watch* was making fun of politicians, just as Americans were sensing their own impotence over the nation's political process. Not only did the snappy put-downs report the thinking of Washington's insiders, they gave voice to the public's contempt for those who fancied themselves the nation's leaders.

But the *CW Watch* and the growing derision toward politics that it spoke to further cheapened the campaign debate. Conventional wisdom obsessed over personality flaws, emotional issues and outright trivia. Candidates of substance got little hearing. Those who staked out gutsy positions on controversial issues found their seriousness rated not for its wisdom but for its effectiveness as a political gimmick.

Former Arizona governor Bruce Babbitt ran a colorless, issues-oriented campaign for the 1988 Democratic nomination, which the CW found charming but hopeless. Early in the primary season, Babbitt got a sideways arrow with the puckish observation: "Good news: ideas being examined. Bad news: ideas being examined." A week later as the Iowa caucuses neared, Babbitt was arrowed down, with the observation: "Live by the CW, die by the CW. Bruce Babbitt was praised as too-candid-to-win. Now he's dismissed as too-candid-to-win." After poor showings in Iowa and New Hampshire, Babbitt was "x'd" off the *CW Watch*'s list of candidates: "Just shows best man can't win."

Candidates suffered, too, when they took positions that lacked the blessing of Washington's insider community. Congressman Richard Gephardt raised the CW's hackles over his "protectionist" trade policies. For some reason, possibly connected to the number of Washington power brokers on the Japanese payroll, the CW has long been hostile to any populist message aimed at limiting "free trade." The CW's hammering on Gephardt grew so numbing that Alter cited it as one of the worst CW excesses of 1988. "Sometimes there was piling on," he said of the Gephardt experience.

But the CW was mixed on the reddish-haired, fair-complexioned Gephardt. While regarded favorably as a Thoroughbred entry in the political horserace, he suffered a bashing, ironically for the CW, as a man lacking in conviction. In the *CW Watch,* the insiders' ambivalence about Gephardt often showed in his receipt of simultaneous arrows up and negative comments. "Of course he'll win Iowa. But then what? Is he the foe of the establishment or part of it?" the chart commented while giving him an up arrow before the Iowa caucuses. Later, after solid early showings, Gephardt earned another up arrow, but a critical observation: "He seems a phony flip-flopper, but N.H. blue-collar voters didn't mind acrobatics." Prior to the Super Tuesday primaries in the South, Gephardt again was arrowed up, with the comment: "Only lack of money and unconvincing eyebrows holding him back now." A few weeks later, his candidacy pummeled by his opponents and the CW for his alleged "flip-flopping," Gephardt was earning a big arrow down and out. "The CW won't have Dick Gephardt to kick around anymore," the *Watch* lamented. Gephardt was just one more out-of-luck candidate given the bum's rush from the campaign.

The conventional wisdom likes nothing more than a winner. "It's like the stock market," Kaus says about the CW. "It registers the dominant expectations of the future. But in Washington, a lot of what power is, is how much power you are expected to have in the future." Thus, if the CW reports that a candidate is in trouble, he is besieged with questions about pulling out of the race—which might leave him little choice but to pull out of the race. Fascinated with who's up and who's down or what's hot and what's not, the conventional wisdom revels in the triviality of politics: tactics, trends, the latest poll results.

To take the measure of this political stock market, Kaus and Alter would start their CW monitoring a week early by watching *The McLaughlin Group* shout-fest on Saturday night. There, they would hear the latest punditries from the likes of Morton Kondracke and Fred Barnes, neoconservatives from *The New Republic;* mainstream centrist-liberals such as *Newsweek*'s Eleanor Clift and columnist Jack Germond; and hardline conservatives Robert Novak,

Patrick Buchanan and John McLaughlin himself. On Sunday morning, they would tune in the more highbrow *This Week with David Brinkley* to hear the insights of the thinking man's conservative, George Will, the irascible Sam Donaldson, the effervescent Cokie Roberts and the ever-acerbic Brinkley.

In an earlier era, reporters would sit on panels, such as *Face the Nation* or *Meet the Press*, and simply ask news makers what they thought about issues or events. However, the new format, pioneered in the 1970's by *Agronsky and Company*, dispensed with or minimized the role of the news maker and let the journalists pontificate. The format spread in the 1980's, achieving its purest form in the "food fight" atmosphere of *The McLaughlin Group*. Its regular participants achieved more influence in setting the national agenda—and the CW—than almost any member of Congress. They also became inviting targets for the White House, which would feed its pundit friends tidbits that, when repeated on the shows, would seem to be independent opinion, not just government propaganda.

Although the numbers of such shows proliferated during the l980's, the punditry programs represented a remarkably small sampling of available political thought. The regulars on one show often turn up on other, supposedly competitor shows, giving these anointed pontificators a wildly disproportionate chance to sound off on their personal opinions.

A television viewer wired for cable, for instance, could tune in McLaughlin for about a half-dozen hours a week. Besides appearing on *The McLaughlin Group* and *Capital Gang,** Buchanan would also cohost CNN's *Crossfire*. Novak, too, could scarcely be missed while sampling the channels on any given night. The repetition of punditry appearances guarantees that few truly challenging or original ideas will find their way onto the nation's airways.

That the familiar faces tend politically toward the right side of the American spectrum is less important to the CW than that the credentialed commentators will endlessly reprise the same predictable thoughts. Alan Hirsch, author of *Talking Heads*, a book about TV's star pundits, sees this televised political scrimmage

---

*A CNN promo for the *Capital Gang* opens with a darkened set and the chat show's participants, in silhouette, moving to their places around a table. The announcer intones about the profound significance of what will take place at that weekly gathering. "A select few," he says, referring to the *Gang*, "make judgments that affect us all."

pushing the ball only between the forty-yard lines. "The accept-
ability factor and the celebrity status achieved by some commentators create a situation where certain journalists become ubiquitous
while others never receive public exposure," Hirsch observed.
"Even within the forty yard lines, we would benefit from more
player substitution."[2] Despite the hogging of playing time by a few
conservative veterans and chronic liberal laments about the political
imbalance, the CW setters show few inclinations to send in some
rookies off the bench.

This small, opinion-shaping team of talking heads amounts to
what another pundit watcher, Eric Alterman, terms a *punditocracy:*
"Composed of journalists, columnists, former government officials
and wanna-be experts, the punditocracy is Washington's varsity
talking team, the boys everybody turns out to see. The favored
members of this tiny but influential squad are offered the emotionally satisfying opportunity to mouth off about the issues of the
day on television . . . and make piles of money for it."[3]

As Kaus and Alter followed the CW trail through the week,
they would check up on the latest campaign shifts by reading
Hotline, the equivalent of a stock ticker for the 1988 race. A new
computerized newsletter, *Hotline* summarized the top political stories around the country and delivered this roundup early each morning to the computer terminals of political reporters in every major
news organization. By highlighting pivotal news stories from around
the nation, publishing overnight-poll results and spotting campaign
trends, *Hotline* gave momentum to the CW as it lurched first in one
direction and then another.

One of the *Hotline*'s founders, Ron Rosenblith, said that en-
ergizing the CW was not his intent. He saw the computerized
newsletter as a way to "democratize" campaign coverage by giving
national attention to stories from smaller newspapers that had broken a politically important story. Rosenblith was fond of recalling
one comment about the publication: "After *Hotline,* there was no
such thing as a local story."

For instance, when the *Buffalo* (New York) *Evening News* zeroed in on Congressman Jack Kemp's right-wing religious supporters, that story was quickly communicated to the national campaign press corps. When the *Wilmington* (Delaware) *News-Journal*
nailed Senator Paul Simon on his budget figures, the "Simon-

omics" story was flagged for the attention of the big media. "We were waiting for someone to say it and when they did, we played it fairly prominently," Rosenblith recalled. "We tried to create the opposite of pack journalism."

But the *Hotline* also ensured that all major political reporters were now reading from the same menu of available leads and stories. Further, if one candidate were on the downward slide toward oblivion, a flurry of stories about his demise would be summarized in the *Hotline*, speeding his elimination. The never-ending progression of overnight-poll results were a *Hotline* staple. That, too, accelerated the CW process.

"There was a debate within a very tight circle of people [covering the campaign] as to whether we exacerbated pack journalism or did the opposite, whether we were an echo chamber or the opposite," Rosenblith said. Despite its best intentions, *Hotline* created a formal means to communicate the CW trends, which is one of the reasons the *CW Watch*ers kept such a close eye on whether a candidate's value was slipping on the *Hotline*'s political stock ticker.

After a week of taking the CW soundings, Kaus and Alter would consult with Howard Fineman by phone. Fineman, based in *Newsweek*'s Washington bureau, is a rare political reporter. He is thoughtful and self-effacing with an intellect and a sense of decency strong enough to be horrified by how the CW was mindlessly distorting the way Washington works and political campaigns are fought. But steeped in the political atmosphere of Washington, he could no more escape inhaling the conventional wisdom than he could stop breathing.

Kaus and Alter would count on Fineman to sniff out the latest wind shifts in the CW. On Fridays, Fineman would report in to Kaus and Alter before the two *CW Watch*ers would slip out to Burger Heaven or some equally greasy dinner spot and chew over some lukewarm burgers and the hot CW. Divining the CW "was never very hard to do," Kaus recalled. "It was always pretty obvious."

Kaus and Alter, though both in their thirties, had long been skeptics about the way Washington worked. Both honors graduates from Harvard, they embodied the image of the hip, irreverent, intellectual outsider. They were glib, adept at cramming their clever insights into very few words. They were bright, feeling a bemused sense of superiority over the campaign they followed.

Though hard to pin down ideologically, they tended more to the left side of the political spectrum, yet their professional detachment let them gauge the CW impartially.*

The pair defended their weekly compilation of Washington's predictable thoughts as part satire. "The comic point is to lampoon the self-centered certainty with which people make pronouncements in Washington," said Alter. "The more serious point is that through Old CW–New CW, you can tell the reader how fallible this supposedly professional judgment is. That's the not-so-subliminal message that we're trying to send to the reader: 'Be more skeptical about the high and mighty.' "

But through its clever, derisive tone, the chart has oddly given new momentum to the CW. It commits to paper what might otherwise be picked up only by devotees of the chat shows or others attuned to Washington's insider culture. It's like a printout of the Washington pecking order—and no one wants to find himself on the bottom. Though "most people get the joke," *Newsweek*'s Alter said, "there's a certain percentage of our readers who don't understand it." That is, they take the chart and its CW judgments seriously.

Certainly no more seriously than the conventional wisdom makers take themselves. "The shapers of the CW have an extraordinarily short attention span and an enormous confidence that they know what the American people are interested in," said Alter. Yet even as opinion polls constantly reflect a public desire for more issues-oriented campaigns, the national media offers up shorter

---

*In a thoughtful look back on the sixties—part of a *Newsweek* retrospective package on the controversial decade—Kaus defended what the youthful antiwar activists had accomplished, while freely admitting the many mistakes. Though the article is entitled "Confessions of an Ex-Radical," Kaus comes across more as a thoughtful intellectual than a rock-throwing crazy. But instead of joining the trendy parade of so-called Second Thoughters and denouncing the decade, Kaus offered a tempered defense, complaining that "the memory of the era—my era—has been slowly poisoned." Kaus said he missed out on the supposedly wanton sex ("I couldn't find it, and believe me I tried") and spurned at least the harder drugs. "Mainly my friends and I cared about politics. Left politics," he wrote. "We were quite serious at learning, and thinking, in the soft-core, democratic, neo-Marxist tradition with which we were aligned." Like many young Americans who came of age in the sixties, Kaus was shaped by the Vietnam War. "Ultimately, opposing the war—not sex or drugs or rock and roll or Marx—was what gave a clarity and purpose to our lives that, for many, has been missing ever since," he remembered. "We really did feel the future would be something completely different. We were very wrong. And that makes the future a disappointment" (*Newsweek*, Sept. 5, 1988).

sound bites, greater fascination with politicians' private lives and endless analysis of political tactics.

"The CW is not very interested in history," observes Alter. His *CW Watch* cofounder Kaus adds that the conventional wisdom is equally uninterested in originality of thought about the future. The CW likes insights only when they are safe enough to be embraced by other Washington insiders.

"There is no honor in being right too soon," Kaus observes. "People just remember that you were out of step and crazy. The way to have impact as a journalist is to state the conventional wisdom a day before everybody else does. The way to have impact is to write the article that crystallizes the CW."

The best in the CW business understand this rule and would never plunge into uncharted waters where other pundits dare not go. But as with every darting school of fish, there must be one that darts first, and in today's politics, that honored position goes to the TV pundits, especially those who double-whammy the process with a syndicated column or regular space in a premier newspaper, such as *The Washington Post*, or in a hip, influential magazine, such as *The New Republic*. Although *Newsweek* charts the CW and liberally sprinkles its news columns with companion observations, it is less likely to crystallize the CW than to consolidate the conventional wisdom after it has been defined by others.

Near the top of Kaus's list of CW swamis is Morton Kondracke, a broadfaced, bespectacled *New Republic* writer in his early fifties who is a regular on *The McLaughlin Group*. McLaughlin, the show's ringmaster, often will tease Kondracke by drawing out his first name as "Mor-*ton*," with the emphasis on the second syllable. Amid the show's verbal mud wrestling, Kondracke often expounds his latest certitude over clamor and interruptions. (Sometimes it seems that the most commonly heard statement on the show is "Let me finish my sentence.")

Despite the Geraldo Rivera decorum of the show, Kondracke exploits his prized television seat to articulate the newest in conventional wisdom, not too far ahead of the CW pack. "Mort is rarely right too soon or remains a holdover too long after the conventional wisdom has shifted," Kaus explained, with amused admiration. It is just that agility of principle that is looked for in a CW MVP.

Jefferson Morley, formerly an editor at *The New Republic*, recalls Kondracke earlier in his career as a vaguely liberal fellow who was never widely regarded as having keen insights or strongly held beliefs. "He wasn't trying to go against the grain," Morley said to me in an interview about Kondracke and the conventional wisdom. "By the early eighties, he is invited onto *The McLaughlin Group* because they needed a liberal, but for a guy like Kondracke, liberalism was kind of a memory. As for the defining moments of the sixties, like the antiwar movement, he wasn't affected by it. He was a straight guy from the Midwest."

As *The New Republic* lurched rightward in the Reagan era, so did Kondracke. "He is caught in the updraft of conservatism," Morley explained. "Mort never had that kind of confidence" in his opinions, so "when there was this intellectual rationale for Reagan's policies, this gives him the confidence to say these things."

Then, of course, there were the financial rewards of punditry stardom. "Suddenly his speaking fees went up," Morley said. "The week-in and week-out rewards were just reinforcing. The rewards on a personal level were enormous. A guy like Mort could go out and make $2,500 or $5,000 for saying what he'd be saying anywhere. . . . The question is not why someone would not go along, the question is more why wouldn't anybody go along with this. . . . The importance of opinionmakers was going up fast."

For Kondracke, an undistinguished journalist until he was anointed a punditry star, the Washington roulette wheel of power and success had clicked to a stop right on his number. He suddenly, fortuitously, had influence, like a real-life Chauncey Gardiner. Gardiner was the lead character in Jerzy Kosinski's *Being There*, a novel—and later a Peter Sellers movie—in which the pretensions of Washington enable a simpleminded gardener to rise accidentally to power and influence. The character, uneducated and addicted to TV watching, gets his first break when he inherits an expensive wardrobe from his dead employer. Dressed as a gentleman and measured of speech, Chauncey Gardiner impresses the president with his earthy wisdoms about his garden. His simple observations about tending plants are revered as profound insights into current affairs, and Gardiner unexpectedly finds himself welcomed into the halls of power.

Kondracke, too, stumbled luckily into his fame and influence.

A plodding moderate with a hazy take on the world, he was the perfect foil for fast-talking conservatives like Robert Novak and Patrick Buchanan. Kondracke was like the slow-footed basketball team that would take the floor against the razzling-dazzling Harlem Globetrotters. But he learned how to survive. He found he could hold his own in the eye-scratching arguments if his pronouncements followed the line of Ronald Reagan's White House. He could protect against the right wingers' attacks, in effect, by shielding himself behind the conservative president.

In a flattering profile in the Unification Church–owned *Washington Times*, his friends praised him for, well, his malleability. "What's diferent about Mort," said pal and fellow pundit Fred Barnes, "is that whereas most Washington writers have developed a strong, consistent set of political beliefs to guide them in their columns and so on, Mort really is open to persuasion." Kondracke himself recognized his intellectual limits. "Mort doesn't think he's made it," his wife, Millie, was quoted as saying. "I think he's made it, but Mort thinks that any day people will stop wanting to hear what he has to say. He accuses himself of being lazy, of not being deep enough. No matter what he does, it's never good enough."[4]

After covering national affairs for the *Chicago Sun-Times*, Kondracke jumped to *The New Republic*, a small-circulation political journal, and became its executive editor in 1977. But his real break came in 1982 when he won his hot seat on the newly formed *McLaughlin Group*. He departed *The New Republic* for an unhappy one-year stint as *Newsweek*'s Washington bureau chief in 1985, returning to *The New Republic* in 1986. But his greatest public impact was through his television appearances, which established his celebrity status.

"Reagan even picked out Morton at a news conference [once] and said Mor-*ton*," like McLaughlin did, Morley recalled. "It floored him. . . . He grew beyond the point that his abilities warranted. Mort was often over his head." It was just such assertive mediocrity that is at the core of conventional wisdom. As *The McLaughlin Group* is taped on Fridays, the plodding Kondracke proved amazingly adept at stating what more high-powered thinkers may have been telling each other—and him—about the past week's events and how to perceive the week ahead. He was a perfect vessel for the CW.

*   *   *

Tracking the CW was "not a reporting function," Alter felt. "It was an antennae function. You would smell the CW. You can't see it or touch it but you can smell the CW." Despite this reliance on olfactory skills, Alter and Kaus still saw the chart as legitimate journalism, reporting what the Washington insiders were thinking. That, they argued, could be valuable to both the public and the candidates, by raising warning flags that, if ignored, could mean a candidate's ruin.

Historically, in an earlier, slower-paced political time, Senator Edmund Muskie saw his 1972 presidential hopes dashed in the snows of New Hampshire because his behavior in denouncing personal attacks directed against himself and his wife coincided with an impression of Muskie among the campaign press corps that he was unstable and thin-skinned.

As Timothy Crouse recounts in his classic book on the press and the 1972 presidential campaign, *The Boys on the Bus*, the image of Muskie derived from a series of cozy, get-to-know-you dinners between the candidates and the press. The dinners generated little news but let the campaign press meet the candidates firsthand. "The dinners provided only one solid insight—that Ed Muskie had a bad temper. At his first guest shot, in 1970, the members gave him the old George Romney treatment, boring in with question after question about Vietnam. Muskie kept giving equivocal answers and finally he blew up, attacking the group for trying to trap him. They were trying to trap him, but Presidential candidates were supposed to stay cool in the face of such questioning. Some of the members knew about Muskie's temper from covering his vice-presidential campaign in 1968, but most were stunned."[5]

In the pivotal New Hampshire primary, this underlying impression came back to haunt Muskie when he tried to defend his wife from personal attacks directed against her in the only statewide newspaper, William Loeb's ultraright *Manchester Union Leader*. Standing on a flatbed truck in a snowstorm in front of the newspaper plant, Muskie shed a few tears—and that was his undoing. "Muskie's crying sank him because it played into the CW on Muskie," Kaus explained.

The nation would learn only years later, in the Watergate scandal, that President Nixon's political hit men also understood Muskie's weaknesses, as well as his potential to mount the strongest

Democratic challenge to Nixon's quest for four more years. So they "rat-fucked" Muskie's campaign with sabotage, such as the infamous "Canuck" letter, which falsely quoted Muskie as using the slur against French-Canadians, an important voting bloc in New Hampshire. The letter was published in the ever-cooperative *Manchester Union Leader*.

The 1972 Muskie experience is a good, though extreme, example of how CW can dominate politics. Muskie's CW was his short fuse, so the Nixon campaign started lighting matches. Eventually, Muskie exploded, reminding everyone of his CW and sending him flying out of the presidential race. So, while Kaus sees a negative CW arrow as a warning flag to a politician, it is conversely an invitation for an opponent to attack.

In the modern world of politics, with its fast-paced punches and counterpunches, the winner is usually the one who defines, exaggerates and exploits his opponent's negative CW. In 1988, Dukakis's CW was that he was a nerd, a well-intentioned, automatonic nerd—a cruel, exaggerated, but not entirely false image. So when the Massachusetts governor donned a soldier's helmet and clambered into a tank, he opened himself up to a devastating Bush counterattack, because the tank ride looked nerdy. The Bush campaign even reprised the tank footage in Republican television commercials that spotlighted Dukakis's unappealing-personality CW.

In the same way, Gary Hart's campaign collapsed because of an ill-timed tryst with an attractive model. Although the CW perception of the former Colorado senator as aloof and even weird dated back to his surprisingly successful 1984 run for the Democratic nomination, the womanizing issue surfaced publicly in Fineman's *Newsweek* profile of Hart in April 1987. In a generally sympathetic and perceptive piece, Fineman called Hart "a complex man in what has become a game of simplification. . . . Hart's refusal to reduce himself to a 30-second sound bite is an admirable— and difficult—stance in an age of media politics." But at the heart of the story, Fineman observed that "Hart bridles at being defined by convention—even the institution of marriage. . . . The Harts' marriage has been a long but precarious one, and he has been haunted by rumors of womanizing. Friends contend that his dating has been confined to marital separations—he and Lee have had two—nonetheless many political observers expect the rumors to emerge as a campaign issue."[6]

Possibly the most controversial line of Fineman's piece was a quote from John McEvoy, a key Hart adviser from the 1984 campaign, who confided that Hart's "always in jeopardy of having the sex issue raised if he can't keep his pants on." While McEvoy's comment may seem prescient, given Hart's flameout over his rendezvous with model Donna Rice, the acceptance of Hart's CW as a womanizer also made the explosion more likely and more deadly.

"The Donna Rice episode played on the pre-existing notion of Hart being weird somehow and playing around with the ladies," said Kaus. "If it had been some other candidate, it wouldn't have been so important. It might not have been reported at all." But Hart's CW was that he couldn't keep his pants on, and even though that is not an unheard-of problem among national politicians or journalists, the correlation between the CW and the Donna Rice episode proved devastating.

Senator Joseph Biden, too, was drummed out of the Democratic primary race in 1988 when a plagiarism flap coincided with his CW as somehow intellectually superficial. Biden's supposed reputation for mental vacuity may have been one of the more unjust CWs attached to any candidate. The Delaware Democrat had displayed a first-rate interrogating technique when he questioned Reagan administration foreign-policy and law-enforcement appointees who appeared before the Senate Foreign Relations Committee and the Senate Judiciary Committee, respectively.

Biden's incisive questioning of President Reagan's crony William Clark for a senior State Department post forced Clark's embarrassed admissions that he was ignorant of even basic facts about important foreign nations. After Clark gave a stock, Cold War answer to Biden's question about "the compelling issues concerning U.S. interest in southern Africa," Biden asked bluntly, "Can you tell me who is the prime minister of South Africa?" "No, sir, I cannot," responded Clark. "Can you tell me who the prime minister of Zimbabwe is?" asked Biden. "It would be a guess," Clark answered. Polite, but relentless, Biden pressed on: "What are the countries in Europe, in NATO, that are most reluctant to go along with theater nuclear force modernization?" "I am not in a position . . . to categorize them from the standpoint of acceptance on the one hand and resistance on the other." Biden had made his point: Clark was a know-nothing on foreign affairs.[7]

But the CW on Biden, widely accepted by Washington insiders, was that the senator was intellectually light and that coupled with disclosures that he lifted a heart-rending story about his working-class ancestors from a British Labour party politician was Biden's downfall. "If the CW is that important," Kaus reasoned, "that you get bounced out of the race, it was important to know what the conventional wisdom was."

But charting the political conventional wisdom is not like following a ballplayer's batting average for the course of the season. There, a fan's observation that the player has enjoyed a hot spring but tailed off in July will not affect the player's likely performance in August. On the other hand, a politician's rating in the *CW Watch* or on the multitude of TV chat shows directly influences how that politician will be treated by journalists, by other politicians and by the voters. When your arrow's up, you get respect; when your arrow's down, it's like having a knife wound and being dumped into shark-infested waters.

So divining the prevailing CW—what the insiders are thinkings—and awarding a politician an arrow up or an arrow down represented a new kind of journalism. Instead of recounting what someone did or said, the *CW Watch* assesses how the power brokers in Washington "feel" about that individual—or as Alter put it, "You would smell the CW."

An arrow down means that the recipient is on the outs or at least on the skids. It is like pasting a "kick me" sign to the jerky kid carrying seven books under his arm as he hurries to his next junior high school class. In a nearly endless variety of ways, the *Newsweek* CW chart being just one, Washington keeps track of who is wearing the "kick me" sign. That, in turn, clues in even those who aren't normally "in" enough to know who is "out," generating even more ostracism and humiliation for the poor fellow who is "out."

But *Newsweek*'s Alter argues that the *CW Watch* and its clever twelve-or-so-word judgments are not intended to bolster the CW's influence. Rather, he sees it as a way to expose the superficiality of conventional wisdom and highlight the frequency of its errors. Those, like Alter, who have bothered to chronicle the mindlessness of Washington's self-important CW are the most concerned about its corrosive effect on government.

"It crowds out original thinking," Alter concludes. "It is frequently proven wrong by reality. And it feeds a lazy-mindedness." But there is a corollary to Kaus's CW dictum that "there is no honor in being right too soon," and that is, "There is no penalty for being wrong too often, as long as the error is shared by other members of the darting CW school of fish." As Alter puts it, "The CW motto is 'Never apologize, never explain.' "

To the possibility that his snappy CW commentaries could actually make it more difficult to break away from the conventional wisdom, that it could discourage original thought, that his chart is a public "kick me" sign, Alter turns suddenly reticent. "You have identified a danger," he responds.

Despite its frequent errors, the CW emerged as the driving force of the 1988 presidential campaign. As the candidates slogged through the primaries and into the general election, they were bedeviled by CW expectations and predictions. Who was up? Who was down? Who was about to drop out?

Top aides to the candidates devoted hours of their working days trying to shape the CW, finesse it or stomp on it. But mostly the candidates were controlled by it. Perhaps because he was a Washington outsider, Democratic nominee Dukakis seemed particularly mesmerized—or intimidated—by it. Certainly, he let the CW dictate some of his worst decisions.

With Vice-President Bush down by 14 percentage points in late-spring 1988 polls and 17 points after the Democratic convention, Dukakis trusted the CW that Bush could not possibly erase his high negative ratings. The prospective Republican nominee, after all, was described as "reminding every woman of her first husband." So while Dukakis played it safe with his ringing slogan, "Good jobs for good wages," Bush countered with a desperate but effective strategy. First, he ate pork rinds and tried to act like a regular guy, rather than some blue-blood preppie who belonged to creepy Yale social clubs like the necrophiliac Skull and Bones. And second, he negated his own negatives by elevating those of Dukakis.

Bush and his ad team struck pay dirt when they zeroed in on Willie Horton, the black convict who had raped a white woman while on a Massachusetts prison furlough program that Dukakis had supported as governor. Bush also pointedly pledged the flag at the end of his acceptance speech at the Republican convention, highlighting Dukakis's veto of a compulsory pledge-of-allegiance law for Massachusetts schools. In effect, Bush attacked his CW. Instead of accepting his CW image as an Ivy League wimp, he transformed himself into a belly-scratching bully.

As Kaus and Alter would later recall, "Unfortunately for the Democrats, Dukakis accepted the CW of his early invincibility and ignored Bush's attacks. Within weeks, in total defiance of the CW, Bush's poll numbers improved. The experts soon began to hail the negative strategy as brilliant. As for the gender gap, it ceased to be decisive (just as it had in 1984). And somehow, everyone forgot Bush went to prep school."[8]

Before long, Dukakis couldn't win with the CW. If he defended his positions (as he did on constitutional grounds about the pledge-of-allegiance veto), he was ridiculed as defensive and legalistic. If he ignored Bush's bashings, he was excoriated for failing to defuse the attacks. Bush, playing the CW flawlessly, whipsawed Dukakis, and the governor's inexperience with national politics made him an easy victim.

Instead of counterattacking to put Bush on the defensive, Dukakis trusted that the Washington press corps would dig up the more than ample dirt on Bush, particularly his association with Panama's drug-tainted dictator Manuel Noriega and Bush's carefully concealed role in the Iran-contra scandal. What Dukakis, the stranger to Washington, didn't realize was that since Watergate, the national press corps had lost its shovel. The press would go after these important, still-under-reported stories about the future president only if Dukakis goaded reporters into it by raising the questions sharply and pointedly. For instance, Dukakis could have challenged Bush to divulge the full contents of his meeting with Noriega and the Panamanian puppet president in December 1983, a conversation Bush has refused to discuss. But the well-behaved Dukakis didn't. He hoped the story would first appear on *The New York Times* front page, making it acceptable to discuss.

But the major news media feared being labeled too tough on Bush, who after all had a good chance to become president, so they waited for Dukakis to define the issues. This Alphonse-and-Gaston routine led to no one pressing Bush hard for answers about his clearly newsworthy relationships with Noriega, the Nicaraguan contras and other secret deals.*

While Dukakis played the role of immigrant gentleman, the patrician Bush took to the low road and reshaped the CW of the 1988 presidential campaign. As he posed in flag factories and used Clint Eastwood tough talk in pledging "Read my lips: no new taxes," Bush surged in the polls through the late summer and early fall.

The press quickly adopted the new CW that the race was over, that Bush would romp to victory and that Dukakis was a passionless robot who couldn't even work up an emotion if his wife were raped. Bush proved himself as a man who could get things done—even if that meant slinging mud and ducking any serious debate over the future of the nation.

The presidential contest proved once again that taking the high road and offering responsible positions on complex issues can be very dangerous politics. Despite the Horton atrocity, prison furloughs are widely regarded in prison management as a useful tool for controlling prison populations and easing inmates' reintegration into society. Bush knew this, and as Dukakis's people plaintively and belatedly pointed out, the federal government too had a furlough program that had suffered a few abuses.

But Bush's ad men recognized, through test-marketing their campaign themes with small voter-focus groups, that Dukakis would be severely damaged by being associated with Horton's atrocity. The ads created a new, deadly CW on Dukakis: he was soft on crime and a patsy to boot. Bush would later mock Dukakis by joking that while Clint Eastwood's gun-toting slogan was "Make my day," Dukakis's prison policy was "Have a nice weekend." That Horton was black and his victim white was another bonus, playing on the nation's unresolved racial fears and antagonisms.

Bush's campaign manager, Lee Atwater, would insist later that he was unaware of Horton's race when the furlough-rape issue was first injected into the campaign. But in Roger Simon's campaign book *Road Show*, Atwater is quoted as declaring that "The Horton

*The one notable exception was Dan Rather's confrontational interview with Bush about the vice-president's Iran-contra role. But the questioning turned into a shouting match, with media analysts declaring Bush the winner for his tough reaction to Rather's inquiries. The substance of the debate was largely ignored.

case is one of those gut issues that are value issues, particularly in the South. . . . And if we hammer at these over and over, we are going to win."

As Simon, a *Baltimore Sun* columnist, added, "Nobody had to ask what Atwater meant by 'particularly in the South.' Everybody knew how the Bubba vote would react to a black man raping a white woman."[9] Once the soft-on-crime CW was established, Dukakis could protest the injustice of it all, but he could not escape.

As Dukakis would painfully learn, a CW is very hard to shake—and can only be shed by attacking it aggressively, as Bush had done. "If you want to battle CW, you have to do it through controversy," concluded the *Hotline*'s Rosenblith. "If you want to fight CW, you have to make sure that controversial stories are reported, by making them controversial."

But Dukakis had played it safe on Bush's vulnerabilities, not wanting to take the lead in exposing Bush's hidden hand in Iran-contra and the Noriega debacle. Dukakis raised those issues only tepidly and inconsistently, choosing to retreat to his safe slogan, "Good jobs for good wages," and casting himself as a spunky man of the people. It didn't work.

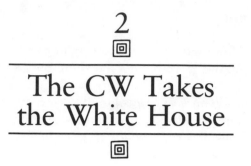

2

The CW Takes
the White House

"**Y**ou can strategically design a campaign to protect from being a victim of the CW, as you can strategically design a campaign to benefit from the CW," theorized *Hotline*'s Ron Rosenblith. By late in the 1988 presidential campaign, the CW had attained such a vaunted status among inside-Washington junkies that it was now the talk of political theory.

Indeed, the race for the White House demonstrated the danger for a candidate who failed to understand, let alone protect himself from, the slashing CW. It also showed how the other candidate could sharpen the CW into a lethal weapon. The key to Bush's victory, Rosenblith believes, was how he manipulated press coverage to highlight the CW that was most favorable to him and most unflattering to Michael Dukakis.

"What you saw [in the 1988 Bush campaign] was a strategy for how to deal with the press, to take a hard line with the press and then do some good-cop approach behind the scenes," Rosenblith said. "The Bush campaign was less concerned about being beaten by Michael Dukakis than it was about being beaten by the press. The campaign had a strategy to be very tough with the press."

In the most famous press-politician confrontation in 1988—a live interview on *CBS Evening News* on January 25—anchorman Dan Rather questioned Bush toughly about the vice-president's evasive and unsatisfactory answers on the Iran-contra scandal. Bush counterattacked fiercely, staggering Rather with a pointed reference to the anchorman's infamous desertion of a *CBS News* set in Miami in September 1987.

Like most of the press, *Newsweek* treated the confrontation as a heavyweight slugfest, with Bush declared the winner by a TKO. But Bush's retaliation against Rather was not done on impulse, the magazine reported. It was a carefully designed strategy to counter Bush's "wimp" image. Bush's cornermen, particularly his slash-and-burn political adviser Roger Ailes, had whispered in Bush's ear to be ready to throw a punch below the belt if Rather came on with a flurry of Iran-contra hooks and jabs.

Ailes and Bush came up with the plan on a car ride back from Andrews Air Force Base, *Newsweek* reported at the time. "Bush aides, including Ailes, claim that the vice president himself . . . hatched the idea of whacking Rather with the reference to the anchor's highly publicized walk off the *CBS News* set," *Newsweek* said. "In fact, the idea should be credited to Ailes. It was only the latest of several prepackaged quips designed by the New York consultant to help the vice president look tougher."[1]

The newsmagazine followed its account of the Bush-Rather confrontation with an article that I wrote about Bush's unanswered Iran-contra questions, the issue that had gotten lost in "the great TV shout-out." Bush had claimed that he was "out of the loop" on the scheme to trade arms to Iran for American hostages held by Islamic extremists in Lebanon. And, of course, he denied any knowledge of the diversion of arms-sales profits to buy other weapons for the Nicaraguan contras.

Bush, the ex-CIA chief and self-proclaimed foreign-policy expert, even insisted that he had no idea about the secret White House project to supply guns to the contras during its two-year operation. He dated his discovery of that secret to December 20, 1986, two and a half months *after* one of the supply planes was shot down over Nicaragua and nearly a month *after* Attorney General Edwin Meese III announced discovery of the Iran-contra diversion.

Bush's determined ignorance of the scandal that had rocked the White House ran headlong into a wall of documentary evidence and plain ol' common sense. For instance, Bush's claim that he believed the administration had been bartering with Iranian "moderates" was directly challenged by notes taken by one of his aides for a July 29, 1986, briefing Bush received from Israeli counterterrorism adviser Amiram Nir. Nir had bluntly described the Iranian side of those negotiations as "the most radical elements."

Even less plausible was the vice-president's memory blank about Oliver North's contra flyboy operation. A key participant, Bay of Pigs veteran Felix Rodriguez, had been placed in Central America by Bush's office and the CIA veteran had met personally with Bush. A memo for one of those meetings had listed the discussion topic as "resupply of the contras." But Bush and his advisers still professed ignorance that Rodriguez was participating in that operation. Even after Rodriguez called a senior Bush aide to warn the White House that one of its supply planes had been shot down over Nicaragua on October 5, 1986, the vice-president and his men still claimed they didn't figure the scheme out—and acquiesced to false public statements denying any U.S. government connection to the flight. Bush said he stayed in the dark until almost Christmastime, when a Republican senator, David Durenberger, filled the vice-president in on what had been happening all around him at the White House.

My article concluded that "in effect, the public must choose between two equally unflattering self-portraits by a man who would be president: either Bush knew a lot about the Iran affair and will not admit it, or he allowed himself to be duped by schemers like Oliver North and John Poindexter." The story further soured the already acid relations between *Newsweek* and the Bush campaign.[2]

But Bush and his media aides understood that the substance of the Iran-contra issue was less important than how it affected Bush's public image. Bush's implausible claim that he was "out of the loop" on Iran-contra contributed to what *Newsweek* had early on labeled the "wimp factor." His cop-out Iran-contra defense, besides being patently dishonest damage control, sounded chicken. Here was the vice-president, who claimed the courage to be president, hiding behind flimsy excuses, while other White House officials, like Marine lieutenant colonel Oliver North and national security adviser John Poindexter, took the heat from Congress and the independent prosecutor.

The "wimp" image had dogged Bush for months, at least since *Newsweek* established that CW in its October 19, 1987, issue. The magazine was showing off the spit-in-your-eye irreverence that had proved so deadly the previous spring to Gary Hart when *Newsweek* publicly charted Hart's CW as a womanizer. The Bush profile, written by Margaret Garrard Warner, portrayed the vice-president as a public-spirited patrician who was raised on his private day school's principle of "claims no more than his fair share of time and attention." This pleasant, preppie image, however, had a dangerous political downside, the article discerned. "Bush suffers from a potentially crippling handicap—a perception that he isn't strong enough or tough enough for the challenges of the Oval Office. That he is, in a single mean word, a wimp."[3] But the well-written, carefully balanced article was not what upset Bush the most. It was the cover.

Normally, appearing on the cover of *Time* or *Newsweek* is a moment that public figures relish as shorthand affirmation that they have attained national stardom. They routinely frame the covers for display in their personal offices. It is a moment to bask in the adulation of sea-to-shining-sea publicity. For politicians, it is a rare chance to define an image far more lasting than a fleeting appearance on television. But this *Newsweek* cover was not destined for a favored spot on an Oval Office wall.

According to accounts that later filtered back to *Newsweek*'s offices, the then vice-president even took some friends to the newsstand to pick up an early copy of the magazine. Worse yet, the magazine hit the streets on the day Bush was scheduled to announce his candidacy for president. At first glance, there should have been nothing to upset even a thin-skinned politician like Bush. The cover picture showed Bush piloting his powerboat and staring steely-eyed out to sea. He was wearing a yellow slicker and scowling slightly.

But it was not the picture but the caption that drained the color from Bush's face and turned his anger white-hot. "George Bush: Fighting the 'Wimp Factor,' " the cover language read. The dreaded "*w* word" had splashed into prominent national view. Bush's public-relations problem could have been worse, however. *Newsweek* had asked—and been denied—permission to photograph Bush on the tennis courts, a request that the Bushites felt was cruelly intended to highlight the vice-president's preppie roots.

Years later, as Bush took the nation to war twice in his first two years in the presidency, pop psychologists would wonder if Bush's belligerence might not flow from a residual fear that his old, wimp CW might otherwise be resurrected. Certainly, his tough-talking, mudslinging campaign for the White House had as one of its chief goals to negate the "wimp factor." Bush's top aides recounted later that he took the "wimp" cover very personally.

In Roger Simon's *Road Show*, a book about the 1988 campaign, media guru Roger Ailes claimed that Bush's anger over the magazine kept him up all night. "Now it was on the floor of his room, cover down, so he would not have to see the hated word," Simon wrote. "All he [Bush] could see was the word 'wimp' swimming up before him, even when he shut his eyes against it. He had not slept. He had not yet shaved. He sat there in his bathrobe in the predawn gloom looking like a sick, tired man."[4] Bush considered the "wimp" cover a cheap shot, especially dirty coming on the day he was to launch his race for the White House. But the greater danger for Bush was that the *Newsweek* cover might set in motion a highly negative CW that could doom his candidacy. Bush and Ailes knew the candidate could not lie down on this one.

Within days of the "wimp" cover, an angry Bush was exacting revenge against *Newsweek*. Demonstrating a firm grasp of power politics, Bush struck *Newsweek* where it hurt the magazine most and damaged him the least. *Newsweek* had launched what was known internally as "the book project." It called for a team of *Newsweek* reporters and writers to prepare an inside account of the 1988 presidential election. These reporters would get access to the internal strategy sessions of the various campaigns but agree not to write what they learned until after the election. While this technique can help reporters better capture the feel and nuances of a campaign, the premise that this approach gives a truly insider look is dubious. If a candidate is planning an action that would be particularly dirty or possibly illegal, he is not going to let reporters know about it under any circumstances.

But Bush shrewdly recognized the "book project" as a *Newsweek* vulnerability. In retaliation for the "wimp" cover, Bush ordered the project's staff barred from his campaign, although he continued to allow the magazine's regular weekly reporters to cover him. "Right after that, they [the Bush campaign] just put the lid on the project," recalled Bill Turque, a member of *Newsweek*'s book project team. "They were furious. Bush was furious."

Bush's ban meant the team could not get cooperation from the five or six top people on the campaign, such as Roger Ailes or campaign manager Lee Atwater. "These people would not do anything as long as they knew that the book project was persona non grata with Bush," Turque said. "We all agreed that this was important. We needed access to a handful of key people."

Newsweek was faced with a major investment in the book project and getting only inside looks at the losing campaigns. Senior *Newsweek* editors insisted that Bush's maneuver had no effect on the tenor of the magazine's coverage. But they were effusively grateful when James Baker left his post as Treasury secretary in mid-1988 to run the Bush campaign. Baker offered to intervene to smooth the vice-president's feathers. Soon, Baker and *Newsweek* editor in chief Richard M. Smith were spotted in a friendly tête-à-tête over lunch in the dark-paneled, manly surroundings of the Hay Room restaurant at the Hay-Adams Hotel, a few blocks from the White House.

But even the influential Baker had trouble persuading Bush to give *Newsweek* a reprieve. "Full cooperation was not restored until September 1988," only two months before the general election, Turque said. "Even Baker underestimated the depth of the anger." *Newsweek* won a reprieve only after a summit with Smith, Washington Post Company chairman Katharine Graham, and *Newsweek* Washington bureau chief Evan Thomas on one side, and Bush and Baker on the other.

The pressure on the magazine had built over the nearly year-long banishment of the book project as Bush wrapped up the Republican nomination and then headed toward a victory in November. Bush's campaign would, after all, be the one that readers would be most interested in, not the failed efforts of Paul Simon or Jack Kemp.

At the summit meeting, Bush, still harboring a deep-burning anger, chastised *Newsweek* for using that "ugly word," apparently unwilling to say "wimp" out loud. "It was a chance for Bush to yell at us in front of Mrs. G.," recalled Thomas. The Republican presidential candidate was demanding an outright apology. *Newsweek* would not go that far. Eventually, Baker and Rick Smith glossed over the differences and the *Newsweek* book project team was let back in, though much of the damage was irreparable. "A lot of color and texture was permanently lost to us," Turque said. "We were making the best of a bad situation."

As the "wimp" dispute bubbled, Bush's aides also steamed over my continuing examinations of the vice-president's Iran-contra role and his ties to Noriega's nest of drug traffickers. They deri-

sively dismissed my stories as a "rehash," a term appreciated by
journalists almost as much as "wimp" is liked by politicians. Besides
the article in the week of the Bush-Rather dustup, another story
in the May 23, 1988, issue explored allegations that Bush's national
security adviser and former CIA man, Donald Gregg, had helped
organize a pre–Oliver North contra-aid network that had ties to
Noriega and his drug crowd. The story started out as follows:

> From the outside, they were three anonymous ware-
> houses in San Pedro Sula, the steamy industrial capital of
> Honduras. Inside, they were stacked high with cases of
> weapons from the East bloc—$20 million worth, by one
> estimate, originally destined for the Nicaraguan contras.
> That's what remains of an enterprise called the Arms
> Supermarket, and it is generating new and potentially
> damaging questions about the role of Vice President
> George Bush and his staff in keeping the contras supplied
> during the congressional aid cutbacks of 1984–86, before
> Oliver North set up the Iran-contra connection. The Arms
> Supermarket was an unlikely partnership involving long-
> time CIA arms merchants, agents of the Israeli Mossad
> secret service and the intelligence arm of the Honduran
> military. And according to government documents and
> high-level administration officials, it was financed at least
> in part with drug money.[5]

The article, however, violated a slew of CW rules, first among
them an abhorrence at any suggestion that prim-and-proper American government officials might get their hands dirty with unsavory
drug dealers. The story also revived the Iran-contra allegations
about Bush at a time the CW had dismissed the scandal as ancient
and boring history. "For some years now," *Newsweek*'s Alter would
recall in 1991, "the CW [on Iran-contra] has been 'Hey, give it a
rest, that's history.' Every story about Iran-contra has had trouble
making its way in the world because that's a very powerful conventional wisdom." So the Bush men had some CW muscle behind
them when they attacked the story for quoting an arms dealer who
had given a sworn deposition to the Senate but whom they dis-

missed as a liar. The story would be the magazine's last investigative piece on Bush for the duration of the campaign.

While *Newsweek* editors denied that their high-level kiss-and-make-up strategy with Bush over the "wimp" issue influenced any news decisions, they were not about to make the same mistake the next time they put Bush on the cover. So as Bush headed for the Republican National Convention in New Orleans in August, *Newsweek* featured the vice-president in a pressed white shirt, dark blue tie with thin red stripes. The backdrop was blue sky, fluffy white clouds and an American flag fluttering in the distance. In the August GOP convention issue, the respectful cover language read: "Bush. High Stakes in New Orleans. A Revealing Interview. Nixon on the Race." Nothing that could possibly offend this time.*

Also, gone were several critical stories on Bush that had been originally slated for convention week but instead were whisked away. One of the stories was to be written by Ann McDaniels about Bush's light footprints at President Reagan's White House, a second by Margaret Warner, who had authored the "wimp" cover story, and a third that I had prepared on Bush's not-so-glorious year as CIA director.

Since I had gotten the word late about the stories being killed, mine was the only one actually written. Like many *Newsweek* stories headed for oblivion, it was first limited in length, to only a single page or three columns, in *Newsweek*'s layout. That is equivalent to about 650 words, depending on the size of the picture and other graphics. Of course, not much can be said, even by *Newsweek* wordsmiths, in that small space, particularly when introducing new, controversial information that must be treated carefully.

The story draft started out citing praise for how Bush restored the CIA's esprit de corps after taking over the scandal-battered spy agency in 1976. But it also examined the darker side of Bush's formative CIA year. As columnist Tom Wicker had asked on *The New York Times* op-ed page, "Do the American people really want to elect a former director of the CIA as their president?" Wicker reasoned that "a CIA chief might well be privy to the kind of

*Not to be partisan, *Newsweek* had given similarly puffy treatment to Dukakis before the Democratic convention. The same blue sky, only no fluffy clouds and no flag.

'black' secrets that could later make him—as a public figure—
subject to blackmail."[6] But Bush's year running the spy agency
received scant attention throughout the presidential campaign,
either from the press or the Democrats.

Appointed by President Ford, Bush directed the CIA from
January 1976 to the start of the Carter administration a year later.
Bush took over the spy agency at a difficult time, following unprecedented disclosures about CIA misdeeds ranging from assassination plots to drug experiments on unsuspecting subjects. Two
congressional committees—one chaired by Senator Frank Church
and the other by Congressman Otis Pike—had pulled back the
curtain of secrecy that had protected the CIA since its inception
in the Cold War days of the late 1940's. The disclosures had made
the proud agency the butt of jokes about cockamamie spy plots
bungled by ham-handed incompetents.

By all accounts, Bush moved quickly and effectively to reas-
sure the badly shaken agency that its role and mission were still
valued. He defended the CIA on Capitol Hill while cooperating
in the establishment of a permanent congressional oversight process. He boosted morale within the agency, exercising a light but
firm management touch, according to more than a dozen CIA veterans interviewed for the piece. He was so popular that toward the
end of Admiral Stansfield Turner's reign as President Carter's CIA
chief four years later, "The seventh floor of Langley was plastered
with 'Bush for President' signs," said George Carver, then a senior
CIA analyst. Another ex-CIA hand, Miles Copeland, even launched
a movement called "Spooks for Bush."

Theodore Shackley, then a top official in the CIA's clandestine
services, said, "For that period, Bush did a remarkable job. He
was very warm, very human, very interested. You could get in to
see him without difficulty." Another senior CIA veteran, John Horton, said Bush "was good for morale [among CIA employees]. He
didn't treat them like animals, which they weren't." Thomas Polgar, who was then CIA station chief in Mexico, called Bush "very
charming, personable, very friendly, very enthusiastic about everything [but] never with a direct hand in operations. He was more
like the Queen of England. He ruled but he didn't govern."

But as with his tenure as vice-president, Bush's year at the
CIA was marred by incidents that have never been fully explained.
That year missed the scrutiny that earlier and subsequent CIA

directors faced because Bush's term fell between the Church-Pike investigations into past abuses and the work of fully operational congressional oversight committees. Yet it was a violent and controversial year. CIA-trained Cuban exiles indulged in a final spasm of anti-Castro terrorism that included the fatal bombing of a civilian airliner and attacks on Cuban diplomats. The Argentine military seized power and launched its "dirty war" against leftist dissidents. Led by Chile's right-wing military dictatorship, like-minded Latin governments banded together in Operation Condor to strike violently at political critics seeking refuge outside their home nations.

It was the most notorious of those Chilean-sponsored international assassinations that caused Bush's CIA the most grief—the car-bomb murder of former Chilean ambassador Orlando Letelier and a woman coworker, Ronni Moffitt, as they drove down Embassy Row in Washington on the morning of September 21, 1976. Letelier had been part of the democratically elected socialist government of Salvador Allende, which had been destabilized by the CIA and overthrown in 1973 by a bloody military coup. The Letelier bombing represented the worst case of international terrorism in Washington's history—a black mark in itself for the CIA, which is responsible for monitoring and thwarting such threats from overseas. But as FBI investigators subsequently discovered, vital clues to the assassination were in the hands of top CIA officials—apparently including Bush himself—two months *before* the bombing.

The first clue that a terrorist operation was afoot came from Paraguay, where two Chilean DINA (Directorate of National Intelligence) operatives went to obtain U.S. visas for their false Paraguayan passports in July 1976. An alarmed U.S. ambassador George Landau was told by a senior Paraguayan official that the Chilean operatives were undertaking a mission to the United States to investigate front corporations being used by dissident Chilean groups—and that they planned to meet with Bush's deputy, Vernon Walters. Landau immediately recognized that the visa request was highly unusual, since such operations are normally coordinated through the CIA station in the host country and are cleared with CIA headquarters in Langley, Virginia. Landau fired off an urgent cable to Walters—and as an extra precaution, he photostated the fake passports and sent copies to Langley.

Landau said he received an urgent cable back signed by the CIA director, George Bush, and reporting that Walters, who was in the process of retiring, was out of town. When Walters returned a few days later, he cabled Landau that he had "nothing to do with this" mission. Landau said he immediately canceled the visas. However, Bush's CIA apparently never followed up to find out what the bizarre mission was all about. Meanwhile, DINA, worried that its initial plan had been exposed, arranged for a new identity for its chief assassin, Michael Townley, and slipped him into the United States. According to Townley's testimony in later trials, he contacted Cuban exiles who had developed close ties to Chile and other rightist governments in South America. With the Cubans' help, Townley taped a bomb underneath Letelier's car and exploded it by remote control device as the dissident diplomat and two associates drove to work.

After the assassination, Letelier's friends and coworkers immediately pointed the finger at DINA, which had already been accused of similar attacks against Chilean dissidents in Argentina and Rome. At a dinner at the Jordanian embassy the night after the bombing, Senator James Abourezk recalls telling Bush that Letelier had been a friend and asking the CIA's help "to find the bastards who killed him." Abourezk said Bush responded: "I'll see what I can do. We are not without assets in Chile." According to U.S. intelligence sources, one of those assets was General Manuel Contreras, the head of DINA. The CIA dispatched its Santiago station chief Wiley Gilstrap to DINA headquarters to question Contreras about the bombing. Gilstrap cabled Langley with Contreras's assurance that the Chilean government was not involved and that the killing was probably the work of communists trying to make Letelier into a martyr.

Two years later, Contreras would be indicted in the United States for masterminding the Letelier bombing. But in 1976, Contreras's explanation was promptly adopted as the CIA's take on the murder and was leaked to leading news organizations, including *Newsweek*. The magazine's *Periscope* section reported the CIA's assessment in the October 11, 1976, issue that "the Chilean secret police were not involved. . . . The [Central Intelligence] agency reached its decision because the bomb was too crude to be the work of experts and because the murder, coming while Chile's rulers were wooing U.S. support, could only damage the Santiago regime." A top FBI investigator on the case determined that the leak had come from the CIA, although he had no evidence that

Bush had authorized planting the story. But whoever authorized the leak, it was dead wrong and helped divert attention from the actual murderers.

Federal investigators who solved the mystery over the next two years said the CIA did provide information about the backgrounds of suspect individuals and groups, but, according to prosecutor Eugene Propper, "Nothing the agency gave us helped us break this case." In particular, the CIA never volunteered Landau's memo about DINA's highly unusual intelligence operation planned for the summer of 1976 or copies of the fake passports that included the photo of the chief assassin, Michael Townley. The CIA's handling of the Paraguay gambit was especially strange because the spy agency had been aware for at least a year that Chilean intelligence operatives were engaged in cross-border assassinations, according to a still-secret Senate report. The report, prepared for the Senate Foreign Relations Committee in 1979, found that the CIA knew that South American rightist governments had banded together to track down and eliminate troublesome dissidents, according to a source familiar with those findings.

Called Operation Condor, the assassination program was blamed for the 1974 bomb murder in Argentina of exiled Chilean general Carlos Prats, a rival to Chilean dictator General Augusto Pinochet, and the attempted murder in Rome in 1975 of Christian Democratic leader Bernardo Leighton. The source said the CIA had warned Portugal and France of two other assassinations planned under Operation Condor in 1975, enabling authorities in those countries to head them off. Despite this history, the CIA apparently failed to put two and two together and warn the FBI about the mysterious Chilean plan for sneaking into the United States. The first word the Letelier case investigators got about Operation Condor came not from the CIA, but from an FBI agent stationed in Buenos Aires, Argentina.

Two weeks after the Letelier assassination, on October 6, 1976, a Cubana Airlines DC-8 with seventy-three people aboard, including the Cuban national fencing team, took off from Barbados. Nine minutes after takeoff, a bomb exploded, plunging the plane into the Caribbean. No one survived. Two Cuban exiles, Hernán Ricardo and Freddy Lugo, who had left the plane on a stop in Barbados, confessed that they had planted the bomb. They named two prominent anti-Castro extremists, Orlando Bosch and Luis Posada Carrilles, as the architects of the attack.[7]

A search of Posada's apartment in Venezuela turned up Cubana Airlines timetables and other incriminating documents. Although Posada was a CIA-trained Bay of Pigs veteran and remained in close touch with some of his former colleagues, again senior CIA officials pleaded ignorance. For the second time in barely two weeks, Bush's CIA had failed to deter a major terrorist incident, even though it had long-standing ties to the perpetrators. Thomas Polgar, who headed the Mexico City CIA station at the time, said simply, "It cannot be assumed that the CIA keeps track of these activities."

Though considered ironclad by the FBI, the cases against Bosch and Posada languished in Venezuela. Bosch was eventually acquitted, returning to Miami a Cuban-American hero. Posada was still in jail in 1985 when he escaped, fled to Central America and joined up with other anti-Castro Cubans working with Oliver North's secret contra-support operation in El Salvador. Another CIA-trained Cuban exile, Felix Rodriguez, appointed Posada the number two man in the air supply operation based at Ilopango airfield outside of San Salvador. Posada, the fugitive terrorist, was put in charge of military supplies.

Rodriguez, Posada and the entire fly-boy operation were exposed when former Air America freight handler Eugene Hasenfus was shot down over Nicaragua on October 5, 1986, and blurted out their two code names—Max Gomez for Rodriguez and Ramón Medina for Posada. Rodriguez, it turned out, had been placed in Central America by Vice-President Bush's national security adviser, Donald Gregg, but Bush and his aides stuck to their story that they had been ignorant of Rodriguez's work with the contras. Although the contra aid operation was rolled up after the Hasenfus plane crash, Posada was never captured.

After the Cubana Airlines bombing in 1976, CIA director Bush appeared to become more concerned about anti-Castro Cuban terrorism. In early November, Bush and a senior FBI official, James Adams, flew to Miami to hear field reports on the problem from FBI and CIA officers. Bush then visited Little Havana, but is unclear whom he talked with or what his message was. One anti-Castro Cuban activist said the CIA's message at the time was to carry out no more attacks inside the United States, although, this

Cuban exile insisted, the CIA put no bars on anti-Castro attacks outside U.S. borders.

For his part, Bush refused to respond to written questions from *Newsweek* about his CIA experience, even though his campaign frequently touted that line of his long, personal résumé as demonstrating the vice-president's capability to handle tough jobs. Bush's chief of staff, Craig Fuller, wrote to me at *Newsweek* that "the Vice President generally does not comment on issues related to the time he was at the Central Intelligence Agency and he will have no comment on the specific issues raised in your letter."

Although my proposed story contained new information and was a stab at examining Bush's most important operational job, it again violated a host of CW rules. First, it was historical and, as Alter says, "the CW is not very interested in history." Second, it touched on Iran-contra (although only slightly, in mentioning Posada's tie-in) and by mid-1988, the CW despised the scandal as too old, too complicated and too boring. Third, it raised troubling questions about American government ties to unsavory characters, and the CW hates anything suggesting fundamental flaws in the nation's elite.

It is one thing for the CW to accept personal foibles of the rich and powerful—too much drinking, too much sex, too much extravagance. But it is another to suggest that the Washington elite cozies up to terrorists or drug traffickers. After all, that same elite plays a big role in setting the CW and moves in a social milieu that does not permit such crass thinking about one's social partners. Upon reading the draft of the story, *Newsweek* editor Maynard Parker told my Washington superiors that I must be "out to get Bush," and the story died. *Newsweek*, however, was not alone in its lack of interest in Bush's year at the CIA. Amid the millions of words written by the mainstream press on the 1988 election, there was no serious examination of the CIA's blunders during Bush's tenure.

Through the 1988 campaign's crucial days in late summer and early fall, the CW embraced Bush as the candidate on the roll. The conventional wisdom is, after all, the "stock market" of expected future success. The vice-president was spared the kind of tough examination that he and the other candidates had experienced during the primary season. Some *Newsweek* reporters covering the campaign even suspected an editorial tilt *toward* the vice-president as a result of the so-called "wimp accord." At least one confronted a senior editor with the suspicion, which was heatedly denied.

Bush's one nasty snafu with the CW in the postprimary phase of the 1988 campaign was his choice of Indiana's Senator Dan Quayle as the GOP vice-presidential running mate. On the fateful day, when Quayle was tapped by Bush for the number two slot, Quayle had been meeting with *Newsweek* editors. Never to miss a judgment on a politician's CW mettle, the *Newsweek* editors came away from the encounter saying the forty-one-year-old, blond-haired, blue-eyed Ken-doll look-alike needed "rocks in his pockets." That was *Newsweek*ese to suggest that a politician lacked the requisite gravity to earn a high rank in the CW standings. Quayle quickly proved the *Newsweek* editors right.

When Bush chose an out-of-doors rally in New Orleans to introduce his surprise vice-presidential choice, Quayle bounded up on stage, looking like an overeager contestant on a TV game show whose name had been called and told to "come on down." Bush, in a white, short-sleeve shirt, congratulated his new understudy as Quayle placed a hand on his mentor's shoulder and offered an admiring, almost adoring gaze. It would become known derisively as "The Look" and be compared to Nancy Reagan's loving expression when she was watching her husband give a speech.

As Quayle made the rounds of the television anchors that night, he found himself battered with questions about his past, particularly how he ducked the Vietnam War by maneuvering his way into the Indiana National Guard. Quayle's image of the privileged son of a rich and powerful family would add to the fire, leaving Quayle feebly trying to douse the flames by suggesting that his accusers were impugning the patriotism of the National Guard. However logically suspect, Quayle's counterattack did salvage some CW initiative for the Bush campaign. He shifted some of the public-relations heat onto the "feeding frenzy" press.

Recognizing that the CW is a dangerous but ever-changing dynamic, the Bush campaign staged an unruly, impromptu press conference for Quayle in his hometown of Huntington, Indiana. Surrounded by a crowd of six thousand Quayle friends and supporters, dozens of reporters and cameramen pressed in on Quayle with microphones, shoulder-held cameras and tough questions. Some of the toughest questioning came from the *Wall Street Jour-*

nal's Ellen Hume, a tall, red-haired woman whose no-nonsense style could make her a model for the television newswoman character Murphy Brown. Hume and others refused to let Quayle slide the question from his alleged draft dodging to the integrity of the National Guard. But the pro-Quayle crowd shouted down the reporters' questions with howls of "boring, boring" and screams at "the redhead," Hume, to lay off.

While Quayle would never escape his flighty image as a Vietnam-era "chicken hawk"—a man who eagerly wants others to go fight America's enemies—the attack-the-press strategy worked. *Newsweek* led its convention summary piece with the press-Quayle confrontation. The *CW Watch* did give Bush and Quayle arrows down that week—Bush got his for "great speech, lousy veep. Hopes words speak louder than actions," and Quayle was nailed: "He ain't heavy. Down arrow insufficent to express the CW's contempt." But Quayle's interrogators fared no better. In a slap at a reporter, the *CW Watch* gave an arrow down to Ellen Hume: "*Wall Street Journal* reporter's shrill queries looked biased on TV."

The fallout from the Huntington, Indiana, scene prompted a warning from Hume's boss, Al Hunt, that she should lie low for a while and avoid talking about the confrontation during her usual appearances on *Washington Week in Review*, the stuffy PBS entry in the weekend reporter-talk-show circuit. Soon after, Hume left the *Journal*, having already made plans to depart before the Quayle dustup. She moved on to a post as a media analyst at the Kennedy School of Government at Harvard University. But several years later, she was still smarting over the *CW Watch* slap: "That's the worst thing that you can call a reporter: biased." Hume considered the *Newsweek* comment a betrayal by journalistic colleagues. Hume felt she had simply stood up to a politician trying to duck responsibility for his own actions, even if the messy confrontation did not make for pretty TV.*

Demonstrating again its CW prowess, the Bush campaign had made the best out of a bad situation. As with the Rather-Bush confrontation, the Republican PR wizards had shifted the Quayle debate from an examination of the young senator's competence to the question of press fairness. By doing so, they deflected the CW

CW Watch writers Jonathan Alter and Mickey Kaus would later agree that the Hume CW was one they wished they hadn't written.

onslaught that had been threatening the Republican vice-presidential candidate and conceivably the entire Bush campaign.

Bush's team proved even more able in managing to mount the far nastier barrage of negative television commercials while only sharing the blame, roughly equally, for the mudslinging. On this central controversy of the 1988 general election campaign—the nasty television commercials—*Newsweek* avoided singling out Bush for criticism as even *Time* magazine, a more establishment-oriented magazine, had done. Like most of the news media, *Newsweek* instead limply chastised both candidates equally for their negative ads, even though Bush had struck more often, more savagely and far more effectively.

In a postelection article entitled "How the Media Blew It," Alter castigated the press for its overall campaign performance— tolerating sound bites over issues, obsessing on the horse race to the exclusion of probing articles, and sitting mute as the candidates ducked live questioning so their answers wouldn't disrupt the carefully crafted "line of the day."

"Equally troubling was the decision of reporters to censor themselves when it came to sorting out misleading TV ads," Alter complained. "Bush's Boston Harbor ad was usually analyzed— including by *Newsweek*—in terms of its effectiveness. Because it wasn't technically false, reporters didn't feel comfortable 'correcting' it. But the larger point it conveyed—of Dukakis as the polluter and Bush as the environmentalist—was absurd. Again fear of seeming slanted overcame any interest in reporting a larger truth."[8]

While some national publications challenged various ads on inaccuracies, *Newsweek* chose to evaluate the commericals for style and mass appeal, an approach in line with the hip CW, which disdains substance at nearly all costs. In several preelection issues, *Newsweek* rated a selection of thirty-second campaign ads like movies, giving one star for poor ones and three stars for good ones. The stars were awarded, however, for production values and how slickly manipulative the ads were. Ads were not marked down for distortions or unfairness.

Special contempt was reserved for positive ads that tried to discuss issues. One Dukakis ad, entitled "Real Answers," drew this review: "Another weak national ad. The warm, I'm-not-packaged Dukakis talks about America 'getting out of shape.' Text eloquent, but energy level low. Lighting so poor the press nicknamed this ad 'Shadows.' " Scorned for its lousy production values, the face-to-the-camera Dukakis ad got one star.

Besides Dukakis's timidity and ineptness in campaigning, Bush had one other great advantage: Bush and his top advisers, particularly his estimable campaign chairman James Baker, had proven Washington contacts and backers in important circles. The hapless Dukakis did not. His campaign manager, Susan Estrich, was an academic running her first national campaign and drew little respect from Washington insiders.

In contrast, Baker, former White House chief of staff and Treasury secretary, ranked as a first-rate power broker, and nothing impresses a Washington CW votary more than does a master of power. Baker could chat comfortably at an intimate power lunch with *Newsweek*'s editor in chief Richard Smith, and whether consciously or not, such friendly contacts influence the way senior news executives make their day-to-day decisions about how stories will be handled. While Estrich didn't have the foggiest notion of how to play the Washington power game, Baker and his patron, Bush, had knocked around that league for years. They understood the nuances of power, how to get even and how to induce others to do their bidding—all particularly valuable in shaping the CW.

Bush and Baker may or may not have earned their campaign kinder and gentler coverage from *Newsweek* by playing political good cop–bad cop over the "book project." But at minimum, they had maneuvered *Newsweek* into a compromising position and instilled enough fear within the magazine that it would not want to wear out its welcome a second time. In doing so, the Bush-Baker team showed that it knew how to play hardball at the major-league levels of Washington power politics. Dukakis and Estrich could barely qualify for minor-league A ball. These were strengths and weaknesses that the ever-perceptive CW could not miss.

On Election Night 1988, President-elect Bush basked in his resounding victory. Once 17 points down in the opinion polls, he had registered a solid 8-percentage-point win in the popular vote and a lopsided 426-111 margin of victory in the Electoral College. "The people have spoken," the wimpy-preppie-turned-pork-rind-chomper declared. But given the paucity of meaningful debate, it wasn't entirely clear what the people were trying to say. They apparently did not want their taxes raised (a pledge Bush would break a year into his presidency), and they surely did not want furloughed black prisoners raping white women. But except for that, the mandate was muddled.

The trivialized campaign had been dominated by the CW, a newly defined force in American public life (although by no means a new force entirely). Obsessed with cleverness over seriousness, style over substance, and trends over meaningful debate, the CW had contributed its smug, all-knowing share to the capping of a decade-long debasement of American politics. But as Jonathan Alter says, "The CW's motto is, 'Never apologize, never explain.' " To the CW, after all, being on top is everything. Though the 1988 presidential election may be remembered as one of the nastiest and emptiest in American history, it will also not be forgotten who won.

3

◙

The Governing CW

◙

Only days after winning the presidency, a sweaty George Bush was padding along on a late-morning run through a lush, green golf course in Gulf Stream, Florida. It was one of those balmy Florida days when the sea air rustles the palm trees and it is eminently clear why so many rich people—from the haughtiest of upper crust to the slimiest of crime chieftains—have made south Florida the American Gold Coast.

The president-elect had sought Florida's delightful refuge to wind down after the grueling campaign. He was staying at the beachfront, pastel-painted-stucco winter home of longtime friend and millionaire horse breeder William Stamps Farish III. But Bush is not a man who turns sedentary or circumspect in his free time, even when a rest is well earned. On vacations, he enters a kind of personal pentathlon, finishing one athletic exercise only to undertake another and then another—from jogging to boating to golf to tennis to fishing to horseshoes. His frenetic pace would sometimes be unnerving—particularly during national crises—as he plunges ahead almost obsessively with a high-speed golf game so he can make time for an unrelaxing turn at a fishing rod. George Bush is not the sort of man for careful reflection or deep reading.

But on that November morning, the nation was just waking up to the man it had elected president. For months, his appearances had been tightly controlled by political handlers who knew that the way to win elections was to put the candidate out in public only in positive settings or in special situations, like the confrontation with Dan Rather, that advance a favorable conventional wis-

dom. Most important, the candidate's appearance should comple-
ment, never detract from, the carefully scripted "line of the day."
The campaign's chosen theme must not be interrupted by some
boisterous reporter who might shout an embarrassing question that
can make a candidate look defensive. The image of a candidate
brushing past a knot of inquisitors with a strained smile or dismis-
sive wave has been known to set in motion dangerous CWs.

Bush's team, many with experience on the state-of-the-art
Reagan media shows of 1980 and 1984, fully recognized the risks
of the campaign trail. For the past year, Bush's handlers had
masterfully controlled the images, using them to highlight Bush's
favorable CWs while spotlighting Dukakis's negatives. As embarrassing as his isn't-this-a-step-too-far trip to a flag factory might
have been for Bush, the visit forced journalists to recap the flap
over Dukakis's vetoing of a mandatory pledge-of-allegiance law
and remind voters that Bush stood foursquare for patriotism—both
important pluses for Bush.

But with the election behind him, Bush was a newly liberated
man as he jogged through the golf course near the beach. In his
head, he was already ticking off the day's checklist of recreational
activities. Then, he unexpectedly spotted another avid jogger, Associated Press reporter Rita Beamish, who had covered Bush frequently during the campaign. Beamish, a tall, outdoorsy blonde
from California, had thought that a run past Bush's quarters might
give her some color for a story about what the president-elect was
up to after winning the most powerful office on Earth. By doing
her reconnaissance by jogging, rather than a more formal approach,
she was able to observe Bush's surroundings without raising the
ire of his protective press officers.

Bush recognized Beamish from the campaign and struck up a
conversation. "He came across the street and said, 'Hello,' " Beamish recalled, still with some surprise in her voice. Beamish's initiative had paid off in a way she had never expected: an exclusive
chat with the president-elect. Showing the conviviality that would
win over the Washington press corps in the weeks ahead, Bush
invited Beamish to join him, his wife and other members of his
entourage for a visit to the Coast Guard cutter patrolling along the
Florida coast.

"One thing that was odd," Beamish said. "He turned around

and asked, 'Hey, can she go in the water with us?' But it wasn't clear who he was talking to. The Secret Service guys weren't going to object. It was like he wasn't sure that he was in charge yet." His campaign handlers had disappeared.

After months under the CW-shaping wing of image molders who had sold him to the electorate as a slightly boorish tough guy, Bush was returning to his earlier CW self: the upbeat civil servant who had left cagey CIA veterans pleased but uninspired twelve years earlier. Again, he was the friendly preppie who lived by his day-school principle of "claims no more than his fair share of time and attention." "During the campaign, he was told to keep away from us [reporters] when that was the politically right thing," said Beamish. "In the postelection period, he was feeling somewhat untethered."

While her less enterprising colleagues were still reading the morning paper or downing a second cup of coffee, Rita Beamish was joining the president-elect on leg two of that day's recreational pentathlon. "He went straight from running to swimming," Beamish remembered. "It was like he had several things to do that day." The high-level personages kicked off their shoes and clambered into rubber boats to make their way to the yacht-sized Coast Guard cutter, about one-half mile offshore.

Bush took a quick tour around the boat to greet the captain and thank the crew for keeping watch over his safety. "He was clearly unwinding from the campaign," Beamish said. "He was chatty, convivial." But he also had in mind a swim to shore. Still wearing his running gear, Bush peeled off his T-shirt and dove into the turquoise-colored water. Mrs. Bush, an accomplished swimmer, was already in. Not one to leave a potential story behind, Beamish quickly jumped in, too.

Fighting choppy water, the president-elect and the reporter accepted a tow from one of the rubber boats part way to shore, while Mrs. Bush completed the swim unaided. As the dripping swimmers made their way across the beach to the well-manicured lawn around the Farishes' vacation home, Beamish tried to get Bush to answer some substantive questions about his plans for Cabinet appointments, but he fended off the news questions. He pointed out the sunny courtyard and swimming pool where he had been accepting congratulatory phone calls from the likes of ex-president Nixon and Senate majority leader Robert Byrd. "That's where I was all morning, talking on the phone," Bush told Beamish. "So you can tell them how we're roughing it."

Later that morning, Beamish briefed her press colleagues about her encounter with the president-elect. To her chagrin, the remark that drew the most attention was her offhand comment that Bush had "really good legs for his age," an assessment the athletic Beamish meant as a compliment to Bush's sound conditioning, "not some sexist remark," she would later explain. When *The New York Times* carried her "good legs" comment, Beamish felt compelled to apologize to Mrs. Bush to ensure that the remark was not misinterpreted.

But what Beamish had run into that November morning on a Florida beach was Bush's new public persona, a kinder-gentler public figure than the cheap-shot artist of the presidential campaign. In the first weeks of Bush's presidency, the Washington press corps would be wined and dined at the White House, would queue up for Polaroid shots in the Lincoln Bedroom (taken by the new president himself), and toss horseshoes with their new First Pal. The revised Bush CW—that he was an amiable, noblesse oblige, regular guy—was taking hold. The Washington CW, which had grudgingly admired his no-holds barred mugging of Michael Dukakis, changed again, almost as if the in-the-gutter 1988 presidential campaign had never happened. *How* George Bush had made it to power was far less important to the CW than that he *was* in power.

The Washington press corps was delighted, too, suddenly to have an entrée to the White House. Though a few members of the press had been close to President Reagan, most reporters had been on the outside looking in, peering through an ornate window at lavish parties for some of the nation's richest citizens. Bush, the blue-blood patrician, was far less snobby than the lower-bred Reagans, who seemed most comfortable when surrounded by the nouveau riche opulence of their friendly California tycoons.

The coziness that grew up between Bush and the White House press corps would eventually prompt some disapproving tittering from journalism critics, who felt reporters should maintain a greater distance from the personable president and strike a more adversarial posture. Helen Thomas, the legendary White House reporter for AP's rival, United Press International, harrumphed in April 1991 about AP's Rita Beamish, ABC TV's Brit Hume and Gannett's Jessica Lee riding with the president on his exercise trips. In Thomas's *Backstairs at the White House* column, she wrote: "President Bush does not mind sharing his armored limousine with reporters. But there is a condition. They have to go jogging with him first. That's the payoff."[1]

Even earlier, the new president had come to expect the traveling White House press corps to accompany him on his routine jogs. At a stopover in Columbia, South Carolina, in May 1990, reporters got a 7:00 A.M. wake-up call and were told that Bush was going for his morning romp in fifteen minutes. When the bleary-eyed reporters showed up, the president urged them to join him, but found no takers. He then picked out Beamish and asked her several times before she finally relented. Beamish had already gone jogging that morning and had changed into her work clothes. But she agreed to trot along with the president as he lapped a football field thirteen times in about twenty-five minutes.

Returning to the knot of unwilling reporters, Bush chastised the laggards. "The rest of you lazy guys, get out there and run," Bush said, apparently half in jest. "A fit America is a fine America. A fit America is a strong America. A fit America should include photo dogs [his term for photographers] as well as print reporters who slovenly sit back in the grandstands while some of us are out running." Some of the reporters, who were putting in marathon days covering the presidential trip, were not amused.[2]

But playing friend to the news media had helped win Bush an extended political honeymoon and sustain very positive CWs through his first three years in office. Yet, the question of cozying up too much with a politician is an age-old debate among journalists.

Many reporters defend the need to get close to any powerful political figure as the only way to report knowingly about his thinking and actions. Even though many politician-press contacts are carefully managed to show the press only the best side of the politician, up-close-and-personal reporting can give a discerning journalist valuable insights into a leader's character not visible from more formal distances.

The coziness between the new president and the press, however, may have obscured rather than clarified the personality of the real George Bush. Amid the reporting about his gosh-gee preppie persona, the White House press corps has overlooked the calculating, secretive, sometimes vindictive side of Bush's character. Even though he touted the joys of listening to country-and-western music and insisted that he really did love pork rinds, the president was above all else an elitist. He believed in decision making by a closed coterie of White House advisers and world leaders, with little meaningful consultation with the elected representatives of the public or with the people themselves.

When Bush dispatched a half-million men to the Persian Gulf, he only grudgingly consulted with Congress at the eleventh hour—and even then warned that he was prepared to go to war regardless of the congressional vote. On the domestic front, Bush's first two Supreme Court nominees, David Souter and Clarence Thomas, were jurists with almost no legal track record on national issues, frustrating the Senate's attempt to gauge their positions on abortion and other pressing questions. Bush's choices became known as "stealth" candidates because of their hard-to-detect opinions.

Even more than the secrecy-obsessed Reagan administration, the Bush White House hoarded information, the staple of any democracy. Instead, the public was fed a steady diet of highly processed images concocted to shape popular acceptance of the hierarchy's decisions. The Bush team did not believe in giving the people the raw data so they could make up their own minds about the lunch-bucket choices on the economy or the life-and-death decisions of war and peace.

Although the press faced unprecedented limits on its ability to assess facts independently during the Panama and Persian Gulf wars, reporters around the president seemed downright relieved not to be pummeled as they often were by Reagan and his ultra-conservative political allies. Asked about the coziness issue at the start of the Bush presidency, Beamish, who landed a regular assignment on the AP's coveted White House staff, offhandedly responded, "It sure beats being adversarial all the time." (Despite Bush's frequent jogging invitations, Beamish would develop into a tough and persistent questioner of the president in the years ahead.)

As the White House press corps got more accustomed to its nonadversarial surroundings, the CW, too, adjusted to the post-election period. At *Newsweek*, Jonathan Alter, the *CW Watch* co-founder, concluded that even after the election, it still made sense to track the conventional wisdom, although the focus would shift each week from one topic to another. "There's a CW on everything," Alter says. But whether there was or wasn't, the *CW Watch* had become a big winner for *Newsweek*. It was a favorite among the younger readers, whose potential longtime allegiance was coveted by *Newsweek* and its competitors. Besides selling magazines, the *CW Watch* earned praise in the *1989 Media Guide* published by neoconservative press critic Jude Wanniski, who called the box "the most successful new idea in newsweekly journalism."[3]

Though the conventional wisdom diviners were adjusting to postelection realities, they were still relying on the same old pundits, a cast of know-it-alls that was even less informed about key foreign and domestic issues than it was about the gossip of the 1988 campaign. This dependence on the tired team of aging white men prompted the *CW Watch* to doze through one "hot topic" that would later burn up the radio talk shows and thoroughly embarrass both Congress and the White House. In the December 26, 1988, issue of *Newsweek*, the *CW Watch* sympathized with the federal pay raise that Congress had snuck through, hoping no one would notice. "Why does the CW yawn?" the *Watch* asked. "Because pundits, once working class, are now quite well paid themselves."

Endeavoring to sound cute and insightful on more demanding topics than the presidential election race often stretched the *CW Watch*'s capabilities. On a Palestine Liberation Organization peace initiative, for instance, Yasir Arafat got an arrow up, with the summary: "Old CW: Terrorist. New CW: Diplomat. He signed nothing, but it's all on tape." In another *Newsweek*, the *CW Watch* tried to divine the conventional wisdom in Czechoslovakia, presumably tuning into the Czechoslovakian equivalent of *The McLaughlin Group*. The *Watch* gave an arrow down to Alexander Dubček, the Czechoslovakian communist reformer who was ousted by Soviet tanks in 1968. As communism finally crumbled twenty-one years later, the *CW Watch* aphoristically mocked Dubček with the snappy comment, "Old CW: Hero of Prague Spring. New CW: Has-been." Alter would readily concede the unevenness of many postelection *CW Watch*es. "It's more difficult when you don't have a strong story going," he explained.

Regardless of its misses, the popularity of the weekly chart turned the heads of *Newsweek*'s circulation-conscious editors. They decided to recast the entire *Periscope* section in the jazzy *CW Watch* style. "The key to this venture, I think, is really the voice: information with an engaging, irreverent edge," wrote senior editor Tony Fuller in an internal memo. The *Periscope* page, which for more than fifty years had been a home in the magazine for late-breaking exclusives, would be overhauled into a mishmash of lists and *Spy* magazine–type put-downs.

Periscope, the so-called front of the front of the book, would be divided into minisections with categories suggesting a never-ending variety of ways to express the ups and downs of conventional wisdom. One category, "Hero/Zero," might take a topic like show business, the memo said, and cite a hero ("Peter Pan for his triumphant return") and a zero ("William Hurt for allegations by his former live-in companion, Sandra Jennings, that the actor 'spit at me and called me names and abused me physically' "). Another category, "Out of Bounds," would "be an example of outrageous conduct, a particularly grotesque bit of sleaze, an outrageous statement, etc." An example cited in the memo: "Actor Cary Grant, who died in 1986, for his 'profound romantic friendship,' with Howard Hughes, alleged in a new biography by Charles Higham. How could the star of 'Philadelphia Story' hang out with someone who wore a dirty bathrobe, Kleenex boxes for shoes and had eight-inch-long fingernails? Judy, Judy, Judy, where are you?" It apparently never crossed *Newsweek* editors' minds that it might be their magazine that was stepping "out of bounds."

Another example of the "irreverent edge" would be "Sizzle/ Fizzle," a category to keep track of "what's hot and what's not," the memo said. Yet another was "His or Her 15 Minutes" for "spotlighting personalities who suddenly are hot." To zero in on a hot topic in any major metropolitan area, there was still another category entitled, "People in (Atlanta, Boston, Chicago, Los Angeles, etc.) Are Talking About . . ."

A later memo added other CW brainstorms, such as "Overexposed . . . It's a version of 'Oh, please shut up' and should feature figures the public is, or should be, sick of." Other tabloid possibilities were "Odd Couples, Hot Couples or Uncoupled" and "Signs of the Times . . . What we want to do with this is periodically run a collection of bumper stickers, billboards, buttons, etc. that reflect local controversies, issues, whacky causes and so on, [such as] the bumper stickers aimed at [San Diego Padre baseball player] Steve Garvey's fathering of two children by unwed mothers:

'Steve Garvey Really Is a Padre' and 'Honk If You're Carrying Steve Garvey's Baby.' "

The *CW Watch*, in all its new variations, had become the feature that devoured the *Periscope* page. Like the sprawling of a suburban subdivision into an environmentally fragile wetland, the CW's obsession with what's hot and what's not was encroaching on the ever-shrinking space in news publications where real news could be shared with the American public. The revamped *Periscope* page was phased in during the spring of 1989.

Newsweek was not alone in its overheated fascination with what's hot and what's not. By the late 1980's and early 1990's, the *Periscope*'s new voice—the "engaging, irreverent edge"—was heard everywhere. Serious was out, snide was in. *The Washington Post*'s "Style" section featured a "personalities" column and other cattily written articles. *Spy* delighted the sadistic socialites of New York who loved to see other socialites carved up by the magazine's serrated sarcasm. *The New Republic* adopted a neo-Leninist writing style that advanced the magazine's neoconservative foreign policy goals by ridiculing its enemies. Even the once-staid *U.S. News and World Report*, following *Newsweek*'s lead, jazzed up its front-of-the-magazine section with short, clever segments, including one entitled, amazingly, "conventional wisdom."

The weekend talk shows continued to bandy about any number of hot topics, with the regular characters sounding more and more like caricatures of themselves. Scant knowledge about any given topic would never stop a *McLaughlin Group* participant from venturing a thumb up or down, or a rating of some current event on a scale of one to ten. The *Group*'s frenetic, arm-waving rantings about the week's events earned even a satirical treatment on NBC's *Saturday Night Live* comedy show. But the *Group* and its CW certainties had long since passed beyond satire.

Fred Barnes, sporting round-rim glasses and a cooperative expression, skipped over the complexities of excessive defense spending and the ballooning federal budget when asked by McLaughlin to judge the B-2 bomber, the bat-shaped "stealth" aircraft expected to cost a quarter billion dollars a copy. Recognizing the CW rule that ideal pundits should look like George Will and sound like Clint Eastwood, Barnes extended a thumb up and declared: "Good plane. Let's build it."

The CW's demand for pithy cleverness guaranteed an exaggerated interest in personalities, especially those in public disfavor. But once a news figure becomes the regular butt of Washington insider jokes, he is a goner from what passes as serious public respect, whether he deserves the opprobrium or not. Many politicians had already learned that lesson. The nasty smirks that followed the mere mentioning of names Hart and Dukakis had marginalized those two Democratic presidential hopefuls to the farthest fringes of American political life.

Similar yucking has dogged Bush's number two man, Dan Quayle, almost from the moment he bounded, Irish setter–like, to Bush's side at the impromptu rally before the 1988 GOP convention in New Orleans. The Bush-Quayle victory in November didn't stop the derision. Partly due to Quayle's own goofs and partly because he was a much easier target than the poll-protected Bush, the vice-president remained a national joke. The Quayle tittering even gave rise to a reasonably successful magazine, *The Quayle Quarterly*, that chronicled the vice-president's misadventures and after one year boasted a total circulation of fifteen thousand.

During one vice-presidential shakedown cruise to Latin America, Quayle picked out a wooden doll of a male Indian on a "shop-op" in Santiago, Chile. The doll, who would get the name "Pedro" in later *Doonesbury* cartoons, sported a wide grin and colorful headdress. But when Pedro's head was lifted, a large, erect phallus sprang out, showing the doll to be anatomically exaggerated. Quayle turned to his wife, Marilyn, displayed the doll, and said, "I could take this home, Marilyn, this is something teenage boys might find of interest."

"Dan, you're not getting that," a stricken Marilyn Quayle wailed. "I didn't buy it," the vice-president replied, with a look of feigned innocence on his face. But his wife replied, "I just saw you give him the money." Stunned journalists, always on the lookout for Quayle to reinforce his lightweight CW, agreed with Marilyn. Quayle had slipped $4 to a Secret Service agent to buy the doll. "You're so sick," Marilyn told her husband.[4]

Other Quayleisms became legendary, like his garbling of the United Negro College Fund slogan "A Mind Is a Terrible Thing to Waste." From Quayle, it came out: "What a waste it is to lose one's mind or not to have a mind." Other entrepreneurs rushed in to tap the anti-Dan Fan Club. There were Dan Quayle calendars, joke books, even a T-shirt with Quayle's head grafted to James Dean's body with the wording: "Rebel Without A Clue."

Whether fairly or not, Quayle suffered from a nineties populist backlash against the garish privilege of the Reagan years. The vice-president was seen as a rich young man who had been spared the trials and tribulations common to lesser-born Americans. His face, while regularly handsome, lacked the wrinkle lines that reveal a man who has overcome day-to-day worries. He seemed to have spent his young life floating above the fray, relying on his pedigree and family fortune to escape everyday pressures, but also failing to make use of his privilege to make himself a worldly, educated man. In that sense, he was indeed "no Jack Kennedy," as Senator Lloyd Bentsen had pointedly reminded the nation in the 1988 vice-presidential debate.

After Bush suffered an irregular heartbeat in May 1991, Quayle's qualifications came under renewed scrutiny. As *The Washington Post*'s Joel Achenbach said, Quayle "has become a kind of stock character, a harlequin. He is an official object of derision, the Dummy Laureate of the United States. . . . The real, corporeal Dan Quayle made the front page again only because his boss started fibrillating, atrially."[5]

But some CW shapers have come to Quayle's defense, even using tried-and-true CW techniques to rescue the hapless, golf-a-dope vice-president from national derision. Columnist Charles Krauthammer, the neoconservative intellectual from *The New Republic*, struck out boldly in a *Washington Post* column, attacking "Dan Quayle's Bum Rap." Krauthammer cited with an awed reverence that Carnes Lord, one of Quayle's foreign policy advisers, had translated Aristotle's *Politics* into English. Although that was no evidence that Quayle even knew who Aristotle was, Krauthammer insisted that "Quayle's real liability is not intellectual but emotional." The columnist traced the public's nervousness about Quayle to Quayle's nervousness about the public. "The standard today is Peter Jennings cool," Krauthammer theorized. "A democratic public, used to the soothing reassurance of its television presences, positively demands it of a president."

In polishing up Quayle's CW, Krauthammer cited the earlier-era CW that Harry Truman, President Franklin Roosevelt's VP choice in 1944, was, in *Time* magazine's words, "the mousy-looking

little man from Missouri." But Krauthammer noted Truman overcame his CW slams, like "To err is Truman," to emerge as a
respected president of the twentieth century. Krauthammer saved
his CW-altering pièce de résistance for last, charging that the Democrats were showing their political desperation by "reaching for the
Quayle issue." He then dredged up the Dukakis CW to counteract
the Quayle CW. "It will be doubly interesting to see a campaign
based on the proposition that Dan Quayle is not qualified to be
president coming from a party that last campaigned on the proposition that Michael Dukakis was."[6] There it was, negative CW
versus negative CW.

Even worse CW abuse would be in store for foreign adversaries—like Panama's Manuel Noriega, Nicaragua's Daniel Ortega
or Iraq's Saddam Hussein—who crossed the CW line into permanent arrow-down status. And unlike Quayle, they would have
no CW-sanctioned defender to ride to their rescue. The national
frenzy that accompanied American military activities against their
countries effectively foreclosed any realistic assessment of those
Third World leaders or the threat to U.S. national security posed
by their nations.

When Noriega's drug-trafficking indictment was handed down
in 1988, the marching orders from *Newsweek*'s New York headquarters were: file any negative information we have about the
Panamanian strongman no matter how scurrilous. Noriega was
heading toward that CW nadir where any accusation from any source
is fair game for publication, no checking necessary. In such cases,
the CW's "irreverent edge" creates a climate hostile to all but the
most disparaging remarks. Any balancing comment is precluded,
and an American public figure foolish enough to say something
positive would automatically be labeled a "Noriega sympathizer,"
unfit for a seat on a premier television chat show.

Moreover, with the eclipse of the Cold War, this personal
ridiculing of foreign enemies replaced any larger philosophical
framework as a justification for war. Instead of weighing the delicate
pros and cons of a foreign military intervention, American opinion-
leaders now were reacting viscerally—and personally—to international adversaries. At those times, halfway measures have no
place in the minds of the nation's rhetorical gladiators.

The only permissible criticism of a hard-line U.S. policy can come from an even more hard-line stance. "Why not assassinate the S.O.B.?" the talk-show commentator wonders. "How could we have ever been friends with this guy?" the liberal skeptics complain. "Why not drop a nuclear bomb to save the lives of American boys?" a few wild-eyed congressmen argue. But there is never a question about resolving disputes diplomatically. That is for wimps, the language of the malaise days of Jimmy Carter. As President Bush neared the end of his first year in office, the nation was ready, even eager, to march to war under the jingoistic banner of conventional wisdom.

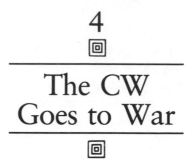

4

The CW
Goes to War

A commercial break had just ended when the familiar singsong sardonic Southern drawl of David Brinkley introduced the next topic for the journalist-pundits on *This Week with David Brinkley*, the upscale CW-setting show. "Well, the other day, the Panamanian government, to the extent it has a government—I think the American view is that it does not—anyway, announced it was at war with the United States," Brinkley rambled. "I don't know what that means, if it means anything. And then last night, a group of American officers in civilian clothes—unarmed or out for a lark, I guess—took a wrong turn and one of them wound up getting killed by a Panamanian mob. So what are we to do about this? George?"

The date was December 17, 1989, and what "we" were going to do about this was invade Panama. But that reality had not struck me until I heard the Brinkley team lightly and sloppily bandy about the options of war and peace. The famous "declaration of war," it turned out, came from press accounts of a resolution from the Panamanian assembly charging that U.S. economic sanctions and aggressive military maneuvers had created "a state of war" in Panama.[1] For his part, Panamanian general Manuel Noriega vowed to use new powers granted him judiciously, adding: "The North American scheme, through constant psychological and military harassment, has created a state of war in Panama," according to a Reuters dispatch.[2] Panama had not declared war against the United States or launched any hostile act against American territory. In the past, the very idea of a banana republic like Panama going to

war against the United States would have been the stuff of fanciful
novels, like *The Mouse That Roared*. But in today's Washington, the
bombastic CW took the threat seriously.

ABC News's mercurial Sam Donaldson joined the Brinkley war
debate, picking up the "declaration of war" theme. "Well, I guess
if you're talking about international law—although it sounds ridiculous here—if they declare war on us, we can declare war on them
and then we can send in the troops with impunity," he mused.
He apparently never thought to read Panama's purported declaration of war or assess the relevant terms of international law before
launching his verbal counteroffensive.

But the pundits failed to follow their own logic: that war was
in the offing. Instead, they talked tough about eliminating Noriega
through some covert military action or sponsoring a coup in Panama.
"I have no doubt that the Bush administration finally is going to
do something about Noriega," Donaldson declared. "Even as we
speak, I'm certain they're making some sort of plan to remove
him." But the sprightly Cokie Roberts was a skeptic. "Well, so
far, their plans haven't done very well," she sniped, referring to
an abortive coup against Noriega two months earlier.

"Yeah, but they've got a legal finding now, they say, that
they're going to be able to give help to groups as long as there's
no direct assassination connection, even though the assassination
of a government leader like Noriega could result from a coup,"
responded Donaldson.

Brinkley interjected the CW contempt for the finicky U.S.
prohibition against assassinating foreign leaders. "Can you imagine
a conversation among a group of military people trying to follow
that rule?" Brinkley harrumphed. " 'It's okay to kill him so long
as it was incidental and was not our principal purpose in shooting
him'? Now, come on." The impetuous Donaldson had another
idea: "Well, let's seize him. We now have decided, the Bush
administration in this extraterritorial dispute—territoriality dispute,
we can go anywhere and seize someone like Noriega wherever we
find him."

Donaldson was referring to a secret legal opinion that the
Justice Department had promulgated in June 1989 and then stone-
walledly refused to share with the American people or Congress.
It leaked two years later, however, and one could understand why
it had been kept secret. Its dubious arguments asserted an "in-

herent constitutional power" for the president and attorney general to violate international law whenever they identified "serious threats" to U.S. domestic security from "international terrorist groups or narcotics traffickers." Considering the administration's broad definition of "terrorism"—any act or threatened act of violence to influence any government's policy—and the vagueness of evidence required to prove drug smuggling, the secret power could be used to justify almost any extraterritorial action a president might desire. The Office of Legal Counsel opinion argued that "as a matter of domestic law, the executive has the power to authorize actions inconsistent" with international law, including the United Nations Charter and other treaties. Although the opinion gave a legal framework for the invasion of Panama, the twenty-nine-page document was withheld from Congress on the grounds that its release would discourage Justice Department lawyers from writing internal opinions.[3]

Surprisingly, it was conservative icon George Will who adopted a more cautious approach to the Panamanian crisis, recommending that the United States simply delay implementing the treaty relinquishing U.S. control over the Panama Canal. But responding to Brinkley's opening question, "What are we to do about this? George?," Will accepted the premises that Panama had declared war and the American soldier had been killed without provocation. "Well, you say you don't know what it means," Will said. "It means we're running out of cheeks to turn when they do disagreeable things to us. We're on a schedule, David, for turning over the canal to Panama by the end of this decade and removing the Southern Command, our forces, from Panama. What we should do now that they, on their own initiative, unprovoked, have said they're in a state of war with us, is stop the clock." "Of course," agreed Brinkley. "So that would be—that's one thing to do," Will continued with his prescription to punish Panama.

Roberts, a female voice for restraint among the bellicose men, argued against abrogating the canal treaty, but in true CW form, her reasoning was that the move would only help America's enemy, Noriega. "Stopping the clock, I think, is a bad idea because the truth is that that will just play into Noriega's hands," Roberts contended. "He's the one who's been saying all along that what the United States is really after is retaining control of the canal, that it's not really him. And every time he says that, he gets the support of the people of Panama. There's no better way to shore up Noriega than to say that we're going to keep the canal.''

Will partially agreed: "That is a danger, but that's a task, then, for public diplomacy, for us to say that our good faith has been proven. We signed the treaties, we complied with them right up to the point where they declared war on us. And if they want to start the clock again, we're perfectly willing to do it. We don't need to prove our good faith on that. They just have to get rid of Noriega and we're here to help.''

"All right," Brinkley said in wrapping up the prewar pontificating, "the other thing that's had Washington excited in recent days was the visit to China by the president's national security adviser . . .'' What had been typical and chilling about the CW posturing was that on this, the Brinkley show, perhaps the most civilized and erudite of the chat shows, no one had stopped to question the premises for war. No one had thought to insist on a precise reading of the "declaration of war," no one had cautioned against leaping to conclusions based on a murky shooting incident where many of the facts were in doubt and dispute. The concept of international law which prohibits one nation from invading another was pooh-poohed as an irrelevant inconvenience when a tinhorn dictator like Noriega was seen as thumbing his nose at the United States.

Perhaps, no principle of international law is more explicitly defined than the prohibition against invasions. Article 2 of the United Nations Charter states: "All members shall refrain in their international relations from the threat or use of force against the territorial integrity or political independence of any state." Article 20 of the Charter to the Organization of American States, to which the United States is also a signatory, declares, "The territory of a state is inviolable. It may not be the object, even temporarily, of military occupation or other measures of force taken by another state directly or indirectly on any grounds whatsoever." But with the flick of a pen, the Justice Department had secretly granted President Bush the power to waive these solemn commitments at his personal discretion—and the CW found little to fear from this remarkable expansion of executive power.

For that matter, whenever the question is U.S. prerogatives in its sphere of influence—Latin America and the Caribbean—Washington insiders have shown only impatience with the precepts of international law. In 1983, the invasion of leftist-ruled Grenada, a tiny tourist-and-nutmeg island, won warm approval throughout Washington as an effective application of power. For most of the last decade, the Reagan administration sponsored a proxy war against Nicaragua's Sandinista government, and the pundits saw the bloody exercise as a useful lesson in realpolitik.

Even outside the Western Hemisphere, the CW shapers displayed a manly understanding of American interventions. The CIA ran covert operations from Angola to Afghanistan to Cambodia with hardly a whimper from the Washington CW. Indeed, throughout the eighties, enthusiasm for sponsoring wars and violently meddling in other nations' affairs had become a test of a CW pundit's mettle.

One of the few times a TV pundit or top columnist could feel politically safe criticizing the Reagan-Bush administrations was when the White House refrained from intervention. Then, the chat-show talkers could posture against "softness" and show off their harder-line-than-thou credentials. In the months before the Panama invasion, these Clint Eastwood–talk-alike contestants saved their most venomous contempt for the timid souls who urged negotiated solutions. Such wimpy concerns were brushed aside in the he-man world of Washington punditry.

Yet the same pundits who would have guffawed at an international law argument in December 1989 turned almost reverential in their profound respect for the United Nations Charter in August 1990. Then, Iraq, similarly irked by a small neighbor to the south, launched a brutal invasion of Kuwait—and that act of aggression justified the United States again going to war, this time to defend international law. The CW would take no note of the inconsistency.

Throughout the brief but violent Panama invasion, dubbed Operation Just Cause, Washington's leading pundits showed little skepticism for the U.S. version of events. "When during the past few days [Noriega] declared war on the United States and some of his followers then killed a U.S. Marine, roughed up another American serviceman, also threatening that man's wife, strong public support for a reprisal was all but guaranteed," commented *Nightline*'s Ted Koppel on December 20, summing up the dubious rationalizations for the invasion. "Noriega's reputation as a brutal drug-dealing bully who reveled in his public contempt for the United States all but begged for strong retribution."[4]

The CW scrutinized the shooting of the Marine officer on December 16 almost as little as it did Noriega's purported "declaration of war." The curious case of the lost carload of Marines who ran a roadblock in front of the Panamanian Defense Force headquarters had followed weeks of mounting tensions, during which the CIA was implementing a $3 million covert program to oust Noriega from power. U.S. special operations personnel were also monitoring Noriega's minute-to-minute movements in case the orders came for his kidnapping.

Although presumably a miscalculation on all sides, the roadblock incident ending in the shooting death of Marine lieutenant Robert Paz ignited the long-smoldering tensions. Another U.S. military officer, Navy lieutenant Adam J. Curtis, and his wife, Bonnie, had been stopped at the same checkpoint while Panamanian soldiers verified their identification. Possibly suspecting some connection between the two groups of Americans or possibly in the excitement over the shooting, Panamanian soldiers then roughly questioned the Curtises. According to the Curtises' account of the four-hour ordeal, Lieutenant Curtis was accused of working for the CIA, gagged and kicked in the groin; Mrs. Curtis was fondled by Panamanian soldiers, who lewdly asked if she wanted to have sex with them. The couple was then abruptly released.

According to Bob Woodward's *The Commanders*, Lieutenant General Thomas W. Kelly did not consider the Paz shooting a deliberate provocation by Noriega, who had apparently been going out of his way to avoid giving the United States a casus belli for an invasion. "Kelly saw that the Paz incident wasn't a clear-cut incident of unprovoked PDF [Panamanian Defense Force] aggression—the car sped away from a legitimate roadblock, lending an element of ambiguity," Woodward reported.[5]

It was the brutal interrogation of the Curtises that grabbed the attention of Washington decision-makers, partly because a senior PDF officer reportedly participated and partly because the lurid story that included sexual propositioning of Mrs. Curtis was so revolting. Although the Curtises had been freed by PDF higher-ups and no sexual assault had actually occurred, the incident had been an affront to American manhood and a stark reminder of the months of U.S. impotence as the machete-waving Noriega publicly denounced American imperialism.

Left unsaid perhaps, but surely in the minds of President Bush and his advisers, was the certain reaction by Washington CW-setters if strong reprisals did not follow. The "wimp factor" would rear its ugly head again. There would be a resurgence of articles suggesting that Noriega was right when he boasted of having "Bush by the balls." Bush, after all, understood the political power of rape from his exploitation of the Willie Horton issue in the 1988 campaign. The recurring image of a black man raping a white woman while her male protector stood by helplessly had played well among American men who transferred their disgust onto the hapless Michael Dukakis, just as Bush's political advisers had hoped. Now the picture of dark-skinned Panamanians fondling an American woman while beating her soldier-husband was equally powerful—and dangerous.

Bush had undergone a CW pummeling when he chose not to back a spur-of-the-moment coup attempt against Noriega in early October. Political critics on both the right and left attacked him for first encouraging the Panamanians to oust Noriega themselves and then extending inadequate help when one PDF officer, Major Moises Giroldi, tried to do just that. The Giroldi coup failed and the PDF major was promptly executed. Bush's prudence "makes Jimmy Carter look like a man of resolve," chortled Congressman Dave McCurdy, a moderate-to-conservative Democrat from Oklahoma. "There's a resurgence of the wimp factor."[6]

The chat shows had been equally unforgiving. Conservative columnist and author Ben Wattenberg, pinch-punditing on *The McLaughlin Group*, charged that Bush's only policy was "prudence, prudence, prudence. Prudence is not a policy. . . . We ought to have a policy that 'floats like a butterfly and stings like a bee.' "[7]

Preppie-pundit Fred Barnes joined in swarming all over his usual allies with ridicule and contempt for their inaction. "I think they do have a policy," Barnes smirked. "The policy is, 'When in doubt, do nothing.' And that's what they did—nothing here. It was a massive failure of nerve. And then to come up with these whiny excuses about, 'Gee, it wasn't the right time, and rapidly changing circumstances, and it wasn't our plan,' that's ridiculous. If this were a baseball game, the fans would be going—the choke sign." Laugher all around.

Morton Kondracke, recognizing that the one safe time to break with the White House is when it urges caution, piled on with his own the-more-macho-the-better policy prescription: "Look, if your policy is to get rid of Noriega, you better get rid of Noriega. And it's quite clear that the civilians can't get rid of Noriega. Now if we want the military to get rid of Noriega, let us have a plan and let's get us to sponsor the coup, and get it done and get it done right. Where is the CIA in all of this?"

Only the crotchety Jack Germond called for cooler heads, but it was like he was speaking to an earlier, pre-CW era. "It seems to me that the mistake was made in the rhetoric—in the original rhetoric—of the Reagan administration and of vice-president, and now President Bush, about Noriega," Germond said. "You're never going to convince me that we have a compelling national interest in getting rid of Noriega that is so overwhelming that we substitute for it sponsorship of some junta that we don't know about."

Kondracke was almost speechless at such a heresy toward the prevailing CW. "We put our—we have now put our national prestige on the line on this issue," he blustered.

"What do you mean, we put our prestige on the line?" Germond shot back. "That's nonsense."

Kondracke: "Because we have gone so far down the line."

Kondracke then took his pro-interventionist club to the certifiably conservative Defense secretary, Dick Cheney. "The other bad thing that's happened here is that Dick Cheney, who used to masquerade as a hard-liner, is now saying things like, 'All we use force for is to protect American lives. We don't use force to install governments in other countries,' " Kondracke concluded in amazement. Nowhere was there even the slightest tip of the hat to the principle of international law.

On the next week's show, the clamor hadn't died down; it just got more personal for Bush. "The problem is," complained right-wing Patrick Buchanan, "that Mr. Bush has been going along with 'read my lips, Noriega must go,' again and again and again. When a chance came, now we get all this legalism about whether or not he should be taken out."[8]

"And look," jumped in Kondracke, "this guy was supposedly the crisis manager during the Reagan administration. He's been in office nine months screaming for Noriega's head, and they didn't have a plan, and they did not execute it when they did have a plan. You know, what's going to happen when they have a big crisis like East Germany or something?"

After McLaughlin inserted a clip of liberal Democratic congresswoman Patricia Schroeder taunting Bush as the "Revlon president," for offering only cosmetic solutions, Kondracke came back with even better insults. "I got two better lines than that," he said. "One is from Hendrik Hertzberg, the editor of *The New Republic*, who said, 'After complaining about Willie Horton, George Bush has now furloughed Manuel Noriega.' That's not bad, is it? The other one is that 'most of what comes from George Bush's bully pulpit is bull.' "

Listening to procoup CW barrage, Colin Powell, chairman of the Joint Chiefs of Staff, thought Washington had lost its senses. Woodward reported in *The Commanders* that Powell "had seen emotional foreign-policy battles before, but never piling on of this intensity, and across the whole political spectrum. It was as if there was a lynch mob out there."[9]

With that backdrop, a tepid response to the abuse of the Curtises would have brought the CW roar to even higher decibels. Instead, Bush chose to lead the CW chorus rather than be deafened by it. He would repeatedly cite the "threatened rape" as the clearest justification for invading Panama. Responding to the Soviet denunciation of the invasion, Bush said he would tell Soviet president Mikhail Gorbachev, "Look, if they kill an American Marine, that's real bad. And if they threaten and brutalize the wife of an American citizen, sexually threatening the lieutenant's wife while kicking him in the groin over and over again, then, Mr. Gorbachev, please understand this president is going to do something about it."

Amid the CW's drum-beating for war, no one seemed to give much thought to the possibility that the Panamanian soldiers simply might have overreacted after the Marines panicked and sped through the roadblock. It seems that Washington's CW can forgive human mistakes only when committed by American troops in pressure-cooker situations. For instance, the CW was very understanding on July 3, 1988, when U.S. naval crewmen blew an Iranian civilian airliner out of the sky after mistaking it for an attack aircraft during a naval skirmish in the Persian Gulf.

The attitude toward rape can also vary when done by friends as opposed to enemies. In December 1980, when Salvadoran soldiers raped and murdered four American churchwomen, representatives of the incoming Reagan-Bush administration offered up rationalizations, rather than revulsion. UN-ambassador-to-be Jeane

Kirkpatrick called the victims "not just nuns. The nuns were political activists . . . on behalf of the [leftist opposition] Frente and
somebody who is using violence to oppose the Frente killed these
nuns," according to an article in the *Tampa* (Florida) *Tribune*. Kirkpatrick would later insist that the quote was "taken out of context"
when she was confronted with it by a human rights lawyer and a
relative of one of the victims.[10] But if accurate, Mrs. Kirkpatrick's
comments suggest that it's not so bad to rape and murder left-wing
political activists.

Early in his tenure, Secretary of State Alexander Haig also
went to bat for the Salvadoran military, offering another explanation
for the premeditated slaughter of the churchwomen. "The nuns
may have run through a roadblock or may have accidentally been
perceived to have been doing so, and there may have been an
exchange of fire," Haig told the House Foreign Affairs Committee.[11] Even at the time, State Department officials responsible for
the investigation were horrified. All the evidence pointed to a cold-
blooded murder: the women had been taken to a remote location,
they had been sexually assaulted and then shot to death at close
range. But the anticommunist hard-liners of the Reagan administration had bent over backwards to be understanding.

Even more on point was a tragic incident on December 24,
1989, four days after the Panama invasion. A nine-months-pregnant
Panamanian woman, Otilia López de Perea, went into labor shortly
after midnight. She was helped into the family Volkswagen and
with her husband, her mother-in-law, and a neighbor, headed to
the hospital. Their car flew a white flag and stopped at a U.S.
military roadblock on the Transisthmian Highway. The four Panamanians requested an escort, but were told that it wasn't necessary. They were waved through, but after driving another five
hundred yards, American troops at a second checkpoint opened
fire, mistaking the Volkswagen for a hostile vehicle. The ten-
second barrage killed López de Perea and her twenty-five-year-old
husband Ismael. The neighbor was wounded in the stomach, and
the mother-in-law, though unhurt, was hysterical. The unborn baby
was dead.[12]

Though acknowledging the facts of the incident, the U.S.
military refused any compensation to the family with a terse form
letter. The U.S. Southern Command said its investigation found
that the incident "although tragic in nature, indicate[s] that the

U.S. personnel acted within the parameters of the rules of engagement in effect at that time." Mistakes happen. Almost certainly,
the young American troops panicked at the sight of a fast-moving
car speeding along the darkened highway. But the CW forgives
human foibles only among Americans, it seems.

     The CW showed no recognition that young Panamanian troops
could also overreact after the tragic shooting at the PDF roadblock
a week earlier. That incident justified an invasion, even though
American officials had recognized that Noriega had been trying to
avoid giving the United States a pretext for war. The Panamanians
had concluded, correctly, that the Bush White House was spoiling
for a fight. *The New York Times* reported on December 24 that "the
Bush administration laid the foundation for the attack against Gen.
Manuel Antonio Noriega weeks ago by drafting new military plans,
rehearsing them and secretly moving tanks and helicopters to Panama in case President Bush decided to order United States forces
into action, senior administration officials said."[13] The overheated
CW atmosphere—and Bush's open animosity toward Noriega—
had made the invasion of Panama a war waiting for an excuse. The
roadblock incident was it.

     On the night of December 19–20, 1989, the U.S. military
demonstrated the newly embraced concept of "overwhelming
force." Employing sophisticated weaponry, including the maiden
attack voyage of the F-117 Stealth fighter, American forces poured
down terrifying firepower not only on Panamanian troops but on
civilian neighborhoods that abutted the military targets. The brief,
violent war was a larger-scale version of the 1983 U.S. invasion of
Grenada and would be a prelude to the even larger conflict in the
Persian Gulf a year later.

     Although little noted amid the excitement, the Panamanian
invasion was also a repudiation of the concept of low-intensity
conflict, which had been in military vogue during much of the
1980's. LIC, as it is known to its devotees, emphasized use of
indigenous forces trained and supported by the United States. The
idea was to keep the American role in the background while U.S.
proxy forces wore down an adversary of America and emerged as
a viable nationalist force to govern a country.

     LIC, however, had achieved only limited success and often
left unpleasant messes along the way. The Nicaraguan contras

required constant public-relations assistance to cloak their reputation as a brutal, undemocratic, corrupt, drug-tainted army. The
Afghan rebels, though idolized by the Washington CW crowd,
proved themselves to be contralike inept when the Soviet army
withdrew and the fractious guerrillas spent as much energy fighting
each other and protecting their heroin-smuggling routes as ousting
the Soviet puppet government in Kabul. Even model guerrilla
leader Jonas Savimbi in Angola fell short of his Washington press
clippings when former supporters began recounting grisly human-
rights abuses, including the burning of rebel dissidents at the stake.

So when the U.S. military was called on to remove Noriega
from power, the old-line Pentagon commanders eschewed the advice of the LIC advocates and brought Armageddon down on the
heads of the PDF and many nearby civilians. By all accounts,
civilian deaths were heavy in the first hours of fighting, as fires
raged through the El Chorillo slums near Noriega's *comandancia*.
But the White House public-relations specialists solved that problem by just making sure the bodies weren't counted. The CW
crowd showed little concern about death and destruction when it
was Washington's military machine inflicting the devastation.

As U.S. troops and aircraft pounced on Noriega's pathetic
defense forces, American newsmen shed any pretense of objectivity
and joined in the enthusiasm for war. CBS anchorman Dan Rather
put Noriega "at the top of the list of the world's drug thieves and
scums," an assessment shared by no expert on international narcotics trafficking. ABC's Peter Jennings termed the Panamanian
dictator "one of the more odious creatures with whom the United
States has had a relationship." NBC's John Chancellor wondered,
"Do we bring him here and put him on trial . . . or do we just
neutralize him in some way?"[14]

In those first days, the American press corps virtually ignored
the questions of Panamanian civilian casualties, a marked contrast
to the routine printing of even wildly erroneous estimates of dead
in other circumstances, from political fighting in Romania to ty-
phoon devastation in Bangladesh.

Oddly, it was a former Reagan administration image-molder,
David Gergen, who first noticed this oversight as well as the widely
reported error announcing Panama's "declaration of war." Appearing by satellite from Mexico for his weekly commentary on
PBS's *MacNeil/Lehrer NewsHour,* Gergen marveled at how diamet-

rically opposed were Latin America's reality and Washington's. "As you remember last week, we understood in the American press that Noriega had declared war against us and that is what we all reported," Gergen said. "Their understanding here in Mexico was that Noriega had said we are in a state of war with the United States. Not that he had declared war."

The former Reagan communications director observed that while Latin Americans were fixated on the large numbers of civilians believed dead, he could find almost no estimates in the American news media. "We see this as a surgical strike to grab Noriega and restore democracy," Gergen reported. "They see it as an occupation by American forces, yet another example of Yanqui imperialism. We see this in terms of the number of American soldiers being killed, and we watched the bodies return with great sadness. Here in Mexico, they talk almost entirely about the number of Panamanian civilians being killed, and the newspapers display bodies of civilians. And they have pictures of buildings that appear to be civilian buildings with great clouds of smoke over them and people in the street."[15]

Days after the fighting had died down, human-rights groups and critics of the war began working on their own count of the civilian dead, eventually estimating about 2,000 killed. In response, the U.S. military finally offered a competing estimate of 202 Panamanian civilians dead, compared with 23 American servicemen and 315 Panamanian soldiers. Although unable to fix a reliable number, the U.S.-based human-rights group Americas Watch denounced the American bombardment of Noriega's military headquarters as indiscriminate. "Under the Geneva Accords, the attacking party has the obligation to minimize harm to civilians," an Americas Watch investigator told me at the time. He complained that American commanders showed "a great preoccupation with minimizing American casualties because it would not go over politically here to have a large number of U.S. military deaths."

But that blasé concern about Panamanian lives matched exactly the attitude of the CW. Once the war was won and Noriega captured to face drug charges in Miami, the CW cared little about establishing such historical details as the number of bystanders who were gunned down during the arrest. Plus it wasn't easy to get a reasonable count of civilian deaths, because the U.S. military and the new Panamanian government quickly bulldozed the remains of hundreds of dead, dumped uncounted into mass graves. To avoid the unsightly public relations of this gruesome cover-up, news cameras were forcibly prevented from filming the burials.

The American press did not revisit the grisly cost of the glorious victory for nine months. Then only in the run-up to the Bush administration's next war in the Persian Gulf did CBS's *60 Minutes* ask the question, How many Panamanian civilians died to get Manuel Noriega? "If civilian casualties are an issue in the war that the U.S. seems to be edging closer to in the Middle East, perhaps it's a good time to take a hard look at what happened to civilians the last time the United States went to war: the invasion of Panama, Operation Just Cause," intoned correspondent Mike Wallace.[16]

The popular CBS newsmagazine cited an estimate of four thousand civilian dead from Isabelle Coro, a Panamanian activist who had raised money to dig up two of an estimated six or seven mass graves. Other religious and human-rights groups considered Coro's figure exaggerated, estimating instead the numbers at between five hundred and two thousand civilians killed. "But how in the world was the U.S. Army able to hide the number of civilian deaths in a country with a population of only two million people?" asked Wallace. "One way was to bury the bodies secretly in mass graves and to attempt to stop reporters from taking pictures like this." The program then showed an American soldier blocking a reporter and cameraman from filming a mass burial.

Although the CW had been fast to embrace President Bush's assurance that "the way we went after some of these targets was to minimize civilian casualties," Wallace's team uncovered a different reality, more in line with Americas Watch's complaint. "One of the targets hardest hit was the *comandancia*, the military headquarters of Manuel Noriega's Panama Defense Forces," Wallace reported. "It sat in the middle of a Panama City slum known as El Chorillo. Twenty-five thousand people lived here and they were asleep in their beds when the world around them began to incinerate."

Wallace interviewed a former U.S. Army lawyer who was representing some of the war's Panamanian victims. "I personally was surprised that we invaded Panama in the way and in the scale that we did," said the lawyer, John Kiyonaga. "In a scenario like that, a planner has to know that there's going to be heavy loss of noncombatant life." The American aerial assault on El Chorillo ignited fires that raged out of control. By morning, "reports had already begun to circulate that hundreds of civilians had been killed and thousands wounded in El Chorillo alone," Wallace said. "When the fires finally burned themselves out, El Chorillo had ceased to exist."

Even at the time, American military critics warned about the dangers of such a brutal victory. Retired Special Forces sergeant Bruce Hazelwood, who spent much of his Green Beret career in Central America and Panama, told me shortly after the invasion that reliance on massive firepower would only generate anti-Americanism down the road. "We have given a chance for nationalism to grow in Panama," cautioned Hazelwood, an advocate of surgical special operations and a critic of the conventional tactics used in the invasion. "We have saddled ourselves with the responsibility of running Panama."

The Bush administration and its stable of paid rationalizers, however, denied any mistakes. There were "no mass graves and never were," declared Assistant Secretary of State Bernard Aronson, a protégé and successor of the notorious dissembler Elliott Abrams. The press reports, Aronson told a House panel on July 30, 1991, were sheer "demagoguery."[17]

Insisting on instant analysis and swaggering about the need to teach "our enemies" a lesson, the CW can be counted on to play into the hands of any White House call for war, if not go out in front and provoke the call. Since the TV pundits comment on issues that they often know little about, they rely heavily on a quick reading of the daily newspapers, absorbing enough about a subject to form a fast opinion but not enough to complicate their thought processes. They are also fed tidbits of information from their White House friends so they can sound like they have actually done some reporting. The CW, even on life-and-death issues like war, is shaped without serious reflection on the other side's case or the historical realities that underlie many disputes. The pundits recognize that it is politically safest to strike a belligerently pro-American stance on any foreign conflict.

Only later—often much later—do less heated commentaries about the war's prelude expose the exaggerations and even falsehoods that incited the nation to war. For instance, amid the Noriega vilification, the American press trumpeted the discovery of 110 pounds of cocaine in a house used by Noriega. It later turned out to be tamale flour.[18] But Jonathan Alter's dictum that the CW "never apologizes, never explains" fits the conventional wisdom about momentous decisions like war and peace as much as it does the twists and turns of a presidential campaign. Only the consequences are different.

In the year after Operation Just Cause, anti-Americanism was growing as thousands of war refugees marched in Panama's streets protesting the squalor of their temporary housing. A coup against the U.S.-installed president, Guillermo Endara, was put down only by the intervention of American troops. The pudgy Endara, the apparent winner in the May 1989 election that had been voided by Noriega, proved an inept administrator, more devoted to his young bride than to governing Panama. The jobless rate lingered at from one quarter to one third of the work force. Crime waves swept the nation, prompting even the attorney general to show off his gold-plated Uzi submachine gun to visitors. The automatic money-counters were humming again at the shadowy banks that had long been the backbone of Panama's service economy.

Worse yet for the United States, Panama's central role in cocaine trafficking—long blamed on Noriega—was flourishing again, even as the deposed military strongman sat in a Florida jail awaiting trial. Police asserted that the Colombian drug cartels had opened a new cocaine-processing plant in the Panamanian jungles along the Colombian border.[19] The General Accounting Office reported that in the months after the invasion, the flow of drugs and drug money through Panama rose dramatically. The GAO noted that in the first quarter of 1991, cocaine seizures in Panama tripled over the previous three months.

The dirty Panamanian banks again were busy laundering millions in drug profits—bank deposits soared to $21 billion by mid-1991 from a 1989 low of $8.5 billion—and the nation's sleazier lawyers were churning out corporate fronts to hide criminal activity, a two-thirds increase in the paper corporations from late 1989. "Panama's money-laundering center has recovered briskly," wrote author James S. Henry. "Its several hundred lawyers and bankers are among the few groups in the economy that are unambiguously better off. As one lawyer now says, 'Noriega was bad for business—no one wanted to bring dollars here anymore.' "[20]

Even more embarrassing, local press reports linked senior Panamanian officials to the laundering of millions of dollars in drug profits, both before and after the invasion. As it turned out, President Endara had even served as a lawyer, director and board secretary for Interbanco, a Panama City bank that Henry describes as "virtually a wholly-owned subsidiary of the cartel." Endara, of course, denied knowing anything about the drug money and announced that he had resigned from Interbanco's board three months before the story broke in August 1990 in *El Siglo,* a local newspaper. The reporter who dug out the story was then jailed by Endara's democratic government for one week. Although declaring his ignorance about Interbanco's drug taint, Endara was also mentioned in a 1991 Florida indictment as the lawyer who set up several companies used by two big-time drug traffickers to launder an alleged $2.4 billion in drug profits.[21]

In another odd twist of history, Henry reported that Endara had worked as a lawyer for Manuel Contreras, the chief of DINA, Chile's brutal secret police under the military dictatorship of General Augusto Pinochet. Lawyer Endara had arranged companies and accounts for Contreras to funnel money to foreign agents, including those who assassinated dissident diplomat Orlando Letelier on the streets of Washington. Contreras, at the time, was considered an intelligence asset by the CIA, which was under the direction of George Bush.

Administration officials naturally sought to minimize the continuing drug-trafficking problem, just as they had maximized it in 1989. Aronson dismissed the GAO's findings, arguing that cocaine trafficking was on the rise in a half-dozen countries in the region, so why single out Panama? "There's more drugs moving through Brazil, there's more drugs moving through Venezuela, . . . there's more drugs moving through parts of the Caribbean," Aronson lamented to *The Washington Post.*[22] "But that's because it's being stamped out elsewhere. That doesn't prove anything about the will of the [Panamanian] government to combat trafficking."

But Aronson's apologia conflicted with observations by others who kept a post-invasion eye on Panama. As Henry more accurately concluded in the wake of the invasion to capture Manuel Noriega: "So the general may have been brought to justice, but Panama remains on the loose." And eighteen months after Operation Just Cause, Congressman John Conyers, Jr., chairman of the House Government Operations Committee, warned that "with almost no notice in Washington, a foreign policy disaster is brewing in Panama. What is being lost is the chance to give life to a sovereign, independent and democratic Panama and to stop drug trafficking and money laundering. . . . More money laundering and drug trafficking are going on now than before the invasion. Even the Department of State has called the current Panamanian record on drugs 'spotty.' There is a shortfall in the political will needed to break the back of sweetheart deals between the money launderers and the banks of Panama."[23]

But the last thing the Washington CW and its pundits possess is staying power. Within days of the exciting Panama invasion, the CW had pushed on to new adventures, forgetting to count the dead or take note of the havoc the wildly popular invasion had just caused. That the most significant "success" of the invasion, to put a crimp in Panama's lucrative role as a drug and money-laundering way station, had backfired was of little interest to the CW. It could count on government spokesmen like Aronson to explain away the facts.

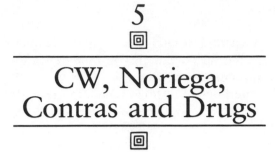

5

CW, Noriega,
Contras and Drugs

Reporters from dozens of newspapers and television stations pushed toward the doorway of the Miami courtroom of U.S. district judge William Hoeveler. Some were pleading with the marshals, begging for one of the few precious seats reserved for the news media. They all wanted to see Panama's newly deposed dictator, General Manuel Noriega. Like many pack-journalism scenes, this one resembled the crush of children at a zoo as the kids wriggle and shove their way to the bars of a cage to get the best look at a rare animal that had just ventured into view.

On this occasion, Noriega's arraignment, only a handful of reporters would get in, either those from the principal daily newspapers and TV networks or a lucky few who had won a lottery for the remaining open seats. That, however, would not check the forces of pack journalism, which drew the overflow crowd of journalists, including me as a *Newsweek* correspondent. A principal law of pack journalism is that the more obvious a story and the less resourcefulness needed to get it, the more reporters it will draw. The arraignment of Manuel Noriega was a case in point.

Conventional wisdom and pack journalism, of course, share a common lineage, the tendency for editors to want the same story that all their competitors want. It comes from the basic law of supply and demand. The recognition that others want a story drives up its value, much as the impression in Washington that a candidate is on the skids will push him out of the race. If, as Mickey Kaus says, the CW is the political stock market, then pack journalism is the crush in the pit as stock traders shout their buy and sell orders.

While the CW manifests itself through the television pundits and newspaper columnists who reinforce each others' silly points of view, pack journalism is a physical presence, literally a pack of journalists baying after a controversial news figure or hot story.

At such moments of journalistic frenzy, teams of newsmen will camp out on the target's lawn, sometimes scaling trees to peek through windows. Cameras swing into action, opening swaths of clear sight lines before them. Boom microphones are shoved into people's faces. Print reporters press close enough to catch a few words or shout a question. Indeed, many reporters who participate in such mob scenes actually believe they have covered the story because they have been at the scene of the action.

Invariably, though, little is learned that's enlightening or new. But the pack-journalism media event itself has come to define what is considered news. Increasingly, editors demand first-person accounts from the scene, even if that's not where the truly important information is to be found. This on-scene reporting is a necessity for broadcast journalists who need the backdrop for their television reports. But print reporters, too, have learned the value of "being there" for the color that allows them to write in the personal style that editors so encourage, even when nothing of note is actually happening.

Sitting in the "front row of history" is an understandable desire of journalists, but it is what happens offstage that is usually more important to understanding history. And it is the offstage events that have received less and less attention in a television-dominated age. Yet if only a tiny fraction of the money spent on covering Noriega's arraignment had been spent five years earlier to investigate the dictator's cozy relationship with senior U.S. officials, the entire tragedy of Panama might have been averted. But exposing Noriega's wrongdoing was not in the White House's interest at the time and, by the mid-1980's, the CW-dominated Washington press corps had been well-trained to take its lead on defining news from the White House.

Only for the past three years had the unflattering spotlight of notoriety fallen on Noriega. The legendary investigative reporter Seymour Hersh had started Noriega's fall from grace with a front-page exposé of Noriega's alleged drug links. The story ran in *The New York Times* on June 12, 1986, and charged that "the army commander of Panama, a country vital to United States interests in Latin America, is extensively involved in illicit money laundering and drug activities and has provided a Latin American guerrilla group with arms, according to evidence collected by American intelligence agencies." The army commander, of course, was Noriega, and the guerrilla group was the Colombian M-19 leftist rebels.[1]

But the article also quoted administration officials as saying "they had overlooked General Noriega's illegal activities because of his cooperation with American intelligence and his willingness to permit the American military extensive leeway in Panama. They said, for example, that General Noriega had been a valuable asset to Washington in countering insurgencies in Central America and was now cooperating with the Central Intelligence Agency in providing sensitive information from Nicaragua."

Noriega saw the sudden unflattering attention as a warning from his White House friends that they were tired of his double-dealing on Nicaragua and Cuba. Having grown up in the shadowy world of intelligence dirty tricks, Noriega suspected that Hersh's *New York Times* article had been planted to punish him for his independence.

Instead of kowtowing to Washington, however, he lashed back. According to a former top intelligence aide for Noriega, José Blandon, the general ordered the seizure of a Danish freighter, the *Pia Vesta*, that was carrying a load of East bloc rifles and grenade launchers. Blandon claimed the White House intended to plant the weapons in El Salvador so they could be "discovered" as evidence of Nicaraguan support of leftist Salvadoran rebels. The predictable CW fury against the Sandinistas that would have followed discovery of the long-elusive "smoking gun" of Sandinista support for the Salvadoran guerrillas would presumably have swung enough congressional swing votes in June 1986 to guarantee a reauthorization of the then-suspended CIA contra funding.

The man who arranged the *Pia Vesta* shipment, French arms dealer George Starckmann, told me five years later that the shipment had been coordinated with White House officials close to Oliver North. Starckmann said the Americans had ordered that the weapons be shipped to El Salvador through Noriega, just as Blandon had alleged. But as the *Pia Vesta* lumbered into Panama's waters en route to El Salvador on June 14—two days after Hersh's article—Noriega had the boat seized and its cargo emptied.

As official Washington tired of Noriega's game-playing, the

little dictator fell deeper into CW disfavor. By 1988, he had been indicted on drug-trafficking charges and publicly denounced in Senate hearings. Noriega was well on his way to a CW rating which might be summarized, "Old CW: Wily ally. New CW: Satan." By December 1989, when U.S. troops invaded Panama, the machete-waving general had become the dictator the CW loved to hate.

Noriega was that little pock-faced demon whose very existence drove the CW setters to their thesauruses in search of fresh insults. Noriega inspired supposedly objective journalists to use words like "slither," "thug," "scum," "odious." A *Newsweek* excerpt from a book by *Wall Street Journal* reporter Frederick Kempe was typical in its venomous contempt for Noriega. Kempe recalled Noriega's origins as "mean-streets Mestizo, the bastard son of his father's domestic." Kempe cast the low-life Noriega as a stark contrast to the blue-blood Bush when the two met in 1976 during Bush's one-year stint as CIA director. "Noriega offered his usual damp, limp handshake to Bush's firm grip," Kempe wrote.[2]

A month before Noriega's capture, an American visitor, human-rights activist Larry Birns, had a different, CW-clashing view of the Panamanian dictator. Birns found Noriega a nervous but charismatic man, who saw "himself as the great national liberation figure of the hemisphere [who is] doomed to be martyred for standing for the inviolable Latin American principle of sovereignty and independence." Noriega spoke spiritually, Birns recalled. "He made constant references to the church and Christianity. . . . He looked like a man possessed. He had that look of Jeanne d'Arc as they lit the fire. He had that look of doom on his face."

Birns, the iconoclastic director of the liberal Council on Hemispheric Affairs, had been invited to meet with Noriega apparently because Birns was one of the few voices in Washington to challenge the prevailing CW that international law should be cast aside to get Noriega. Birns considered the U.S. strangulation of the Panamanian economy and other pressures to drive Noriega from power a violation of the country's sovereignty.

But Birns was no Noriega patsy. He had long criticized Noriega's human-rights record and used his preinvasion visit to meet with opposition figures who claimed that Noriega had executed fifty-five to seventy-five rebellious officers after the failed Giroldi coup in October. Birns said one captain was reportedly

killed when he infuriated Noriega by turning in his Mercedes automobile as a protest against the government's corruption.

The CW, however, felt little patience toward the subtleties
of Noriega's complex personality. After his capture, the press reveled in his humiliation. His mug shot graced the covers of newspapers and newsmagazines, including that of *Newsweek*. He had
been reduced to federal prisoner #41586.

In Judge Hoeveler's packed courtroom, Noriega tried to maintain an air of self-assurance, dressing in a formal military shirt with
his general's stars on each shoulder. His lead attorney, Frank Rubino, termed him a "political prisoner" and declared that Noriega
refused to recognize the jurisdiction of the American court. Rubino,
an experienced member of what is called in Miami the "white
powder bar," charged that Noriega had been captured illegally by
U.S. authorities in violation of international law. The general's
apprehension "was made under coercion and intimidation," Rubino
said. He claimed Noriega had been forced into surrender by a threat
that the Panamanian government would lift the diplomatic sanc-
tuary of the Vatican nunciature, where Noriega was holed up. That
could have left Noriega and his associates at the mercy of angry
mobs of Panamanian citizens, the lawyer contended. "Many lives
could have been lost," Rubino said.

The arraignment marked the start of complex legal machin-
ations that would grind on under the patient eye of Judge Hoeveler
for many months. Much of the defense maneuvering would focus
on Noriega's so-called CIA defense, his claim that his contact with
drug traffickers was authorized for intelligence-gathering purposes
by the U.S. government. Even before Noriega's capture, Rubino
had told me that the general had discussed with his attorneys which
U.S. government documents should be subpoenaed. "A great por-
tion will be on Nicaragua," Rubino said. "The Reagan administration was tremendously preoccupied with waging a war in
Nicaragua."

Noriega's name-dropping—his disclosures of connections with
powerful Americans—was another inconvenient detail about the
Panama invasion that the CW-pundits had played down during the
patriotic upsurge around the invasion. To the CW, this nagging
question was best explained by simply asserting that the U.S. government turned on Noriega after it learned that he might be tied

to drug trafficking. ABC's Peter Jennings summed up this explanation: "Let's remember that the United States was very close to Mr. Noriega before the whole question of drugs came up."[3] This sanitized version of history allowed Americans to think that their government may have misjudged Noriega initially but rejected him as soon as he revealed himself as a man who would assist drug traffickers. That rendition of reality, however, conflicted with accounts even from longtime Noriega boosters in Washington that U.S. intelligence first learned of his assistance to the drug trade in the early 1970's.

According to U.S. intelligence sources, the CIA had begun to receive allegations linking Noriega to illicit activities, including drug trafficking, by 1973. But the sources said those reports were not considered solid enough to drop what the CIA saw as a promising intelligence informant. After all, Panama's hospitality to drug lords and revolutionaries made it an ideal intelligence window. When Bush met personally with Noriega in 1976—feeling the Mestizo bastard's "damp, limp handshake"—Bush sought Noriega's help in obtaining intelligence about Castro's Cuba, which had used Panamanian corporations to circumvent the U.S. trade embargo.

Besides Noriega's ties to drug traffickers, the dictator had long been active in undercover arms shipments, both for U.S. friends and enemies. According to Blandon, the weapons often were purchased in Europe by former Israeli Mossad officer Michael Harrari, a mysterious and sinister figure in Noriega's security apparatus. Harrari had been fired by the Mossad after one of his assassination teams bungled a 1973 attempt to kill a suspected Palestinian terrorist. Harrari's assassins had murdered the wrong man, a Moroccan waiter who worked at a restaurant in Lillehammer, Norway.[4] Until the U.S. invasion in 1989, Harrari had directed Noriega's personal security details and, after the invasion, he was quietly allowed to flee Panama and return to Israel.

Although working for U.S. intelligence, Noriega allowed weapons shipments to the leftist Nicaraguan Sandinista rebels before they overthrew U.S.-backed dictator Anastasio Somoza in 1979 and later to Marxist-led guerrillas in El Salvador. One of Noriega's arms-laden planes even crashed in El Salvador, prompting the Salvadoran government to protest to Panama.[5] Noriega's inconsistency annoyed some elements of U.S. intelligence, but his ability to glean secrets from American adversaries and Panama's strategic location made him invaluable to others. Noriega was dropped from the CIA's payroll by President Carter's exasperated CIA director Stansfield Turner, but was reactivated in 1981 by President Reagan's CIA chief, William J. Casey.

Rewarding Casey's trust, Noriega soon put his pilots to work flying arms from Panama to Costa Rica for the anti-Sandinista contras. One Noriega pilot, Werner Lotz, said the flights mixed drugs and guns, with the guns dropped off in northern Costa Rica and the drugs flown on to the United States.[6] Other cocaine traffickers and contra fighters have made similar statements to federal authorities and American reporters, although the Reagan-Bush administrations sought to shield the contras from blame for the drug flow.

The recurring allegations, tying Noriega to drug trafficking, would lead eventually to his indictment and his extraordinary arrest. But it was Noriega's support for a negotiated settlement to Central America's bloody conflicts that would offend his Reagan-administration patrons and resurrect his image as an unreliable ally. Ever playing both sides, Noriega promoted diplomatic efforts by the so-called Contadora group, consisting of four Latin American countries (Venezuela, Mexico, Colombia and Panama) and named for an island off Panama where the negotiations began. The idea behind the Contadora peace effort was to bring a halt to the contra war in Nicaragua and a political settlement to the bloody conflict in El Salvador. The plan, however, was viewed with disfavor in the United States, where the Reagan administration had set its sights on the outright ouster of Nicaragua's Sandinistas.

On a warm December day in 1983, *Air Force Two* touched down in Panama for a refueling stop. It had carried Vice-President Bush from the inauguration of the new Argentinian president and would next fly to El Salvador, another Latin American crisis point. Bush bounded from the plane and into a crowded airport reception area. After shaking hands with Panamanian and American dignitaries, he was guided into a small, blue-painted meeting room. He sat on one end of a large sofa, under the painting of a large white bird. Next to him was Panama's president, Ricardo de la Espriella. On another sofa, at Bush's left elbow, sat Manuel Noriega, leaning intently forward. Across the room was a senior Noriega aide, Colonel Roberto Díaz-Herrara. When the door closed, even some senior

American officials who had hoped to join the meeting found themselves on the outside.

The men sat around a wooden coffee table, adorned with a Christmas-season poinsettia. Looking at ease and in charge, Bush stretched his right arm over the back of the sofa and crossed his long legs. He talked in the direction of de la Espriella, but his message was meant less for the figurehead president than the military strongman, Noriega, whom Bush had known since both headed their nations' intelligence services in 1976. Noriega, wearing a light brown military shirt with epaulets on his shoulders and the PDF insignia on his sleeve, perched attentively on the edge of his seat, a marked contrast to the relaxed Bush. What was said during that meeting on December 11, 1983, might go a long way to explain what Bush knew about the mounting drug corruption in Panama and when he knew it. But the conversation has been treated as something of a state secret by Bush and his advisers. The Washington press corps has never pried too hard to get answers.

During the 1988 U.S. presidential campaign, while working at *Newsweek*, I contacted Díaz-Herrara, who had been present, and another top Noriega aide, José Blandon, who claimed to have received a full briefing about the meeting shortly after the talk ended. Díaz-Herrara was reluctant to discuss Bush's role in the meeting. After splitting with Noriega, he had fled to Venezuela, where American sources have said he was receiving at least indirect financial support from the U.S. government.

After much coaxing, however, he agreed to give his recollection of the discussion. He said Bush had complained about drug-money laundering in Panama and pressed for Panamanian help against the leftist Sandinista government. "Bush had two basic messages for Noriega," Díaz-Herrara said, paraphrasing the vice-president's statements. " 'We will be behind you as long as you behave yourself. We are aware of some of your unscrupulous activities, and those do not bother us so much. But you must stop your support for Cuba and Nicaragua, and get firmly behind the contra effort. That is the principal U.S. objective in Central America.' "

In a separate interview, Blandon, a small, owlish-looking man who had served as Noriega's intelligence chief, agreed that Bush

had complained about Panamanian money-laundering and had simultaneously sought support for the White House's anti-Sandinista
position. Neither Díaz-Herrara nor Blandon contended that the
vice-president had explicitly linked the drugs and contra issues as
a trade-off. An American participant at the meeting, then-ambas-
sador Everett Briggs, confirmed only that Bush expressed concern
about Panama's handling of drug money. Briggs added that Bush
may have requested diplomatic support on Nicaragua but never
asked for military assistance.

Although Bush has refused to divulge the full contents of the
meeting, it makes sense that Nicaragua would have been one of
the topics. By December 1983, the Reagan White House was in a
tizzy over how to sustain the growing contra army. Congress had
already voted to put the CIA on a $24 million contra allowance,
and the Reagan administration had begun panhandling allies to
supplement the contra stipend. Bush spokesmen acknowledge that
the vice-president complained about laundering drug money, but
they have stopped there on the grounds that the talk was a "privileged" communication with a head of state, de la Espriella. For
his part, Noriega, even before falling into American custody, had
told his lawyer, Frank Rubino, that Bush indeed had sought Panama's assistance on the White House's front-burner issue, ousting
the leftist Sandinistas in Nicaragua.

After the Bush meeting, Blandon said it was ex–Mossad officer
Harrari who put two and two together and advised Noriega that
the way to lessen U.S. pressure on the drug issue was to help the
Americans on Nicaragua. Blandon said that on Noriega's instructions in early 1984, he contacted the office of Donald Gregg, Vice-
President Bush's national security adviser and a longtime CIA
officer. Blandon said those contacts led to Noriega's assistance to
contra units, especially those fighting from Costa Rican bases under
former Sandinista hero Eden Pastora. Gregg has emphatically denied Blandon's claim, contending that he and Bush knew nothing
about illegal efforts to sustain the contras during the 1984–86
congressional aid cutoff.

Two conservative American arms dealers who supplied the
contras during the cutoff told me, however, that Gregg had overseen the original network for funneling non–U.S. government aid
to the contras prior to the arrival on the scene of Lieutenant Colonel
Oliver L. North. They even gave me a hand-drawn chart, showing

Bush and Gregg at the top of the early contra support network, which purportedly used CIA-trained Cuban exiles, including Felix Rodriguez and Mario Delamico, and Honduran intelligence officers to distribute the equipment in the region. Responsibility for the contra supplies, they said, was later given to North, who incorporated some of the Cubans, like Rodriguez, into his network but also relied heavily on former CIA logistical experts, including Richard Secord and Thomas Clines.

Despite the vociferous denials from both Gregg and Bush about playing any role in the contra supply operation, the evidence is clear that Noriega did pitch in with a helping hand. In July 1984, Noriega funneled a $100,000 contribution to contras on the southern front, according to documents released at North's Iran-contra criminal trial. A stipulation of facts in that trial said Noriega even volunteered in August 1986 to supply Panamanian military assistance in the assassination of the Sandinista leadership. The document said North informed Noriega's representative that assassinations are prohibited under American law. "The representative responded that Noriega had numerous assets in place in Nicaragua and could accomplish many essential things, just as Noriega had helped the previous year in blowing up a Sandinista arsenal," the document said. It added that although rejecting the assassination scheme, North and his boss, national security adviser John Poindexter, sought Noriega's help on sabotage raids inside Nicaragua.

Noriega recognized that his on-again-off-again contra support relationship with the White House had been stormy. His lawyer, Rubino, told me in 1989 that it was only after Noriega balked in 1985 at a proposal from Poindexter for Panamanian troops to participate directly in the Nicaraguan conflict that the Reagan administration began to promote drug allegations against him. Noriega made the same assertion to his visitor, Larry Birns, before the invasion in 1989, claiming then that Poindexter had demanded that Panamanian troops act as "an arrowhead" against the Sandinistas.

Although President Bush has escaped serious political damage over his Noriega ties, a Senate panel that cataloged the long history of American tolerance of Noriega found that "General Noriega provides the best example in recent U.S. foreign policy of how a foreign leader is able to manipulate the United States to the detriment of our own interests." The December 1988 report by the

Senate Foreign Relations subcommittee on narcotics, chaired by Senator John Kerry of Massachusetts, added: "In the mid-1980s, this meant that our government did nothing regarding Noriega's drug business and substantial criminal involvement because the first priority was the contra war. This decision resulted in at least some drugs entering the United States as a hidden cost of the war."[7]

The panel's findings were echoed by others who even held senior posts in the Reagan administration. "Clear and incontrovertible evidence was, at best, ignored, and at worst, hidden and denied by many different agencies and departments of the government of the United States in such a way as to provide cover and protection for [Noriega's] activities," said former National Security Council aide Norman Bailey in testimony to a House narcotics panel in 1988.[8] Likewise, former U.S. ambassador to Costa Rica Francis J. McNeil charged that American authorities were "coddling . . . Noriega beyond any time when one could reasonably doubt Noriega's involvement in drug trafficking to the United States" because of his help to the contra cause.[9]

The Senate report said that even as the United States lost patience with Noriega in 1985, the dictator received "mixed messages" from administration officials. Noriega was still rubbing shoulders with some of the White House's heaviest hitters. According to ex–Panamanian intelligence aide Blandon, Noriega met with North in June 1985 on a boat anchored off Panama City again to discuss cooperation in the Nicaraguan conflict. Blandon said Noriega agreed to train contra troops and to permit contra leaders to enter and exit Panama freely.[10]

Ambassador McNeil said that after the meetings with North, Noriega met with CIA director Casey on November 1, 1985. And according to a Casey memo, cited in the Senate report, Noriega was "reassured," apparently because the narcotics issue was not raised. Casey justified not mentioning drugs by reasoning that Noriega was providing valuable support for U.S. policies in Central America. Casey felt the drug matter could be handled through the ambassador. Other U.S. officials, however, concluded that Casey had "let Noriega off the hook," McNeil testified.[11]

But Casey was not just letting Noriega off the hook on narcotics in December 1985. The wily old CIA director was giving Noriega a hand on another political crisis that had been boiling up around the dictator since September. The CIA had stepped in to help its intelligence ally after a respected former Panamanian health minister, Dr. Hugo Spadafora, threatened to denounce both Noriega and President Reagan's beloved contras for complicity in drug trafficking.

Hugo Spadafora headed out of his house in Costa Rica at eight o'clock in the morning on September 13, 1985. A romantic revolutionary who had joined an independent-minded band of contras to fight the Sandinistas, Spadafora was returning to Panama to denounce Manuel Noriega. Spadafora planned to accuse Noriega of responsibility for the flow of drugs through Central America that had tainted some of the contra forces fighting along the Nicaragua–Costa Rica border. Only days earlier, he had briefed Robert Nieves, the head of the Drug Enforcement Administration office at the U.S. embassy in San José. Nieves, however, would later recall that Spadafora seemed short on the kind of specifics that the DEA needed to launch a full-scale investigation.

By about one o'clock in the afternoon, Spadafora had crossed the Costa Rican border into Panama, where he boarded a bus headed for Panama City. At the first PDF checkpoint, there was the first sign of trouble. He was taken from the bus for questioning but allowed to reboard. Then, at the town of La Concepción in the border province of Chiriquí, he was escorted off the bus again by a member of Panama's G-2 military intelligence unit. When the bus driver called for Spadafora to pay his fare, Spadafora shouted his own name and tried to show the driver his identification card. It was the last time Spadafora would be seen alive.[12]

At about six o'clock that evening, another local resident, Alvaro Sequeira Ramírez, spotted a white Toyota jeep driving along the Costa Rican side of the border near the La Vaca River. Suspecting smugglers, he crept close to the vehicle and recognized three soldiers who were laughing and hoisting a heavy bag into the jeep. The vehicle then drove off in the direction of Roble de Laurel, a Costa Rican town along the Roblito River.

The next afternoon, at about one-thirty P.M., the decapitated body of Dr. Hugo Spadafora was found under a bridge of the Roblito River near Roble de Laurel. The body showed extensive signs of torture. It had been slashed by a knife from the neck down to the chest, back and left shoulder. The left side of the chest was heavily bruised, three ribs were cracked, and "F-8"—an apparent reference to a Panamanian intelligence hit team—had been carved into his back. The body was covered by a green canvas bag from the waist up. On the bag was printed "Domestic U.S. Mail, J-469."

Two weeks after Spadafora's disappearance, on September 26, in New York, Noriega met with his then-trusted aide, Blandon. Noriega identified a senior PDF officer in Chiriquí as Spadafora's assassin. Blandon said Noriega wanted details about the murder so the information could be provided to a German living in Panama who would then concoct a cover story. Blandon added that this man did go to the Panamanian press and try to blame Spadafora's murder on leftist Salvadoran guerrillas.

A later Costa Rican prosecutor's report would identify this German individual as working for Joseph Fernandez, who was then CIA station chief in Costa Rica and an important figure in Oliver North's secret contra resupply operation. Fernandez, a heavyset, blustering man, would eventually be indicted by Iran-contra prosecutor Lawrence Walsh on charges of lying to federal authorities about the contra resupply operation. But the charges were dismissed when the Bush administration refused to allow evidence in the case to be declassified. Fernandez would then go into business with North, selling bulletproof vests.

But the White House decision to torpedo the Fernandez trial guaranteed that the mystery would never be clarified as to why a CIA operative would have allegedly aided a cover-up of a political murder in Panama.

Another one of the dirty secrets that dismissal of the Fernandez trial apparently protected was how far the CIA had gone in subverting the democratic process in Costa Rica, the Central American nation with the longest and strongest tradition of political freedom. In pursuit of the Reagan administration's passionate commitment to the contras, the CIA had even established a special intelligence unit operating inside the Costa Rican government and against Costa Rica's leaders.

The CIA-trained Costa Rican agents had originally been organized with the mandate to help the Costa Rican government counter a supposed communist threat from Nicaragua. The Costa Rican authorities tapped a select group of fifteen agents to work under the tutelage of a CIA trainer. But one of its unstated jobs, a Costa Rican government report would later charge, was to spy on the nation's president and other leaders. According to a document in the Fernandez case, some of the protected secrets that led the Bush administration to scuttle the trial related to this same intelligence team, described innocently enough as "a joint Costa Rica/United States . . . program [designed] to provide better intelligence to the Costa Rican government about the intentions of the Nicaraguan government."[13]

Costa Rica's CIA-trained unit, which allegedly had been turned against its own democratic government, had been given the nickname "The Babies," because it was trained by a CIA officer known as Dimitrius Papas. A pun on his last name made him "papa" to the "babies." The unit was formed in 1984 to develop "pure intelligence" on the possibly hostile intentions of neighboring Nicaragua.

But the Costa Rican prosecutor's report said the Babies were soon turned against top Costa Rican officials who committed the heresy of favoring neutrality on the war in Nicaragua. The Babies apparently felt more loyalty to the Americans, who were paying the bills. Enjoying the U.S. largesse, the special unit moved into its own building, rented by the American embassy. The embassy also supplied desks, telephones, typewriters and two motor vehicles. With its finances cared for by Washington, the intelligence team soon became a force answerable only to hard-line Costa Rican officials and to its CIA trainer. "The Babies, who lost loyalty to their superiors, were used to run surveillance" on top officials, including President Luis Alberto Monge, the Costa Rican report charged. As evidence, it cited declarations by two senior officials from the Ministry of Public Security.

But Papas and the CIA didn't stop there. The Costa Rican investigation determined that Papas also built ties to the police through antiterrorism training taught to the Organization of Judicial Investigations, the OIJ, Costa Rica's FBI. The prosecutor's report said "a close bond" developed between Papas and the OIJ's Office of Special Affairs, which handled all state-security crimes. "That relationship turned into a true economic dependency," the prosecutor found, with the police office receiving telephone-tapping equipment, recorders and photographic equipment as well as cash for supplies, car rentals, apartments and per diems. The money for these purchases came from the Costa Rican intelligence service, but its ultimate source was allegedly the CIA.

The prosecutor discovered that the CIA-trained agents and

the intelligence service's administrators were receiving $32,000 a month in cash payments funneled through a San José, Costa Rica, law firm which, in turn, received its money from a shadowy New York organization identified as the "Cardenal Association." No listing for the group exists in New York City directories. The prosecutor said the U.S. embassy received a secret accounting of these payments, and U.S. government sources told me that the money for the unit did come from the CIA. Through a spokesman, the CIA would say only that "our policy is not to comment on such allegations."

But the strange happenings in Costa Rica—and the behind-the-scenes American role—may have gone further than simply spying on a democratic ally. The prosecutor's report recommended the indictment of CIA asset John Hull, an American farmer living near the Nicaraguan border, and a Cuban-American contra backer named Felipe Vidal. The proposed charge would be the terrorist bombing of renegade contra leader Eden Pastora while he was giving a news conference at a base camp in the border village of La Penca on May 30, 1984. Pastora was wounded, but several journalists, including American Linda Frazier, and several contra rebels were killed.

The Costa Rican report criticized Papas and the Babies for interfering in the La Penca investigation by steering suspicion away from rival contra groups hostile to Pastora. Papas sent Costa Rican investigators after time-consuming false leads that sought to implicate the Sandinista government in the bombing, the prosecutor complained. For his part, Pastora has expressed near certainty that CIA-backed contra factions were behind the assassination attempt. His reasoning was that the bomber had been infiltrated into the press conference by associates of the spy agency. But the case has never been solved.

At the time of the bombing, the CIA and Noriega were trying to pressure Pastora, a disenchanted former Sandinista, to line up with more conservative contra forces operating in Honduras. But Pastora had refused, charging that those contras were led by officers of the National Guard of Nicaragua's longtime dictator, Anastasio Somoza Debayle. Fighting with the Sandinistas, Pastora had helped oust Somoza in 1979, and he wanted nothing to do with restoring Somoza's friends to power. To advance contra unity, however, the CIA's Latin American chief Duane Clarridge brought Pastora and three other contra leaders to Panama in 1983 so Noriega could press them into an alliance with the Honduran-based contras, Pastora told the Costa Rican investigators. Pastora refused, angering the CIA and prompting the agency's repeated—and ultimately successful—attempts over the next three years to purge him from the contra movement. Hull and Vidal have denied a role in the Pastora bombing.

In a separate probe, U.S. Senate investigators got another look at the tangled espionage world that had enveloped peaceful Costa Rica. Noriega pilot Floyd Carlton told startled investigators in 1988 that the Panamanian dictator had gone beyond lending a hand to help his CIA friends cope with the independent-minded Costa Ricans. "I'm saying," Carlton declared, "the intelligence in Costa Rica is directed by Noriega." Then, echoing the findings of the Costa Rican report, Carlton said, "In intelligence in Costa Rica, many things are done that the superiors don't know and the president doesn't know." For one telling example, Carlton alleged that in September 1985, Costa Rican intelligence officials tipped off Noriega to Spadafora's plans to denounce drug trafficking by Noriega and the contras—allegations that Spadafora had outlined to the U.S. embassy.

As intriguing and newsworthy as this tale of corruption and espionage may have been, it received scant attention in the CW-dominated national press corps. The Costa Rican report, with its remarkable disclosures, passed almost unnoticed in the United States. The former, hard-line U.S. ambassador to Costa Rica, Curtin Winsor, Jr., labeled the report "whole-cloth lies"—despite its multiplicity of named sources and documentary support. Bored with anything that smacked of Iran-contra, the American press did no follow-up.

Even with the American invasion of Panama and Noriega's capture, the CW setters showed little interest in the dictator's relationship with President Bush, the CIA or Costa Rican intelligence. The housebroken Washington press corps preferred to see the world through eyes that view American adversaries only as black-hat villains and American friends as white-hat good guys—with scant regard for the fascinating complexities of the real world outside the Washington Beltway.

6

The CW Fights
a Middle East
Bad Guy

In the predawn dark, the carefree lives of the al-Sabahs suddenly turned terrifying and frantic. Mercedes limousines queued up in front of the palace as servants scurried to pack suitcases and load them into the waiting cars. As the night wore on, the news for Kuwait's royal family went from bad to worse. A war of words and threats with Kuwait's truculent neighbor to the north, Iraq, had turned into a war of fast-moving tanks and 100,000 battle-hardened Iraqi soldiers.

Over the past weeks, Iraq's leader, Saddam Hussein, had positioned his armor and troops in a coil along the Kuwaiti border, poised to strike. The aggressive move had followed months of escalating charges from Saddam that Kuwait had committed economic sabotage against Iraq. Saddam had angrily accused the emir, Sheikh Jaber al-Ahmed al-Sabah, of exceeding oil production quotas and stealing oil from the rich Rumaillah field that rested mostly in Iraq but dipped slightly into Kuwait.

Saddam also wanted relief on Iraq's war debt and guaranteed access to the sea through two unpopulated islands, Bubiyan and Warbah, that obstructed Iraq's entrance to the Persian Gulf. "O God almighty, be witness that we have warned them," Saddam had railed in the days before the invasion.

Saddam, his country's economy reeling from the $70 billion debt due to his long war with Iran, had taken his complaint about the Kuwaitis to the Arab League and to individual Arab leaders. Throughout the late spring and early summer of 1990, Saddam pressed the Kuwaitis to negotiate on oil prices and his demands for massive financial relief, including billions from Kuwait's petrodollar-flush treasury.

"We cannot tolerate this type of economic warfare which is being waged against Iraq," Saddam warned at an Arab League summit meeting in late May. "We have reached a state of affairs where we cannot take the pressure."[1] In mid-July, Saddam renewed his charges against Kuwait and the emirates for alleged overproduction of oil. He charged that some Persian Gulf states had stabbed Iraq in the back "with a poison dagger" as part of a U.S.-led conspiracy to drive down oil prices. Over the first half of 1990, Saddam claimed the United States and its Gulf friends had engineered a sharp drop in oil prices from $21 a barrel to $16 a barrel, costing Iraq $14 billion in revenues. The goal of this "subversive policy," he charged, was to "secure the flow of oil . . . at the cheapest price."

Then, in an ominous warning that he would use military force, Saddam declared, "If words fail to protect Iraqis, something effective must be done to return things to their natural course and return usurped rights to their owners."[2] But the emir of Kuwait showed no willingness to make concessions.

In *Secret Dossier: The Hidden Agenda Behind the Gulf War*, ABC correspondent Pierre Salinger and French journalist Eric Laurent quote Kuwait's foreign minister as telling Jordan's King Hussein five days before the invasion: "We cannot bargain over an inch of territory. It's against our constitution. If Saddam comes across the border, let him come. The Americans will get him out."[3]

Yet even at that late date, most observers in the Middle East and Washington believed that Saddam's bellicosity and show of military muscle on the border was only to intimidate the emir, not take his country. Like a Mafia godfather with a million-man army, Saddam was saying, "Show me some respect." He just wanted to squeeze a few concessions from the headstrong al-Sabahs.

But Saddam, a mercurial and brutal tyrant who fancied himself a great Arab nationalist leader, was not bluffing. The coiled tank columns sprang across the border in the early-morning hours of August 2 and sliced through Kuwait's soft and undermanned defenses. The emir's 25,000-man army was in disarray.

It became clear to the Kuwaiti royal family that Saddam had no intention of halting his troops in the disputed border region. Iraqi armored units were speeding right into Kuwait City, the sheikhdom's capital. Behind the high walls of the luxurious Dasman Palace, the royal family was in a panic about what to do. The al-Sabahs, long one of the most self-indulgent monarchies in the Middle East, issued emergency orders and then countermanded them. The U.S.-trained Royal Guard took up positions around the palace, but Saddam had control of the air and Kuwait's few dependable troops were no match for Iraq's battle-tested legions. The al-Sabahs placed frantic calls to the U.S. embassy, but there was little help the Americans could offer, except a means of escape.[4]

As the boom of artillery closed in on Kuwait City like a fast-moving thunderstorm, the al-Sabahs took the escape option. Servants rushed to finish loading a long line of Mercedes limousines. Then, the white-robed al-Sabahs swept into the cars, which took off at high speeds through the plush royal gardens and into the darkened, deserted streets of Kuwait City.

The odd cavalcade of rich soon-to-be exiles stopped first at the U.S. embassy where it was greeted by the American ambassador. The emir, the crown prince and several other dignitaries scrambled on board an American helicopter, its blades already churning. The helicopter rose quickly and headed south. The rest of the royal entourage sped south by Mercedes, leaving a stream of dust as the cars raced the thirty miles to the Saudi border.[5]

In one of the few critical postinvasion articles about the al-Sabahs, Christopher Dickey, a respected correspondent at *The Washington Post* and later *Newsweek*, wrote in *Vanity Fair* that the royalty abandoned the country with such haste that they did not even bother to sound the emergency-warning sirens.

The dutiful servants were left behind, as was one of the emir's brothers, the popular head of Kuwait's Olympic committee, who died fighting at the royal palace. "Some say he was chosen to make a last stand defending hearth and home," Dickey wrote. "According to others, he was left behind by an oversight when the rest of the family roared out of the country in their Mercedes convoy, leaving their people to be pillaged by the invaders."[6] The emir, known for his dark, black beard, piercing eyes and wanton womanizing, moved in to Taif, the luxurious summer refuge of the Saudi royalty, to wait out the war.

Back in Kuwait, Saddam's victory seemed total. His troops had crushed the outmatched Kuwaiti army in hours and pushed unhindered up to the Saudi border. His nemesis, the emir, whose intransigence over oil had so infuriated Saddam, had fled in a humiliating panic. Literally overnight, the Iraqi dictator had expanded his nation's already vast oil reserves. Between Iraq and occupied Kuwait, Saddam now sat on one of the largest known oil reserves, 20 percent of the world's total. But it would be the breathtaking scope of his oil conquest that would prove his undoing.

Those who knew the most about the explosive politics of oil were the least surprised by Iraq's invasion of Kuwait. Oil historian Anthony Sampson, for one, recognized how the developed world's pressure for cheap oil in the late 1980's had squeezed Iraq, Iran, Mexico and other heavily populated oil-producing states.

"Inside the United States, the arguments about the proper oil price had been decisively won by the politicians and consumers who saw cheap oil as the basis of the industrial boom and the popular vote, while the advocates of a higher price—whether for conservation, or their own profit—had been effectively undermined," Sampson wrote.[7]

The combination of cheap oil and the willingness of some of the lightly populated oil sheikhdoms, like Kuwait, to exceed OPEC quotas put Iraq in a vise.

"The two Gulf republics with much bigger populations, Iran and Iraq, could not pump more oil and were both pressing for a higher price at OPEC meetings," Sampson noted. "But they had lost their arguments. It was exasperating for Iraq, the most powerful Arab nation in military terms, second only to Israel in the Middle East. The price of oil had become a ferocious issue for its president, Saddam Hussein. . . . Now, as Saddam saw it, the price of oil was being deliberately kept down, in what amounted to economic warfare against Iraq."[8]

What longtime students of oil politics understood is that oil, the lifeblood of the world's economy, is the stuff that wars are fought over. Not only had the Western economic giants clashed in world warfare over the control of the Middle East oil fields, but the Big Powers had frequently intervened when producing states moved too aggressively to control their own resources. The British and American intelligence services, for example, had teamed up to overthrow the elected Iranian government in 1953 and reinstall the shah in a bare-knuckled reaction to Iran's audacity in nationalizing its own oil fields.

For even longer, the history of Kuwait and the al-Sabah clan had been one of service to Western dominance, first the British, who relied on Kuwait as a seaport to the east, and later the Americans, who wanted access to its oil. The al-Sabahs had originally served as an elite police force and governing class for Kuwait's wealthier merchant families. But with the discovery of oil in the 1920's and the military support of the British, the al-Sabahs began to consolidate both wealth and power.

The oil money changed the al-Sabahs as it did Kuwait. By the time Great Britain granted Kuwait its independence in 1961, the al-Sabahs were widely despised as one of the most arrogant ruling families in the Middle East. As Kuwait amassed a giant oil fortune, its foreign investments—believed to exceed $100 billion—gave the tiny nation the unflattering nickname "Kuwait, Inc." Radical Arabs regarded Kuwait's leaders as pawns of the West.

For Saddam and many Arab oil producers, the crisis in the Persian Gulf region was set against this historical backdrop of Western domination of Arab oil. While his fulminations about an American conspiracy against him may have sounded fanciful to Western ears, the British, French and Americans have long played complex power games in the Middle East. Famed CIA officer Miles Copeland, who worked on the Iran operation, liked to call these interventions "the game of nations."

Oil is, after all, the ultimate international prize. When Syria or Israel invades hapless Lebanon, the international community might cluck disapprovingly, but it will not dispatch hundreds of thousands of combat troops to right the wrong. Lebanon might have been a lovely country once, but it does not sit atop a subterranean ocean of oil.

As the storm clouds built and then exploded over the Persian Gulf in the last half of 1990, the conventional wisdom showed its usual lack of interest in the situation's complexities. There are few realities of international or domestic affairs that the CW disdains more than complexity. After all, complexity cannot be summed up in a two-sentence opinion shouted over interruptions on *The McLaughlin Group* or captured in a catchy twelve-word putdown in *Newsweek*'s *CW Watch*.

Yet it is in the rich history of oil politics that the invasion of Kuwait could be best understood and appreciated. The motivations of men and nations are far more interesting—and the news story far more compelling—when viewed as the clash of fundamental interests. That, however, often shades the event with the grays of truth, rather than the blacks and whites of CW.

Washington's conventional wisdom sketched Saddam, cartoon-style, as a madman. After all, the Iraqi dictator had violated international law, which the CW suddenly revered. Only months earlier, of course, the conventional wisdom had felt that finicky international law should not hamstring America's dealings with Nicaragua, Panama or a host of other Third World nuisances. The CW took seriously President Bush's declaration that Soviet president Mikhail Gorbachev should understand the American invasion of Panama because some Panamanian toughs had kicked an American officer in the groin and threatened his wife with rape.

The CW possesses an inexhaustible ability to bring varied moral standards to otherwise comparable situations. Many of the same CW realpolitik pundits who would ridicule any sentimental preoccupation with human rights now abhorred Saddam's long history of brutality. The CW liked one ringing phrase in particular. Citing Iraq's use of chemical weapons against the Kurdish minority, Saddam was denounced as someone who would "kill his own people." Why this is worse than killing someone else's people was never explained. Nor did the CW setters extend this condemnation to American allies, such as the U.S.-backed armies of El Salvador and Guatemala, which routinely "kill their own people."

Like many historic moments, Saddam's invasion of Kuwait caught Washington's conventional wisdom as off guard as it did the emir of Kuwait. Only a few columnists, particularly those with close ties to Israel, had been raising the Saddam alarm. Three months before the invasion, conservative *New York Times* columnist William Safire complained of "the relentlessly pro-Iraq tilt of the Bush White House" and lashed out at "Saddam Hussein's new supporter, Senate Minority Leader Bob Dole of corn-producing Kansas." Noting Iraq's purchase of corn at 10 percent above the world market price, Safire mused that a combination of Dole's "old anti-Israeli resentments and Kansas corn interests suddenly let the dark out."[9]

Charles Krauthammer, another neoconservative entry from the *New Republic* stable, launched the Saddam-as-Hitler analogy in a *Washington Post* column on July 27, a week before the invasion.

"Hitler analogies are not to be used lightly," Krauthammer began. "To be compared to Hitler is too high a compliment in evil to pay most tyrants. The time has come, however, to bestow the compliment on a tyrant who is truly a nightmare out of the 1930s: Saddam Hussein, president (soon for life) of Iraq."[10]

Krauthammer spelled out in this remarkable column what would become the CW line against Saddam Hussein. Ticking off Saddam's domestic crimes—"the wholesale murder of political opponents, the poison gas attacks on his own Kurdish minority"— Krauthammer then argued that the dictator's unbridled regional aggression made him a Hitleresque danger.

"What makes him truly Hitlerian is his way of dealing with neighboring states," Krauthammer argued. "In a chilling echo of the '30s, Iraq, a regional superpower, accuses a powerless neighbor of a 'deliberate policy of aggression against Iraq,' precisely the kind of absurd accusation Hitler lodged against helpless Czechoslovakia and Poland as a prelude to their dismemberment."[11]

If Mickey Kaus is right, that what gives a journalist power in today's Washington is to be the first to crystallize a new CW, then Krauthammer is truly an influential columnist. Certainly much of Krauthammer's bleak assessment of Saddam would prove correct. But what is so troubling about Krauthammer's body of work is his unblushing double standard: he denounces as Hitlerian in one context what he embraces in another. In the mid-1980's, Krauthammer coined the phrase *Reagan Doctrine* to put a gloss of legitimacy over a string of U.S. military interventions. Yet surely, the Reagan Doctrine's paranoia about threats to Harlingen, Texas, from the Nicaraguan army; the bloody covert war against the Marxist government in Angola, originally to "protect American sea-lanes"; the exaggerated drug-smuggling danger from Noriega's Panama; or the "9,000-foot-runway" theme used to suggest a strategic threat from tiny Grenada were as illogical as Saddam's feigned fears about Kuwait. But on one hand, Krauthammer adored the American covert and overt actions while comparing Saddam's thuggery to the darkest days of world history.

Yet for Krauthammer, now in his early forties, the reference to Hitler was not simply a clever rhetorical touch. The columnist and regular on the pundit show *Inside Washington* was the son of Jewish refugees who had fled Hitler's totalitarianism. His father, an Austro-Hungarian by birth, and his mother, a Belgian-born Jew,

wended their way to Cuba to escape the Nazis. His father later
settled the family in Montreal, Canada, where he established a
successful real estate business.[12]

"Krauthammer came from a family with very vivid memories
of fascism," recalled Jefferson Morley, a former colleague at *The
New Republic*. Krauthammer grew up with firsthand stories about
the evils of the Nazis. And like many American Jews born in the
post–World War II era, he transferred his family's hatred of German
fascism into an intensely anti-Soviet ideology and a disgust for
radical Arab states threatening Israel. Krauthammer became the
archetypal neoconservative, a Democrat who espouses a more activist social agenda than do most Republicans, yet a believer in an
interventionist foreign policy, which reached full flower in his
paeans to Pax Americana during the Persian Gulf crisis.

After graduating with high honors at McGill University in Montreal, Krauthammer entered Harvard Medical School, where he
looked forward to a promising career in medicine. But one hot
summer day when he was twenty-two, he sprang off a diving board
at an outdoor swimming pool. The water was too shallow and he
struck his head on the pool's concrete floor, breaking his neck and
damaging his spinal cord. Though rescued from the pool, Krauthammer was left paralyzed and wheelchair-bound. Only through
hard work and rehabilitation did he regain partial use of his hands.
Despite his handicap, he finished medical school and went to work
as a psychiatrist. He later won an out-of-court settlement from the
pool company for $1 million.[13]

Krauthammer's injury did not stop his driving ambition. Tiring
of psychiatry, he entered a new career as a writer. He landed an
offer from *The New Republic* to submit some articles, concentrating
at first on issues of medical ethics. "He was very thoughtful, a
good sharp writer," Morley remembered. But soon Krauthammer
branched out into foreign-policy issues. Enamored of the Reagan
administration's militarism, he was soon denouncing the Soviet
Union as "an empire of evil," endorsing the invasion of Grenada
and urging CIA assistance to the Nicaraguan contras.

Krauthammer became a hero to the Reagan administration
with his CW-defining article that identified the U.S. policy of sponsoring anticommunist wars as "the Reagan Doctrine." The clever
wordsmith gave the heretofore covert military adventures an intellectual veneer. "Krauthammer coined the phrase the *Reagan*

Doctrine," Morley said about the influential article. "It gave public coherence to something that was already going on. [In this and other writings] Krauthammer attacks the role of international law as a harmful fraud."

The New Republic's new-found role as intellectual rationalizer for the Reagan administration's aggressive foreign policy was heady stuff for the magazine's young polemicists, like Barnes, Kondracke and Krauthammer. It also brought expanded influence and power. Krauthammer won a prized spot on *The Washington Post*'s increasingly neoconservative op-ed page in 1984 and syndicated his writings in 1985, leading to a 1986 Pulitzer Prize for commentary. *The New Republic* was riding the wave of resurgent American military might. "Anyone around *The New Republic* had to be struck by an attitude of militant triumphalism," Morley said. "Krauthammer really pours it on for the contras throughout 1985. By early 1986, you see *The New Republic* advancing the extralegal foreign policy goals," some of which would later become known as the Iran-contra scandal.

The magazine's old liberal image, put to the service of a right-wing White House, brought rewards in access and glamour to the rising stars at *The New Republic*. "These guys were on the road to power," Morley said, recalling his colleagues' sudden entrée to the circles of power. "Krauthammer was in the White House. Fred Barnes was in the White House." Through op-ed columns, appearances on TV chat shows and their *New Republic* writings, the magazine's pundits pressed relentlessly in support of the Reagan administration's interventionism.

Krauthammer's only real break with Reagan policy came on issues touchy to Israel, such as the U.S. tilt toward Saddam's Iraq during the Iran-Iraq war. For instance, Krauthammer scored the U.S. policy of putting U.S. flags on Kuwaiti tankers so they could carry Iraqi oil out of the Gulf. "The United States did not go into the Gulf to defend the principle of 'free navigation,' " he argued in August 1987, "That is a fool's mission. The Gulf, the world and the oil trade lived quite nicely for three years with the unfree navigation brought on by the Persian Gulf tanker war. [The United States] is defending the shipping of Kuwait, Iraq's closest ally. If the reflagging plan has a purpose, it is to help shore up Iraq, the weaker side of the Iran-Iraq war."[14] The column was typical in expressing Krauthammer's realpolitik disdain for the principles of international law, what in this context he dismisses as a "fool's mission."

Unlike Kondracke and Barnes, whose greatest influence derived from their televised *McLaughlin Group* appearances, Krauthammer shaped the CW more through the written than the shouted word. He championed the cause of American interventionism through his syndicated column and, especially, through its high-status spot on *The Washington Post*'s opinion page. Having a column on the well-read *Post* op-ed page was like getting a choice corner table at Maison Blanche. It meant power in Washington. And Krauthammer's rise as a leading intellectualizer for neoconservative causes corresponded to a simultaneous rightward shift at the *Post*.

Though still disdained by some right-wingers as part of the Eastern liberal establishment and hated for its Watergate coverage, the *Post* had quietly rid itself of its liberal baggage. By midway through the Reagan years, its editorial writers routinely endorsed the Reagan administration's overseas adventures and the newspaper's regular contributors on the op-ed page reinforced those opinions. By the mid-1980's, the *Post*'s columnists seemed to range from Jeane Kirkpatrick to James Kilpatrick, from neoconservative to paleoconservative. It was a comfortable home for leading right-wing pundits, such as Rowland Evans, Robert Novak, George F. Will and Krauthammer.

The *Post*'s home-grown opinion leaders embraced Reagan's anticommunist activism as well. Stephen S. Rosenfeld, the *Post*'s chief editorial writer on foreign affairs, shared Krauthammer's situational ethics when it came to bloody Third World conflicts. In one by-lined opinion piece in 1990, Rosenfeld offered his view on a news story alleging an American hand in the slaughter of an estimated quarter-million communists and suspected leftists by the Indonesian army in 1965. Although the vast majority of the victims were executed in cold blood, Rosenfeld defended the bloodbath as a valuable exercise in realpolitik. "This fearsome slaughter . . . was and still is widely regarded as the grim but earned fate of a conspiratorial revolutionary party that represented the same communist juggernaut that was on the march in Vietnam," Rosenfeld wrote. "Though the means were grievously tainted, we—the fastidious among us as well as the hard-headed and cynical—can be said to have enjoyed the fruits in the geopolitical stability of that important part of Asia, in the revolution that never happened."

Rosenfeld scolded one historian, Gabriel Kolko, who criticized U.S. help to the Indonesian military, for "his typical revisionist blame-America-first point of view."[15]

Throughout the past decade, there had been scant America-blaming—first, second, or ever—anywhere on the *Post* op-ed pages. During the Persian Gulf crisis, the *Post*'s columnists were even more a one-note chorus than usual. Another *Post* regular, Jim Hoagland, and one of the page's few liberals, Richard Cohen, both enthusiastically supported a military solution, leaving conservative columnists Evans and Novak as virtually the only op-ed writers questioning the march to war.

One of the newspaper's few remaining dissenters against the prevailing CW was Mary McGrory, who wrote a regular column that appeared on page 2, not on the op-ed section normally reserved for opinion articles. While McGrory's skeptical voice was a lonely one in the *Post*, it still raised the hackles of the touchy president, George Bush. *Post* editor Ben Bradlee recounted shortly before retiring in 1991 how he had been invited to lunch at the White House. Bush used the occasion to complain about McGrory's sprightly columns. "He told me in the course of that [lunch] that he wasn't making any progress with Mary," Bradlee said in an interview on C-SPAN. "They want 'em all. They don't want to have a handful of columnists to agree with them. They want a hundred of them. If you've got a hundred, you want two hundred." Bush had come as close as any modern president to having them all, especially during the Persian Gulf War, but he was still annoyed with McGrory's resistance.

While the *Post* was tacking ever rightward during the 1980's, the capital's other daily paper was *The Washington Times*, a far-right journal financed and controlled by the Unification Church cult. The cult's founder, Sun-Yung Moon of South Korea, espoused a totalitarian rightist vision of the world's future. His domination over the lives of his followers was so complete that he would select their spouses and preside over their weddings in bizarre mass ceremonies.

Moon's organization covered the paper's annual losses, estimated in the tens of millions of dollars, but the original sources for that money remained shrouded in secrecy. Though the cult had close ties to South Korean intelligence, most of its money appeared to flow from rightist Japanese business interests. Besides financing a virulent brand of right-wing journalism, *The Washington Times* and Moon's cult had institutionalized a means of buying influence for its extremist points of view. Through conferences, contributions, and salaries, the Unification Church and its panoply of front groups put money into the pockets of right-wing thinkers, conservative journalists and pro-military political organizations. During the 1980s, the Reagan White House often used *The Washington Times* as a billboard for its conservative strategies or as a weapon to attack administration critics.

The joint effect of the *Post*'s drift into neoconservatism and the introduction of an ultra-right publication, *The Washington Times*, was to shift the capital's predominant thinking ever-further rightward. The CW followed.

In 1989, some of the traditional conservatives lost influence with the departure of Ronald Reagan, but the neoconservatives from *The New Republic* kept up their intimacy with the preppier crowd around George Bush. As the Cold War faded and the old-line conservatives pulled back from interventionism to an America-first outlook stressing attention to the nation's domestic and economic shortcomings, the neocons continued to ply their skills in the service of American military and ideological activism abroad.

With the Iraqi invasion of Kuwait, this split between the two groupings that had monopolized the foreign-policy CW for a decade left Washington's opinion elite in temporary disarray. Many influential figures from the America first group favored the soft line toward Saddam that could be found in the wimpy signals the Iraqi dictator had gotten from the State Department before the war. Meanwhile, the neocons had sided with Israel and its alarmist warnings about the Butcher of Baghdad, Saddam Hussein. This split in the elite Washington CW went public as the crisis broke. But even *The New Republic* crowd never envisioned how far George Bush was ready to go.

On the weekend prior to Saddam's invasion, *The McLaughlin Group* chewed over the crisis as a second segment of the show. "It would be crazy to think that if . . . Iraq . . . sends its five hundred thousand troops in that we're going to send troops over there and defend Kuwait," declared *The New Republic*'s Fred Barnes. He called instead for "a little gunboat diplomacy, but not troops on the ground for combat." His *New Republic* colleague, Morton Kondracke, agreed with the administration's move of "putting ships in the Persian Gulf."[16]

Representing the America-first crowd, the pugnacious conservative Patrick J. Buchanan objected even to raising this caution flag. "Let me bring some realism to this," the ex–Reagan communications director offered. "Look, you have the gunboat liberals over here in Mr. Kondracke's—but we can't stop Iraq if it moves into Kuwait and takes over that [disputed border] territory. What could we do? Blockade the coast. If we do that, the price of oil will shoot up. As a practical matter, Iraq and Iran are going to be the dominant powers in the Persian Gulf, and there's not a great deal the United States can do about it." Untethered from his anticommunist interventionism, Buchanan was sounding downright isolationist.

Yet, even as the Persian Gulf teetered on the brink of war, *The McLaughlin Group* could not escape its usual CW silliness. For what moderator McLaughlin terms his "exit question" from a topic, the *Group*ers gave their guesstimates on whether Iraq would invade Kuwait. Buchanan: "Eventually, it's going to take part of it." Barnes: "No . . . it's a bluff and it's working." Jack Germond: "No." Kondracke: "If they're not bluffed out of it, they will." McLaughlin: "I say no, at least for the forseeable future." Score one for the plodding Kondracke, the Chauncey Gardiner of Washington journalism.

Saddam was not bluffed out of it. At a crucial meeting on July 25, 1990, eight days before the invasion, U.S. Ambassador April Glaspie seemed more eager to assuage Saddam's anger than draw a line in the sand. A transcript of the meeting released by the Iraqis suggested a U.S. policy of conciliation, not confrontation. "We have no opinion on the Arab-Arab conflicts, like your border disagreement with Kuwait," Glaspie said in her most controversial remarks to Saddam. "I was in the American Embassy in Kuwait during the late '60s. The instruction we had during this period was that we should express no opinion on this issue and that the issue is not associated with America."[17]

Glaspie, a career foreign-service officer and fluent speaker of Arabic, also sympathized with Saddam's anger over critical stories about him in the American news media. "I am pleased that you add your voice to the diplomats who stand up to the media," said the ambassador in her first face-to-face meeting with the dictator. "If the American president had control of the media, his job would be much easier." Glaspie even found time to tell Saddam, "I spent four beautiful years in Egypt."[18]

Although the State Department chose not to challenge the transcript's accuracy, Glaspie insisted to Congress after the war that she had given Saddam repeated warnings which had been deleted from the transcript. Talking tougher than she did to Saddam's face, she argued that the U.S. policy of deterrence failed because "we foolishly did not realize he was stupid, that he did not believe our clear and repeated warnings that we would support our vital interests."[19]

But Glaspie's State Department secret cables, grudgingly turned over to Congress almost a year after her pivotal meeting with the dictator, revealed that her message to Saddam indeed had been more reassurance than rebuke. She stressed President Bush's "desire for friendship," and when she asked about his intentions toward Kuwait, she assured Saddam that the question was posed "in the spirit of friendship, not confrontation." Glaspie's meeting was followed by mixed signals from Bush himself three days later. In a message to the Iraqi leader, Bush reiterated his hope for better relations, though warning Iraq not to pursue "threats involving military force" against Kuwait. Saddam did not believe the Americans were staring him down. He thought instead they were blinking or winking. The crisis lurched forward. But as the CW took shape in late summer of 1990, the administration's bungled diplomacy was still a secret.*

As for predicting Saddam's plans, Glaspie ranked with most of *The McLaughlin Group* in misjudging his intentions. "His emphasis that he wants peaceful settlement is surely sincere," she cabled back to Washington.[20]

---

*The first comprehensive press account of President Bush's spurned courtship of Saddam Hussein did not appear in the mainstream press until February 23, 1992. Then, the *Los Angeles Times* printed a lead article by Douglas Frantz and Murray Waas detailing Bush's longstanding secret policy of facilitating U.S. loan guarantees and dual-purpose technology shipments to Baghdad. In fall 1989, only nine months before Iraq's invasion of Kuwait, Bush signed a top-secret directive ordering closer ties with Saddam's government and clearing the way for $1 billion in new U.S. aid.

*   *   *

After Saddam's forces crashed across the Kuwaiti border and gobbled up the little sheikhdom, the CW squealed its objections, but uncertainty prevailed about what to do and what the war meant. On the August 3, 1990, *McLaughlin* show—taped the day after the invasion—Buchanan voiced a detached ambivalence. "Well, first, John, the day of the dictator is certainly not over.* The United States is no longer policeman of the Gulf. The Carter Doctrine is dead. And I think Al Capone basically is the big man in the Gulf.

"Where is it headed?" Buchanan asked himself rhetorically. "Iraq is going to get the reparations they want, they're going to get the oil field they want; they're going to get the outlet to the Persian Gulf that they want; they're going to put in a provisional government, my guess is a little protectorate in Kuwait; and then their army is going to withdraw and they're going to have a total victory."[21] Seldom has even a CW pundit been this wrong, or so openly advocated an American policy of accommodation. Buchanan seemed to have forgotten that Clint Eastwood is the ideological model for a true CW master. Others in *The McLaughlin Group* hadn't.

"Well, I remember when you used to condemn that stuff and urge American intervention in cases like that," scolded Fred Barnes, who proposed measured steps to punish Iraq economically and to protect Saudi Arabia with American air power. Kondracke urged, "by whatever means necessary and possible, we've got to organize a buffer against this guy, Saddam Hussein . . . who wants to dominate the whole Gulf."

Still, Buchanan insisted on his unusual role of appeaser: "My point is, people ought to sit back and use their heads. In the long run, Iran and Iraq are going to be the powers on the Gulf." That line drew a rebuke from McLaughlin himself: "There he is, Neville Chamberlain in the Gulf!"—a response followed by derisive laughter toward Buchanan.[22]

McLaughlin, whose career odyssey had wound its twisted way from Jesuit priest to President Nixon's loyal Watergate defender to his lucrative resurrection as megasuccessful chat-show host, had not lost his instincts for the CW. Even in the midst of war, with all its terrible gravity, McLaughlin did not forget a fundamental

---

*Buchanan's line was a pointed gibe at President Bush's inaugural-address claim that "the day of the dictator is over."

principle of the conventional wisdom: all events must be summed up as "winners and losers"—"who's up, who's down"; or "what's hot and what's not."

"Is Egypt a winner or a loser, I ask you?" McLaughlin quizzed his pundit panel.

> BARNES: Oh, a big loser.
> McLAUGHLIN: A big loser.
> BARNES: Egypt—Mubarak wanted to be the big cheese in the Middle East. He ain't.
> McLAUGHLIN: Hey, what about the other Hussein over—what about Assad over—
> BUCHANAN: No, Hussein—the other Hussein is in bed with this Hussein right now.
> McLAUGHLIN: Jordan.
> BUCHANAN: Assad's a winner—let me tell you a winner—
> McLAUGHLIN: King Hussein, what?
> BUCHANAN: A winner. There's been savage cutting of SDI in the House—almost 50 percent. You'll get a good deal of that back.
> McLAUGHLIN: Another winner. But what about Assad? Assad is a big loser.
> KONDRACKE: Loser.
> McLAUGHLIN: In fact, you could see—you could see Saddam Hussein moving in the direction of Syria, could you not?
> *Newsweek*'s ELEANOR CLIFT: Right.
> KONDRACKE: You could see the United States moving in the direction of Syria. You could see Israel moving in the direction of Syria.[23]

So went the CW debate in the early hours of the crisis. The CW was definitely a loser.

The Washington CW didn't get its feet on the ground until President Bush's helicopter landed on the White House lawn on Sunday, August 5, returning him from a work-filled weekend at Camp David. An angry president waved his finger and left no doubt about his intent: "This will not stand. This will not stand, this aggression against Kuwait." Bush ruled out any compromise and summed up the attitudes of the world leaders he had talked to by phone. "What's emerging is nobody seems to be showing up as willing to accept anything less than total withdrawal from Kuwait of Iraqi forces, and no puppet regime," the president told reporters.

Once President Bush lashed out at Saddam, the CW quickly took shape. Some columnists compared Saddam to Mussolini, if not Hitler. Others called him a madman, an image that Saddam fostered by taking hundreds of Westerners hostage as "human shields." Saddam even assumed animal characteristics. "Look, Saddam Hussein is a big fat rat and he has been cornered," explained Kondracke on *The McLaughlin Group* a week after the invasion.[24]

Other pundits saw the problem as whiny, destructive Arabs. "Saddam's political 'strength' is built on a thirst for revenge by Arabs who blame the West for their vast problems and want payback," wrote *The Washington Post*'s Jim Hoagland. "It is a 'strength' that can create nothing. It can only destroy. Or be destroyed."[25]

A few lonely Arabist voices urged giving diplomacy a chance. "The dispatch of American troops was a hasty act based on misunderstanding of the people and politics of the region; ill-conceived analogies fit for poetry not policy and an atavistic tendency for intervention that has not yet adjusted to the spirit of globalism, which many people around the world are hoping for," cautioned Sharif S. Elmusa, a Washington-based specialist in Arab economic development.[26] But the CW easily shrugged off such high-minded idealism.

The chief resistance to the Get Saddam CW continued from some of the CW's most red-blooded interventionists, Buchanan, Robert Novak and other, lesser-known conservatives. Since the Persian Gulf War was the first post–Cold War world crisis, these anticommunists had lost their East-West-only compasses that had guided their predictably militant reactions in the past. Without the Soviet threat to predetermine their outlook, these conservatives emerged as the most cautious pundits in Washington.

"Where is the political basis for Americans to go out there and lay down their lives, eventually, if it comes to that, for oil that primarily goes to Europeans, Japanese and East Asians?" asked Edward N. Luttwak, a foreign-policy expert for the conservative Center for Strategic and International Studies. "And where is the political basis to defend the regime of Saudi Arabia, which with

the possible exception of Albania, is the most oppressive and re-
actionary and absolutist regime in the world?"[27]

The two heads of the conservative pundit team of Rowland
Evans and Robert Novak both talked up the chance for peace in
late August 1990. "Although the ton of bricks that hit Saddam
Hussein when Iraq annexed Kuwait did not deck him, its cumu-
lative weight is leading his government to consider remedies in-
conceivable three weeks ago," Evans and Novak reported from
Baghdad four weeks into the crisis. "In order to reduce or get rid
of the U.S. military power accumulating in the Gulf, Iraq might
offer what one Arab head of state—not Saddam—calls a 'commitment to withdraw' by Iraq. . . . If this Arab solution also dealt with
long-standing, recognized territorial disputes, Saddam might give
the commitment. . . . That would rid Kuwait of Iraqi control and
thus be a major victory for President Bush."[28] Contrary to their
normal interventionist impulses, the conservative columnists were
looking at practical alternatives to war.

Novak, who is the more public of the two-man team, carried
his take-it-easy message to his television pundit show *Capital Gang*
on CNN. There, centrist Al Hunt hung the nickname "Neville
Novak" around his neck, a clever alliteration that had Washington
tittering over the sudden turn of fate for the pundit once known
as the "prince of darkness."*

In the early days of the crisis, the conservative doubters were
overwhelmed by a CW consensus that tolerated no dissent. While
Novak suffered the smirking comparisons of him with Britain's
appeasement prime minister, Buchanan felt an even more painful
lash. His CW whipping came after he argued that Israel and its
U.S. backers were pushing for a hasty war. "There are only two
groups that are beating the drums for war in the Middle East: the
Israeli defense ministry and its amen corner in the United States,"
he said three weeks into the crisis. "The Israelis want this war
desperately because they want the United States to destroy the
Iraqi war machine. They want us to finish them off. They don't
care about our relations with the Arab world."[29] He later spelled

---

*Hunt defended his "Neville Novak" line as a fitting rejoinder for all the times Novak had
baited opponents for their softness against communism. "After years of battling Novak from
the left, to have gotten to his right, I enjoyed that," Hunt told me.

out that he considered *The New Republic* part of the "amen corner."

Buchanan's comments contained large elements of truth. The Israelis did want Saddam's ears pinned back. They did favor the destruction of his war machine. They understandably did place their own national security ahead of how popular the United States was with the Arab world. But Buchanan had crossed an invisible CW line. He had gone too far in challenging the coalescing of conventional wisdom behind President Bush's hard-line stand. For once, the conservative pundit would find himself at the receiving end of the CW.

A. M. Rosenthal, former executive editor of *The New York Times* who had moved the newspaper's news columns to the right during in the 1980's, would lower the boom. In his *New York Times* column, Rosenthal leveled the ugly charge that *The Mc-Laughlin Group* regular was an anti-Semite. A strong backer of Israel, Rosenthal accused Buchanan of spreading a "venom about Jews."

Rosenthal took aim at Buchanan's pattern of alleged anti-Semitic sins: "the demeaning of the Holocaust, the phony 'evidence' to question a crime of the gas chambers, the smarmy defense of war criminals* and the attacks on American prosecutors who dared chase them down, the crack that Congress was 'Israeli-occupied' territory."[30]

But it was Buchanan's objection to the rush to war that brought Rosenthal's and the CW's animosity pouring onto Buchanan. "We are not dealing here with country-club anti-Semitism but with the blood libel that often grows out of it: Jews are not like us but are others, with alien loyalties for which they will sacrifice the lives of Americans," Rosenthal concluded.

Buchanan, whose verbal and physical posture suggests a man who is always ready for a fight, had been doing battle in Washington since his college days at Georgetown University. After getting a

---

*Buchanan's most notable defense of an accused Nazi war criminal was mounted on behalf of John Demjanjuk, who was convicted in 1988 by an Israeli court for the slaughter of Jews at the Treblinka death camp. Buchanan argued that Demjanjuk had been mistakenly identified as Ivan the Terrible, a notoriously brutal camp guard. In January 1992, the Israeli prosecutor submitted documents bolstering the defense claim that Demjanjuk was, indeed, not Ivan the Terrible but a guard at a different concentration camp. Buchanan's skepticism seemed vindicated, though attacks on him as an anti-Semite continued to dog him when he challenged President George Bush in the Republican primaries in 1992.

speeding ticket one night, the twenty-year-old Buchanan took on a couple of Washington policemen in the back of a squad car. The cops finally subdued the rambunctious student with their night-sticks. He was bloodied but unbowed. According to his flippant recollection of the incident years later, "I was ahead on points—until they brought out the sticks."[31] For the next three decades, Buchanan would treat the political world as if it were wrestling with him in the back of that police car. A conservative hitman, he would mix it up with any punk liberal who dared go after Richard Nixon, Spiro Agnew, Ronald Reagan or any of his conservative icons.

So it was not surprising when Buchanan, no more mellow in his early fifties, struck back, accusing Rosenthal of carrying out a "contract hit" for the staunchly pro-Israel Anti-Defamation League of B'nai B'rith. In effect, he complained that the Israeli lobby was manufacturing a CW against him. Rosenthal's weapon was "the branding iron wielded by a tiny clique, to burn horribly heretics from their agreed-upon political orthodoxy," Buchanan wrote. "It is used to frighten, intimidate, censor and silence . . . to scar men so indelibly that no one will ever look at them again without saying, 'Say, isn't he an anti-Semite?' "[32]

The only humor to this ugly episode was that, for years, Buchanan had happily pressed his own branding iron into the flesh of others who had violated the orthodoxy of anticommunist interventionism. In 1985, demanding the Congress resume funding President Reagan's proxy war in Nicaragua, he had written that "the Democratic Party will reveal whether it stands with Ronald Reagan and the [contra] resistance—or with Daniel Ortega and the communists." Just as Buchanan had loved firing up the CW branding iron in the cause of White House propaganda, he was now feeling the same scorching heat himself.

Although many *McLaughlin Group*ers disagreed with Buchanan on Iraq, his chat-show colleagues rallied to his personal defense. "I say that calling somebody an 'anti-Semite' is the worst, one of the worst things you could possibly call him and you have to have lots of proof, and Abe Rosenthal does not have the proof," summed up Kondracke. Eleanor Clift, a semiregular *Group*er and a thoughtful *Newsweek* correspondent, saw a bigger picture: "U.S. policy has been geared, strategically, towards Israeli interest in that region and we are shifting away from that, and it is a painful transition, and this kind of ugly name-calling is going to happen as we do it."[33]

Despite the branding, Buchanan remained the highest-profile skeptic about the war. On November 9, 1990, as Bush unilaterally doubled the number of American troops in Saudi Arabia and opened up the "offensive option," Buchanan protested: "The president hasn't told us what we're going to war for and what all the guys are going to die for."[34]

Kondracke filled him in by ticking off the White House's finely honed prowar themes. "For one last time," Kondracke, the pundit's pundit, lectured: "This is a monster who is going to have nuclear weapons two to three years from now . . ."

Moderator McLaughlin interrupted, "There are other ways to control that."

But Kondracke continued, ". . . who is trying to control the world's oil supply. It's not just a matter of gasoline being $1.20 a gallon. It's a matter of poor countries all over the world not being able to feed their own people."

Buchanan broke in, "Oh, stop it. Stop it." Still, Kondracke wasn't finished. "It's a question of barbarism prevails in the world. That's what we are fighting for." For even McLaughlin, that was a bit rich. "Thank you for your sermonette of the week," he told Kondracke.[35]

Led by the *New Republic* neoconservatives—what Buchanan had termed Israel's "amen corner"—the CW rallied behind Bush early in the crisis and never wavered. Even though the American public and much of Congress harbored doubts about the wisdom of going to war, President Bush maneuvered the nation in that one direction. By controlling the flow of information, by keeping embarrassing diplomatic gaffes out of the news, by escalating troop levels unilaterally so that a withdrawal would be a national disgrace, Bush left the country no choice but to press forward. It was like the spikes used at rental car lots that click down to let you drive a car in but would shred the tires if you backed out.

In a perceptive postwar column, Krauthammer lauded Bush for his stealth in guiding the nation to war. "Cast your mind back exactly seven months," Krauthammer wrote. "On August 1, you would have thought crazy anyone who suggested (a) that President Bush would send more than 500,000 troops into the Arabian desert,

(b) that he would launch them in a massive ground offensive and (c) at the point of maximum danger, 90 percent of the American people would support his conduct."[36]

The columnist marveled at Bush's leadership, especially in view of the president's handicap with the oratory thing. "At every stage, he brought the country with him," Krauthammer enthused. "It was a remarkable feat of domestic diplomacy, all the more remarkable for being almost imperceptible." By first introducing troops for defensive purposes, then doubling their number, and finally arranging a United Nations deadline for Iraqi withdrawal, Bush set up those rows of tire slashers that gave the country no choice but to go forward.

Even in the last stage, the ground war, barely 11 percent of the American people, according to a CBS–*New York Times* survey, favored launching one. Yet when the ground war started, 75 percent rallied to Bush's side. "Bush managed to rally a reluctant nation to a successful war not with soaring visions, but with a series of shrewd and forcing actions," Krauthammer concluded.[37]

But in limiting America's choices and shielding the secrets that would have informed a meaningful debate, Bush made a mockery of the democratic process. Cleverly, "almost imperceptibly," in Krauthammer's view, Bush bypassed even Congress until—on the eve of the U.N. deadline—it too had no choice but to click over the last row of tire shredders and turn over the keys to the president.

Throughout, Bush was aided by Washington's CW, which has never met a macho solution that it didn't like. While Bush led the reluctant nation to war, the CW ignored the president's long record of pre–August 2 accommodations to Saddam's Iraq, including help in equipping its war machine. The CW showed little interest in the preinvasion diplomacy that had failed to tell Saddam: "Read our lips, no attack on Kuwait." And the CW paid no serious attention to Evans and Novak's concern about finding a less violent, less costly way to pry the Iraqis out of Kuwait. Instead, the CW tucked these disastrous miscalculations and unresolved questions into its old kit bag and marched, verbally speaking, off to war.

7

The CW,
the al-Sabahs
and the CIA

No sooner had the Kuwaiti elite climbed out of the dusty Mercedes limousines that had carried them to safety in Saudi Arabia than they were planning the first vital step to liberate their homeland: they began scouting for the right Washington public-relations/lobbying firm. The Kuwaitis settled on perhaps the most potent "government affairs" company in the United States, namely, Hill and Knowlton, Inc.

The powerhouse firm is located in a futuristic office complex on the Potomac River below fashionable Georgetown. It sports a bipartisan all-star team of Washington connections. On the Republican side are power brokers like Robert Gray, who was tight with the Reagan White House, and Craig Fuller, who had been Vice-President Bush's chief of staff. The firm's big-name Democrat is Frank Mankiewicz, who ran George McGovern's failed presidential campaign in 1972 and went on to get rich as a lobbyist.

By August 20, less than three weeks after the invasion, the Kuwaitis had pulled out their still-ample checkbooks and retained Hill and Knowlton. The firm hastily threw about fifty representatives, virtually its entire available staff, into the Kuwaiti account. By November 10, less than three months later, the firm had run the bill to $5.6 million, according to Foreign Agent Registration records on file at the Justice Department.

Of that healthy sum, $1.1 million had been funneled to the polling firm of Richard Wirthlin, who had been President Reagan's personal pollster. Wirthlin, a teetotaling Mormon who abstains even from coffee, was the resident conservative genius at melding political-poll results with public-relations strategy. For the state-of-the-art Reagan media management, Wirthlin had been a kind of political aerospace engineer who could study his poll data and know exactly what would fly with the American people, what modifications were needed to get a PR campaign off the ground.

Wirthlin put into practice the same tactics for the Kuwaitis that he had applied so successfully to Reagan's two victorious presidential campaigns and to policy debates during the president's two terms. Wirthlin's team arranged "focus groups" to test out public-relations themes on representative Americans to see which arguments generated the most favorable response. As these themes were then pitched to the general public, Wirthlin would gauge the effectiveness of the message through nightly tracking polls. That way, the Kuwaitis and their allies in the Bush White House could keep track of which arguments were working and which ones needed to be refined or dropped altogether.

What worked best, a Wirthlin pollster told me, were "anti–Saddam Hussein messages," not sympathetic tales about the exiled Kuwaiti government. Attempts to depict preinvasion Kuwait as "progressive with a strong human-rights and democratic record," he said, suffered "a lack of credibility" because of American skepticism about Arab nations in general. But warnings about Saddam's aggressiveness struck a raw nerve among Americans, who feared that his control of vast oil resources could threaten America's prosperity. Shared with the White House, the Wirthlin findings helped shape the case for going to war.

One theme that the Wirthlin team advised President Bush to downplay was the Saddam-Hitler analogy, which the polls found was not taken too seriously by the American public. "It trivializes both Saddam and Hitler," the Wirthlin pollster told me. "It's too easy a straw man to knock down." Whether or not influenced by the poll results, Bush did drop the Hitler reference from many of his later speeches on the war.

The Kuwaiti influence-buying splurge rekindled a long-simmering argument in Washington power circles about whether foreign clients get their money's worth from Washington influence-peddlers. Some, like *Newsweek*'s Washington bureau chief Evan Thomas, believe that the business of selling connections is mostly a sham, with the foreigner paying far more than the supposed influence is worth. Others, like former TRW executive Pat Choate,

maintain that Japan and other foreign competitors have bought the
freedom to plunder the American market with well-paid Washington insiders working as lookout men and getaway drivers.

For the evicted Kuwaitis with worldwide investments estimated at $100 billion, the spending of a few million on Washing-
ton's largest PR and lobbying firm was pocket change. What Hill
and Knowlton could guarantee, at a minimum, was a loyal cadre
of well-connected people who would relentlessly pitch the latest
Kuwaiti public-relations line to journalists and politicians alike. It
was a battle for the Washington cocktail parties and pundit talk
shows. And it would end in a Kuwaiti victory as decisive as Saddam's initial conquest of the oil-rich sheikhdom.

After studying the Wirthlin poll results, Hill and Knowlton
organized public-relations forums on Iraqi atrocities. With Hill and
Knowlton and the White House taking the lead, the Iraqi soldiers
were pictured as little more than animals. They raped helpless
women; they summarily executed young Kuwaitis in front of their
families; they even ripped infants from incubators so the machinery
could be shipped to Iraq. (After the war, this incubator story would
be debunked as an invention, but it was a very effective image of
Iraqi savagery during the prewar buildup.) Simultaneously, the
Kuwaiti monarchs were cast in a sympathetic role, appealing to the
world as the most innocent of victims. The lobbying firm helped
arrange both the congressional hearings on Iraqi abuses and the
highly unusual presentation to the United Nations.* Hill and
Knowlton set up teams for "message development," "grass roots"
organizing, government contacts and a "national media program."

The contest between the Kuwaitis and Saddam for the hearts
and minds of the American people went lopsidedly against the Iraqi
tyrant. But the decision to commit U.S. troops to battle was decided
by only a few votes in the Senate. A less intense hatred of Saddam

---

*A key witness, who alleged that babies were left to die after being pulled from incubators,
was introduced at congressional hearings only as "Nayirah," her last name withheld supposedly for security reasons. But in January 1992, in a *New York Times* opinion article, John
R. MacArthur reported that the witness was, in reality, the daughter of the Kuwaiti ambassador to Washington. Her emotional accusations were cast into grave doubt. Exhaustive
studies of the incubator issue by Middle East Watch and other human rights groups concluded that the incubator claims were false propaganda. However, as the war clouds built
in late 1990, the charges were effectively exploited by the Kuwaiti government-in-exile and
repeated by President Bush in speeches, whetting the public's demand for revenge against
Saddam Hussein and his army.

and a less romanticized image of Kuwait's rulers might have tipped that vote the other way, favoring continued use of economic sanctions to compel Saddam's withdrawal. Thus, the one-sided CW on the Persian Gulf crisis proved critical to the commitment of American military power. That black-and-white picture might have changed if the American people had taken a close, hard look at whom America's young men and women were being sent to fight— and maybe die—for. If the CW had ever zeroed in on the al-Sabahs and their jet-set feudal monarchy, the public might have wished a plague on both their houses, not the ambivalence a president wants when taking a nation to war.

At the beginning of the Persian Gulf crisis, the Bush administration struggled to explain why it was committing hundreds of thousands of American troops to the Saudi desert. President Bush spoke vaguely of defending "our way of life." But by that, Bush testily insisted he did not just mean cheap oil, even though to many Americans that might have been reason enough to fight. Stung by other Americans who picked up the slogan "no blood for oil," Bush ruled out oil as a crass motive for the far-off intervention. He later modified that stance, agreeing that "oil is part of it, but it is not a main reason—a main reason we are there is to see that aggression is unrewarded."

But as the White House embraced a combination of high-sounding motives and practical self-interest, it also understood that its CW weak point was the Kuwaiti royal family. *The New York Times*'s correspondent Thomas L. Friedman captured this dilemma in a prewar article. "If war breaks out," Friedman wrote,

> the Administration's political Achilles heel could well lie in the stark contrast [Secretary of State James] Baker was exposed to [in Saudi Arabia]: The American troops he visited . . . are dug in on the harsh Saudi desert floor, while the Kuwaiti ruling family . . . is ensconced in the Presidential Suite of the Taif Sheraton Hotel.
>
> In wartime, it could be difficult to explain the contrast between American troops in camouflage garb fighting in the desert and white-robed Kuwaitis sitting around hotel lobbies in Taif, Paris, London, Geneva, Monaco and Bahrain, sipping coffee and applauding the liberation

of their homeland by others. . . . "I know, I know," said
a senior Administration official traveling with Mr. Baker.
"That's why if the war starts, it has to go well for us from
the very start, and by well I mean it has to be over fast."[1]

   The administration's fears about a press focus on the pampered
al-Sabahs turned out to be misplaced. The American press, fully
absorbed in the CW hype of the military buildup, discreetly averted
its eyes from how little the Kuwaiti royal exiles were exerting
themselves toward the liberation of their sheikhdom. Whatever TV
news attention the al-Sabahs received focused on the few young
Kuwaiti princes who joined the war effort as a tiny adjunct to the
American, British and other allied forces.
   The all-important conventional wisdom dutifully followed the
press guidance from the White House, ignoring the occasional story
that would catch the exiled al-Sabahs discoing the night away in
chic Cairo clubs. As mentioned earlier, one of the few in-depth
articles that took an unflattering look at the al-Sabahs' decadent
lives was written by Christopher Dickey for *Vanity Fair*. From his
home in Paris and previous assignments in the Middle East, Dickey
had come to know the al-Sabahs with a detached disgust.
   "Some of the al-Sabah's black sheep have lived here in Paris
for a long time," Dickey wrote, "the world's richest remittance
men, finding on the boulevards a welcome respite from the arid
society of home, where men judge one another's mettle by the cut
of their crisp white dish-dashas, the folds of their headdresses, the
gleam of the Cartier pens in their pockets. One young al-Sabah
spent his time delving into 'European cultural studies' at the Left
Bank's American College in the early eighties and became 'one of
the centers of *le tout Paris homosexuel*,' as a classmate recalls; he
adorned himself with extravagant jewelry, and even posed for portraits by Helmut Newton."[2]
   But the young al-Sabahs in the fashionable centers of European
extravagance were not the only members of the clan who knew
how to enjoy themselves. They had an estimable mentor in Sheikh
Jaber al-Ahmed al-Sabah, the emir of Kuwait since 1977. Dickey
found that even amid the notorious womanizing of the Persian Gulf
sheikhs, the rakish, bearded emir "is reported to delight in his
harem, perhaps more than any other modern ruler in the Middle

East. Islam allows him four wives, and he has used the allotment for business and pleasure."[3]

Dickey quoted sources in the Western diplomatic community as saying that the emir stretches his wife quota by reserving one of the slots for a new bride each week and sometimes fitting two girls into the rotating spot. "The old bugger, the emir, he used to get married once a week—every Thursday night was the lore around the community," one former Canadian envoy told Dickey. "A Bedouin girl. And if she got pregnant, they sent her back with presents, back to the tribe. You know, I think Saddam is right when he says the emir doesn't even know how many [children] he's got."

The self-indulgent life-style of the al-Sabahs was no secret to official Washington. It was just an inconvenient reality that the White House felt was best sheltered from the view of the American people. As touchy as President Bush was about his critics' slogan "no blood for oil," the administration recognized that the public would feel even less passion for fighting a war so the emir could again impregnate Bedouin virgins.

So the CW stayed focused on the unsavory Saddam Hussein and the al-Sabahs entered the picture only rarely, as humble figures, swathed in their white robes, coached by Hill and Knowlton experts, recounting the horrors of the Iraqi occupation. Out of the CW's camera frame was the U.S. government's knowledge of the al-Sabah's personal corruption—as well as their behind-the-scenes relationship with the CIA. Typically, the CW was missing a good story.

For Robert M. Sensi, the balancing act ended abruptly at 4:15 A.M. on August 22, 1986, at the Gloucester Hotel in the drab Kensington section of London. Two blank-faced plainclothesmen from Scotland Yard knocked on his hotel room door. They informed the groggy Sensi that he was under arrest and ordered him to dress quickly. He was wanted, they said, by the American FBI, back in Washington, for embezzling $2.5 million from his employer, Kuwait Airways.

Sensi, a beefy fellow whose view of life is tinged with the cynicism of having seen too much, would spend the next four months in London jails. His gloomy, damp, rat-infested cells recalled some nineteenth-century novel by Dickens. But he never lost hope that any day he would be rescued by his other, secret superiors—in the CIA.

It was, however, Sensi's misfortune that his high-level contact in the spy agency, its director, William J. Casey, had other problems to worry about. The wild-eyed Iran-contra schemes, in which Sensi had played a bit part, were starting to unravel, and Casey's own health was in serious decline. Sensi, like many others recruited by Casey, would find himself both dispensable and deniable after running into trouble.

Sensi's value to Casey had been his ability to bridge two worlds. On one side, Sensi worked and partied with some of the highest-rollers of the Middle East. He was a fixer for the Kuwaiti royal family and boasted of other well-placed contacts in the Arab world. And inside the United States, he had influential contacts within the Republican party and Casey's spy world.

Though normally discreet, with a knack for saying little even when talking a great deal, Sensi detailed many of his odd jobs for the Kuwaitis and the CIA in a remarkable sworn deposition, given on October 10–11, 1987, prior to his embezzlement trial. Testifying in a civil suit connected to his criminal case, he described how his $22,000-a-year job as a Washington office manager for Kuwait Airways gave him the keys to a $2.5 million slush fund.

Born on November 22, 1950, in Blue Island, Illinois, Sensi attended Catholic schools and briefly studied opera in Rome. But instead of an opera career, he returned to Chicago, where he graduated from Loyola University in 1971 with a political science degree. After graduation, he held short-term jobs, repossessing cars and working in a grocery store before landing a position at a travel agency. By 1976, he was a sales manager for Gulf Air and already was using his contacts in Customs to help out influential Kuwaitis.

Sensi always trafficked in contacts, doing favors for wealthy people who in turn introduced him to other wealthy people. One of his Kuwaiti associates led him to his job as Kuwait Airways' Mr. Fix-It in Washington. "I always wanted to move to Washington anyway, because I had friends there," Sensi explained in his deposition.

As Sensi polished his collection of contacts, he went through two marriages. The first, lasting three years, produced a daughter now in her teens. The second, after Sensi moved to Washington, also ended in divorce after a couple of years. In 1986, he had a son with another woman who lived in the stylish Foggy Bottom neighborhood of Washington. His son was born while Sensi was awaiting extradition in a London jail.

According to Sensi, the Kuwaiti slush fund grew out of his after-hours work providing for the all-purpose care and feeding of rich Kuwaitis living in or visiting Washington. He would arrange an occasional prostitute for a lonely sheikh, pay off a professor to boost the grade of a royal student, take the sheikhs' wives on shopping trips, and help arrange quiet medical treatment for embarrassing social diseases.

"What was happening," Sensi told a battery of lawyers at the deposition, "I was spending a lot of money out of my own pocket in the early years from '77 to '80. . . . Trips to New York with the wife of the crown prince, traffic citations for some 'muddy' from the royal family. I mean you name it."[4]

In 1980, Sensi said he took his plight to the Kuwaiti ambassador to the United States, Khalid Jaffar. Sensi said that although he technically worked for Kuwait Airways, the ambassador from the royal family was "basically your boss. . . . The ambassador provided me with authority to open that account because of the amounts of money that I was spending prior to opening that account on behalf of the royal family."[5]

Sensi claimed that upon the ambassador's oral instructions, he began diverting Kuwait Airways money into a special account. The money came from air fare payments that the embassy's cultural division made to Kuwait Airways.[6] Sensi maintained that other airline company officials knew of and approved of his actions.

Skeptical lawyers asked Sensi why he had not obtained the ambassador's written instructions, a normal precaution in the Western world. "It wasn't necessary," Sensi answered. "Because he [the ambassador] was the ultimate authority in this country,"[7] and in the Middle East such arrangements are handled differently. National airlines are virtually an extension of the government and the ruling families. To bolster his claim, Sensi argued that repeated discoveries of the missing money over the next six years were ignored as he continued to pay for unorthodox personal expenses of the royal family. If the slush fund were not approved, he asked, why wouldn't he have been cashiered years ago?

Typical of his experiences at Kuwait Airways, Sensi said in the deposition, the ambassador sent him on a trip once to San

Francisco with a royal delegation. "He was testing me to see how secretive I would be," Sensi said. "He was testing me in terms of my knowledge . . . of general life, whether I knew how to, you know, book a room, whether I knew how to find a prostitute, whether I knew how to clear a seat when they were completely full."

"Did you know how to find a prostitute?" inquired one lawyer. "I would say so," responded Sensi.[8] According to Sensi, the ambassador's curiosity on the question of female traveling companions wasn't entirely academic. One of the documents introduced as evidence in the civil case contained a list of women that Sensi acknowledged he "knew over the years".[9] On the paper was a note, reading, "San Francisco with Jaffar, Sonoma and maid." Sensi testified that sheet "refers to the fact that the ambassador had a liaison with one of the women that I am referring to here. . . . Sonoma would have been [for] Jaffar, and the maid would have been mine."

In the early days, pimping seemed to be a big part of Sensi's after-hours work. A canceled check from the Kuwait Airways slush fund showed Sensi paying $1,000 to the president of a travel agency. Sensi said the man "was also very involved in the procurement of prostitutes for various Kuwaitis that were coming to town. . . . He had a string of telephone numbers of very discreet young ladies that the Kuwaitis would be very interested in."[10]

According to Sensi, the price of the "young ladies" varied from "$500 to $1,000 depending on the quality." "Was it a one night or a couple of nights?" asked one interested lawyer. "Sometimes for just a couple of hours," Sensi answered.[11] For his part, former ambassador Jaffar declined to be interviewed, conveying through his son that he knew Sensi but did not authorize any of Sensi's payments.

Sensi's greatest challenge in caring for the royal family seems to have been Fahed al-Sabah, the son of Kuwait's crown prince. In the sworn deposition, Sensi called Fahed "demented, not nuts. Extremely demented."[12] Sensi said Fahed, who had trouble staying in school, was accepted by a college in North Carolina only after the Kuwaitis forwarded a generous donation.

The son's Watergate neighbors, including former Senator Edward Brooke, needed calming down, Sensi said, when Fahed insisted on feeding a pet cobra on the balcony. "It was going to hit the media that the son of the Kuwait crown prince had a cobra on his balcony at the Watergate and he was feeding him birds," Sensi testified.[13] "At any rate, I took care of the problem to the extent that nothing ever happened. We disposed of the snake."

Less easily handled was Fahed's problem with his servants. One driver quit, Sensi told the lawyers, "because what he [Fahed] would do, he'd throw balloons, water balloons, at the driver while he was driving," nearly causing accidents.[14] A "servant/slave" from Kuwait suffered even worse abuse, Sensi said. Fahed "periodically decided to starve him and to use him as a punching bag," Sensi testified. "He would hang him in his closet, and he would telephone me and say, 'Bob, come over right away. I want you to see something.' And the poor servant would be hanging by his hands on top of the closet."

The servant/slave also ended up on the wrong end of Fahed's brief fascination with boxing, Sensi said. Fahed "bought boxing gloves," Sensi testified. "He decided he was going to be Muhammad Ali. So this poor guy [the servant/slave] had black marks all over his eyes. He was just beaten to a pulp. I said, 'Fahed, you can't do these kinds of things. This is America. You're going to be in a lot of trouble.' . . . He says, 'Never mind. My father is the crown prince. I'll do whatever I want. This is my slave.' "[15]

At no time has the Kuwaiti government officially responded to Sensi's claims.* Even at his trial in early 1988, key Kuwaiti officials refused to testify. Nevertheless, Sensi was convicted of embezzlement in a federal jury trial in Washington. Just before sentencing, however, one of Sensi's superiors at Kuwait Airways did come forward with a written affidavit. The superior, Inder Sethi, delicately acknowledged that on top of Sensi's normal duties, he "performed additional tasks for some members of the royal family. . . . On certain occasions, some members of the royal fam-

---

*Written questions about Sensi's deposition were sent to both the Kuwaiti Embassy in Washington and to Fahed personally. There was no response. Human rights observers, however, told me that Fahed's actions may have gone from bad to worse. Aziz Abu-Hamad, senior researcher for Middle East Watch, said, "There have been many allegations linking Fahed to human rights abuses" against Palestinians and others in postwar Kuwait who were suspected of Iraqi collaboration. According to press reports, a gang of young al-Sabahs had organized armed squads to beat, torture and murder suspected collaborators. After public disclosure of these abuses, the Kuwaiti leadership, including Fahed's father, the crown prince, cracked down on the royal gang. According to one Fahed associate, Fahed denied any connection to these actions, but blame for the abuses was never fixed.

ily of Kuwait, when they were in the United States, requested Mr. Sensi to undertake duties on their behalf." Further, Sethi said he "never questioned or doubted the legitimacy of the account and of Mr. Sensi's use of it. It was clear to me that many people, both in the United States and in Kuwait, were aware of Mr. Sensi's activities."

Those people in the United States also knew that the slush fund was not just for social occasions. According to records in the case, Sensi dipped into the money to pay for his own business contacts with Iran, activities which he claimed had the CIA's blessings.

But during the trial, Sensi found the CIA unwilling to lend a helping hand. The spy agency agreed, finally, to submit only a brief statement admitting to a "relationship" with Sensi from March 1983 until his arrest in August 1986. The agency also released records documenting a June 9, 1986, meeting between Casey and Sensi that was attended by Republican party activist Robert Carter. But the agency refused to take responsibility for the alleged embezzlement. Sensi, for his part, agreed not to disclose the names of CIA agents or call them as witnesses.

Sensi, who looks a bit like Saddam Hussein except a lot less sinister, believes the Kuwaitis risked the public embarrassment that his story could bring them—for the pittance of $2.5 million— because they objected to his last assignment for Casey. When arrested in London, he was on his way to meet with high-ranking Iranian officials, possibly including Ayatollah Khomeini, Sensi said. The Kuwaitis had ordered him to stay away from Iran, fearing that that trip could backfire and inflame their already incendiary relations with Teheran.

Yet Sensi followed his hustler instincts still farther out onto the high wire of international intrigue. He found that playing the espionage game offered excitement and quick riches. But like many free-lancers, Sensi also discovered that when trouble hit, he was just another highly expendable asset cooling his heels in jail.

Sensi maintained that many of the slush-fund withdrawals covered business expenses related to his Iran initiatives for the CIA. The documents from the civil case do show large sums going to Sensi's front companies that he ran with Iranian exile Habib Moallem and others. But what is not clear is whether Sensi exaggerated his ties to Casey and the CIA as part of a moneymaking scam—or whether he was following explicit orders from senior CIA men.

Beyond the CIA's limited acknowledgment of a "relationship" with Sensi dating back to 1983, Sensi had worked with CIA-connected individuals even earlier. In fall 1982, for instance, Sensi arranged a business deal—the purchase of a Costa Rican hotel—for Francisco "Chicano" Cardenal, one of the founders of the CIA-financed Nicaraguan contra army. Some expenses for that venture were paid out of the Kuwait Airways slush fund.[16]

In another curious 1982 deal, Sensi bought an unprofitable mine in the West African nation of Sierra Leone. Sensi testified that the idea behind that scheme was to "penetrate the Sierra Leone government" by funneling money through the mine to some political leaders. That, he claimed, would grease the CIA's relocation of sensitive listening posts to Sierra Leone if instability in nearby Liberia forced the closing of the electronic-eavesdropping facility there. The Kuwaiti slush fund, again, covered the several-hundred-thousand-dollar loss from that investment.

What brought Sensi directly into the CIA camp, however, was Iran—and Casey's desperate need to establish intelligence contacts inside that Islamic republic. Sensi, with his Middle Eastern friends, seemed a logical choice. To expand his contacts with Iran, Sensi set up purchasing companies in London and Teheran, again financed discreetly through the Kuwaiti money.

But bankrolling Sensi was not Kuwait Airways only assistance to the CIA's Iranian operations. When the ex–CIA airline, Southern Air Transport, needed cargo jets to carry missiles to Iran and weapons to the Nicaraguan contras, it found them in the inventories of Kuwait Airways. The Kuwaitis sold three Boeing 707's to Southern Air in 1985.

By late 1985, Casey was entertaining other plans to deal with the Iranian problem. The aging spymaster was listening to two very different schemes. One called for a covert action to overthrow—and possibly kill—the ever-troublesome Khomeini. The other would arrange for the United States to sell weapons directly to the Islamic republic in exchange for Teheran's help in reining in fundamentalist terrorists in Lebanon and winning the freedom of American hostages.

Sensi's group appeared to have a wheel on each track. On

December 1, 1985, Sensi's associates met with the U.S. ambassador to the Vatican, William Wilson, one of Reagan's closest personal friends, according to sources familiar with the meeting. Their pitch to Wilson was for him to urge Reagan to back U.S.-to-Iran arms sales, a decision that the president was weighing at the time. Wilson told me later that he had no specific recollection of the meeting, but found a notation on his calendar for that day that could have referred to the appointment.

Another meeting to consider the two Iranian options—confrontation or collaboration—was set for late December 1985 at the Watergate Hotel. This time, according to testimony at Sensi's trial, the participants were to include Casey and Vice-President George Bush. But the meeting was canceled after a decision was made to first test out the quality of Sensi's contacts by asking his help to resolve a $20 million claim that Ingersoll-Rand, a major engineering firm, had filed against the Iranian government.

But Ingersoll-Rand executives weren't sure, either, what to make of Sensi, so they sought assurances that Sensi did indeed have powerful connections in Washington, according to trial testimony of Barry Parnum, an Ingersoll-Rand consultant. Parnum said he traveled to Washington in the spring of 1986 to reconnoiter. Sensi escorted Parnum around town and into the offices of several former senior government officials. Later in the day, Sensi pulled some strings to get Parnum an Oval Office tour. But the main event was still to come.

Sensi invited Parnum, along with another Ingersoll-Rand executive and their wives, to a $5,000-a-couple White House soiree in June 1986 to benefit the Ford Theater. As the limousine approached the White House gate, Parnum wondered, "What on earth is Sensi up to?" But as the car window came down and the guard recognized Sensi, the car was quickly waved through. The impressed Ingersoll-Rand executives were soon inside the White House at an intimate reception attended by the Reagan Cabinet.

"We were at one end of the White House, where the tables were laid out with the drinks to serve all of the guests," Parnum testified. "Bob Sensi said, 'One moment. That's my friend over there, Bill Casey. He likes to drink scotch. Why don't I get him a scotch because we are here and I will give it to him and why don't I introduce you?'" After chatting with Casey for several minutes, Sensi led the tall, stooped, shuffling, white-haired man back to the Ingersoll-Rand group. "Mr. Casey started to chuckle," Parnum recalled. "He said, 'Seems as though Ingersoll-Rand gets everywhere, doesn't it, Barry?' " The company execs were convinced. Sensi, they concluded, was for real. The tickets for the reception were paid with $15,000 from the Kuwait Airways slush fund.

Immediately after the White House reception, Sensi and Robert Carter visited Casey at CIA headquarters in Langley, Virginia. This was the meeting of June 9, 1986, confirmed by the CIA. The topic of discussion was a trip by Sensi to Iran on behalf of Ingersoll-Rand. Sensi told me that he intended to meet with senior Iranians, possibly including Ayatollah Khomeini, whose failing health and likely successor were hot topics around the CIA.

Preparing for the trip, Sensi said he flew to London, where a Kuwait Airways superior ordered him to cancel the Iran visit for fear that Sensi's actions could worsen the already tense relations between Iran and Kuwait. Kuwait, fearing the spread of Islamic fundamentalism in the Gulf, had quietly sided with Iraq in the Iran-Iraq war. The little sheikhdom also had shown some spunk by imprisoning seventeen Islamic fundamentalist terrorists who had bombed Western embassies in Kuwait City. But Kuwait didn't need any more trouble with Iran, particularly when Iran had gained the upper hand in the war and had moved troops within marching range of Kuwait's border.

Sensi claimed that after he refused to bail out on Casey's project, Kuwait Airways blew the whistle on his six-year-old slush fund, leading to his early-morning arrest by Scotland Yard. Sensi's lawyer, Stephen A. Saltzburg, argued at the embezzlement trial that his client's mistake was to "put his own government and his own country ahead of his job. He basically said . . . to the Kuwaitis for whom he worked, 'I will not do what you want because I have a higher obligation to my government.' " However, the federal jury, presumably taking note that some slush-fund money had found its way into the pockets of Sensi's family and friends, judged him guilty of theft and mail fraud.

Before his sentencing on July 1, 1988, Sensi told U.S. district judge George H. Revercomb that "I solemnly swear before the court and Almighty God, the true judge of our deeds, that I am a patriot and that which I did, was done for the benefit of my country and my fellowman. And what have I to show for this effort? I am now a convicted felon. . . . I have brought disgrace and despair to my parents and siblings, and my infant son will now grow to manhood with the stigma of having a father who is a common criminal."

Revercomb responded sympathetically, but noted that "you did spend too much money for personal use to support a conclusion that you believed it was all in the name of business—or for that matter, in the name of intelligence work." The judge did accept Sensi's claim that some of his activities were authorized. "The court is satisfied that there was some knowledge, indeed some acquiescence or perhaps complicity on the part of others," Revercomb said. "And for whatever reason, the victim, [Kuwait] Airways, in this case, has not made available the witnesses who were knowledgeable of your duties at the Airways and your relationship to the Kuwait government." He handed Sensi a light sentence of six months in jail and five years probation. Counting pretrial time served in London, Sensi was out of a minimum-security prison in Loretto, Pennsylvania, in less than two months.

Sensi and his trial opened a window into the covert relationship between the CIA and oil-rich Kuwait. But the CW press had decided by 1988 that the Iran-contra scandal was just too boring. Sensi's trial received scant attention when it occurred and none at all during the Persian Gulf crisis, when the secret intelligence connections between the Kuwaiti royal family and the CIA would seem to have deserved a fresh examination.

The recent CIA-Kuwait history was certainly relevant when the Iraqis accused Kuwait of collaborating with another Reagan-Bush plan to advance U.S. interests in the Middle East. But the CW's obsessive hatred of Saddam precluded any serious attention to the covert side of American relations with the al-Sabahs. The CW's subtle effect on editors, convincing them to avert their eyes from issues that the White House had not given legitimacy, kept press attention on the war's buildup, not its background.

Yet the United States did seem to be playing a role in the Iraq-Kuwait tensions that led up to the war. After the Iran-Iraq war ended in 1989, the administration pursued a carrot-and-stick strategy with Saddam that simultaneously assisted Iraq's military and economic expansion while undermining Saddam's ability to finance his nation's needs.

According to Israeli intelligence officials, the U.S. goal was to exact concessions from Saddam on a Middle East peace settlement—in effect, to draw Iraq into the Camp David process. But where Washington saw an opportunity to lessen the region's tensions, Israel saw danger. The Jewish state feared the continued expansion of Saddam's military might, particularly his chemical, nuclear and ballistic capabilities, as a deadly threat to Israel. Prime Minister Yitzhak Shamir also opposed the American peace plan, which he felt would carve up Israel by returning the West Bank, Golan Heights and Gaza Strip to the Arabs.

Indeed, the Bush administration had been pressing for a land-for-peace swap between Israel and its Arab enemies—a deal that would have deprived Israel of biblical territory captured in the 1967 war from Jordan and Syria in exchange for Arab assurances that they would respect Israel's right to exist. A running joke among the Israelis was that the American land-for-peace scheme simply meant giving up pieces of Israeli land for empty promises from the Arab enemy. Reduced to a thin strip of territory along the Mediterranean Sea, Israel would again be vulnerable to renewed Arab attacks.

As for the Persian Gulf oil states, U.S. policy might be summarized as "They sell us oil at a decent price and we bail them out whenever they get in trouble." Indeed, a secret State Department cable that fell into the hands of Iranian radicals when they overran the U.S. embassy in 1979 said almost exactly that. Dated July 5, 1979, the cable stated that despite differences over Israel, the Saudis wanted to continue their "special relationship" with the United States. "The basis of this relationship," the cable said, "our need for oil and the Saudi need for security. . . . Oil for security is still the essence of the special relationship." Ironically, the cable was directed to April Glaspie, then a Middle East specialist based in London.

The same deal applied to Kuwait and the tiny Gulf sheikhdoms. Late in the Iran-Iraq war, the United States committed its naval forces in the Persian Gulf to reflag Kuwaiti oil tankers and safeguard their passage through the war zone. Conceivably, the Kuwaiti government, counting on unquestioned U.S. backing, simply pushed Saddam a step too far.

                                    *   *   *

The CW showed scant curiosity about these underlying relationships and thus offered the American people little historical
context for understanding the daily rush of events. Saddam was
simply a villain and the Western powers were just righting an un-
justifiable wrong, the invasion of a defenseless little country. It
was, as President Bush explained in a simplified way that the CW
could grasp, "Hitler revisited."

Those Americans who still didn't get it, who went into the
streets to march, carry signs and shout antiwar slogans, drew a
special contempt from the CW set. "I believe this is Vietnam
movement redux," observed Kondracke on *The McLaughlin Group*.
"All of this is trying to re-create the joy of the sixties and it's going
to fail." To the *Group*'s other *New Republic*ker, Fred Barnes, the
antiwar protests were even worse than a lark. "Their complaint is
not against anything," Barnes explained. "They don't like the
United States and they don't want it to have a role in the world.
What they need to be effective as an antiwar [movement] is a long
war that's not going well. This ain't it."[17]

It was simple. The antiwar protesters were just fun-seeking
America-haters who hoped for a long and bloody war so they could
re-create the joyous sixties. One of the protesters' chief demands
drew special derision: that give-and-take negotiations be tried before the killing started. Whenever tepidly raised, even by bona fide
conservatives like Evans and Novak, that idea was greeted by a
CW chorus that anything short of total, unconditional and humiliating Iraqi withdrawal would be "rewarding Saddam for his aggression." Saddam would not get even a tiny fig leaf to cover his
withdrawal from Kuwait.

As the CW has grown to dominate the Washington political
debate, only fools dare take on the riskiest of all mantles, that of
peacemaker. In the Clint Eastwood verbalisms of CW talk, negotiations are for sissies. No sane political figure in Washington—
still hearing snickers about that weakling Jimmy Carter—needed
reminding about the political dangers of conciliation. War was now
the first resort, diplomacy the last. That reasonable negotiations
might have averted the calamity of war never got more than a
derisive back of the hand.

Yet peace had always been a possibility. As the next chapter
will show, both before and after August 2, 1990, the day Saddam's

army charged into Kuwait, a full-scale war might have been averted and international law respected. But only in the wake of the 100,000 dead, the widespread environmental damage, the heartbreaking Kurdish uprising, the billions of dollars wasted, the torture and the sickening show trials in "liberated" Kuwait would the CW consider the possibility that there might have been an alternative to war. And as usual, by then it was too late.

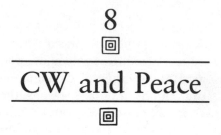

8

CW and Peace

Ayear after Iraq's invasion of Kuwait, Saddam's sinister and slightly puffy visage was staring down again from the magazine and newspaper racks. On the first anniversary of the crisis, *Time* magazine superimposed Saddam's brooding face on an oil fire in Kuwait. Across the red and orange cover, *Time* raised the long-forbidden question: "Was It Worth It?"[1] The CW was changing.

While the *Time* account nudged the long-standing CW that had just loved the war, the magazine would not go so far as to suggest that it and the other CW setters had rallied too rabidly around the flag when war was in the offing. Though acknowledging that the price had been high to restore the Gulf's status quo, *Time* added that that "is not to say the gulf war wasn't worth it. A crucial principle was defended: aggression will be checked—at least when the victim sits atop the commodity Clemenceau said was 'as necessary as blood.' But on most other fronts the euphoria of the allied victory has given way to the region's traditional pessimism."

Time noted that the Middle East was still home to long-harbored grievances against the West. Despite the catastrophe of war, the Kuwaiti government could summon up little energy or initiative. The U.S. Army Corps of Engineers restored the water and power "illustrating a dependency of little consequence to most Kuwaitis, who rarely lift a finger except to point it. Those who had hoped for a New Kuwait, a more democratic, self-reliant and purposeful society, have been forced to concede the obvious: the rush is in the opposite direction—back to the past."[2]

Describing this "mess in Kuwait," the *Time* article cited the mistreatment of thousands of Palestinians and other nationals considered disloyal who had been imprisoned without trial or forcibly deported. Some had been sentenced to death or to life sentences after circuslike show trials where the flimsiest of evidence (such as a man's wearing a Saddam T-shirt) had justified the harshest of punishments.

Time noted how the old Kuwaiti traditions of corruption (the need to pay agents to act as middlemen) had slowed the vital effort to extinguish the fires set by Saddam's retreating forces. Even as 732 of the sheikhdom's 1,000 oil wells burned, profit-making off the disaster came first. Fully five months after Kuwait's liberation, only about one third of the fires had been doused, and the trickiest fires in the high-pressure wells had yet to be tackled. Meanwhile, giant lakes of crude oil had spread over 1.2 billion cubic feet of soil, covering Iraqi antipersonnel mines and sinking into the sand. In the air, dark oil clouds hovered over the country and spread their greasy stain wherever the wind blew them. (The last of the oil fires would finally be snuffed out in early November 1991.)

The political horizon looked no more promising. The monarchy had made only token steps toward opening up the nation's medieval system of awarding all key positions of power to members of the al-Sabah clan. At the top, the government still functioned under the principle of "one emir, one vote," as *Time* noted. Although many of the royal courtiers were contemptuously nicknamed the "runners" by the lesser-born Kuwaitis who stayed behind to endure and resist the Iraqi occupation, it was the "runners" who returned to retake the positions of power, wealth and influence. Many arrived back at the airport with replacement servants in tow.

Time, however, tried to be understanding. "The Kuwaiti government is behaving as would most regimes in similar circumstances," the article sympathized. "Its overriding priority has been the reassertion of its authority." Still, the magazine criticized the gross mistakes and foot-dragging that had characterized the postliberation period.

Time was downright pessimistic about the possibility that the war might spread the principles of democracy to Kuwait and the other filthily oil-rich sheikhdoms of the Persian Gulf. The emir did hold out the promise of a new parliamentary election in October 1992, but the opposition groups complained that the far-off date simply defused the public pressure for more freedoms.

"In all this," admitted one U.S. diplomat to *Time,* "the anti-Sabah factions have been hurt by President Bush's saying that the Gulf war was not fought in order to bring democracy to Kuwait. . . . When the president, who's considered a saint in Kuwait, downplayed democracy, the Emir won a cushion that will protect him at least until the '92 vote."

Time found the Kuwaitis more interested in restoring their pampered life-style where every care is tended to by foreign servants and paid for by the oil riches beneath their deserts. "If ever they bear down at all," *Time* observed, "most Kuwaitis will probably work hardest in the service of the one goal they all understand instinctively: making their nation safe for the making of money. Democracy can wait."

Despite *Time*'s bleak assessment of postwar Kuwait, the magazine's rhetorical query of "was it worth it?" went only so far in taking a revisionist glance at the wartime CW. *Time* did not count against the "worth it" question the thousands of civilians killed in the not-so-precise American bombardment of Iraq, the horrifying slaughter of tens of thousands of retreating Iraqi troops, the devastation of Iraq, the spreading hunger and disease, and the deaths of several hundred American, British and other allied soldiers.

But *Time*'s criticism marked the crystallizing of a new CW on Kuwait and the war—a shoulder-shrugging recognition that not much had changed other than the bloody destruction of much of Saddam's army and war machine. But why hadn't the opinion shapers understood that likelihood when the devastation could have been averted? *Time,* like other mainstream publications and pundits, had acted as little more than flag-wavers on the bandwagon for war as it sped downhill in the fall of 1990 and early winter 1991.

In a sanguine prewar prequel to its sober postwar review, *Time* had asked in its December 24, 1990, issue: "What is Kuwait? And is it worth dying for?" But unlike its downbeat assessment in August 1991, the prewar image of Kuwait was glowing. As if reading from a script written by Kuwait's public-relations firm, that article depicted Kuwait as a valiant little city-state governed wisely by kings and princes who seemed to have stepped out of a Walt Disney classic. *Time* warmly praised the al-Sabahs for their wise management of the nation's vast wealth, the country's generous social programs and, remarkably, even the royal family's frugality. The answer to the life-and-death question was an unqualified yes.

"Unlike other nations, which spend their oil revenues almost as fast as they come in, Kuwait long ago decided to save for the future," *Time* said in praise. It then quoted a rich Kuwaiti businessman flattering his patrons, the al-Sabahs. "Other rulers in other places have kept the money for themselves and their friends, doling out just enough to keep their populations contained during their reigns," the businessman said. "Our rulers, the Sabahs, have earned our loyalty by providing for our grandchildren."

The lengthy *Time* cover story made scant mention of the dark side of this magical kingdom. The magazine acknowledged only at the very end that foreign residents—more than half the total population of nearly two million—had few rights, though they performed nearly all of the sheikhdom's work. Only males whose forebears had lived in Kuwait before 1920 could vote. That meant that out of the 826,500 Kuwaiti-born citizens, only about one tenth possessed the franchise. Women and lesser-born men were barred from voting altogether.

But, of course, the franchise held little value in Kuwait because the al-Sabahs had banned political parties, forcibly dispersed protest demonstrations, censored newspapers and suspended the nation's parliament for criticizing the al-Sabahs' rule. There was little change in this depressingly undemocratic picture in the days after liberation.

But the corollary to *Time*'s positing of the prewar question in December 1990 "Is it worth dying for?" or the postwar query in August 1991 "Was it worth it?" must be a question that the CW has never been willing to ask: "Was there another way to reverse Saddam's aggression without the terrible human suffering and environmental damage?" The answer is, "Maybe, yes."

There were moments even after Saddam's gross miscalculation in invading Kuwait when creative diplomacy might have engineered his full retreat, possibly by the end of August 1990. That would have saved the Kuwaitis the horror of the Iraqi occupation as well as the devastation of their "liberated" country. The hundreds of Iraqi civilians killed by the occasional dumb American bomb might be alive and the survivors in Iraq might still be living in the twentieth century. The children of Iraq might not have had

to face a two-to-three-times higher chance of death from such diseases as typhoid, cholera and malnutrition, as reported by a Harvard
medical team.[3] There might not be hundreds of mass graves
stretched across the desert covering the charred remains of tens of
thousands of uncounted Iraqi young men. The 148 American military men and women who weren't lucky enough to celebrate the
"miraculously light casualties" that the U.S. forces had suffered
might still be among us. And Iraq's Kurdish minority—urged by
Bush and the CIA to rise up against Saddam—might have been
spared their latest betrayal by the West, a postwar double cross
which allowed the still-potent remnants of the Iraqi army to crush
their rebellion while the United States did little more than air-
dump pallets of food on their refugee camps.

In short, if the war had been averted, untold thousands of
innocents on all sides might have been spared. But it would have
meant satisfying some of Iraq's legitimate objections against Kuwait—and as the CW would tell us throughout the crisis, that would
have been "rewarding Saddam for his aggression."

Saddam's first peace overture came the same day as the invasion, with a call to King Hussein of Jordan. "We had to go in,"
Saddam told King Hussein, according to Salinger and Laurent's
Secret Dossier.[4] "I am committed to withdrawal from Kuwait. It will
start within days and will last several weeks. Please do whatever
you can with the Arabs to persuade them that condemnations and
threats don't work with us. We may end up with Kuwait being part
of Iraq."

King Hussein then began a round of telephone calls to Arab
leaders, proposing a minisummit on August 4 and asking them to
refrain from denouncing Saddam's actions. The little king of Jordan
placed a similar call to President Bush, who was aboard *Air Force
One* on his way to meet Prime Minister Margaret Thatcher in Aspen,
Colorado. "We just need a little time," King Hussein implored,
quoting Bush's reply as, "You've got it." But Bush would also state
publicly that he told King Hussein and Egypt's President Hosni
Mubarak "that it had gone beyond simply a regional dispute because of the naked aggression."[5]

In Aspen, Thatcher, known as the "Iron Lady," urged the
president to take the strongest possible stance against Saddam's
aggression. "She spoke of Saddam Hussein rather as one of her

predecessors, Anthony Eden, had spoken of Gamal Abdel Nasser during the Suez crisis, comparing him to Hitler," according to an eyewitness.[6] Back in Washington, the president and his men began planning for a military response to Saddam's invasion.

In Egypt, meanwhile, plans for the Arab minisummit were coming unglued. The Egyptian Foreign Ministry, apparently responding to Washington's desire for a harder line against Saddam, denounced the invasion. "This destroys everything," King Hussein would later recall thinking as he returned to Jordan from his meeting with Saddam. "And it gives all chances of broadening the conflict."[7] Under mounting U.S. pressure, Mubarak apparently had concluded that Saddam could not be trusted to live up to a promised withdrawal even if the minisummit had occurred. But others in the Arab world insist that Saddam was prepared to withdraw from Kuwait if the meeting had achieved an agreement.

On August 4, the day when King Hussein had hoped to engineer an end to the crisis, a divided Arab League adopted a resolution condemning Iraq and demanding an unconditional withdrawal. The next day, in Washington, a visibly angry President Bush wagged his finger and denounced the Iraqis for lying. "They said they were going to start moving out today, and we have no evidence of their moving out," Bush told reporters. "I view very seriously our determination to reverse out this aggression. . . . This will not stand. This will not stand, this aggression against Kuwait."

The CW that took shape in Washington in those dog days of August would rest heavily on Saddam's deceit. Bush would also accuse him of falsely assuring Mubarak that he would not invade Kuwait in the first place. But as in all diplomacy, careful reading of precise language is crucial. Salinger and Laurent would report that Saddam's promise to Mubarak on July 24 went as follows: "As long as discussions last between Iraq and Kuwait, I won't use force. I won't intervene with force before I have exhausted all the possibilities for negotiation."[8] When those last-ditch talks collapsed a week later, on August 1, Mubarak should have been aware of the heightened danger of an Iraqi attack.

A tyrant as ruthless as Saddam would not hesitate to mislead friends and foes alike when it suited his purposes. But it will never be known whether an Arab solution to the crisis was possible in those early hours, had Egypt and other U.S. allies not sensed pressure from Washington for an uncompromising stand against

Iraq. Saddam's invasion of Kuwait and the denunciation from the Arab League shattered the always fragile unity of the Arab states and moved any hope of a peaceful settlement into the international arena.

By the time of President Bush's finger-waving pledge that "this will not stand," Saddam was realizing that his actions had exploded into a major world crisis. He began exploring channels to the United States to extricate himself from the mess he had created. Secretly, Iraq conveyed diplomatic messages to the United States, both through traditional and unconventional channels, trying to establish talks with President Bush about an Iraqi withdrawal.

Saddam's hope, it seems, was to have used the Kuwait invasion like a two-by-four across the front of a mule's head to get its attention—and then trade freedom for Kuwait for settlement of his economic grievances. But after getting mule-kicked by world opinion for his invasion, Saddam began to signal frantically that pretty much any sort of trade might do.

Salinger and Laurent recounted how Iraqi deputy foreign minister Nizar Hamdoon used PLO chief Yasir Arafat to deliver a message on August 7, 1990, in Vienna to a Palestinian businessman with close contacts inside the White House. The message, from Saddam Hussein to President Bush, "confirmed that Saddam Hussein was ready to pull out of Kuwait but needed to resolve problems with Kuwait first," the two journalists wrote. "The businessman called John Sununu, the White House chief of staff, and told him he was forwarding the message. 'It's OK, but I don't want anyone to know such a message has been passed on,' Sununu said. When the message got to Washington, there was no reply."[9]

A similar fate awaited another Iraqi initiative. One week after the invasion, the Iraqis dispatched a peace feeler to Washington through a back channel of two Arab-American businessmen, Michael Saba and Samir Vincent. After an oral briefing on the plan from Hamdoon, the two were allowed to "escape" from Iraq on August 9. After driving by car out of Iraq, the pair flew immediately to Washington and, through separate arrangements, contacted the White House. Hamdoon, who had served as Iraq's ambassador to Washington, was considered a pro-Western moderate. But according to participants in the initiative and a confidential congressional summary, Hamdoon's proposed settlement reflected the thinking of Saddam himself.

The Hamdoon proposal offered a complete military pullout from Kuwait in exchange for guaranteed Iraqi access to the Persian Gulf through some formula on Kuwait's Bubiyan and Warbah islands, total Iraqi control of the Rumaillah oil field, which dips slightly into Kuwaiti territory, and negotiations on oil prices with the United States. Gone were the demands for a multibillion-dollar economic bailout.

Immediately upon his arrival in Washington, a travel-weary Saba went to the White House to meet with Sununu, whom Saba knew through Arab-American cultural activities. As with the other peace feeler, Sununu apparently wanted, more than anything, to keep the initiative a secret. For his part, Saba has refused to divulge what he told Sununu, except to say "that Hamdoon had said that Iraq had no quarrel with the U.S." In a letter, Saba denied that he carried "a formal proposal or any other document from the Iraqi government." When I called him back, however, he declined to comment on whether he conveyed an informal, oral peace proposal from Hamdoon. Even after the war, the fate of those early peace proposals remained a closely guarded secret.

On a separate track, Vincent, a onetime Olympic athlete for Iraq and a Boston College graduate, arranged other contacts with the White House through a retired U.S. Army colonel, Carl Bernard, and through ex–CIA director Richard Helms. Bernard set up a meeting for Vincent with National Security Council staffers, but Bernard recalled later that the staffers seemed more interested in arguing against the Hamdoon plan than copying down its terms.

Disappointed with that approach, Vincent and Bernard turned to Helms, who also had served as U.S. ambassador to Iran and was a respected expert on Middle East politics. As the crisis built, Helms feared its dangerous long-term consequences and agreed to raise the Iraqi peace plan at a previously scheduled lunch with national security adviser Brent Scowcroft. According to accounts of that August 21, 1990, meeting, Scowcroft told Helms that while the White House was not blind to negotiations, it first wanted to assess the results of economic sanctions against Iraq. Scowcroft added that he already knew of the peace feelers. "Scowcroft advised him that he had learned of the initiative from Saba as of Aug. 10," the congressional summary said.

When Helms relayed Scowcroft's equivocal response back to Vincent and the Iraqis, Hamdoon saw hope. He updated the plan on August 23 to include release of all Western hostages, on the Iraqi side, and the lifting of United Nations sanctions against Iraq, on the American side. The Iraqis also wanted talks with the United States about how to improve stability in the Gulf and ease Iraq's severe economic problems. But the chief points remained the same: full military withdrawal from Kuwait, in exchange for the disputed oil field and access to the Gulf. Helms promptly delivered this new message to the White House, too.

Though the Americans were cool, the Iraqis still hoped this back-channel contact might lead to a breakthrough. Hamdoon, anxious about the White House reaction, called the Iraqi embassy in Washington the next day, August 24, to make sure his latest message had been delivered. Impatient, Vincent turned back to Bernard, an army expert in special operations who runs a small defense-consulting business in Alexandria, Virginia. On August 27, Bernard contacted a Scowcroft aide to get an answer to the Iraqi initiative and urge the use of Vincent as a future mediator. But as with the earlier initiative funneled through the PLO, there was no White House response. The Bush administration seemed most interested in keeping the peace feeler secret.

The initiative, however, did not stay secret long. An enterprising investigative reporter for *Newsday*, Knut Royce, got wind of the back channel and wrote an article for his Long Island newspaper on August 29.[10] Royce is a hardworking throwback to an earlier age of journalism. He takes a perverse pleasure in confounding the conventional wisdom, not conforming to it. His exclusive on the peace feeler correctly outlined the initiative but without mentioning the names of the participants or the intrigue that surrounded the plan.

After the *Newsday* report, the White House "steered" the easily maneuvered Washington press corps away from the story. Only late in the day, too late for the evening TV news shows, the White House acknowledged that there was something to Royce's story after all. But the administration noted, stiffly, that "there was nothing in this particular proposal that merited its pursuit."[11] And the White House advised Iraq to convey any future messages through normal State Department channels. The Iraqis had chosen to circumvent State, participants in the back channel said, because they considered the department too sympathetic to Israel.

Though the Kuwait invasion was the hottest story of August,

the national news media showed no follow-up interest in Royce's scoop. The White House had dumped cold water on it, and as usual, the CW would take its lead from the president. The Washington press ignored this practical initiative that conceivably could have resolved the crisis before the two sides had hardened their positions. Within weeks, President Bush had elevated Saddam above Hitler on history's list of most-evil villains, accused the Iraqi army of "crimes against humanity," and declared: "I am more determined than ever to see that this invading dictator gets out of Kuwait with no compromise of any kind whatsoever."[12] For his part, Saddam was ranting about making American soldiers "swim in their own blood."

The American press would later focus on Saddam's grandiose demands that the Iraq-Kuwait problem be settled only as part of an overall Middle East peace conference. That thoroughly impractical proposal served Saddam's rhetorical and political needs of appealing to the Arab masses, but would have required the untangling of hopelessly twisted conflicts, like the Lebanese civil war and the Israeli-Palestinian problem, before Kuwait would be freed. Citing Saddam's political "linkage" as evidence of insincerity, the CW concluded that Saddam was never interested in negotiations.

Striking in its pragmatism and flexibility, the Hamdoon back channel contained practical elements that clearly were open to negotiation. And Hamdoon's eagerness to revamp the proposal to make it more attractive to Washington reveals an Iraqi government drooling to engage the United States in some sort of talks. Although possibly just a stall to buy time, key leaders in Baghdad appeared to want desperately to extricate Iraq from the trap that Saddam had sprung. But instead of testing out Iraqi sincerity or exploiting it to create divisions in Iraq, the White House chose to do nothing with the plan.

Secretary of State James Baker formally rejected the idea of trading any Kuwaiti concessions for an Iraqi withdrawal on October 16, 1990. Baker warned against succumbing to the "siren song" of appeasement and objected to any "negotiated arrangement that would enable [Saddam] to claim benefits from his unprovoked aggression."[13] The widely publicized "negotiations" that Bush promoted in the days before his January 15, 1991, war deadline were actually ultimatums demanding Saddam's full withdrawal and total humiliation. Iraq's foreign minister Tariq Aziz would leave Bush's last prewar ultimatum on a desk in Geneva, throwing the TV chat shows into a fury, but the best chance for peace had passed almost unnoticed five months earlier.

After the war, I stumbled onto the existence of Hamdoon's back-channel proposal and interviewed many of the participants. "I think the message was real," Bernard, the former army colonel, told me. The problem, he thought, was cultural. "In the camel-trading business, ultimatums aren't the same as trading camels," Bernard remarked. "Certainly, the guys in Iraq . . . were offering this and offering that. [But] they were dealing with a New Englander who didn't trade camels much."

The congressional summary, prepared in early January 1991 by a Democratic aide with intelligence-oversight responsibilities, said Saddam may have seen the invasion only as a dramatic opening shot in negotiations to resolve his long-simmering border dispute with Kuwait. "The Iraqis apparently believed that having invaded Kuwait, they would get everyone's attention, negotiate improvements to their economic situation and pull out," the summary said. It added that if the White House had been interested, "a diplomatic solution satisfactory to the interests of the United States may well have been possible since the earliest days of the invasion."

Instead, the summary said, "the NSC apparently concluded on the basis of a psychological profile of Saddam Hussein, and to avoid seeming to in any way reward the invasion, to refuse any negotiations with him, concluding that they would be fruitless until the U.S. had backed Saddam Hussein into a corner from which he could not escape."

Former CIA chief Helms assessed the dead end more succinctly: "The U.S. government didn't want to make a deal." For his part, Vincent, one of the couriers, would say only, "It was a serious attempt. . . . Unfortunately, it didn't succeed."

9

CW Versus the Vietnam Syndrome

He had been Hitler, Mussolini, a monster, a madman, even "a big fat rat," but what never sank in to the egotistical Saddam Hussein was that he was only a bit player in a larger drama that surrounded the Persian Gulf crisis. Saddam was the accidental villain and his pathetic country an unfortunate scene on location. The more important strategic war that Saddam stumbled into by invading Kuwait was a long-fought battle for the hearts and minds of the American people. Waged for a decade by the Reagan and Bush administrations, it was a struggle to subdue, once and for all, the Vietnam Syndrome.

From the earliest days of the Reagan-Bush era, the White House had recognized that the greatest check on its ability to commit American forces abroad was not a foreign enemy. It was heartland America. The Vietnam War—its endless casualties, bitter generational divisions, the cheery public relations which would be exposed as lies—had deeply scarred the country's psyche and American willingness to dispatch soldiers abroad. Breaking the people of this syndrome, this national reflex to pull away from the flame of foreign conflict, had been at the center of the Reagan-Bush international agenda.

Saddam may have thought he invaded Kuwait, but in truth, he had marched his troops to the center of an American psychological struggle over the use of the nation's awesome military power. His rash decision was worse than a Waterloo, for even a defeated general can retreat from a military debacle. Saddam had put himself and his army in the middle of American celluloid reality. He was the snarling movie villain—and George Bush could finally be Clint Eastwood.

As 100,000 or so Iraqi men were obliterated on the hard desert ground of Kuwait and Iraq, the United States felt not horror, but the catharsis that moviegoers experience at the end of an action thriller. Saddam had invaded and raped helpless Kuwait. When confronted by the forces of law and order, Saddam had vowed, vaingloriously, that the heroes would "swim in their own blood" and were facing "the mother of all battles." Cornered in the finale, Saddam and his gang got a good and thorough thrashing. It was a formula that Americans knew from their TV sets, their VCRs and their movie theaters. Only this time, they were transported into the true-life adventure. This time, the killing was real.

Even before the carnage in the desert, President Bush had announced that the war had a demonstration value. In one pre-ground-war stump speech before an excited crowd at Fort Stewart, Georgia, Bush explained that the conflict's outcome would erase any doubts about American will. "When we win, and we will, we will have taught a dangerous dictator and any tyrant tempted to follow in his footsteps, that the U.S. has a new credibility, and that what we say goes, and that there is no place for lawless aggression in the Persian Gulf."[1]

But the memory of Vietnam was never far in the background as 500,000 American troops again were dispatched to a faraway land. *Washington Post* columnist Jim Hoagland, who beat the war drum early and often, was typical in depicting the confrontation as a test, simply put, of "America's mettle."

"Iraq's refusal to abandon its plan to erase Kuwait from the map and to seize the emirate's oil wealth confronts Americans with a moment of decision," he wrote a month after Saddam's invasion. "The extended crisis in the Persian Gulf forces Americans to define who they are, in global terms, for a long time to come."[2]

Hoagland framed the question as a two-bit dictator taunting America for its weakness and indecision. It was a reprise of America as a "pitiful helpless giant" in Richard Nixon's formulation two decades earlier at the start of the Vietnam Syndrome.

"Saddam's America," Hoagland wrote, "does not have the resolve, discipline or confidence to endure a protracted confrontation with a medium-size Arab nation willing to use poison gas to retain its conquests. Saddam's America was so badly burned by

Vietnam that it can support only quick, easy operations in the Third World like Grenada and Panama. There is already enough second-guessing of George Bush's swift response to Iraqi aggression to encourage Saddam and others abroad that this view of America will prevail."

That the evidence shows Saddam's Iraq desperately seeking an accommodation with the United States is missed by Hoagland. Instead, a dispute between two Arab nations, both ruled by arrogant tyrants, is transformed into a test of America's post–Vietnam War resolve. To fit the adventure-movie script, the enemy must intentionally and cynically demean the hero's power.

Yet the repeated and frantic peace initiatives coming from deputy foreign minister Nizar Hamdoon through a variety of channels would suggest an Iraqi leadership terrified of—not tempting—that military might.

But CIA psychological profiles had correctly analyzed Saddam's prideful character as refusing to budge if his manhood or his nation's honor were being challenged. So the contemptuous American attitude—from comparing him to Hitler to allowing him no graceful exit—locked the dictator into a decision to keep his hapless army in Kuwait and extend the misery of the Kuwaiti people. The Bush administration's policy seemed geared, at key moments, to guaranteeing an opportunity to demonstrate American resolve and the power of the U.S. military.

Even when a bombed and battered Iraq accepted a Soviet-sponsored plan for abandoning Kuwait in late February, the White House pressed ahead with its devastating final offensive. The allied air and ground slaughter of the retreating Iraqi army would be the Vietnam Syndrome–cleansing catharsis that Bush and his advisers seem to have desired from day one.

Columnists Evans and Novak, shedding their dovish doubts about the wisdom of the entire enterprise, applauded Bush's strategy in a remarkably candid report entitled "No Vietnam Syndrome."[3] They wrote that the last-minute Soviet peace plan had "stirred fears" among Bush's advisers that the Vietnam Syndrome might yet survive the Gulf War.

> There was considerable relief, therefore, when the president returned . . . made clear he was having nothing to

do with the deal that would enable Saddam Hussein to bring his troops out of Kuwait with flags flying. . . .

Fear of a peace deal at the Bush White House had less to do with oil, Israel and Iraqi expansionism than with the bitter legacy of a lost war. "This is the chance to get rid of the Vietnam Syndrome," one senior aide told us. "We can show that we are capable of winning a war." The desire is intense among youthful administration aides and conservative members of Congress who grew up in the Vietnam era of flawed potency by the American military. But even older officials from the start have viewed the cost in lost American lives and hatred by the Arab "street" as worth the renewed credibility of a country willing and able to use its military prowess.

If Saddam had not still sought some face-saving cover for his retreat, Evans and Novak wrote that the White House might have been denied the chance "for the exhibition of American will and valor that, once and for all, would remove the heavy hand of Vietnam inhibiting U.S. leadership in the world." In other words, Evans and Novak, two quintessential White House insiders, discovered that American forces were ordered to massacre a retreating Arab army as a palliative for a war lost in Asia sixteen years earlier.

Thanks to the military censorship and discretion of network executives, the American people were spared the most graphic, gruesome images from that slaughter. The U.S. Army restricted access to the killing fields, and the networks voluntarily withheld the grisliest scenes for fear of a negative public reaction. But even the written accounts were chilling.

From the Kuwaiti town of Mutlaa, *Washington Post* reporters William Claiborne and Caryle Murphy reported that "as far as the eye can see along this road to Iraq is a tangled sea of scorched, twisted metal littered with bodies of Iraqi soldiers. . . . The carnage and destruction, resembling a great martial demolition derby, is the gruesome remnant of a mile-long Iraqi convoy that once had been a battalion-sized column of more than 1,000 vehicles."[4]

With the lead T-55 tank destroyed, other vehicles veered off the roadway into the sand, only to meet the same destructive fate. "The grim scene is at once fascinating and horrifying, offering a first-hand look at the devastation that likely exists on an even grander scale farther north, where Iraqi military positions came under concentrated U.S. and allied bombing for weeks," the *Post* account said. "The number of Iraqi casualties caused by the bombing raids is still unknown." Even months later, no reliable estimate of Iraqi dead had been tabulated.

"I got a little bit sick when I saw this," U.S. Army sergeant Roy Brown told the *Post* reporters. Near him lay the scorched bodies of thirty-nine Iraqis, now little more than ashes. An American officer said twenty-five others had already been buried down the road, one of many quickly excavated mass graves dotting the Kuwaiti desert. From the air, American pilots compared the scene in Mutlaa to "the road to Daytona Beach at spring break" or "like shooting fish in a barrel."

Some photos appeared in European publications, showing Iraqi bodies torn apart by the devilishly lethal American ordnance. High-tech cluster bombs had spewed metal bomblets over a wide area, ripping through the frames of the Iraqi vehicles and their inhabitants. Other Iraqis were consumed in flames. One gruesome photo that was widely seen in Europe but not in the U.S. mass media showed a grotesquely smiling skeleton at the wheel of a burned-out Iraqi truck.

But amid the carnage, PR theatrics were never far away. As a capstone to the victorious offensive, Marines were landed by helicopter on the roof of the U.S. embassy in Kuwait. The symbolism could not be missed. The image was the exact opposite of the scene a decade and a half earlier when the last helicopter lifted away from the U.S. embassy in Saigon as North Vietnamese troops overran the city. The *Post* observed correctly the significance of the act. "From the beginning, President Bush opened a second front in this war, aimed squarely at the audience at home," the newspaper reported. "He led a fierce assault against what had been called 'the Vietnam Syndrome.' "[5]

Indeed, in his first remarks about the military victory, Bush confirmed that the Vietnam Syndrome had been near the top of his thinking. To a political group visiting the White House after hostilities ended on March 1, 1991, Bush bubbled with enthusiasm: "I know you share this wonderful feeling that I have of joy in my heart. But it is overwhelmed by the gratitude I feel—not just to the troops overseas but to those who have assisted the United States of America, like our secretary of defense, like our chairman of our Joint Chiefs, and so many other unsung heroes who have made all this possible. It's a proud day for America. And by God, we've kicked the Vietnam Syndrome once and for all."

On the same day, *The McLaughlin Group*, too, celebrated the victory of Desert Storm and the eclipse of the Vietnam Syndrome. President Bush got straight A-pluses and was lavished with so much praise that columnist Jack Germond harrumphed about "all the boot licking."[6]

But the *New Republic*kers, Kondracke and Barnes, were unabashed and unashamed. "This was flawless leadership," oohed Barnes. "In fact, I think it was one of the greatest presidential performances ever over six months, a fantastic performance."

"There will be some people who will say that, 'Oh, well, Bush had it easy. This was a second-rate army.' After all, Bush did not know that. It required vision on his part, guts, grace in the end," aahed Kondracke.

"It's getting pretty deep in here," growled Germond. "Well," responded Kondracke, "that's all right. Look, this guy deserves it."

Even Patrick J. Buchanan, the conservative doubter, joined in the applause. "I don't think anyone suspected that he had the determination, drive, resolve from day one to push this thing all the way through to military victory," Buchanan effused. "It was Mr. Bush's war and it is Mr. Bush's triumph."

McLaughlin then reprised the predictions that the show's participants had made on February 1, about when the war would end. Kondracke had foreseen the Iraqi army cracking by the end of February and the moderator in chief had prognosticated March 1, which, McLaughlin noted, turned out to be the exact date of the provisional cease-fire.

"You're shameless, John," joshed a blushing Kondracke. But McLaughlin wouldn't be stopped, "This means that [it's] McLaughlin and Kondracke . . . who have . . . made the precision hits. . . . Barnes and Arnaud de Borchgrave [who was pinch-punditing on February 1] scudded in two weeks off . . . and Germond's missile landed in the Persian Gulf." McLaughlin did not mention that many of the *Group*'s earlier predictions about the war's duration would have required intermediate-range missiles to plunk into the Bay of Bengal. McLaughlin had originally foreseen the war's wrap-up in the first week of February, and Kondracke's crystal ball had revealed the end of January.

But nothing could dampen the towel-snapping enthusiasm of this group of middle-age pundits celebrating a big win for Team USA. Like upsetting an old nemesis on the gridiron, the victory in the Persian Gulf had gotten the Vietnam Syndrome monkey off the nation's back.

"Do you think that this Operation Desert Storm has put to bed permanently the Vietnam Syndrome, which may be defined as the perception by our allies that we won't live up to our obligations plus the chronic malaise that settled over this country that we were unable to win a war?" asked McLaughlin.

"John, there's no question, in a sense, yes," responded Buchanan. "But let me mention this. Look, Vitenam is a wound . . . and everybody of our generation is going to carry it with them to their grave. However, the kids who are now from ten years old to twenty-one years old, have no memories of Vietnam. Their memories are going to be the great victory over Iraq."

Fred Barnes was even more sanguine. "The Vietnam Syndrome is gone, except among Democrats," observed the *Group*er in preppie glasses. "They're just unwilling to use force, that's the problem for the Democratic party. . . . That's why people think they're weak on defense or they are weak on defense."

Fellow *New Republic* pundit Kondracke, too, chose to bury the syndrome, not praise it. "It's clearly gone," he exulted. "The idea that American arms don't work, that American generals are stupid. . . . It's why all the Democrats voted against this war. They thought we'd lose."

Only columnist Jack Germond objected, questioning even McLaughlin's definition. "You defined the Vietnam Syndrome wrong," he groused. "The Vietnam Syndrome was a reluctance to get involved in a long, complicated, painful war and . . . this was an easy war, obviously. I don't think it's gone at all."

After the war, Evans and Novak submitted to a Maoist-style self-criticism. They admitted to their "early anxiety" and doubts about the best means to "shut down a tyrant not because he menaced the future of America but because he posed a regional danger." They acknowledged a shift from their Cold War "hawkish support of U.S. intervention in the Dominican Republic, Vietnam, El Salvador, Grenada, Angola and Afghanistan." In those cases, they saw "an undeniable Soviet attempt to expand the Communist empire." But in the Persian Gulf that was gone.

"We cling to that assessment and to our procedural concerns over Bush's course to war, while freely admitting gross error in miscalculating the war's brilliant outcome and its beneficial results," they concluded like reluctant students in a reeducation camp.[7]

In its postwar edition, *Newsweek* devoted a whole page to a special Desert Storm *CW Watch*. George Bush, as might be expected, got an arrow up with the snappy comment: "Master of all he surveys. Look on my polls, ye Democrats, and despair." Equally unsurprising, Saddam Hussein got an arrow down: "Hitler? Try Custer. A monster, a madman, but most of all a moron." For his last-minute stab at a negotiated Iraqi withdrawal, Soviet president Mikhail Gorbachev earned an arrow down, too: "Give back your Nobel, Comrade Backstabber. P.S. Your tanks stink."[8]

Despite getting their country back, the Kuwaiti Elite came in for a down arrow: "Welcome back from Cairo disco. Now, democratize, and make it snappy." For their hope that economic sanctions might have done the job, the Democrats, too, got a down arrow: "Aaaaaiiiiiiieeeeeee!!!! Help, I've fallen and I can't get up." Although freed from the shadow of the war, Domestic Issues joined the ranks of the down arrows: "CW distinterested while the flavor lasts. Let the parades begin." And, of course, a down arrow for Vietnam: "Where's that? You mean there was a war there too? Who cares?"

Whether anyone cared or not, the Vietnam Syndrome would never be the same. Americans had been pulled into the life-and-death drama of war, feeling all the excitement but few of the risks. The Persian Gulf War had succeeded beyond a public relationist's wildest dreams. It had fused the Washington CW's fondness for tough-talking intervention with a nation's pride in its fighting men and women.

The America that emerged from Desert Storm was a nation that had, at least temporarily, overcome its many divisions for a larger cause. America had bonded over the crisis, sharing fear over the fate of its young soldiers and relief at the small number of casualties. With the omnipresent yellow ribbons, red-white-and-blue flags and Desert Storm collector's cards and other paraphernalia, America had learned to relish war—at least those that could be won easily against outmatched enemies.

Criticism of the war effort had been thoroughly marginalized in the mass media. The liberal press-critics from Fairness and Accuracy in Reporting conducted a survey of ABC, CBS and NBC nightly news and reported "that of 878 on-air sources, only one was a representative of a national peace organization—Bill Monning of Physicians Against Nuclear War. By contrast, seven players from the Super Bowl were brought on to comment on the war." The only news coverage of the antiwar arguments came from the "nature footage" of marching protesters, the group complained.[9] Rarely had the nation seemed so united or euphoric.

The victory-parade extravaganzas that stretched into June added to the image that war is fun. Hundreds of thousands jammed Washington for what was called, naturally, "the mother of all parades," although New York City promptly tried to grand-mother it. Troops marched in desert fatigues; Americans bought Desert Storm T-shirts by the caseload; military hardware was on display for children to ogle at and climb on; and the day ended with, yes, the "mother of all fireworks displays." Featured in the night sky over Washington were special fireworks that exploded in the shape of yellow ribbons.

A *Washington Post* story the next day captured the mood. Headlined "Love Affair on the Mall: People and War Machines," the article started: "How many people can stand atop an M1A1 Abrams tank: Fifty-one. And there they stood in total bliss, shoulder to shoulder, clutching babies, posing for pictures—and grinning." War machines, mostly in desert camouflage, stretched across the Washington Mall, on display for the Desert Storm celebrants. "For the hundreds of thousands at the Mall it was a day to feel part of a winning team—to wear, wave and salute the flag," the *Post* reported.[10]

The national bonding extended to the Washington press corps, which happily shed its professional burden of objectivity to join the national celebration. In late March, three weeks after the end of hostilities, the press's patriotism spilled over at the annual Gridiron Club dinner, where senior government officials and top journalists get to rub shoulders for a fun-filled evening. The newsmen and newswomen applauded wildly everything military. An NBC executive asked President Bush to sign a Desert Storm collector's card, a signature which presumably would boost the card's value.

The highlight of the evening was a special tribute to the Persian Gulf troops. First, there was a reading of a soldier's letter home, and then a spotlight fell on a violinist who played the haunting strains of Jay Ungar's "Ashokan Farewell," the theme of the PBS series, *The Civil War*. Special lyrics honoring Desert Storm were put to the music and the Gridiron singers joined in the chorus:

> Through the fog of distant war
> Shines the strength of their devotion
> To honor, to duty,
> To sweet liberty.

After the program, Defense Secretary Dick Cheney praised the journalists for the tribute, but noted how unusual it was. "If there's a tough, cynical crowd, it's this crowd," Cheney said, "and that tribute to the troops, it was very moving. You would not ordinarily expect that kind of unrestrained comment by the press."[11]

Former national security adviser Zbigniew Brzezinski summed up the evening, which traditionally pokes fun at politicians of both parties, as "pretty benign, not nasty. It's a symptom of the transitional deification of the president."[12]

A month later, at the White House Correspondents Dinner, another press-government get-together, the campaign's commander, General H. Norman Schwarzkopf, starred. He was bathed in spotlights and cheers when he was introduced. "It was like a Hollywood opening," recalled one journalist about the spotlights swirling around the general whom everyone simply calls "the Bear." When Schwarzkopf arrived at the *U.S. News and World Report*'s predinner cocktail party, political reporter Gloria Borger pulled from her satin evening bag a Desert Storm collector's card featuring Stormin' Norman for him to autograph. But Schwarzkopf declined, saying it would be too commercial.[13]

Krauthammer and the *New Republic* crowd, who had long espoused an era of American interventionism, gloried in the patriotic hoopla. Voicing the overpowering CW favoring a new "Pax Americana," Krauthammer argued that "if we want relative stability and tranquillity in the world, we are going to have to work for it. It will come neither by itself nor as a gift from the Security Council. It will only come from an American foreign policy of 'robust and difficult interventionism.' "[14]

Not surprisingly, Krauthammer lectured those "grumbling amid the scribbling set about the endless stream of homecoming parades for Desert Storm vets." He mocked this minority's concern about "the glorification of war, warriors and war machines" and about the "excessive wallowing in glee over a military victory." Krauthammer advised, "loosen up, guys. . . . Raise a glass, tip a hat, wave a pom-pom to the heroes of Desert Storm. If that makes you feel you're living in Sparta, have another glass."[15]

To the CW set, the postwar answer to fears about America glorifying warfare was a reprise of Bush's reggae campaign slogan: "Don't worry, be happy." But the danger to America's future from a reliance on military solutions is clear. As the United States in a "unipolar" world becomes the SWAT team on the block, Washington's fascination with expensive weapons continues to give America's economic competitors a head start over U.S. industry. Burdened with the expense of a huge war industry which siphons off many of the nation's best engineering minds, whole business sectors of the U.S. economy have collapsed.

Spared from major investments in military technology, Japan, Germany and other up-and-coming nations in both Europe and Asia have poured their capital and talent into new factories, education, training, highways and rail systems—the sinews of economic might. In the emerging global village, Japan is becoming the banker and the high-tech industrialist. Germany produces specialty machine tools and quality cars. Second-tier economies from Italy to Korea market a vast array of products that have aced out American goods. With its continued emphasis on military power, the United States is carving out a job in the global village as night watchman. Even to the CW, it should be clear where the higher salaries lie.

Yet the CW still pushes the nation toward more interventionism. Krauthammer and other Pax Americana pundits raged against Bush's failure to march the allied armies up the Euphrates River, finish off Saddam Hussein and establish an American protectorate in Iraq. The president chose instead to watch Saddam's battered

army finish off the Kurds and other rebels who had revolted at
Bush's urging. As agonizing as the failed Kurdish uprising was, that
leading columnists would demand a breathtaking imperial reach
into the heart of the Arab world showed how far the macho CW
had come. Bush could get criticized only for not being interventionist enough.

The cluster-bombing of the Vietnam Syndrome in the Kuwaiti
desert had removed the chief restraint on the U.S. role as world
policeman. Crystallizing the new CW, Krauthammer observed that
the new Pax Americana "does mean that where our cause is just
and interests are threatened, we should act—even if . . . we must
act unilaterally." Of course, it will be the frenzied CW of any
particular hour that will be judge and jury to the justness of the
American cause and the seriousness of the threat.

But George Bush's larger victory was clear: the decade-long
campaign by the Reagan and Bush administrations to defeat an
invisible enemy, this Vietnam Syndrome, had achieved its objective as fully as American soldiers had in liberating Kuwait. The
significance was not lost on Bush, who exulted on the very day the
Gulf War ended: "By God, we've kicked the Vietnam Syndrome
once and for all."

Though ultimately won through the televised images of brave
American pilots and soldiers standing proud in the Persian Gulf,
this struggle for the hearts and minds of the American people had
been a war of many battles. It had been a war of propaganda,
advertising skills and sometimes intimidation. And it had been
fought outside the normal rules of engagement that bar the federal
government from spending taxpayers' money to propagandize the
American public.

This long war against the Vietnam Syndrome had made America the target of the same techniques for influencing a population
that the CIA historically applies to hostile foreign countries. The
drive to throttle the Vietnam Syndrome had even skirted the rules
that bar CIA propaganda experts from applying their skills do-
mestically. But the American people know next to nothing about
this unprecedented campaign of which they were the targets, this
war to purge the legacy of Vietnam from the American psyche. It
was a war fought in secret, out of public view, in the CW trenches
of Washington.

PART 2

10

CW and the
CIA Director

As always in early August, the Washington weather was hot and muggy. But the request to the ad executives had been unusual enough to bring them trudging through the humidity to the Old Executive Office Building, an ornate, gray, Victorian structure next to the White House. The invitation to attend an informal brainstorming session in that steamy summer of 1983 had come from the director of Central Intelligence, William J. Casey.

Since taking over at CIA in 1981, Casey had pushed for a more aggressive administration strategy to gain public backing for President Reagan's anticommunist interventions abroad. The nation was still possessed by that Vietnam Syndrome CW. Casey understood that his CIA projects could exist only in the shadows until the American people put the past behind them and learned to love intervening again around the world. As recently as December 21, 1982, Casey had appealed to then national security adviser William Clark "for more effective governmental instrumentalities to deal with public diplomacy and informational challenges."

Public diplomacy had emerged as the new code word for influencing the American citizenry, even though, by definition, "diplomacy" governs the relations among nations, not between a government and its own people. But the Reagan administration always saw American public opinion as an entity to be managed, as one might manipulate the events in a less-than-friendly country. The CIA had long ago refined techniques for confusing and manipulating foreign populations through propaganda. Now it was time to employ those techniques at home.

By summer 1983, Casey was taking matters into his own hands. Frustrated by continued public and congressional resistance to the Reagan administration's interventionist proclivities, Casey convened a meeting with five of America's top advertising minds. Casey chose his non-CIA office at the stately OEOB as the place for the get-together. "The overall purpose" behind Casey's idea, according to an internal White House document, "would be to sell a 'new product'—Central America—by generating interest across-the-spectrum."[1]

According to the ad men, a national security aide warmed them up for their Casey meeting with a briefing about the cataclysmic dangers the White House saw coming from Latin America. Unless the United States acted, the aide told them, there would be waves of refugees flooding the borders and communist governments would cynically smuggle drugs into America. The message hit home to the five PR executives.*

After jotting down some ideas over lunch, the PR execs presented their proposals to Casey. William I. Greener, Jr., one of the ad men, told me that Casey mostly listened as others talked. Casey took copious notes. But despite the spymaster's reticence, Greener felt that "Casey was kind of spearheading a recommendation" for a special public-diplomacy campaign to broaden American support for the administration's policies in El Salvador and Nicaragua. The two chief ideas coming from the ad hoc PR team were for a high-powered communications operation based inside the White House and private fund-raising to pay for aggressively selling the case for U.S. activism in Central America.

Over the next three years, Casey would harp on these recommendations over and over as he pushed the White House to sharpen its pro-contra pitch. He would receive periodic reports from his domestic propaganda team about both the big and little pictures, from the broad overview of success to the nitty-gritty of personnel problems and transfers. Casey, a tall, stooped man whose quick

---

*The five PR executives were Kenneth Clark of Duke Power; James Bowling, a senior VP for Philip Morris; Kalman B. Druck, founder of Harse-Rotman and Druck, one of the biggest PR firms in the United States; William I. Greener, Jr., an executive at G. D. Searle and former Nixon administration spokesman; and Kenneth D. Huszar, a senior VP at Burson-Marsteller who was sitting in for the firm's chairman, Harold Burson.

mind was hidden by his inarticulate speech, had run spies and disinformation programs in World War II's Office of Special Services, the CIA's forerunner. At the core of his intelligence experience, he knew the value of effective propaganda, deception and political action.

Much more than the sexy paramilitary operations which attract most of the attention, covert political manipulations are the stock-in-trade of modern intelligence. The CIA had sponsored thousands of these covert operations in foreign countries over more than three decades: planting newspaper stories, secretly funding favored political groups, discrediting opponents, pulling off dirty tricks, and spreading rumors and lies.

But what made this operation different and much more sensitive was that it would take place inside the United States—and would target not some foreign adversary but the American people. It would run counter to the legal prohibition against the spy agency conducting domestic operations. Indeed, President Reagan's own executive order on intelligence activities, numbered 12333, had prohibited CIA activities "intended to influence United States political processes, public opinion . . . or media." More broadly, the administration's campaign would clash with federal law that bars the executive branch from engaging in lobbying or domestic propaganda, a gray area of restrictions that has also included bars on material produced by the U.S. Information Agency being distributed inside the United States. But Bill Casey was never one to worry about the fine print.

Casey had a bigger problem in 1983. A covert war that the CIA was sponsoring against the leftist Sandinista government of Nicaragua was going badly and the Democrats in Congress were growing restless about Casey's less-than-candid explanations of events in the region. An offensive aimed at spreading the contra war from remote border areas to Nicaragua's populous center had fizzled, and the CIA's contra army had been driven back to its camps along the Honduran border. Though President Reagan offered repeated assurances that Central America was not Vietnam, poll after poll showed the American people resisting his clarion call for anticommunist action in the region. The people feared another Vietnam-style quagmire.

What Casey needed now was a way to buy time and fend off Democratic attempts to curb his contra funding. Even before Casey convened the meeting of ad executives, the administration had been batting around proposals on how to reshape the nation's attitudes toward these bloody foreign interventions. Casey needed a way to put the growing opposition in Congress and a skeptical news media on the defensive, while building public support for the CIA's operations. He needed to exorcise, somehow, the hovering specter of Vietnam from the American spirit.

While determined to excise this fear, the Reagan team was, in another sense, still fighting the Vietnam War. The men around the president harbored old wounds from that defeat not only in Indochina, where the North Vietnamese had checked American might, but at home, where young Americans by the millions had marched and chanted against the war. As an article of conservative faith, these Reagan hard-liners believed that the Vietnam War was lost only because North Vietnamese and Soviet propaganda had tricked the American people. And they saw the press's critical reporting on the war and the domestic antiwar movement as parts of this enemy disinformation campaign. The Reagan men were convinced that the antiwar movement had been treasonous and that the American press had acted more as a Viet Cong fifth column than a patriotic Fourth Estate.

Many conservatives also had persuaded themselves that the trendy new concept of low-intensity conflict had cleared away the traditional distinctions between military combat and enemy political action. Under LIC theory, all conflict—violent and nonviolent—stretches across a political-military spectrum that ranges from propaganda activities and political action on one end to conventional warfare and thermonuclear obliteration on the other end. The goal, not surprisingly, is to keep the conflict at the low-intensity end of the spectrum. But the downside of LIC theory is that all conflict, even political debate, is put on the same board with real warfare. In effect, politics is defined as just another manifestation of fighting with the enemy.

So now, an American antiwar activist who undercuts the president's policies at home can be seen in the spectrum of conflict as being on the enemy's side. The same might be true of a reporter who writes an article critical of what the administration is doing. In this embattled view, World War III had already begun and all Americans had to take sides, either with their president or with the nation's foreign enemies.

The administration's inability to find evidence to support this view that millions of Americans were acting as enemy agents or dupes never shook the certainty of this ideological faith.* The Reagan team carried a grudge, too, against the American press corps, blaming it for the spread of defeatism that preceded U.S. military withdrawal from Vietnam. Though this "press lost Vietnam" analysis was more ideological than historical, it had taken root deeply among American conservatives and had reached into the CW as well.†

---

*In the early days of the Reagan administration, the president tasked the FBI's counterintelligence men to ferret out these domestic spies in the antiwar movements, but none were found. The LIC concept, however, shows through in the FBI's March 1983 report on *Soviet Active Measures Relating to the U.S. Peace Movement*. The FBI reported that "through official communiqués, propaganda and active measures operations [the phrase for communist covert actions], the Soviets have maneuvered to align themselves with popular sentiments of the peace movements in the United States and Western Europe, with the prospect that Western public opinion might dissuade Western Governments from deploying the new [intermediate-range nuclear missile] weapons systems." Despite the FBI's ominous warnings about the Soviet intent, the bureau's intelligence division acknowledged that the KGB had little to show for whatever its intent mght have been. The FBI said the KGB is "attempting to develop contacts with religious figures in the United States" and "KGB officers have also collected personal and biographic information on several peace activists in the United States . . . to identify those peace activists who are likely to cooperate with the Soviet Government and to determine if any of these individuals are vulnerable to recruitment operations." Even at this late date, the KGB was still sorting through bios. Yet through the eyes of true believers every antiwar act by Americans somehow fits into Soviet strategy. "The Soviets believe that the participation of American clergy and religious organizations in the peace movement is extremely desirable, since it lends the aura of moral legitimacy to the movement," the FBI said in its report made public through Republicans on the House Intelligence Committee. The FBI contended that the widespread popular movement to freeze nuclear weapons was tainted because one of ten organizations planning a major "freeze" demonstration in New York City on June 12, 1982, the U.S. Peace Council, was a Soviet "front," an allegation the group emphatically denies. But when the New York City rally drew an estimated one million Americans, the FBI accepted that "we do not believe that the Soviet Union and its proxies directly controlled the proceedings of the June 12 rally, nor were they primarily responsible for the large turnout. . . . The overwhelming majority of the nearly one million people that attended the June 12 rally were members of independent peace and civic organizations, and they attended the rally as an expression of legitimate concerns about nuclear weapons." As for the bigger picture, the FBI concluded that "we do not believe the Soviets have achieved a dominant role in the U.S. peace and nuclear freeze movements, or that they directly control or manipulate the movement."
†Not even a 1989 study by the army itself debunking the right-wing thesis could pull this weed from the American political garden. The study, written by army historian William Hammond and published by the U.S. Army Center of Military History, laid the defeat to a poorly designed military strategy and the American people's gradual loss of faith in the Pentagon's rosy public relations. While pointing out flaws in the day-to-day reporting, Hammond found that "press reports were still often more accurate than the public statements of the administration." Most of all, Hammond concluded, the American people turned against the war because of mounting U.S. casualties. "What alienated the American public in both the Korean and Vietnam wars was not news coverage but casualties," he wrote. But old canards die hard. As German right-wingers blamed their nation's defeat in World War I on traitorous politicians, so the rising-up-angry crowd around Ronald Reagan wanted to

*   *   *

As Casey listened to the ad executives give their prescriptions
for curing America's anti-interventionist ills in 1983, he recognized
that his daunting task would be to turn around the antiwar CWs
in Washington and across the nation. It would be an uphill battle.
Despite more than two years of hard-line rhetoric, the public still
didn't understand why it should send guns to a brutal army in El
Salvador and secretly finance a guerrilla army in Nicaragua.

Though "spearheading" a nuts-and-bolts strategy on how to
sell the hard line on Central America, the CIA chief was not alone
in recognizing the Vietnam Syndrome problem. It pervaded the
strategy papers that were circulating inside the administration in
early 1983 on the need for a domestic "public diplomacy" apparatus
to convince the American people that they were surrounded by
hostile forces everywhere—and weakened by enemy agents and
dupes within.

According to a summary memo that surfaced years later during
the Iran-contra scandal, the "common element" in all the proposals
was "the need to counter the Soviet-orchestrated effort to influence
the United States' Congress, the national media and the general
public." The memo, written by Kate Semerad, an external-rela-
tions official at the Agency for International Development (AID),
bemoaned the administration's disadvantages. "The totalitarian
states whose intelligence and propaganda apparatus we face have
no internal problem in denying their citizens access to information
or even flagrantly lying to them," Semerad wrote. "They have
secretive organizations which control the ultimate levels [*sic*] of
power within their countries. We have neither the apparatus nor
the legal mechanism which would allow the success of an effort to
emulate that of Moscow, Habana [*sic*] and Managua."

Nevertheless, Semerad urged, "we can and must go over the
heads of our Marxist opponents directly to the American people.
Our targets would be: within the United States, the Congress,
specifically the Foreign Affairs Committees and their staffs, . . .
the general public [and] the media."

---

find internal enemies to scapegoat for America's lost war. Responding to the army's assessment on the press's role in Vietnam, Reed Irvine, founder of the conservative Accuracy
in Media, would not relent on his certitude about the press's disloyalty. Hammond, Irvine
told me, simply lacked "a very good grasp of psychological warfare and the tactics the enemy
was using over there."

Otherwise, Semerad argued, the Soviets and their allies would continue to overwhelm the United States in "wars of national liberation," like in Vietnam. North Vietnamese general Vo Nguyen Giap was a "dismal" battlefield commander, she argued, but "won his wars because he and his Soviet allies fought the principle [*sic*] campaigns against unaware or, at best, unorganized opposition in Paris, New York, and Washington. Their weapons were propaganda and disinformation and the results are history."

The overriding motive behind the strategy was summed up by J. Michael Kelly, deputy assistant secretary for the air force for force support, in an address that year to a National Defense University forum on low-intensity conflict. "The most critical special operations mission we have . . . today is to persuade the American people that the communists are out to get us," Kelly told the conference, which listed as an attendee an obscure Marine major named Oliver North. "If we win the war of ideas, we will win everywhere else."[2]

Administration theorists agreed that they had to convince the nation that "the communists are out to get us." But the White House faced stubborn obstacles to committing U.S. men and matériel abroad—within Congress, the press and the American people. "Our Central American policy is facing an essentially apathetic and in some particulars hostile U.S. public," an internal May 5, 1983, "public diplomacy strategy paper" observed. "There is serious opposition in Congress as illustrated by the two-month battle over the president's request to reprogram $60 million security assistance funds for El Salvador and the current congressional mark-up of the '83 supplemental and '84 authorization bills," the classified document said. "We are faced with amendments designed to cut security assistance and change the direction of administration policy, particularly vis-a-vis El Salvador and Nicaragua."

An acute problem existed with the nation's press, as well, the strategy paper said. "As far as our Central American policy is concerned, the press <u>perceives</u> [*sic*] that: the USG [U.S. government] is placing too much emphasis on a military solution, as well as being allied with inept, right-wing governments or groups. . . . The focus on Nicaragua has not been the repression of pluralism by the Sandinistas but on the alleged U.S.-backed 'covert' war against the Sandinistas. Moreover, the opposition to the Sandinistas is widely perceived as being led by former Somozistas rather than being

broadbased and including many who initially supported the Sandinista revolution. Further areas of press concentration have been:
the USG is exaggerating the communist threat; the USG is supporting 'covert' efforts to overthrow the Sandinistas in Nicaragua;
the USG is not supporting a political solution of the Salvadoran
'civil war'; the USG is opposed to negotiation with Nicaragua to
solve outstanding issues."

In one way, this candid assessment was directly on the mark.
The press did have many of those perceptions. Those were the
CWs. The trouble for the administration was that the press's perceptions at that stage in 1983 were, by and large, correct. In fact,
the Reagan administration *was* supporting a covert war. The contras
were led by ex–Somoza National Guardsmen. They *had* vowed to
overthrow the Sandinistas.

It would also be a fair assessment that the administration's
scare tactics about Nicaragua's threat to the U.S. security were
exaggerated. Nicaragua was a Third World country of about two
million people, possessing a rudimentary industrial base and dependent on an agricultural economy, no real threat to Harlingen,
Texas, as President Reagan would suggest. And as later events and
statements by American diplomats would make clear, the Reagan
administration had little interest in negotiating a settlement with
the Sandinistas or in working very hard for a political resolution of
the Salvadoran conflict, which raged for eight more years.

To "correct" these press perceptions, however, the "confidential" strategy paper urged that Congress and the news media
be subjected to a persistent "public diplomacy" campaign until
they fell in line with the White House perception of reality. One
administration official who worked on this special project liked to
call the task "perception management." In short, the goal was to
establish a new CW on Central America, one that accepted the dire
threat posed to U.S. national security from the Sandinistas in Nicaragua and other leftist movements in the region.

The "public diplomacy objective" was, the paper said, "to
convince Congress and American opinion leaders that the pursuit
of political stability and economic and social reform in Central
America serve our moral and security interests. Our public diplomacy effort . . . must be directed to: obtaining congressional support for economic and security assistance [and] to foster a climate

of editorial and public opinion that will encourage congressional support of administration policy."

As for the U.S. press, the paper complained that "media reporting and editorial writers can be expected to overly stress human rights abuses and failures by friendly governments that the U.S. supports. Thus, it is going to be difficult to turn the situation around, without irrefutable evidence, to rapidly or entirely reverse this state of affairs. Nevertheless, a comprehensive and responsive strategy, which would take timely advantage of favorable developments in the region, could at least neutralize the prevailing negative climate and perhaps, eventually overcome it."

Even at this early date in 1983, the "public diplomacy" planners envisioned that "the general public could be informed [about Central America] by opinion leaders in the mass media," without doubt, a reference to the influential pundits on *The McLaughlin Group* and the columnists for *The Washington Post* and other leading newspapers. But the strategy also understood the need for more precise targeting of the message. Special approaches were planned for groups of Americans indentified by their ethnic identification or profession. "Themes will obviously have to be tailored to the target audience," the paper said. In addition, an attachment to the planning paper matched up key members of Congress on Central America to their hometown newspapers, which were listed as either supporting or opposing White House policy. By influencing the newspapers' editorial policies, added pressure could be applied to recalcitrant lawmakers. The theoretical underpinnings for a propaganda apparatus were in place.

But in early 1983, the U.S. government lacked the machinery to carry out this kind of domestic propaganda war. Though the White House, State Department, Pentagon and CIA have hundreds of public-relations officers scurrying about, the executive branch lacked a structure for mounting sustained political-action campaigns inside the United States.

"We were not configured effectively to deal with the war of ideas," recalled Walter Raymond, Jr., who had served as the CIA's chief propaganda and disinformation specialist before moving to the National Security Council staff in 1982. The reason the government lacked this capability of waging a "war of ideas" was that federal law forbade taxpayers' money from being spent on spreading domestic propaganda or organizing grass-roots lobbying campaigns to pressure congressional representatives. The president and his men did have vast resources to make their case in public, but by tradition and law, they were restricted to speeches, testimony and one-on-one persuasion of lawmakers.

In January 1983, President Reagan took the initial step to circumvent the rules against a domestic propaganda operation. He authorized creation of an unprecedented peacetime information bureaucracy by signing National Security Decision Directive 77. It was entitled "Management of Public Diplomacy Relative to National Security" and deemed it "necessary to strengthen the organization, planning and coordination of the various aspects of public diplomacy of the United States Government." Reagan ordered the creation of a special planning group within the National Security Council to direct these "public diplomacy" campaigns. One of its principal arms would be a new Latin American Office of Public Diplomacy, housed at the State Department.

Raymond, then the top CIA officer assigned to the White House, contributed his professional advice for establishing what he called this "new art form" in foreign policy. "It is essential that a serious and deep commitment of talent and time be dedicated to this," Raymond argued in a January 25, 1983, planning memorandum to NSC adviser William Clark. "Programs such as Central America, European strategic debate, Yellow Rain* and even Afghanistan have foundered by a failure to orchestrate sufficient resources and forces [for] these efforts." Raymond, a veteran of covert actions against U.S. enemies abroad, added that the goal of the public diplomacy apparatus would be to "provide central focus for insuring greater commitment of resources, greater concentration of effort in support of our foreign policies: call it political action, if you will."

To the CIA, "political action" is a term of art encompassing a wide range of activities, both overt and covert, to achieve a desired political result. Historically, CIA "political action" has combined gradations of propaganda, from white (essentially straight information funneled through a cut-out to give it more credibility) to

---

*The Reagan administration's highly publicized charge that the Soviets had used chemical warfare in Indochina collapsed several years later when scientists concluded that the alleged "yellow rain" microtoxins were not chemical-warfare agents but more likely bee feces from swarms of bees on "cleansing" flights.

gray (the mixing of truth and half-truths to influence an audience) to black (the planting of false stories designed to destroy or discredit an enemy or target).

In 1983, Raymond, a thirty-year career CIA man who had risen through the covert action ranks at Langley, stepped forward as the pivotal "political action" officer in this new "public diplomacy" bureaucracy. He formally retired from the CIA in April 1983 so, he said, "there would be no question whatsoever of any contamination of this." His résumé describes his White House job as "overall responsibility for NSC staff coordination concerning public diplomacy."

Raymond, born in New York in 1929, is a slight man, described by those who know him as soft-spoken, possessing the ability of a John le Carré spy character to blend with his surroundings. "If you didn't know who he was, you would never notice him in a crowd," said one acquaintance. "He easily fades into the woodwork." Yet in small working groups, Raymond is more assertive, pouring forth ideas, always very serious. Associates say his CIA career stayed close to headquarters at Langley because of special care required for a sick child. Still, he rose to senior levels in the CIA's covert action hierarchy, and his last agency job title was considered so revealing of the CIA's darker arts that it has remained a highly classified secret.*

Even before his retirement from the CIA was final, Raymond had turned his propaganda talents to the administration's front-burner issues of Nicaragua and El Salvador. Raymond took over the newly formed Central American Public Diplomacy Task Force, an interagency committee that met every Thursday morning. In that job, he coordinated the "public diplomacy" work of the State Department, the United States Information Agency, AID, the Defense Department, the CIA and the NSC staff. The minutes of those Thursday-morning meetings show Raymond as the bureaucratic taskmaster, making sure documents were released on time, checking the budgets and ensuring adequate staffing levels.

Three years later, he would inform his old boss Casey that the operation "takes its policy guidance from the Central American RIG [restricted interagency group] and pursues an energetic polit-

---

*When Raymond's connection to CIA propaganda and disinformation was leaked in 1988, Raymond complained bitterly about the security breach.

ical and informational agenda." The RIG—then dominated by NSC official Oliver North, CIA Central America Task Force chief Alan Fiers, and Assistant Secretary of State Elliott Abrams—also oversaw the illegal arms-resupply flights to the contras, according to the former U.S. ambassador to Costa Rica Lewis Tambs and sources inside the operation to arm the contras.*

But like the secrecy that would surround those paramilitary operations, the propaganda apparatus also needed to be hidden from the public. From the start, Raymond always recognized the sensitivity of the administration—and particularly the CIA—manipulating domestic public opinion. In private memos, he warned that the White House hand must stay concealed. "The work done within the administration has to, by definition, be at arms length," Raymond confided in an August 29, 1983, memo taking note of legal prohibitions against executive-branch propaganda activities. On other occasions, Raymond would caution about the special sensitivity for senior CIA officials to be participating too directly. Recognizing the statutory prohibition on a CIA role in such shenanigans, Raymond said he hoped "to get [Casey] out of the loop."

Casey, whose fascination with intelligence operations seemed to know no bounds, was not so easily called to the sidelines. Not only did he convene the OEOB meeting with the ad executives, he continued to pepper the operation with suggestions and receive periodic progress reports. Almost to the day the Iran-contra scandal exploded, Casey kept up to speed on how the domestic political action was going. In August 1986, three years after the OEOB meeting, Raymond prepared a memo for Poindexter to sign and send to Casey which reported on even routine bureaucratic changes inside a key State Department "public diplomacy" office.

One of Casey's closest aides also lent a helping hand. On August 26, 1986, Raymond reported by computer message to Poindexter that Casey's counselor at the CIA, former ad man Peter Dailey,

> invited me to breakfast. . . . What he thought was missing was the immediacy of the problem from the American

---

*All three—North, Fiers and Abrams—would acknowledge later having misled Congress about the administration's secret contra supply operations.

domestic perspective. He believes that we are operating with a relatively narrow window in which to turn around American perceptions re Contras—and particularly Nic[aragua]—or we will be chewed up by Congress. We discussed the obvious, which is part of our strategy, including such things as: the need to convince people of the key importance of contras to our national security; the need to glue white hats on our team, etc. . . . The key difference is that he thinks we should run it more like a political/presidential campaign. . . .

Later, in talking to Ollie [North] and Bob Kagan [then head of the State Department's Latin American Office of Public Diplomacy], we focused on what is missing and that is a well-funded, independent outside group—remember the Committee for the Present Danger—that could mobilize people. Peter suggested 10 or 12 very prominent bipartisan Americans. Added to this would need to be a key action officer and a 501-c-3 tax-exempt structure. It is totally understanding that such a structure is needed and also totally understanding why, for discreet political reasons, it was not included in the memo to Bill Casey. I told Pete he was right but we need "a horse" and money!

CIA counselor Dailey, who had worked for Casey on the 1980 Reagan presidential campaign, later defended to me his participation in the PR planning, saying "you don't give up your rights when you go to work for the CIA." But he insisted that his advice "had nothing to do with advertising," nor with "public diplomacy." The overriding problem, Dailey said, was the limitation on the president getting his case across to the public. "It's a joke today that the president has no way to take his message to the American people," Dailey said. The astute advertising executive apparently hadn't noticed the vast array of communication tools that the president and his surrogates possess to dominate any major policy debate.

Besides working through his CIA counselor, Casey kept his oar in, propelling the domestic propaganda campaign forward. "Bill Casey was in this morning," reported NSC adviser Poindexter in a September 13, 1986, computer message to North, "and amongst other things he said that he still felt that we needed somebody in the WH [White House] full time on Central America public affairs. . . . I think what he really has in mind is a political operative that can twist arms and also run a high-powered public affairs campaign."

Even as the lies of the Iran-contra scandal were unraveling in fall 1986, Casey continued to push for a stronger "public diplomacy" apparatus. "There have been several meetings following up on the effort to get a major, bipartisan group formed to help promote an 'educational' program in the U.S. which would help provide understanding (and support) for our Centam policy, particularly vis-a-vis Nicaragua," Raymond wrote in another computer message to Poindexter. "Although Pete Dailey, Bill Casey and Clif White [a well-known GOP political operative] have all been involved in general discussion of what needs to be done, we are going to have to be sure that Pete and Bill are not involved. Pete is getting very nervous on this item. . . . The problem with all of this is that to make it work it really has to be one step removed from our office and, as a result, we have to rely on others to get the job done."

Shrugging his shoulders about the failure to ease Casey out of the picture, Raymond told the Iran-contra committees that "public diplomacy" was "the kind of thing which [Casey] had a broad catholic interest in and understanding of and would encourage." As for the questionable legality of a CIA director assisting in a campaign to influence the American people, Raymond explained that Casey undertook those actions "not so much in his CIA hat, but in his adviser to the president hat."

Whichever hat he was wearing, Casey even joined in bare-knuckle congressional lobbying when he needed to squeeze out a few votes to gain reauthorization of CIA military funding for the contras. At two White House meetings with sixty members of Congress before a February 1986 contra aid vote, Casey showed up carrying a brown paper bag containing a classified report on an alleged Sandinista "disinformation campaign." The Sandinista "disinformation" turned out to be the routine arguments being advanced by a public-relations firm working for the Nicaraguan government. But Casey's tactic delivered a chilling warning to Congress that anyone who opposed the president's demand for more covert money could expect to be labeled a communist dupe.

Even some Republicans felt that Casey's intervention into the legislative process was a bit much. Senator David Durenberger, a moderate Republican from Minnesota and chairman of the Intelligence Committee, called the ploy an "outrageous" attempt "to portray every senator and congressman who votes against lethal aid as a stooge of communism."

But Casey's brown-bag stunt was just part of an overall strategy, covering several years, to reshape the Washington conventional wisdom. If the CW could be structured as pro-contra or at least hostilely anti-Sandinista, Casey understood, then the "swing votes" on the issue in Congress would feel more pressure to fall into line with the White House. As the State Department's Robert Kagan would acknowledge later, the prime targets of the administration's hard-line message were the politicians and journalists in Washington. The sense of reality that they absorbed on a day-to-day basis would decide the contra aid issue. "I always argued that this was an inside-the-Beltway issue," Kagan once told me.

And inside the Washington Beltway is where members of Congress and the press felt the greatest pressure to conform with the White House's desired CW, a CW that would justify financing a war against Nicaragua, a dirt-poor country which had never committed an aggressive act against the United States. The pressure was relentless and uncompromising.

Raymond, the ex–CIA disinformationist, would explain to his propaganda shock troops again and again, the goal "in the specific case of Nica[ragua], concentrate on gluing black hats on the Sandinistas and white hats on UNO [the contras' United Nicaraguan Opposition]." The reality, of course, was that both sides wore gray hats; both sides committed human-rights abuses, both sides were power-hungry. But the public-diplomacy strategy was to insist that the Sandinistas were the embodiment of all evil and the contras were like Gary Cooper in *High Noon*. Following this script, President Reagan would denounce Sandinista-ruled Nicaragua as a "totalitarian dungeon" and extol the contra leaders as the "moral equivalent of the Founding Fathers." Black hats and white hats.

Those participating in this aggressive "political action" campaign had little doubt what they were up to. One NSC official who worked closely with Raymond and North told me that the domestic "public diplomacy" campaign indeed had been modeled after CIA covert operations abroad. "They were trying to manipulate [U.S.]

public opinion . . . using the tools of Walt Raymond's trade craft
which he learned from his career in the CIA covert operation shop,"
the official confided. Another "public diplomacy" official told the
Miami Herald's Alfonso Chardy that "if you look at it as a whole,
the [State Department's Latin American] Office of Public Diplomacy was carrying out a huge psychological operation, the kind the
military conduct to influence the population in denied or enemy
territory."[3] Only this time, the enemy territory was the United
States—and especially the opinion circles of Washington.

After the secret propaganda operation was exposed in 1987
during the investigation of the Iran-contra scandal, the participants
would downplay the importance of what they had done, insisting
that it had little impact on the national debate. But in their private
messages to one another, they celebrated their successes in restructuring the Washington CW and punishing those in the press and
Congress who refused to submit. Otto Reich, who ran the State
Department's Latin American Office of Public Diplomacy (S/LPD)
from 1983 to 1986, volunteered his office for a commendation as a
battered Congress and a housebroken news media shifted into the
pro-contra camp.

"S/LPD has played a key role in setting out the parameters
and defining the terms of the public discussion on Central America
policy," Reich wrote in 1986. "Despite the efforts of the formidable
and well-established Soviet/Cuban/Nicaraguan propaganda apparatus, the achievements of U.S. public diplomacy are clearly visible." In an August 7, 1986, memo, Raymond reported to Casey,
through NSC chief Poindexter, on the success of the CIA director's
brainchild. "It is clear we would not have won the House vote
without the painstaking deliberative effort undertaken by many
people in the government and outside."

Even though polls showed that about 60 percent of the American people still opposed contra aid, the battle inside the Beltway
had been won by the secret operatives of the Reagan White House,
aided by high-level CIA advice and the expertise of a career CIA
propagandist. Maybe the American public was still under the spell
of "the formidable and well-established Soviet/Cuban/Nicaraguan
propaganda apparatus," but the Washington CW had been taught
the grave national-security danger posed by Nicaragua.

11

CW, the
Sandinistas and
Buzz Words

sea of people waving red and black flags filled
the central plaza in Managua. Five scraggly men arrived atop a fire
engine. They were dressed in olive-green fatigues and each carried
a rifle. Most were young and had lived shadowy lives until this
point, the lives of secretive revolutionaries, in and out of government jails, lives under cover or on the run. The five Sandinista
*comandantes** were little known to their countrymen, except for the
whispered legends of a nation undergoing revolution. But on July
19, 1979, they had triumphed over a brutal dictator, Anastasio
Somoza Debayle, the last in a long line of family dictators, imposed
on Nicaragua nearly half a century earlier by the United States.[1]

As these unkempt young revolutionaries were cheered by the
jubilant crowd, the scene had the unruly vibrancy of an antiwar
demonstration at a large American university during the Vietnam
War. The Sandinista triumph looked, on a small scale, like what
America might have resembled if the antiwar students' youthful
dreams of revolution in the sixties had somehow come to pass. It
was, for Nicaragua, as if the SDS had taken power.

Like the student radicals in the United States, the Sandinistas
were a mixed bag of revolutionaries—some Marxist-Leninist hard-
liners, some romantic reformers and some Social Democrats looking
for a Nicaraguan middle course between a feudal capitalism that
had failed in Central America and a communist-style system that

---

*The five original junta members were Tomás Borge, Eden Pastora, Jaime Wheelock and
two brothers, Daniel and Humberto Ortega.

would surely bring down the wrath of the region's historic power to the north.

After the turbulence of revolution, a Sandinista-dominated committee of national reconciliation was established to put the Nicaraguan house back in order. While clearly under the thumb of the *comandantes* who had fought Somoza's troops, the committee included at least the window dressing of moderate civilian representation. It was a profoundly divided coalition from the start, made more acute by the daunting reconstruction task before them.

The country had been devastated by an earthquake in 1972 and then the civil war. Somoza had drained the government's treasury to finance suppression of the mounting dissent. And the wealthiest Nicaraguans, having learned from the bitter experience of the unprepared Cuban elite, had been quietly pulling their money out of the country and transferring it into a Cayman Island bank known as BAC International. As the political situation deteriorated and this monied class fled the country, their foresight would give them a nest egg for restarting their lives in Miami.

In Nicaragua, however, the daily struggle was to put the country back on its feet—and for the Sandinistas to show that their revolution would indeed make life better for the average Nicaraguan. Though unskilled in running a country, the Sandinistas had youth, enthusiasm and the sense that anything was possible. With help from idealistic Europeans and Americans—and the mentor of all Latin leftist revolutionaries, Fidel Castro—the Sandinistas mounted campaigns to eradicate illiteracy and expand medical care. Revolutionary tribunals punished several thousand Somozistas, but without the indiscriminate bloodletting that had so deepened hatreds in Cuba twenty years earlier.

The Sandinistas, for all their faults, had chosen a more moderate revolutionary course than had Castro. They left a large percentage of the country's economy in private hands. They sought to maintain trade and other commercial relations with the United States and Latin neighbors. While the Sandinistas gave moral and practical support to fellow Central American revolutionaries fighting desperate wars against "death squad" armies in El Salvador and Guatemala, the flow of military supplies appears to have been light and intermittent, based at least on U.S. intelligence findings.

Although moderates on the national governing committee quit to protest the Sandinistas' more radical policies, Nicaragua did not suffer the cataclysm predicted by many. U.S. intelligence reports would show a reasonably stable economy into the early 1980's, sources told me, and relatively few Nicaraguans joined the rivers of immigrants flowing toward El Norte from the rightist-controlled nations of El Salvador and Guatemala.

So, when President Reagan took office in 1981, he and his conservative allies faced an uphill fight on several fronts against the Sandinistas. The young revolutionaries seemed popular inside their own country and had gained broad credibility internationally. They were seen as a model and inspiration for millions in Latin America demanding social change. Western European nations sent doctors, development specialists and aid money. A large segment of the American population, too, sympathized with a small country feeling its way toward greater independence. Within the American elite, there was guilt over the long U.S. history of violent intervention in the region. Many Americans hoped for a new, more cooperative relationship with these young leaders.

But the new Reagan administration saw the revolutions sweeping Central America as just another front in the East-West battles between Moscow and Washington. And the Sandinista revolution was a threat to the entrenched oligarchies throughout Central America who shared the president's intense ideological hatred of communism. The Sandinistas had to be stopped, if not openly, then secretly—and that responsibility fell to Bill Casey and his CIA.

Deception was always part of the package. The Reagan administration would justify the contra war initially as a way to interdict alleged Sandinista support of leftist guerrillas in nearby El Salvador. But even administration officials would admit later that the explanation was misleading. "I was absolutely stupefied when I heard how it had been described to Congress," said Craig Johnstone, deputy assistant secretary of state for Central America. "No one thought that we're going to send a group out and capture some guy running across with weapons."[2]

The administration's evidence proving any significant flow of matériel—a kind of Latin American Ho Chi Minh Trail—was always shaky. One shipment of guns was intercepted at the Honduran border in 1980. But for periods of years, despite intensive intelligence coverage of the border areas, the Reagan White House could not produce a single pistol that had traveled from Nicaragua to El Salvador. While some weapons certainly did go from Nicaragua to

El Salvador with the covert blessings of the Sandinistas, the guerrillas seem to have relied at least as much on non-Sandinista supply routes, including the purchase of some guns and ammunition from CIA-supplied contra units in Honduras. Without clear-cut evidence of Sandinista complicity, the administration never sought to make its case before international tribunals. Another reason for that course of inaction was that such a complaint might appear ludicrous given the long history of CIA interventions against governments from Guatemala to Iran to Indochina.

But the administration would advance a host of other arguments against the Sandinistas, again often lacking a convincing case to take to international courts. President Reagan argued, in July 1983, for instance, that the Sandinistas' record on free elections and human rights put them "in violation, literally, of a contract" with the Organization of American States, which had called for Somoza's removal in June 1979 in exchange for Sandinista commitments on democratic reform. But OAS spokesman Dan Cento disagreed. "No, that is not the case," Cento said. The Sandinistas' assurances, he said, had no force of law, since the Sandinistas were not part of the OAS at the time. But like others who crossed the administration on Central America, Cento would find his frankness unappreciated. He promptly lost his job, always an effective way to minimize contradictory information.[3]

So instead of pursuing its case against the Sandinistas in an international forum, the Reagan administration decided to train and finance an army of counterrevolutionaries and disgruntled peasants—and loose them on the people of Nicaragua.

The job was first undertaken in secrecy, through covert military and political operations. In those early days of secret war in late 1981 and early 1982, the CIA planners dreamt of a quick victory over the Sandinistas. Though to Congress and the American people, the administration would insist that its goal was never to overthrow the Sandinistas, privately the CIA's plan foresaw the contras marching into Managua in the latter half of 1983.

Drafted by two senior CIA paramilitary specialists shortly after President Reagan authorized the covert war in December 1981, the plan remained in the CIA's internal Nicaragua policy file for years, U.S. intelligence sources told me later. "There were always two tracks," one intelligence official confided. This official said the overthrow timetable was only discarded in spring 1983 when Casey realized that the rebels could still not mount a serious challenge to the Sandinistas. With the contra failures that pivotal year, it became "clear that [the timetable] was all pie in the sky," the official said.[4]

When that "pie in the sky" assessment proved fanciful—underestimating both the Sandinistas' political strength and the contras' weaknesses—CIA director Casey recognized that a war of attrition would require more. To compensate for the Contras' shortcomings, the CIA intervened more directly than ever before, launching sabotage raids from an offshore "mother ship." The CIA's chief of paramilitary operations, Rudy Enders, one of the authors of the timetable, oversaw these raids, working from the mother ship and a command-and-control helicopter. Specially trained CIA mercenaries recruited from Latin American militaries carried out the raids under direct CIA orders. Casey would call these CIA-directed mercenaries "unilaterally controlled Latino assets" or UCLAs.

In summer and fall 1983, the CIA unveiled its new strategy. Under the false cover that the attacks were the work of the contra army, the CIA paramilitary teams began attacking Nicaraguan coastal targets. The CIA concentrated its attacks on Nicaragua's fragile fuel reserves. One devastating raid on the port city of Corinto in October destroyed 3.2 million gallons of fuel and forced the town's evacuation.

Another raid sabotaged oil pipelines near Puerto Sandino.[5] Then, the country's ports were mined to deter oil tankers from replenishing Nicaragua's oil reserves and drive up insurance costs for the tankers that would brave the mined waters.

Unbeknownst to either the Sandinistas or the U.S. public, American helicopter pilots working for the CIA even engaged in direct combat with Nicaraguan forces twice. On January 6, 1984, at the northern port city of Potosí, CIA-manned helicopters attacked Nicaraguan warehouses allegedly used for military supplies. Then on March 7, 1984, the agency's copters swooped down to protect a CIA boat dropping mines in the harbor at the Pacific-coast town of San Juan del Sur after the boat developed engine trouble and came under fire from Sandinista coastal defenses. In neither case did the Sandinistas know they were fighting Americans. The secret was also kept from the American people until I learned about the clashes from U.S. government sources and wrote a story for the Associated Press wires late that year.[6]

But Casey knew CIA mercenaries could not win the war alone. He would need a stronger contra army, and for that, he would need more money and more U.S. military trainers. To justify this long-term strategy and the increasingly open U.S. violation of international law, Casey would also need to discredit the Sandinistas, at least within the American opinion elite. Simultaneously, the Sandinistas' internal popularity had to be eroded, by bolstering the internal opposition and squeezing the nation's economy. It would be a war of multiple fronts both inside Nicaragua and inside the United States. Casey set out to do it all.

Casey's strategy recognized the need to dirty up the Sandinistas—to raise their negatives, in the vernacular of Washington—while alarming the American public about the danger from leftist revolution in Central America. In effect, the CIA director needed to reshape the Washington CW on Nicaragua. His method would be an uncompromising propaganda campaign. Carefully crafted themes would be selected to appeal to both the general public and special audiences. As one "public diplomacy" strategy paper said, "themes will obviously have to be tailored to the target audience."

An early "target audience" was the influential American Jewish community. To exploit this group's well-founded fear of persecution, the theme chosen was anti-Semitism and the goal was to pin that offense on the Sandinistas. Ex–contra propaganda chief Edgar Chamorro said the anti-Semitism idea originated with the CIA's station in Miami in 1983 as the spy agency was analyzing how to turn parts of the American electorate against the Sandinistas.

Chamorro said the CIA officers fashioned a propaganda campaign that seized on the fact that much of Nicaragua's tiny Jewish population—about fifty people—had left the country after the revolution. There had, indeed, been some ugly anti-Semitic incidents in the months before the Sandinistas took power. Some Jewish residents reported receiving threatening phone calls, and at one point a firebomb was thrown at the front door of the nation's only synagogue. After the revolution, many of Nicaragua's Jews who had worked closely with Somoza's government fled to Miami, leaving so few Jews behind that the synagogue was closed. The building's owner, Abraham Gorn, was among those who left. His property was confiscated and the Sandinistas reopened the old synagogue as a youth center.

At the CIA's urging, Chamorro said, a few Jewish exiles brought their complaints to mainline Jewish organizations like the Anti-Defamation League of B'nai B'rith. Soon, neoconservative Jewish publications were picking up the theme, denouncing the Sandinistas as anti-Semites. The ugly charge was an accusation that, in a more personal context, conservative pundit Pat Buchanan would compare to a "branding iron . . . to burn horribly heretics from [an] agreed-upon political orthodoxy." But in summer 1983, it was the Sandinistas' image that was being scarred.

The only flaw in the administration's PR campaign was that the White House had yet to purge the U.S. embassy in Managua of honest foreign-service officers. The embassy investigated the anti-Semitism charges conscientiously, still assuming apparently that its job was to provide accurate information to U.S. decision-makers. To the White House's dismay, however, the embassy investigation "found no verifiable ground on which to accuse the GRN [Nicaraguan government] of anti-Semitism," according to a cable dated July 28, 1983, and signed by Ambassador Anthony Quainton. The Sandinistas' relations with Israel were cool, the embassy reported, but that was because Somoza had been a close ally of Israel and had obtained weapons from the Jewish state in his desperate war against the Sandinistas.

The Jews who felt persecuted, the embassy further discovered, had been close allies of Somoza, in some cases helping the dictator negotiate his weapons deals. These Jews, the cable said, received much the same harsh treatment as had non-Jews in similar situations. "The FSLN [Frente Sandinista de Liberación Nacional—Sandinista National Liberation Front] does not engage in anti-Semitic rhetoric per se, and it does not harass Jews who are otherwise of no interest," the cable continued.

As for the allegations that the Sandinista government "systematically persecuted Nicaragua's Jewish community and drove all Jews into exile," the cable concluded, "our investigation has uncovered no evidence to confirm these allegations. . . . Although most members of Nicaragua's tiny Jewish community have left the country and some have had their properties confiscated, there is no direct correlation between their Jewish religion and the treatment they received from the FSLN."

The embassy's findings, which were classified as a government secret and thus kept from the American people, did not stop the

White House from continuing its campaign to associate the Nicaraguan government and anti-Semitism. In national addresses on
Central America, Reagan would disregard the findings, which remained secret, and denounce the Sandinistas for "anti-Semitic
acts"[7] and for driving all Jews out of Nicaragua. "The capital's only
synagogue was desecrated and firebombed—the entire Jewish community forced to flee Nicaragua," the president told the nation in
a televised address in 1986.[8] With the embassy's contrary findings
kept hidden, the anti-Semitism theme could still burn into the
Sandinistas' image, particularly among American Jews, whose fear
and disgust of anti-Semitism were being cynically exploited by their
own government.

   Not only were specific ethnic and religious groups targeted by
the "public diplomacy" apparatus, but regional fears were also
played on to rally support for the president's contra cause. In early
1983, White House pollster Richard Wirthlin tested a number of
potential anti-Sandinista themes by polling groups of representative
Americans. Again, this was classic advertising and political strategy.
Polling and focus groups would later be used to identify the potential explosiveness of the Willie Horton issue against Michael
Dukakis and the power of the anti–Saddam Hussein themes in the
Persian Gulf War.
   But Wirthlin, the master political pollster, found little encouraging in his poll results. The American people did not seem
to care or even know that much about Central America. Few of
the anticommunist themes generated the strong fears that the
administration had hoped for. However, Wirthlin discovered one
"hot button" issue: the theme that would become known as the
"feet people."
   Wirthlin's polls found that eight out of ten of those Americans
questioned expressed a "great deal of concern" about the prospect
of millions of Central American refugees flooding into the United
States. Encouraged, White House political operatives felt the private polling showed that the American public would back the president's hard-line stand in Central America if convinced that his
policy was the only way to prevent an influx of brown-skinned,
Spanish-speaking refugees.
   "We may be in a no-lose situation politically," exclaimed Mor-

ton C. Blackwell, then special assistant to the president for public liaison. "If the president's opponents succeed in Congress" in blocking the aid Reagan says is needed to save pro-U.S. governments and challenge Nicaragua, "the refugees are coming—and the public will hold [the Democrats] accountable."[9]

Reagan himself seized on the issue in a June 1983 speech, declaring that "a string of anti-American, Marxist dictatorships" in Central America could lead to "a tidal wave of refugees, and this time, they'll be 'feet people' and not 'boat people' swarming into our country." Elliott Abrams, then assistant secretary of state for human rights, joined the campaign, arguing that communist victories could destabilize Mexico, driving even more than the current 1.5 million immigrants a year across the border. "One hesitates even to think what instability in Mexico would produce in terms of refugees given the current peaceful flow," chimed in Abrams.[10]

Administration officials argued that historically about 10 percent of a population flees after a communist victory. While admitting to having no studies supporting that percentage, they nevertheless applied it to the 100 million people living in Central America to estimate a flood of 10 million "feet people" into the United States if the communists won everywhere.

Despite the power of the "feet people" theme, a few voices were raised in protest. Republican Senator David Durenberger, then Senate Intelligence Committee chairman, said the crass scare tactic employed against border-state voters and congressional representatives was disgraceful. "I despise anybody who uses that kind of tactic, because it turns people against legally admitted refugees and aliens," the senator told me. "You play on the basest and most selfish instincts of humanity." Some Hispanic groups were even more blunt. "The Reagan administration is practicing . . . racism and callousness in its reference to 'feet people,' " complained Arnoldo S. Torres, executive director of the Leage of United Latin American Citizens, the nation's oldest and largest Hispanic organization.[11]

But Reagan's political warriors could not pass up a chance to appeal to American xenophobia any more than Bush's presidential campaign could just say no to the Willie Horton ads. This traditional American fear of losing jobs to foreigners was a deep-seated cultural phobia, the kind of national flaw that psy-op specialists were trained to identify and exploit. For the next several years, the "feet people" theme would be repeated over and over, especially to congressional representatives and senators from southwestern border states.

Although used with zest by the Reagan administration, the "feet people" argument would never have survived serious analysis. The administration blamed the flow of refugees on communism. But historically, long before communism existed, people fled from war and economic deprivation. The Irish emigrated from Ireland in vast numbers in the nineteenth century, not because of communism but because of the Great Potato Famine. Tories fled the original thirteen colonies after the Revolutionary War because they had ended up on the losing side. The examples, of course, are endless, stretching back to the earliest days of human history and continuing into the post–communist era of the 1990's. When threatened with violence, repression and starvation, people tend to move.

But even on the specific cases in Central America, the argument didn't hold up. For years after the Sandinistas took power, the refugee flow from Nicaragua was one of the lowest in the region. The great treks northward came from El Salvador, where a U.S.-backed government ruled with a heavy hand, and from Guatemala, where another American-supported regime launched brutal extermination campaigns through the Indian countryside. Yet all of the Central American refugee flows were dwarfed by that from Mexico, where high unemployment had driven waves of desperate people across the U.S. border looking for even the lowest-paying jobs. The long-predicted flood of Nicaraguan refugees did not materialize until the latter part of the 1980's—after years of an American-sponsored guerrilla war and a potent U.S. economic embargo.

But logic was not the point of "public diplomacy." It was to identify "buzz words," locate "hot buttons," and make the American people react emotionally, viscerally, irrationally. This was how political campaigns were run in the United States, how commercial products were sold—and now how American wars were justified.

Like a series of tropical depressions, the administration's "public diplomacy" whipped up more and more anti-Sandinista turbulence throughout 1984 and 1985. Propaganda swept onto the Washington CW like hurricane-whipped waves upon a coastal island. Each wave of propaganda swelled up along the surf line, rose, crested and crashed upon the Washington opinion circles. The erosion of rational thought was startling.

In 1984, for instance, the administration achieved a propaganda coup by implicating the Sandinista leaders in drug trafficking to the United States. In a "sting" operation overseen by Oliver North and the CIA, a convicted narcotics trafficker, Barry Seal, flew a load of cocaine into Nicaragua, took some grainy photographs of some people moving the sacks from one plane to another, and flew the drugs out again to Florida. The story was promptly leaked to the press. Administration allegations tied Nicaraguan defense minister Humberto Ortega and other senior Sandinistas to the plot.

The incident received front-page play and prompted a Senate hearing to denounce Nicaragua's rulers. In a nationally televised speech, President Reagan accused top Sandinista officials of "exporting drugs to poison our youth." The drug-trafficking theme was another sizzling hot button. But in reality, only one Nicaraguan, a shadowy figure named Federico Vaughan, who supposedly worked at the Nicaraguan Interior Ministry, was ever indicted. Strangely, Vaughan had been calling his American contacts from a phone belonging to either the U.S. or other Western embassies, according to a later congressional probe. It was never entirely clear for whom Vaughan was working.

Drug Enforcement Administration officials later complained that the smuggling investigation had been blown prematurely by the White House to embarrass the Sandinistas before one of those many contra-aid votes. DEA officials also acknowledged that they had no evidence that any other Nicaraguan official besides Vaughan had ever participated in drug trafficking. The only cocaine shipment they were even aware of coming from Nicaragua was Seal's load, and that was brought into and out of Nicaragua by the U.S. government.

There were, of course, two good reasons why Nicaragua was bypassed by drug smugglers, neither relating to the Sandinistas' morality. First, Nicaragua was under constant American surveillance for contraband. It was said that the CIA was so plugged in to Nicaragua that the spy agency could hear a toilet flush. Second, the U.S. trade embargo deprived drug smugglers of commercial shipments in which to hide drugs. With planes leaving Nicaragua under the watchful eye of the CIA and almost no freighters carrying Nicaraguan products to El Norte, no sane drug trafficker would move his narcotics through Nicaragua. Much safer and easier smuggling routes were available in nearly every country that had friendly commercial ties to the United States.

But logic never interfered with the administration's strategy of gluing black hats on the Sandinistas at every turn, whether the Nicaraguan government did anything or not. On the day of the U.S. presidential election in November 1984 (as Nicaraguans were getting ready to go to the polls that same week to elect Daniel Ortega their president), the Reagan administration struck again. The ever-eager image-makers leaked false intelligence reports that the Soviet Union was sending MiG-21 aircraft to Nicaragua. Though the MiG-21s never arrived, the story got big play on the heavily watched news shows on the night of the presidential election. The perception of Nicaragua as some kind of military threat to the United States was advanced again.*

The administration scored another propaganda point when Congress narrowly defeated a contra-aid bill in April 1985 and Daniel Ortega flew to Moscow seeking emergency economic assistance. Although the Moscow trip had been long planned, it was played up as an "insult" to the anti-contra members of Congress, who then were ridiculed as dupes of the Sandinistas. The TV chat shows had a field day ridiculing the Democrats and denouncing Ortega as a diplomatic dunce. The power of ridicule—a major force in the shaping of conventional wisdom—overwhelmed finicky concerns about international law. Congress promptly reversed itself, approving $27 million in nonlethal, "humanitarian" contra aid and again opening the door to CIA "intelligence sharing" with the contras.

Even innocuous actions were grist for this well-oiled propaganda mill. For example, when Ortega visited the United Nations and bought two pairs of glasses for himself and filled other prescriptions for family members, the alert "public diplomacy" team saw an opening. President Reagan, whose wife and friends lavish upon themselves the costliest of designer clothes, seized on the glasses' expense. For weeks afterwards, Reagan would ridicule

---

*Although the State Department's Latin American Public Diplomacy Office has denied being the source for the leak, it certainly was a source. "On a possible Soviet MiG delivery to Nicaragua [S/]LPD provided over 30 background briefings to the media," according to one internal report dated February 8, 1985.

Ortega as "the dictator in designer glasses." The purchase had played into a "public diplomacy" theme to hammer away at the "high living" of the Sandinistas.

Always, the black-hat-gluing campaigns would get stickiest right before key contra-aid votes. In one fourteen-page memorandum, dated March 20, 1985, NSC aide Oliver North informed then national security adviser Robert McFarlane about more than eighty planned publicity events for influencing public and congressional opinion for an upcoming vote. "In addition to the events depicted on the internal chronology," North wrote, "other activities in the region continue as planned—including military operations and political action. Like the chronology, these events are also timed to influence the vote: planned travel by [contra leaders Adolfo] Calero, [Arturo] Cruz and [Alfonso] Robelo [and] special operations attacks against highly visible military targets in Nicaragua. . . . You should also be aware that Director Casey has sent a personal note to [then White House chief of staff] Don Regan on the timing matter" of the vote.

According to North's timetable, in the two months before the vote, U.S. intelligence would research and publicize Sandinista war violations; "public diplomacy" officials would review opinion polls "to see what turns Americans against Sandinistas"; a "dear colleague" letter would be prepared "for signature by a responsible Democrat which counsels against 'negotiating' with" the Sandinistas; the Justice Department would prepare a "document on Nicaraguan narcotics involvement"; interviews with contra fighters would be arranged for the press; and, in one ironic entry, the State Department would "release [a] paper on Nicaraguan media manipulation." North's event checklist also called for coordinated pro-contra activities by ostensibly private groups, including the Gulf and Caribbean Foundation and International Business Communications, which received funding from either the State Department or North's private network.

Even North's private operatives in Central America pitched in to help. In early 1985, North's sidekick, Robert W. Owen, drafted his own "public relations campaign for the freedom fighters." The plan called for a unified contra front "to enhance and reshape their image," Owen recommended in the February 19, 1985, proposal to North. Another Owen brainstorm would build the contras' fighting mystique by getting onto the record charts a toe-tapping contra version of "The Ballad of the Green Beret."*

By December 1985, the administration felt its "public diplomacy" work was making headway. "Informed Americans . . . have become disenchanted with the Sandinistas," said a new "90-day plan" for action. But there was more to do, the paper said, before the showdown votes in 1986 that would restore CIA funding for the contras. The administration's plan called for more public-opinion polls to spot new "buzz words."

In a section on "themes," the "confidential" paper played a medley of old and new propaganda favorites: "Sandinista ties with USSR/Cuba; Sandinista military build-up; Sandinistas blocking Contadora—they oppose provisions affecting the size of their military, democratization, and national reconciliation† Nicaragua, a renegade nation, is clearly distinct from the other Central American countries, which are democratic or moving toward democracy‡ Sandinista chic—Commandantes [*sic*] living a high life style while speaking of the poverty of their people; Corruption and drugs; Ties with PLO, Libya and terrorists."

A special section summed up the strategy of finding a special exploitable theme for nearly every indentifiable interest group in the United States; to this end, the paper cited "Sandinista repression of civil rights of: Church groups—Catholic, Protestants (Evangelicals, Moravians), Jews; lawyers who defend persons charged with violating law for maintenance of public order and security; Nicaraguan employees of American embassy in Managua; press, radio, TV; unions; private enterprise." The hum of emotional buzz words, divorced from any context or balance, had grown deafening.

By December 1985, the "public diplomacy" apparatus also had a clear notion about its "media and tools," the title of another

---

*North followed through on the unity proposal, bringing three rebel leaders together in a Miami hotel and convincing them to draft a unity declaration in March 1985. North then handpicked the three contra politicians—Adolfo Calero, Arturo Cruz and Alfonso Robelo—to serve as directors on the revamped contra leadership panel, the United Nicaraguan Opposition. The contra "Ballad of the Green Beret" never made it.

†Interestingly, North's action plan nine months earlier had sought to block negotiations with the Sandinistas, and Roy Gutman's book, *Banana Diplomacy*, details the long history of White House hostility toward the Contadora and other peace initiatives.

‡The Reagan administration had repudiated Nicaragua's 1984 elections even though many European electoral observers had found them generally fair.

section. To persuade Washington, Congress and the rest of the nation about the rightness of the White House cause, the propaganda campaign would carpet bomb the media through "op-ed pieces; letters to the editors; S/LPD publications; speakers: official, surrogate, defectors; press: chains such as Copley and Hearst; friendly organizations; television: morning and Sunday talk shows, evening news shows, CNN news and talk shows, CBN, including 700 Club; radio: national, syndicated talk shows, local/regional talk shows, direct line interviews." The media blitz would be total.

Besides whipping up pro-contra support and wearing down the anti-contra political opposition, the administration gained another benefit from these propaganda barrages. It could identify its "friends" and "enemies" in the Washington press corps by who would accept and who would challenge these propaganda themes. But as the new pro-contra CW took shape, there were fewer and fewer reporters standing in the way.

By spring 1986, the Washington CW had changed. The domestic "public diplomacy" campaign was working. Even Democrats who opposed contra aid felt obliged to protect their political flanks by haranguing the Sandinistas for their much publicized sins. The Democrats had been maneuvered politically onto a narrow spit of sand—where they now argued that they, too, favored ousting the Sandinistas but hoped to use diplomatic and economic pressure, rather than the contras. But the "public diplomacy" waves were still crashing and the pro-contra tide still rising.

It would be *The New Republic*'s honor to crystallize the new pro-contra CW, with a March 24, 1986, article. "The Case for the Contras." The magazine reprised all the predictable anti-Sandinista propaganda themes, but added a touch of historical inevitability brought about by the long contra war of attrition. "Not even the most anti-contra-aid congressman denies that the Sandinistas have become extremely unpopular," said the magazine's editorial, without examining the U.S. role in creating that national despair.[12]

If contra aid were not restored, *The New Republic* argued, the Sandinistas would crush the rebels and "then, just as certainly, the unarmed resistance, demoralized and abandoned, will follow, leaving the Sandinistas in total, permanent control of Nicaragua. . . . If in Nicaragua transition to democracy were possible without war, we too would oppose any fighting. But that option does not exist. Does anyone believe that the Sandinistas will ever peacefully transfer power or permit free allocation of power by election?"*

The magazine then walked the reader through a list of hypothetical objections to renewed contra support, batting them down one after another. To the question of America's right to preach democracy in a country where it had long backed dictatorship, *The New Republic* editors responded: "This is the 'because of our tainted history we have no moral standing' argument. It is mystifying. . . . Certainly the U.S. has a very blemished history in Nicaragua. It is equally certain that our aims now are different than they were 60, even 20, years ago." As for the future, the editors wrote, "We do not have any illusions about the tragedy that is civil war and the suffering it causes. Guerrilla war is of necessity nasty, brutish and long. . . . A decision to support one side in a civil war is not one to be taken lightly. We come to it in the full realization that, whatever tragedy it brings, the liquidation of the democratic side of Nicaraguan civil war will bring infinitely more tragedy to Nicaragua, to Central America, and ultimately to the rest of the hemisphere."[13]

It was a sign of the CW times that of the ten questions asked and answered, not one dealt with the principles of international law and the United States' solemn treaty commitments against military intervention in the affairs of another state. The Sandinistas had been pleading that case against U.S. intervention before the World Court in The Hague. For two years, with little attention from the U.S. news media, the remarkable case had ground slowly forward.

On June 27, 1986, the World Court ruled by lopsided margins that the United States had broken international law and violated Nicaragua's sovereignty through the contra war. The United States, the World Court ruled, "has acted, against the Republic of Nicaragua, in breach of its obligations under customary international law not to use force against another state, not to intervene in its affairs, not to violate its sovereignty, and not to interrupt peaceful maritime commerce." The court, the judicial arm of the United Nations, ordered the Reagan administration to stop "arming and training" the contras.[14]

---

*As *Newsweek*'s Alter and Kaus recognized, the CW cares little about long-term accuracy. The Sandinistas, who had won the presidential elections in 1984, relinquished power in 1990 after losing to Violeta Chamorro.

The Reagan administration's only legal retort to the allegations of its misdeeds had been to protest stiffly that the World Court had no jurisdiction interfering with U.S. actions in Central America. This response had seemed like the moral equivalent of a child insisting on changing the rules of a game because he owned the ball. But after the ruling, the "public diplomacy" operatives changed strategy. They attacked the integrity and impartiality of the judges.

One might think the unprecedented rebuke of the United States in the premier court of international law would give the Washington opinion-leaders pause and prompt some serious reflection by the press and politicians on the violent U.S. policies in Central America. The United States had, after all, led the long fight to establish the rule of law in relations among nations. Instead, in the age of CW, the ruling was only a blip in the debate.

Ignored or denigrated by the Reagan administration's spinmasters, the World Court ruling quickly faded as an issue. Unlike the anti-Sandinista messages that were relentlessly reprised until they took on the aura of accepted fact, the World Court ruling slipped out of news stories, even those summarizing the history of the CIA-backed contra war. To mention that the United States had been censured by an international tribunal had a discordant ring that editors and opinion-leaders found unpleasant. The ruling soon became a nonfact in the Nicaraguan debate.

Even a greater unmentionable was whether the use of violence to influence the political actions of the Nicaraguan government crossed the line into international terrorism. The legal definition that the U.S. government had adopted for terrorism was any violent act intended to intimidate a civilian population or influence a government's policies through coercion. That definition would seem to apply to the contra war, which sought explicitly to force changes in Nicaraguan government policies through violence. But the CW simply would not countenance the thought that the United States had joined the ranks of international terrorist states. That was simply too unpleasant a thought.

Less than two months after the World Court rebuked the United States for waging an illegal war against Nicaragua, both houses of Congress endorsed a resumption of CIA "covert" aid to the contras. Having reshaped the CW, the administration asked for and got $100 million. In a few months, the CIA paramilitary boys would be back in business.

12

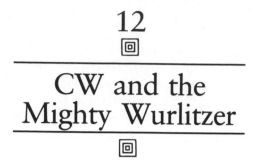

CW and the Mighty Wurlitzer

How the Washington opinion elite acquiesced to an illegal war against a country that posed no significant threat to American security is a chilling story about the fragility of democracy in an age of advertising wizardry—and the CW. Operating under the secrecy of the National Security Council, the Reagan administration had coordinated for three years a wide-ranging propaganda campaign for, in Walter Raymond's words, "gluing black hats on the Sandinistas and gluing white hats" on the contras. It worked like magic.

In an image long used by intelligence officers, it was like playing a mighty Wurlitzer organ. Certain notes and melodies were repeated over and over again, until they imprinted themselves onto the public's brain, like a tune you can't shake out of your head as much as you might want to. Some of the tunes were played with extra resonance. They were picked up and repeated by supposedly independent outside groups. This repetition from nongovernmental organizations lent the pro-contra arguments more credibility than when the public simply heard them from government spokesmen.

Only later, during the Iran-contra scandal, would some of the secret financial relationships between these "private" groups and the White House be discovered. But this network of clandestine relationships remained one of the best-kept secrets of the Iran-contra scandal. Under pressure from three moderate Republicans—Senators Warren Rudman, William Cohen and Paul Trible—Senate Democrats on the congressional investigating committees agreed to drop key parts of a chapter on the explosive topic from the final Iran-contra report. Although seven senior House Democratic members disagreed, the investigators' findings were traded for a measure of bipartisanship and the signature of the three GOP moderates to the Iran-contra majority report.*

Thus, the American public was spared the draft chapter's troubling conclusion—that the Reagan administration's covert propaganda apparatus had employed "one of the CIA's most senior specialists, sent to the NSC by Bill Casey, to create and coordinate an inter-agency public-diplomacy mechanism. [This network] did what a covert CIA operation in a foreign country might do—[it] attempted to manipulate the media, the Congress and public opinion to support the Reagan administration's policies." With the sharp conclusion blunted, the American people never were told clearly how they had been targeted by an intelligence operation run by their own government, a covert action that, in many ways, has never stopped.

Both before and after the Iran-contra scandal, the Mighty Wurlitzer was drowning out competing noises—or at least making them sound discordant and tinny. Once the Washington CW was whistling the same pro-contra melodies all over town, any contra criticism sounded off-key. There was less and less tolerance for—and more and more hostility toward—even the mildest heresy against the new orthodoxy.

Rather than challenge this prevailing pro-contra CW, editors began to question the objectivity of their reporters, whether in the field in Central America or in Washington, a city of consummate conformity. It was not smart to come up with information that conflicted with White House briefings, State Department "white papers" or cocktail-party assurances from senior administration officials. Reporters who crossed the White House too many times would find themselves reassigned or pushed out of jobs altogether.

Throughout Central America, U.S. reporters either lived in a state of career terror—expecting to get the ax at the first wrong move—or they cozied up to the U.S. embassy staffs and planned their job advancement through their companies' bureaucracies. The most famous case of a promising journalistic career done in by aggressive reporting on Central America was the case of *New York*

---

*The other seven Republicans on the Iran-contra committees refused to sign the majority report, submitting instead a minority report defending President Reagan and his actions.

Times correspondent Raymond Bonner. Bonner, who took up journalism as a second career after tiring of law, was hired by the *Times* when Central America began to heat up as an issue in 1980 and the national newspaper of record needed someone who knew the region.

But Bonner quickly annoyed the incoming Reagan administration with frequent articles about death-squad activities in El Salvador. President Reagan had vowed to stop the spread of leftist revolution in the region, and El Salvador was where he first drew a line in the jungle. The reality of the Salvadoran government-run death squads, however, undermined public backing for the president's tough anticommunist policy. Bonner's death-squad stories also made the *Times*'s correspondent a bête noire for Accuracy in Media and other right-wing groups created to pressure the news media to purge itself of an alleged liberal bias.

Already in disfavor, Bonner earned the administration's heartfelt animosity when he and *Washington Post* reporter Alma Guillermoprieto traveled to a remote Salvadoran rebel stronghold, Morazán province, in early 1982. The administration was pushing for more military aid for the Salvadoran military and was readying a document, certifying to Congress that the Salvadoran armed forces were making "a concerted and significant effort" to respect human rights.

In January 1982, the two reporters walked through what remained of villages that had been visited over Christmastime by the U.S.-trained Atlacatl Battalion. The reporters went from hut to hut, finding the grisly remains of men, women and children. They interviewed the horror-struck survivors, who recounted how the soldiers had killed some villagers where they found them, while others were lined up for cold-blooded execution. Bonner put the number of dead at 733; Guillermoprieto tallied 926.

The stories hit the *Post* and *Times* on January 27, 1982, a day before President Reagan sent his formal human-rights certification to Congress. The White House and State Department were furious. Conservative pressure groups, such as AIM, attacked the reporters as communist dupes for accepting the word of villagers who presumably were sympathetic to the guerrillas. Bonner went firmly onto the administration's journalistic hit list.

That fall, while visiting El Salvador on assignment for the Associated Press to interview rightist leader Roberto D'Aubuisson and U.S. embassy officials, I was riding with a senior American military adviser and a top embassy officer when the topic of Bonner came up. "We finally got rid of that sonuvabitch," the military officer bragged. "The embassy finally got him." Several months later, early in 1983, Bonner was reassigned to the *Times*'s bureau in New York, and he eventually left the newspaper altogether. The transfer ordered by executive editor A. M. Rosenthal was described by all parties as routine.

For his part, Bonner refrained from criticizing his superiors. But in an interview with Mark Hertsgaard for the Reagan-*über*-the-press book, *On Bended Knee*, Bonner admitted that the constant attacks from the administration and its ideological allies had a telling effect. He recalled being told by his editors that "we've got to take extra care when your name's on the story."[1] Any misstep by Bonner gave the critics new ammunition to slap into their automatic rifles.

"There was more latitude to write critical stuff before Central America became such a big issue back in Washington and all the indirect political pressure began to be exerted," Bonner told Hertsgaard. "Nobody [in the press corps] wants to go down as soft on communism. . . . But name me one reporter who's been called too soft on [U.S.-backed Chilean dictator Augusto] Pinochet, or [U.S.-backed Philippines dictator Ferdinand] Marcos. It doesn't happen. Who'll criticize them? *The Nation, The Progressive*—the liberals, who've never had power in this country and don't now. But reporters do care about criticism from those who are in power." Bonner had come to recognize the power of the CW. "It's hard to write against the prevailing wisdom in Washington, no matter who's in power," he concluded.[2]

Life for Washington-based reporters who bucked the administration was no more pleasant. In 1986, *ABC News*'s Karen Burnes did a creditable job of following leads about contra corruption and drug smuggling. But like others, she ran into constant resistance. "It takes months and months to do this story," Burnes said in an interview with *Rolling Stone* magazine. "If I'm on the air for [a total of only] five minutes, it doesn't look good on the computer. If you're someone who perceives success as air time, this is not a way to be successful."[3]

The toll was so heavy on reporters like Burnes who took a stab at getting out the facts on Central America that they reached a point where they physically and emotionally wanted to submit to the administration's propaganda themes. "It's easy to become co-opted," Burnes told *Rolling Stone.* "At times you are so desperate and tired that you want to believe anything you hear." For a break from Washington, she opted to cover the civil war and famine in Ethiopia. "It was a relief," she recalled. "I'll take a civil war any day before working in this city."

While working as an investigative reporter for the Associated Press, the nation's largest wire service, I had encountered the same pressures against looking critically into contra misdeeds. In 1986, at the height of the administration's paranoia about the press exposing Oliver North's secret contra-aid network or other unpleasant truths, the *Miami Herald*'s Alfonso Chardy took me aside for a drink at Bullfeather's, a typical dark-wood-and-brass bar on Capitol Hill. "They're trashing the hell out of you," Chardy warned me. The attacks against my journalistic integrity were coming primarily from the "public diplomacy" apparatus.

Chardy, a dogged reporter who had specialized on Latin America and still carried a Mexican passport, advised me to switch off to some other subjects until the pressure subsided. He said, for instance, he was spending more time covering Haiti, another south-of-the-border story making news in 1986. Although well meant, I found Chardy's advice troubling. American reporters, I had always believed, should not be scared off any story by government pressure.

Like Bonner and others before me, I was counted among the administration's journalistic enemies. One government official told me that I was called a "treasonous reporter," because I had published classified information that the administration had not chosen to leak out. My stories—from disclosure of what became known as the CIA "murder manual" to the first reports about Oliver North's private contra network to unearthing, with my AP colleague Brian Barger, contra drug trafficking—had turned out again and again to be true. But behind my back, the administration had tried to persuade my journalistic colleagues that I was unreliable, that I had some dark-spirited "agenda."

A favorite tactic for discrediting out-of-step journalists was ridicule. For instance, after I wrote a story for AP detailing how North, CIA Central American task force chief Alan Fiers and Assistant Secretary of State Elliott Abrams oversaw the secret contra supply network, Abrams's spokesman Greg Lagana came on the phone to another journalist and told him: "That's what happens when you have a wire service reporter who should be writing for the advocacy press. . . . Bob Parry, he's contra obsessed."* Another reporter recounted how an administration official had snidely suggested, about me, that "you get up in the morning thinking of ways to get the contras."

But I was far from alone in being so honored. Once, in 1986, while talking to an official from the State Department's Latin American Office of Public Diplomacy, I was told that my AP colleague Brian Barger was a "Sandinista agent." But when I pressed the official for anything approaching evidence, he acknowledged that he had none. He fell back to an allegation that Barger was "bad news," and recounted three specific charges: (1) Barger had worked for the liberal Pacifica radio network (the truth was that Barger had sold some free-lance articles to Pacific News Service, a different company); (2) *ABC News* had caught him fabricating a story (the truth was that the story in question that Barger had done for ABC was about a contra death squad run by the rebels' intelligence chief, Colonel Ricardo "Chino" Lau, a story the State Department official acknowledged was accurate); and (3) Barger had worked for *Washington Post* foreign editor Karen DeYoung, whom the administration disliked for her reporting on the Nicaraguan revolution in the late 1970's (this last point was correct, although meaningless, since Barger had been an editorial assistant on the *Post* foreign desk when DeYoung was editor).

But in smearing journalists, there was almost no limit in how far the administration and its allies would go. In 1985, the State Department's Latin American Office of Public Diplomacy helped spread a scurrilous story from a Sandinista defector claiming that American reporters had received prostitutes in return for favorable reporting on Nicaragua. "It isn't only women," Otto Reich, the chief of the office, asserted in the July 29, 1985, issue of *New York* magazine. For gay journalists, Reich contended, the Nicaraguans provided men. While such unsubstantiated and baseless charges may seem too crude to work, it is with such quiet back-stabbing that careers are wounded or killed and journalists are scared away from stories.

---

*In 1991, Fiers and Abrams both pleaded guilty to two misdemeanor counts for willfully withholding information from Congress about the administration's secret role in dropping military supplies to the contras during a 1984–86 congressional aid ban.

*   *   *

The administration's Mighty Wurlitzer on Central America played with greater and greater force as aid votes for the contras would arise periodically before Congress. Administration officials would insist that their fortissimo performances were just a reaction to disinformation coming from Managua and Moscow. So, the lead musicians sitting before the grand propaganda organ felt no mercy for the journalists, anti-contra members of Congress, or opposition political groups being drowned out.

Otto Reich, a former Miami businessman and city official who was born in Cuba in 1945, stood out as a star in the propaganda show. Carrying to Washington the anticommunist political extremism that pervades Miami's politics, the heavyset Reich was blustery, zealous and combative. But one acquaintance described Reich as "more than anything else, ambitious." In 1983, Reich was named director of the State Department's newly created Latin American Office of Public Diplomacy (S/LPD), the bureaucratic entity that carried the propaganda fight to a skeptical Washington. To his superiors, he would boast about how tough he could be with journalists who didn't have the right outlook.

In a report to Walter Raymond in March 1986, Reich applauded his S/LPD operation for taking "a very aggressive posture vis-a-vis a sometimes hostile press." His office, he wrote, "generally did not give any quarter in the debate." Reich would also tell Raymond that with his S/LPD gang roaming the ideological waterfront, "attacking the president was no longer cost free."

Indeed, Reich's team literally policed the nation's airways on the lookout for news stories that did not conform with the administration's pronouncements. He took special pride in getting to reporters' editors even before the stories were out so the American people might be spared the confusion of discordant information. His S/LPD report cards bragged of having "killed" purportedly "erroneous news stories" at many news organizations. But when stories did air that challenged the administration's point of view, Reich made sure the offending reporters paid a price.

Reich's modus operandi was to go over the reporters' heads to their editors and dispute every fact in an article no matter how minor. This way, gradually, editors were worn down. The next time the reporter suggested an article on Central America, the editor was likely to remember the contentious struggle to get the last story out and the furious administration complaints that followed. Since editors are, above all else, busy people, the last thing they want is a time-consuming squabble with a legion of government minions plopping down in their offices and contesting every comma of a story on Central America. The end result of the administration's harassment was to discourage critical reporting on White House policies.

In April 1984, Reich made one of his trips to CBS after President Reagan got mad at the network's coverage of El Salvador and Nicaragua. Secretary of State George Shultz sent President Reagan a memo describing how Reich had spent one hour complaining to the correspondent involved and two more hours with his Washington bureau chief "to point out flaws in the information." This was but one example of "what the Office of Public Diplomacy [S/LPD] has been doing to help improve the quality of information the American people are receiving," a proud Shultz told the president. "It has been repeated dozens of times over the past few months."

In another case that raised Reich's ire, National Public Radio aired a lengthy story in 1984 about a Nicaraguan contra attack that slaughtered a truckload of civilians on their way to pick coffee. The NPR segment covered the funeral of the victims and gave voice to the grief of average Nicaraguans trapped in the brutish violence. "It was a long piece and very, very moving," recalled Paul Allen, then NPR's foreign editor. "There was no particular effort to apologize for the contras. This was a story about a bunch of people who got caught in the war and were shot up."

Although there was no allegation that NPR got any facts wrong, Reich and his crew "went ballistic," Allen said, and demanded a meeting with the editors and reporters involved. "It was billed as a brown-bag lunch in [NPR's] editorial conference room." In attendance were Reich and his deputy, Jonathan Miller, on one side and on the other, NPR's news director Robert Siegel, correspondents Bill Buzenberg and Ted Clark, the segment's producer Gary Covino, and Allen.

Reich's chief complaint was that the piece "was too emotional, one-sided, not balanced," Allen remembered. "But it was kind of the last straw" for Reich and his associates, who had been unhappy with the radio network's coverage from the region. "Reich made the point that our broadcasts were being measured," Allen said. "Miller said some ungodly number of minutes were anti-contra.

We said, How could you decide what was anti-contra? But the point was, 'We're monitoring you—holding a stopwatch on you.' The point was, someone was listening and they were doing it with a very critical view."

Buzenberg, then NPR's foreign-affairs correspondent in Washington, said Reich informed the NPR editors that he had "a special consultant service listening to all NPR programs" on Central America, analyzing them for possible bias against U.S. policy. Reich said he had "made similar visits to other unnamed newspapers and major television networks [and] had gotten others to change some of their reporters in the field because of perceived bias," Buzenberg said in a speech a year later in Seattle, Washington.[4]

For Allen, who oversaw NPR's coverage worldwide, the intervention by a government official to pressure the network to change its coverage was unprecedented. "Never in our coverage of Poland, South Africa, Lebanon, Afghanistan had they chosen to come in and remonstrate with us," he said. "We understood what Otto Reich's job was. He was engaged in an effort to alter coverage. It was a special effort."

Though subtly, the pressures had their effect. Allen said that later when Siegel marked down his overall job performance, the coffee-picker-massacre story was one of the points that came in for criticism. As happens in such cases, Allen's subsequent story suggestions found a less-and-less-receptive audience at management levels of the radio network. Still, the administration would complain periodically about NPR's "shrill" coverage on Central America, Allen said. That nagging, combined with NPR's money squeeze, softened NPR's aggressive coverage. A year after the massacre story, Paul Allen quit NPR and left journalism.

To staff his unusual office, Reich drew on Defense Department personnel with experience in intelligence and psychological operations. One, Lieutenant Colonel Daniel "Jake" Jacobowitz, who served as Reich's executive officer, had a "background in psychological warfare," S/LPD's deputy director, Jonathan Miller, told the Iran-contra committees. After Reich asked Raymond for more manpower, the office retained the services of five other army psy-war specialists from the 4th Psychological Operations Group at Fort Bragg in North Carolina.

According to military doctrine, psychological operations iden-

tify cultural and political weaknesses in a target country that can
be exploited to induce the population to comply, whether consciously or not, with those carrying out the psy-op. A classic example from the playbook of legendary CIA psy-warrior, Major
General Edward Lansdale of the U.S. Air Force, was to write phony
astrological reports on communist Vietnamese leaders and then
distribute them to the Vietnamese people whom the CIA considered to be highly superstitious. The phony reports predicted
doom for the communist leaders, thus supposedly undermining
their status among the people.

Reich put his psy-war specialists to work picking out incidents
in Central America that could be used to agitate the American
public and Congress against the Sandinistas. One of these psy-war
specialists, Jacobowitz told Reich in a May 30, 1985, memo, would
be scouring embassy cable reports from the region "looking for
exploitable themes and trends, and [would] inform us of possible
areas for our exploitation." After this work was uncovered by
congressional investigators during the Iran-contra scandal, the State
Department insisted the military personnel did little more than
shuffle papers. A different position, however, was taken internally.
The psy-war men were put up for commendations.

The chief job of Reich's office was to deluge official Washington with reasons to hate the Sandinistas. A typical publication
on "the Soviet-Cuban connection," published in March 1985, carried ominous maps showing the importance of the Caribbean sea-
lanes to America's commerce and security. Just in case World War
III did not end in the expected eruption of mushroom clouds, the
pamphlet noted that "60 percent of total resupply/reinforcement
material" to NATO "in the first 60 days [of World War III] sails
from Gulf ports through Florida Straits." A caption added: "The
Caribbean sea lanes are viewed by the Soviets as the 'strategic rear'
of the United States." In less ideologically passionate times, the
idea of a few Sandinista river-patrol boats bottling up the American
fleet in New Orleans might be considered humorous.

But Reich and his office took themselves very seriously.
"Without blowing our own horn," Reich testified in his Iran-contra
deposition, "it got to the point where the president of the United
States, the national security adviser, Cabinet officials and lots of
other people relied on our information and used it verbatim. I mean,
it was that good."

The office's barrage of one-sided publications and speeches hammered unceasingly at the evils of the Sandinistas or abuses by the leftist guerrillas in El Salvador. In its first year alone, S/LPD activities included booking more than 1,500 speaking engagements from radio appearances to editorial-board interviews. The office published three booklets on Nicaragua and distributed materials to 1,600 libraries, 520 political science faculties, 122 editorial writers and 107 religious organizations.

The public-diplomacy office also understood the CW-shaping value of the weekend talk shows and prominent columnists. "Correspondents participating in programs such as the 'McLaughlin Group,' 'Agronsky and Company,' and 'This Week with David Brinkley' receive special materials such as the report on Nicaragua's Military Build-up expeditiously and have open invitations for personal briefings," according to a February 8, 1985, S/LPD activities report to the NSC.

Reich's office maintained a discreet relationship with private pro-contra groups, such as Friends of the Democratic Center in Central America, known as PRODEMCA. Its president, Penn Kemble, was also a principal in the Institute for Religion and Democracy, which had worked closely with S/LPD and received some money from one S/LPD contractor. At PRODEMCA offices in downtown Washington, Kemble convened legislative strategy sessions for winning contra aid, attended at least once by a senior State Department official.

When PRODEMCA was organizing a pro-contra ad to publish in *The New York Times*, an advance copy along with signatories was slipped to Reich. "This is closely held until Sunday [the publication date] because the signers do not want to alert the 'opposition' since some of them are 'coming out of the closet' for the first time," Reich told Shultz in a confidential memo. "They also do not want to give the appearance of having ties to the administration or of having obtained 'approval' from us."

But even this full-court press to put out the president's case and discourage opposing points of view was not enough. At taxpayers' expense, the public-diplomacy office was even paying for opinion articles to be written under the names of others and then snuck into the American news media, with the government's hand hidden. In a classified May 13, 1985, memo to Patrick Buchanan, then President Reagan's communications director and only later a

star TV pundit, S/LPD's Jonathan Miller boasted about some of
the office's "white propaganda" activities. Miller reported that the
office had been placing anti-Sandinista opinion articles into leading
newspapers. One appeared in the *Wall Street Journal* on March 11,
1985, authored by a Rice University history professor, John Guil-
martin, Jr., who, Miller reported in the memo, had "been a consultant to our office and collaborated with our staff in the writing
of this piece [about Nicaragua's arms buildup]. Officially, this office
had no role in its preparation."

Miller, who would later resign after disclosures that he had
helped cash contra traveler's checks from Oliver North's safe, also
recounted how the office pushed the positive side of the contras
without letting news organizations know who was behind the shov-
ing. "Through a cut-out, we are having the opposition leader Al-
phonso Rubello [*sic*—the real name is Alfonso Robelo] visit the
following news organizations while he is in Washington this week:
Hearst Newspapers, Newsweek magazine, Scripps-Howard newspapers, The Washington Post (editorial board) and USA Today,"
Miller explained. Normally, however, Miller added he would be
too busy to keep Buchanan up to speed. "I will not attempt in the
future to keep you posted on all activities since we have too many
balls in the air at any one time and since the work of our operation
is ensured by our office's keeping a low profile. I merely wanted
to give you a flavor of some of the activities that hit our office on
any one day."

In a deposition before the Iran-contra investigators, Miller
argued that "white propaganda" was "actually putting out [the]
truth, straight information, not deception." For his part, Reich
stated that his office did not ghostwrite articles or engage in illicit
propaganda. But a September 30, 1987, legal opinion by the congressional General Accounting Office concluded that the S/LPD's
"white propaganda" operation amounted to "prohibited covert
propaganda activities designed to influence the media and the public to support the administration's Latin American policies." Federal law prohibits the executive branch from spending taxpayers'
money to lobby Congress or build grass-roots pressure groups.

To give the Mighty Wurlitzer greater resonance, the White
House secretly financed a wide range of "private" organizations
and individuals who joined the chorus in support of President Rea-

gan's contra policies. Again, this was a classic intelligence tactic to spread money around to guarantee a receptive audience for a message. Only instead of some Mideast bazaar or Latin American mob, this time the money was greasing the palms of Americans who would influence the national public debate.

One key member of this "private" apparatus told me that the idea was simple: the American people would trust an outside group—with no visible connection to the government—more than they would the government itself. This source said that once, in 1984, this propaganda strategy paid a surprise bonus when the office of House Speaker Thomas P. O'Neill, Jr., a leading contra critic, called upon Joachim Maitre, the dean of Boston University's communications department, to provide the office with expert advice on Nicaragua. What O'Neill's office didn't know was a trip by Maitre to Central America had been paid for by the Gulf and Caribbean Foundation, which was secretly an adjunct of the administration's propaganda network. Without the trip, O'Neill's office would not have consulted with Maitre or heard his pro-contra views.

At times, S/LPD acted as little more than a laundering mechanism to put money into the hands of these pro-contra activists. The GAO and the House Foreign Affairs Committee investigated secret no-bid contracts given by Reich's office to private organizations, particularly to a Washington-based public-affairs company called International Business Communications, Inc. Between 1984 and 1986, S/LPD awarded IBC and its principals, Francis Gomez and Richard Miller, more than $440,000 in contracts that, on the surface, paid to set up press conferences for contra leaders, draft briefing papers and create a computerized mailing list for S/LPD publications.

But IBC had an even more secret mission, as a September 7, 1988, staff report by the House Foreign Affairs Committee noted. "Supported by the State Department and White House, Miller and Gomez became the outside managers of Carl 'Spitz' Channell's fund-raising and lobbying activities," the report said. "They facilitated the transfer of funds raised by Channell and others to Swiss and offshore bank accounts at the direction of Oliver North. They became the key link between the State Department and the Reagan White House with the private groups and individuals engaged in a myriad of endeavors aimed at influencing the Congress, the media and public opinion. They also became the main funnel for private U.S. money going to the Democratic Resistance in Nicaragua." The "Democratic Resistance" was Washington talk for the contras.

Although most of the contras' financing during the 1984–86 congressional-aid cutoff came from Saudi Arabia and other foreign governments, the Channell-Miller network played an auxiliary role. Relying on North's emotional appeals to donors, the dandyish Spitz Channell raised more than $10 million through his tax-exempt National Endowment for the Preservation of Liberty. Through Miller's IBC and under North's direction, about $1.7 million was laundered via offshore banks into North's Iran-contra accounts.

On the domestic front, IBC's Miller and Gomez advised Channell on how to spend another $2 million of the North-solicited funds* for lobbying, television ads, newspaper ads and grass-roots activities to sway congressmen's votes on contra aid.[5] IBC's connection to North was considered so tight that one White House political aide, John Roberts, called the firm the "White House outside the White House."

North's network took special aim at Congressman Michael Barnes when he ran for the U.S. Senate in the 1986 Maryland Democratic primary. While chairman of the House Foreign Affairs Subcommittee on the Western Hemisphere, Barnes had made troublesome inquiries about North's activities. "We all, of course, wanted to nail Barnes' ass," one of Channell's assistants, Kris Littledale, told Iran-contra investigators. Undated notes taken by one of the participants at Channell's strategy sessions made clear the intent: "destroy Barnes [and] use him as [an] object lesson to others"; "Barnes—wants [to] indict Ollie. Watergate babies—want to get at the Pres. through Ollie. Want another Watergate. Put Barnes out of politics. If we get rid of Barnes we get rid of the ring leader and rid of the problem."

To punish Barnes and make him an example to other members of Congress, Channell placed a series of ads on Washington-area television stations and in local newspapers, portraying Barnes as a

---

*Another $1 million went to accounts controlled by contra director Adolfo Calero. Much of the rest of the $10 million went for salaries, expenses and other overhead and about $500,000 was directed by North to other individuals and offices linked to the contra effort, including North's courier Robert Owen; former congressman Dan Kuykendall, who ran the Gulf and Caribbean Foundation; Thomas Dowling, who once gave pro-contra congressional testimony while dressed as a Roman Catholic priest; and the contras' Washington political office.

Sandinista sympathizer. The night Barnes lost, Channell sent North a telegram proclaiming "an end to much of the disinformation and unwise effort directed at crippling your foreign policy goals." Anti-Barnes ads had a side benefit, too. Their intimidating messages, broadcast throughout the Washington area, were delivered to other members of Congress. And to drive home the point further, similar ads ran in the districts of "swing" voters who had opposed contra aid.

Despite the evidence of its own manipulation, a timid Congress took little action against the public-diplomacy apparatus. Most of the domestic network was protected when the congressional Iran-contra committees refused to expand their investigation beyond the money-for-arms-for-hostages trail. As Congress averted its eyes, the secrecy and stonewalling continued. A year after the Iran-contra investigation ended, a September 1988 House Foreign Affairs staff report noted that

> many of the key individuals involved were never questioned or interviewed by the Iran/contra committees. . . . The State Department Office of Personnel has, for over a year, refused to act on a recommendation by the State Department Inspector General that the former head of S/LPD [Reich] be subjected to disciplinary action. . . .
>
> Key officials of the NSC and S/LPD, who were responsible for many of these improper activities, have been promoted or transferred to senior positions in the U.S. government. A subsequent investigation may be necessary to determine the extent to which the Department of State was used, and perhaps compromised, by the CIA and the NSC to establish, sustain and manage a domestic covert operation designed to lobby the Congress, manipulate the media and influence domestic public opinion.

A few corrective steps were taken, however. A House Foreign Affairs Committee staff report prepared in March 1987, cited the case of IBC and concluded that the State Department had entered into "secret contractual arrangements which might violate prohibitions against lobbying and disseminating government propaganda purposes." Responding to these findings, Congress shut down S/LPD in December 1987. Crusty Congressman Jack Brooks, then chairman of the House Government Operations Committee, called S/LPD "an important cog in the administration's effort to manipulate public opinion and congressional action."

S/LPD, the office that "did not give the critics of the policy any quarter in the debate," was the only bureaucratic casualty of the Iran-contra scandal. But as a senior "public diplomacy" official wryly told me when S/LPD was closed, "they can shut down the public-diplomacy office, but they can't shut down public diplomacy."

Although most of the government officials got a pass, both IBC's Richard Miller and Spitz Channell* pleaded guilty in spring 1987 to charges they violated Internal Revenue Service rules for collecting tax-exempt contributions. They were, however, spared jail time. Oliver North was named in the cases as an unindicted coconspirator and would later be tried on related charges in his 1989 trial. Guilty verdicts on three criminal counts against North were overturned on appeal because Congress had compelled North's testimony about the scandal in 1987.

Even before IBC and Spitz Channell, the strategy of letting ostensibly nongovernmental groups and individuals make the administration's case had been part of the propaganda plans. Like snake-oil salesmen who plant a few cohorts in the audience to whip up excitement for the cure-all elixir, administration propagandists salted some well-paid "private" individuals around Washington to reinforce the White House themes.

This financing of an administration "amen chorus" (to borrow a controversial Pat Buchanan line) started early. In a January 25, 1983, memo, Raymond, while still on the CIA payroll, wrote, "We will move out immediately in our parallel effort to generate private support" for "public diplomacy" operations. Then on May 20, 1983, Raymond recounted in another memo that $400,000 had been raised from private donors brought to the White House situation room by USIA director Charles Wick. According to that memo, the money was divided among several organizations, including the right-wing Accuracy in Media and neoconservative Freedom

*In early 1990, after climbing out of his car on a Washington street, Channell was struck by an automobile. He died two months later on May 7 after developing pneumonia.

House, which frequently has attacked the Sandinistas for human-rights violations.

Raymond later told me that the $400,000 went to support a public-diplomacy campaign in Europe to clear the way for deployment of U.S. intermediate-range missiles. But Accuracy in Media was most active inside the United States, nagging about the alleged liberal bias among reporters who would not toe the administration's line.

For its part, Freedom House has denied receiving any White House money or collaborating with any NSC propaganda campaign. In a letter responding to reports about Raymond's memo, Freedom House official Leonard R. Sussman termed Raymond "a second-hand source" and insisted that "this organization did not need any special funding to take positions on missile deployment or on any other foreign-policy issues." But it is hard to understand why Raymond would have lied to a superior in an internal memo.

Indeed, the evidence is that Raymond saw Freedom House as an important "public diplomacy" ally. In a memo dated August 9, 1983, Raymond outlined plans to arrange private backing for the administration's Central American policies. He said USIA director Wick "via [Australian publishing magnate Rupert] Murdock [*sic*], may be able to draw down added funds" to support pro-Reagan initiatives. Raymond recommended "funding via Freedom House or some other structure that has credibility in the political center."

Raymond, who helped found the government-sponsored National Endowment for Democracy (NED), later pushed NED to give money to Freedom House, according to a June 21, 1985, letter written by Raymond.* Freedom House did become a leading recipient of NED money, starting with a $200,000 grant in 1984 to build "a network of democratic opinion-makers." Its total bounty of taxpayers' money funneled through NED came to $2.6 million from 1984 to 1988, more than one third of Freedom House's total income, according to a tabulation by the liberal Council on Hemispheric Affairs. The writers of the council's report on NED's controversial grants entitled one chapter, "Freedom House: Portrait of a Pass-Through."

Other times, the CIA allegedly lent a direct hand in starting up "independent" organizations. In his 1987 booklet, *Packaging the*

---

*Raymond's letter was obtained by Professor John Nichols of Pennsylvania State University.

Contras: A Case of CIA Disinformation, ex–contra propaganda chief Edgar Chamorro wrote that CIA money was channeled to Nicaraguan exile Humberto Belli to found the Puebla Institute, another "independent" human-rights group. Puebla also published Belli's book attacking the Sandinistas' record for religious intolerance. The book was called *Nicaragua: Christians Under Fire*.

"Of course, the CIA told us to say that the money for the book and the Institute was from private individuals who wanted to remain anonymous," Chamorro wrote. In late 1984, Chamorro was ousted as a contra director in a bitter power struggle after disclosure of a CIA-drafted "murder manual" and his admission that the contras had routinely executed Nicaraguan civilians linked to the Sandinistas.

After departing, Chamorro disclosed how CIA officers would even coach contra leaders on what to tell members of Congress and journalists. They were to play down their goal of overthrowing the Sandinistas, Chamorro said, and stress instead their desire for negotiations and democratic reforms.

The Puebla Institute went on to be an aggressive anti-Sandinista pressure group in Washington and has angrily denounced Chamorro for his statements. When I included Chamorro's remarks in an article I cowrote with Peter Kornbluh for *Foreign Policy* magazine in 1988, Puebla Institute lawyers threatened legal action if the publishers, the Carnegie Endowment for International Peace Institute, did not delete the Puebla references. A Puebla lawyer also offered to let us examine the group's financial records. But when we readily agreed to that proposal, the offer evaporated. The Chamorro quote stayed in, along with a Puebla denial that the group had received any CIA money or had any association with the CIA.

For the next issue of *Foreign Policy*, Puebla's director Nina Shea wrote an angry letter attacking Chamorro's credibility and our article. "As we made clear to *Foreign Policy's* editors on several occassions, the allegations attributed to Edgar Chamorro . . . are utterly unsubstantiated, false and malicious . . . Edgar Chamorro is not a credible source on the Puebla Institute. . . . For *Foreign Policy* to cite solely such a self-evidently mendacious source as Edgar Chamorro in its attacks on Puebla is a disservice to the public dialogue on Nicaragua."

Kornbluh and I replied that Shea "is simply wrong on the

credibility of Edgar Chamorro. . . . Mr. Chamorro has been one of the most credible witnesses on what occurred inside the movement during his time as a contra director. He provided, for instance, the first information on Oliver North's role as a replacement for CIA officers in guiding the contra movement. He has accurately recounted problems with contra human rights violations and corruption. He had disclosed how the CIA hand-picked contra leaders, manipulated the contras' internal actions, and even ordered the contras to claim credit for the CIA's mining of Nicaragua's harbors. All of these assertions, now illuminated by voluminous records, are accepted as historical truth."

But as with all witnesses who came forth with truthful statements about the reality in Nicaragua, Edgar Chamorro had to be blasted by one of the pipes in the administration's Mighty Wurlitzer.

13

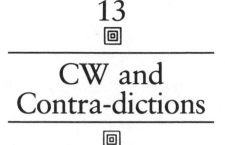

CW and
Contra-dictions

For Edgar Chamorro, a handsome man with a hangdog look, the crisis came over the constant lying. The brutality and mindlessness of the war had eaten at him, but what sent him over the edge were the lying and the personal corruption that went with it. "The policy of the CIA is buying people's will," Chamorro told me once, with a quiet bitterness still in his voice. "They were buying everybody." The CIA bought him for $2,000 a month, plus expenses.*

Chamorro sometimes reminded me of the character that William Holden played in the movie *Network,* Paddy Chayefsky's masterpiece about the TV news media driven mad by ratings. Holden's character, an aging news executive who remembered the profession's principles but had bent to its commercial demands, is part pushed and part pulled out of his job, neither crass enough to submit anymore nor heroic enough to fight. Like Holden's character, Chamorro's craggy face and thoughtful eyes showed a man balanced somewhere between expediency and honor.

A professor in prerevolution Nicaragua, Chamorro had joined other anti-Sandinista nationalists coalescing into organizations in Miami in 1980–81. These were more political exile groups than a counterrevolutionary movement. But the CIA, looking for a less bloody image for the fledgling contra army, saw promise. Chamorro

---

*There was a joke around Miami that if you were a Nicaraguan and needed money, all you had to do was go on a Cuban-American radio station and denounce the contras. That night a CIA man would knock on your door, hand you an envelope with money and ask you to keep quiet.

was recruited by the CIA in 1982 when the spy agency was restructuring the contra movement to make it more sellable to the American people.

The contras saw the bulk of their original political leadership swept aside with the CIA's organization of the Fuerza Democrática Nicaragüense (FDN)—the Nicaraguan Democratic Force. The CIA selected seven directors*—a woman, a soldier, a businessman, a politician, a doctor, a private-sector representative and an academic. The architect of the remodeled contra leadership must have been a CIA officer who believed in job quotas. Later editions of the contra directorate would bring in token Indians and more "moderate" political figures. But one fact would remain the same: the leaders were picked by the CIA, the State Department and the White House, not by the Nicaraguans themselves.

In 1983, the new leadership was announced in a glossy, four-language booklet, complete with color portraits of the seven, all paid for by the U.S. taxpayers. But what the CIA was cloaking with its new directorate—and the ones that would follow—was what would remain a contentious issue throughout the long contra debate in Washington: Who exactly were the contras? Were they brutal reactionaries seeking revenge for the ouster of dictator Anastasio Somoza? Or were they noble freedom-fighters and democratic politicans disillusioned by the repressive policies of the Sandinistas?

Initially, at least, the contras were built around the remnants of Somoza's National Guard. After being routed by the Sandinistas in 1979, the Guard survivors fled to the hills of Honduras, where they began, with the help of Argentine military advisers, to organize to retake Nicaragua. By 1982, the fledgling contra movement, now with covert CIA backing, had begun striking intermittently at border villages inside Nicaragua.

A secret Defense Intelligence Agency report, dated July 16, 1982, reported at least 106 rebel attacks inside Nicaragua in the one hundred days from March 14 to June 21. These included

---

*The directors were Lucia Cardenal de Salazar, the widow of a Sandinista opponent slain in a violent confrontation; Adolfo Calero, a Coca-Cola distributor before the revolution; Alfonso Callejas, a former Somoza vice-president; Indalecio Rodrigues, a veterinarian and ex-Sandinista; Marco Zeledón, a leader of the Nicaraguan business council; Enrique Bermudez, an ex–Somoza National Guard officer; and Chamorro, an ex–Jesuit priest and philosophy professor. However, the directors were mostly frontmen. The real control of the contras remained divided between the contra military command and the CIA.

sabotaging of bridges and fuel tanks, burning of crops and a customs warehouse, sniper fire, small-unit attacks, and "the assassination of minor government officials and a Cuban adviser." One splinter organization of contras, the 15 September Legion, was termed "a terrorist group comprised of a small number of commandos believed to be operating out of Honduras." In December 1981, this group hijacked a Costa Rican airliner, and in February 1982, it planted a bomb in an airplane suitcase, which exploded at Sandino Airport in Managua.

Edgar Chamorro's job was to sell the contras to the American press. Dividing his time between his family's pleasant stucco home on Key Biscayne, Florida, and closer to the front lines in Honduras, Chamorro cultivated journalists who were struck by his intelligence and professorial style. But the CIA had picked badly when it chose Chamorro. He had not overcome his Jesuit training, which stresses rationality and truth. He grew disillusioned with the lies he was routinely ordered to tell the reporters. He felt compromised claiming contra credit for military actions conducted by the CIA. And he was sickened by the brutality of the contra forces.

Chamorro's first moment of crisis came with the contras' kidnapping of an elderly couple. He had pleaded with the contras to spare the lives of Felipe and María Barreda, who had been captured while picking coffee. Chamorro had known the family in prerevolutionary days in Estelí. Despite Chamorro's personal intervention, the couple was executed after "confessing" to serving with Sandinista security. Chamorro was a soft-spoken and somewhat pliable man, but he had a core of integrity that seemed constantly troubled by the hard moral choices that confronted him in the world. After nearly three years as a contra director, he split with the CIA over the so-called murder manual, which a spy agency contractor had written in 1983 and some in the U.S. government blamed Chamorro for leaking a year later. In 1985, Chamorro poured out his CIA experiences in a sworn affidavit to the World Court. He described in detail the CIA's role in uniting the contra movement, paying for Argentine military trainers, creating a special unit for demolitions, and funneling money into the hands of CIA-favored leaders.

"Our first combat units were sent into Nicaraguan territory in December 1981, principally to conduct hit-and-run raids," Chamorro said. By March 1982, the CIA-backed contras had scored their first success, blowing up two bridges in northern Nicaragua. As CIA equipment poured in, the contras expanded their ranks.

"Some Nicaraguans joined the force voluntarily, either because of dissatisfaction with the Nicaraguan government, family ties with leaders of the force, promises of food, clothing, boots and weapons," Chamorro said. "Many other members of the force were recruited forcibly. FDN units would arrive at an undefended village, assemble all the residents in the town square and then proceed to kill—in full view of the others—all persons suspected of working for the Nicaraguan government or the FSLN, including police, local militia members, party members, health workers, teachers and farmers from government-sponsored cooperatives. In this atmosphere, it was not difficult to persuade those able-bodied men left alive to return with the FDN units to their base camps in Honduras and enlist in the force."

But the contra brutality was not confined to suspected Sandinistas. Chamorro expressed strong concerns about the rampant violence inside the contra camps: drunken brawls that ended in shoot-outs, the execution of troublesome rebel fighters, and the sexual abuse of women recruits. With his voice choking one night, Chamorro told me about a visit he had made to a contra base camp in Honduras, where he accompanied a doctor walking the rounds of a contra hospital. There, they encountered two hysterical contra women soldiers who were undergoing treatment. Amid screams and tears, they told Chamorro and the doctor how their contra field commander, known as El Tigrillo, had raped them at knife point. That commander would later rise into the top ranks of the rebel leadership, be brought to Washington for news conferences, and be palmed off to the ever-trusting national press corps as a model commander.*

Despite positive public relations in Washington, senior administration officials knew of the contras' sorry record on human rights. One high-ranking contra handler was fond of privately comparing the rebels to a born-to-be-wild motorcycle gang. "They're always in need of adult supervision," this official would chuckle. As contra

---

*Years later, in 1987, Tigrillo fell from grace as a star contra commander when he was court-martialed for murdering one of his soldiers. Contra human-rights monitors said he was suspected of at least sixteen other murders of fellow contras as well as an unknown number of prisoners of war.

propaganda chief, Chamorro would do his share of pumping up the contra image.

In 1982–83, Chamorro arranged for Western reporters to travel with another model commander, a rough-and-tumble contra who went by the nom de guerre El Suicida. The contra high command, which resided in the distant safety of Tegucigalpa, if not the even more distant comfort of Miami, saw Suicida as one of the few field commanders who displayed aggressiveness and resolve. The trouble was that Suicida was homicidal.

In June 1983, one sweep through Nicaraguan border villages was particularly murderous. Grisly reports began filtering back to CIA headquarters in Langley, Virginia. Congress, too, began to ask questions about Sandinista government reports of contra atrocities. But no one could control Suicida. He continued to fight and love lustily, reportedly raping many of his women captives and sleeping with women under his command. One of his women was his favorite, La Negra, a willful, tough woman who also took her pleasures with other men when Suicida was away.

Like many contra field combatants, Suicida resented the contras' far-to-the-rear general staff. "It's me who's burning his balls down here fighting the communists," Suicida complained to Christopher Dickey, then with the *Washington Post*.[1] In the spring of 1983, as tensions grew between Suicida and the commanders, he sent La Negra to the rear to complain for him. On the road near Cifuentes, a Honduran border-town, as she made her way back to Suicida's base camp, a bullet fired from a .30-caliber machine gun blasted off a chunk of La Negra's head. Although it was never made clear who was responsible for the killing—the Sandinistas later claimed credit—Suicida suspected that his woman was murdered by the contra general staff.

"Suicida's grief was indistinguishable from anger," Dickey wrote, "and it quickly engulfed his forces. . . . His men died now in numbers they had never suffered before." When the grief-stricken Suicida threw his forces onto the hapless Nicaraguan tobacco village of El Porvenir, Suicida had no plan other than fighting and killing. The Sandinistas launched a devastating counterattack, using heavy artillery and mortars to decimate Suicida's troops and force the survivors to flee back to Honduras.

Suicida's constant disobedience finally grew too much for the contra high command and its CIA overlords. A Honduran officer whom Suicida trusted lured the field commander to Tegucigalpa, where he was taken prisoner by his superiors. "My life's in danger," he wrote in a note to a friend. "They want to kill me." According to Dickey's account, Suicida was brought to the contra base camp at La Quinta and court-martialed. The charges ranged from insubordination to rape and murder. Later, Suicida and three of his subordinates were taken to the border. The three underlings were executed immediately, but Dickey received a report that Suicida was first stripped naked and tortured over several days. Then, he too was executed. The exact date of the killing was never nailed down, but was probably in October 1983.

One of the contra officers who judged Suicida and his comrades later told Dickey, "They were people who never accepted any of their mistakes. Not one. They said it was all envy, that it was a confabulation; they had done everything 'for the fatherland.' But 'for the fatherland' is not going around killing people who are fighting for you, your own comrades. 'For the fatherland' is not raping women."[2] The execution of the onetime model contra commander was kept a closely held secret until it was reported by Brian Barger in *The Washington Post* a year later.[3] After trying for so long to keep Suicida's violent excesses secret, the CIA then argued that his punishment proved the contras' commitment to human rights.

A secret result of Suicida's homicidal rampage in June 1983 was the CIA-drafted manual on "Psychological Operations in Guerrilla Warfare." Prepared by a CIA contractor known as John Kirkpatrick, the pamphlet, in slightly varying forms, was printed and distributed to the contras in early fall 1983. It had been ordered by senior CIA officials, including Director William J. Casey, who met in Honduras in mid-1983[4] (the same period when Casey sponsored his "public diplomacy" brainstorming session with advertising executives in Washington). But like other events in that fateful year—Suicida's June slaughters of Nicaraguan citizens and his October execution—the manual, too, would be a tightly guarded secret for more than a year.

In September 1984, I was given a copy of the manual and was able to confirm its CIA authorship. I then wrote the following story for the AP wires: "The CIA produced a psychological warfare manual for Nicaraguan rebels that instructs them to hire professional criminals for 'selective jobs' and says some government officials can be 'neutralized' with the 'selective use of violence,' intelligence sources say. The 90-page manual, written in Spanish, also urges the rebels to create a 'martyr' by arranging a violent demonstration that leads to the death of one of their supporters, and it tells how to coerce Nicaraguans into carrying out assignments against their will."[5]

In my story, FDN political leader Adolfo Calero denied that the CIA had produced the book, but U.S. intelligence sources confirmed that the CIA did. I also noted that "primarily, the manual stresses the need for political propaganda in a guerrilla war and most of it deals with routine instructions on how to conduct psychological operations designed to turn the people against the government."[*]

The manual story was picked up several days later by *The New York Times* and put on the front page. Congressional Democrats lashed the CIA for producing a booklet more befitting the traditions of communist Russia than a democracy. "It espouses the doctrine of Lenin, not Jefferson," charged Congressman Edward P. Boland, chairman of the House Intelligence Committee. "It embraces the communist revolutionary tactics the United States has pledged to defeat throughout the world. Its emphasis on deceiving the populace makes a mockery of American championship of democratic values."[6]

Chamorro compounded the PR problem. He announced to the American press that it was indeed the contras' "practice" to execute Nicaraguan government officials who were deemed "criminals." In an interview, he told me that "in guerrilla war, if you have to exact justice immediately, sometimes you have to do it. We don't have jails. We are in the jungle."[7] Tired of three years of lies and cover-ups, Chamorro suddenly spoke bluntly about what he knew. The Reagan administration was furious and Chamorro's days as a contra spokesman were over.

After a period of high-level embarrassment, the CIA disciplined a handful of agency officials who had overseen the manual's production, and President Reagan dismissed the controversy as "much ado about nothing."[†]

---

*Three months earlier, I had written about another CIA-produced contra manual. This one, printed in a comic-book style, exhorted the Nicaraguan people to sabotage their government by calling in sick to work, clogging up toilets, pouring sand into engines, hurling Molotov cocktails and engaging in other antisocial acts.

†Reagan had made the same assessment of the secret mining of Nicaragua's harbors. Asked about the mining on May 29, 1984, President Reagan had responded disingenuously. "Those

The CIA's odd defense of the manual was built around the agency's insistence that it was needed to encourage the contras to show greater respect for human rights. The level of contra brutality had been so great that urging "selective use of violence" against civilian office-holders seemed like a step in the right direction. That should have tipped the Washington press corps off to a bigger problem, but it didn't.*

Still, the manual furor, following on the heels of the CIA's exposed mining of Nicaragua's harbors in the spring of 1984, emboldened the Democrats to bar a continued CIA role in the contra war. For Reagan's men, the setback convinced them that more work needed to be done on "public diplomacy." But the congressional prohibition, banning the administration from "directly or indirectly" aiding the contras militarily, also laid the groundwork for President Reagan's biggest scandal: the Iran-contra affair.

In the years that followed U.S. entry into the Nicaragua conflict, that little nation would suffer tens of thousands of dead and wounded as both sides committed atrocities in the brutal "low-intensity" war. Nicaragua would see its economy devastated by a combination of contra attacks, Sandanista mismanagement and a fierce American economic embargo. Nicaragua's children would be reduced to picking through garbage dumps for food; unemployment would be rampant; inflation would run into the thousands of percent. The country's educational and health-care systems—the pride of the Sandinista accomplishments—would be pushed back by decades.

There may come a time in future years when Americans will look back in wonder at why their government waged such a vindictive policy against an impoverished country that had done no more harm to the United States than criticize it with a tasteless line in the national anthem.†

But the problem faced by the administration's "public diplo-

---

were homemade mines, as I say, that couldn't sink a ship," the president told a group of journalists. "They were planted in those harbors where they were planted by Nicaraguan rebels. And I think that there was much ado about nothing."

*Another embarrassment for the CIA was its admission during the controversy that it had distributed some of the psy-war manuals by balloon, floating them from Honduras into Nicaragua. U.S. officials said the CIA's apparent purpose was to scare the Sandinistas by creating the impression that the contras were more of a serious threat than they were.

†The Sandinista national anthem criticized the United States as "the enemy of mankind."

macy" campaign in 1983–84 was more immediate: how to deflect widespread reports about the contras' wanton brutality. To counter this correct image, the White House PR strategy began punishing the messengers carrying bad news. First, the administration denounced any human-rights watcher who noticed a problem. Second, when atrocities did happen, government evidence of the abuses was hidden or massaged into clever rationalizations. And third, the administration fielded a team of pro-contra human-rights "experts" who were secretly financed by the U.S. government and affiliated organizations.

The strategy made its debut in 1985 when a former New York State prosecutor, Reed Brody, spent weeks in Nicaragua, traveling to the border areas to document the recurring allegations of contra atrocities. In a ground-breaking study, supported by 145 chilling first-person affidavits, Brody reported a widespread pattern of contra attacks against civilian targets: kidnapping, rapes and cold-blooded executions.

Brody, however, made the mistake of accepting free transportation from the Nicaraguan government and use of its office space. Even though congressional investigators and reporters independently verified Brody's research, the administration pounced on him for his indiscretion. At an April 15, 1985, speech to a pro-contra dinner-rally, President Reagan personally denounced Brody as "one of dictator [Daniel] Ortega's supporters, a sympathizer who has openly embraced Sandinismo." This American citizen was being sized up for a black hat.

Brody's findings, however, did force a CIA review of the pattern of atrocities, which secretly the agency knew to be true. After all, Suicida had been executed, in part, because of his wanton brutality. Nevertheless, the CIA report, kept secret again for another year, offered page after page of rationalizations for the wanton destruction and slaughter. The agency said its report was based on seven hours of interviews with FDN combatants—whose explanations apparently were never challenged, no matter how absurd.

One of the CIA's chief defenses was that the contras lacked the weapons they were accused of using to carry out some of the atrocities. For example, responding to repeated reports that contras slit the throats of their captives and then mutilated the bodies, the CIA argued that "entirely aside from the fact that this runs against the policies of the FDN as an organization, FDN troops are normally not equipped with either bayonets or combat knives." Although photos from the period show many contras marching off to battle with long, nasty-looking knives at their side, the agency interrogators did not contest the point.

When the agency admitted to one of Brody's findings, the report would rationalize or minimize the event. For instance, the CIA did acknowledge the kidnapping of the elderly Nicaraguan couple, Felipe and María Barreda, on December 28, 1982. The Barredas had traveled from their home in Estelí to the countryside over the Christmas holidays to work as volunteer coffee pickers. But during a contra attack they were captured by the contras, force-marched to a contra base camp, tortured—according to other coffee pickers who survived the ordeal—and then executed.

Instead of simply denouncing this atrocity, the CIA tried to justify it, poking fun at Brody's description of the couple as active in their church parish and "deeply religious." The CIA reported that "the 'deeply religious' Barreda couple were senior officers of the Directorate General of State Security in Estelí, and after finally confessing to this fact, were exected on Suicida's orders. . . . They were not tortured."

Then, the CIA uncritically cited the contra panel's other quibbling with Brody's "false statements" on the Barredas. They were not handcuffed during the march, the report declared. (Again, it was an equipment problem. The contras have "few or no handcuffs in inventory," although the panel added "the Barredas may have been handcuffed at the camp." Somehow, a couple of handcuffs had turned up.) And the panel insisted that they were not kept in a tent. (Yes, of course, "there were no tents in any of Suicida's camps," the report stated.)

Beyond the ludicrous niggling over handcuffs and tents, one might wonder why the Barredas would "finally" voluntarily confess to working for Sandinista security when that would seal their doom.* But, as the CIA reported, "they were not tortured"—that would have been against FDN policy. Neither the CIA nor the Reagan administration had much interest in contesting the contras' innocent explanations or admitting to any spots on the contras' white hats.†

---

*The Sandinistas denied the charge that the Barredas were senior state security personnel.
†Although damaged goods after President Reagan's personal denunciation, Brody tried to

* * *

To muddy the human-rights picture, which was looking bad for the contras, the White House threw its ideological and mercenary foot soldiers into the fray. Starting in 1985, pro-contra activists, secretly financed by Oliver North's White House apparatus, began challenging the work of Americas Watch and other independent human-rights groups, which had uncovered more evidence of contra abuses and were not as easily repudiated as Brody. The White House goal was clear: to throw the contra critics onto the defensive while discrediting the recurring stories about the contras slaughtering civilians, torturing captives and raping women. These stories were dampening public enthusiasm in the United States for renewing military assistance to such an unsavory lot of rebels-with-a-pretty-murky-cause.

In 1985 and 1986, as the White House battled congressional Democrats over resuming CIA military aid to the contras, a Brigham Young University student, Wesley Smith, appeared on the scene. He published two human-rights reports alleging Sandinista atrocities and challenging documented accounts of contra abuses. Smith's reports were treated seriously in the mainstream media—and he sometimes was put on network television as a coequal expert with independent human-rights observers. But Smith provided few specifics that could be cross-checked. He claimed to have interviewed hundreds of Nicaraguans, but withheld the names, he said, for security reasons. No one he spoke with had heard a word about contra abuses, only Sandinista ones. Though a secret at the time, his expenses were being paid by North's private funding network, according to Iran-contra documents that surfaced later.

---

respond to the CIA report. No one in the mainstream press took notice. Regarding seven rape cases he investigated, he reviewed the sexual assaults in the wake of the agency's findings. "Digna Barreda—The CIA asserts, without providing detail, that she has given conflicting accounts of her abduction and gang-rape and that they (the CIA or the FDN?) have previously pointed this out. I am unaware of either. Her account to the New York Times and CBS News were consistent with the one she gave to me . . . ; Marta Arauz—Not discussed by the CIA even though this kidnapping of several teachers, of whom only Marta escaped, has been widely publicized by the Nicaraguan government and made the subject of diplomatic inquiries to Honduras; Mirna Cunningham—This gang-rape is admitted by the CIA which places the blame on Brooklyn Rivera [an independent Miskito Indian contra]; Mileydis Salina Azevedo and Ermelina Díaz—Not discussed by the CIA. I learned from friends in El Jicaro (but could not confirm myself) that, two weeks after these girls escaped from the contras (and I interviewed them), the FDN returned to their hamlet and slit their throats; Josefina Inestroza and Abelina Inestroza—Not discussed by the CIA. I interviewed these women in Susacayan the day after their rape."

Another one of North's private surrogates, Thomas Dowling, dressed up as a Roman Catholic priest and gave testimony on alleged Sandinista human-rights violations to the House Foreign Affairs Subcommittee on the Western Hemisphere in spring 1985. In his testimony, Dowling began: "I am Father Thomas Dowling, a Catholic priest." The burly Dowling, his Irish blue eyes flashing, then told the House panel about his inspirational visits to contra camps in Honduras and Costa Rica.

Trying to defuse the charge that contras had committed widespread atrocities, Dowling testified, "There are people in Washington today who can give direct testimony to the fact that the Sandinistas do put on contra uniforms and commit atrocities. . . . The only other thing I can tell you is that the contras are overwhelmingly religious. One sees tremendous artifacts of Christianity, both Catholic and Protestant, tremendous amounts of Bibles, crucifixes, etc."

Two years later, as the Iran-contra scandal exposed North's financial schemes, subcommittee members discovered that Dowling was not an ordained Roman Catholic priest, but belonged instead to an unofficial sect called the Old Catholic Church, which was unrelated to the Roman Catholic Church. The Iran-contra records showed that Dowling had received $2,500 in traveler's checks from North's White House safe and tens of thousands more from contra leaders and other elements of North's Project Democracy apparatus.

A furious Congressman Sam Gejdenson, a subcommittee member, complained that Dowling had been sent to testify by the White House "public diplomacy" officials. "Mr. Dowling testifed dressed in a clerical collar and stated, for the record, that he was a Catholic priest who had ministered to contra combatants," Gejdenson wrote in a letter to the panel's chairman. "This man is not a Catholic priest. He has never been a Catholic priest." Dowling, a Californian, told the *San Francisco Examiner* that he didn't lie when he testified about his religious status. "If I said I was a Roman Catholic priest, then I would have been in error," said Dowling,[8] who normally is seen around San Francisco wearing a sports jacket or other casual attire, not a Roman collar.

The Reagan administration's "public diplomacy" team also gave no quarter in countering human-rights researchers who found neither side wearing white hats.

One respected human-rights organization, Americas Watch, criticized both sides of the war in Nicaragua, but came under administration attack anyway. Juan Mendez, who directed Americas Watch's Latin America monitoring, said the attacks on his organization were "mostly put out by members of the administration, but also by a variety of groups in the administration's camp without being officially part of the administration. It took the form of impugning our integrity and impugning our methodology."

Born in Argentina, Mendez bore the personal brunt of the administration's complaints against Americas Watch. "I would hear rumors that the reason I was leading Americas Watch into the Sandinista camp was that I had some bizarre connections through Argentine leftists," Mendez told me. "They saw some obscure left-wing conspiracy that was affecting the work of Americas Watch."

The repetitious assaults on Americas Watch's objectivity established doubts throughout official Washington that the group could be trusted when it criticized the contras. The administration succeeded in creating a potent CW against not just Americas Watch, but against the community of human-rights activists who faulted the contras for atrocities.

Yet Mendez insisted that the smear campaigns did not influence Americas Watch's continued examination of human rights in Nicaragua. In the late 1980's, the group's reports did get tougher on the Sandinistas, but Mendez said that harder criticism reflected a deterioration of Managua's control over abuses by its troops. "The war got dirtier and dirtier and the Sandinistas started doing some of the things that they had been accused of earlier," Mendez concluded. The Sandinistas would be blamed whatever their true record.

So tensions between the administration and the human-rights community were already high in 1985 when Alvaro José Baldizon Aviles, an official of the Nicaraguan Interior Ministry, slipped across the Honduran border and defected. Baldizon quickly became a prize witness for the Reagan White House campaign to delegitimate the Sandinistas and shift attention away from the contra abuses. He brought stories of government-approved assassinations, "disappeared" opponents, links to drug trafficking, duping of foreign visitors, intimidation of the Catholic Church, widespread Cuban influence and use of criminals for special assignments (a page right out of the CIA "murder manual").

Baldizon, a young man of slight build, jet black hair and dark, piercing eyes, was unveiled in State Department news briefings. By early 1986, he was the hero in a special S/LPD glossy booklet, detailing his charges. For the administration's propagandists, Baldizon seemed almost too good to be true, which is exactly what Americas Watch suspected.

In early December 1985, Mendez began carefully dissecting Baldizon's charges. The human-rights group wondered why, if Sandinista security had executed two thousand people, as Baldizon claimed, so few families had complained. In other countries, Mendez noted, families overcome great hardship and risk to expose such wrongdoing. Why, the human-rights group asked, did Baldizon have only names and details from the much smaller number of human-rights cases that had already been reported publicly? Why, Mendez asked, would Baldizon's office be assigned to investigate alleged killings ordered by senior Sandinistas and prepare reports on those killings for the same superiors who now wanted them covered up? If they had ordered the killings, they would know about them. If they wanted the murders covered up, why would they generate new documents proving their own complicity? Indeed, the few documents that Baldizon brought with him suggested that the killings which did occur were ordered by low-level field officers, not senior officials. None of the killings that Baldizon blamed on top Interior Ministry officials were supported by any documentary evidence. Mendez had written Baldizon a ten-page letter on December 3, 1985, seeking clarification on many of his allegations, but Baldizon did not respond for nearly three months.

But Mendez's query was still secret and Baldizon's star was still rising in January 1986 when *The New Republic's* Fred Barnes used the defection as a club to pound Washington-based human-rights groups. Barnes judged these groups guilty of not accepting Baldizon's word as truth, as Barnes did. In a CW-setting piece called "The Sandinista Lobby," Barnes ripped into what he called "the community" of human-rights groups, which, he argued, was overly sympathetic to the Sandinistas.[9]

Reprising Baldizon's accusations of Managua's misdeeds, Barnes wrote, "Even by Latin American standards, this was quite an indictment, exactly the kind of firsthand account likely to trigger

outrage by groups monitoring human rights in Central America."
But Barnes said the groups' lack of interest "reflects the selective
moral indignation of a phalanx of organizations in Washington that
regularly criticizes the Reagan administration's policy toward Central America and, in particular, Nicaragua. . . . They tirelessly
point out how Guatemala, El Salvador, Honduras and Panama—
all allies of the United States—come up short.* But Nicaragua,
with its increasingly repressive Sandinista regime, is another story."

As for Mendez and Americas Watch, Barnes noted that the
human-rights investigator "went to the trouble of taking Baldizon
to lunch, where they could confer without State Department interference. But Americas Watch seems more interested in countering Reagan's attacks on Nicaragua than checking out Baldizon's
evidence." Barnes himself didn't bother to check out Baldizon's
evidence at all.

After accusing "the community" of a pro-Sandinista double
standard, Barnes rode off to defend the contras against the Brody
report on contra atrocities. Barnes attacked Brody for releasing his
study only a few weeks before a contra-aid vote. The report Barnes
wrote, "was, at best, open to question. A Reagan administration
examination of the report [the CIA review which had yet to be
released to Congress] found that six incidents cited by Brody had
been carried out by a contra officer [Suicida] later executed for
murdering civilians." Four other atrocities were dismissed by
Barnes because they took place before the formal contra military
structure had been put together, although it's not clear how this
bureaucratic quibbling disproved Brody's study. But Barnes was
not yet done. He would dispute another Brody charge that the
contras killed a French doctor with mortar fire. "The contras say
they had no mortars in that incident and that Sandinista fire killed
him," Barnes assured his readers. Again, an equipment problem.
For some reason, Barnes left out that the contras also were short
on combat knives, handcuffs and tents.

But *The New Republic* pundit hadn't heard a contra excuse that
he wouldn't believe. He even rationalized the cold-blooded murder
of the Barredas. Accepting the CIA's cynical justification for the
murders, Barnes parroted that this " 'deeply religious' couple killed

---

*Remember in January 1986, Noriega's Panama was still being defended by the adminis-
tration and its ideological soulmates.

by contras were actually agents of Sandinista state security." Interestingly, Barnes even put into quotes the same words, "deeply religious," that the CIA had in its then-secret report. Barnes expressed no moral qualms about summarily executing an elderly man and woman simply because they had allegedly admitted to being Sandinista security agents. But Barnes omitted one explanation from the CIA report: he forgot to mention that the Barredas "were not tortured."

Despite Barnes's no-questions-asked endorsement, Baldizon's credibility grew shakier. At a news conference on February 27, 1986, before a key contra-aid vote, the defector came up with a startling new allegation that he had forgotten to raise before in his months of CIA debriefings. Echoing an administration claim for which the White House had long needed a source, Baldizon disclosed that the Sandinistas had dressed up like contras to commit a number of the atrocities blamed on the contras. A special Sandinista unit "went into the bush and began operations as if they were part of the resistance," Baldizon explained. "They killed about a dozen campesinos who were known Sandinista collaborators. They burned their houses and even set fire to a government cooperative."

But again, Baldizon could muster few details, could not recall where the incidents happened and could not provide any supporting evidence. Yet President Reagan and his scriptwriters were delighted. They promptly inserted the new charge in his weekend radio broadcast. At least one State Department official was dismayed, telling me at the time that the administration had no credible intelligence to back up the charge.

On February 28, 1986, Baldizon finally responded to Americas Watch's questions from December. In a long, rambling, largely incoherent letter, Baldizon denounced Mendez for his pointed queries. The defector accused Americas Watch of a "docile and, in a sense, collaborative posture of your organization with respect to the Nicaraguan government. . . . You never expected a person such as I would suddenly appear and publicly take apart all of your schemes. . . . It is evident that you began immediately to pursue me like a bloodhound, looking for the slightest opportunity to discredit me through supposed contradictions."

After months of living on a State Department expense account and stipend, Baldizon faded into obscurity. He moved to Los Angeles and shared an apartment with several family members. On the night of June 18, 1988, he returned home late at night and went to bed. The next morning, his sister went to his room to awaken him for a phone call. She found him dead. An autopsy showed that he had died from a massive cerebral hemorrhage due to a ruptured brain aneurysm. He was twenty-nine years of age. His mother reported that he had been suffering from depression in the days before his death, but he had told her that he was "too strong" to commit suicide.

As the Nicaragua debate moved to Washington's center ring in the mid-1980's, Fred Barnes's bouncy pro-contra articles catapulted him to fame and fortune as a pundit. *The New Republic*'s lead writer for the contra cause, Barnes also benefited from the magazine's key role in shaping the Washington CW into a growing animosity toward the Sandinistas and a warming sympathy for the contras.

Murray Waas, who wrote investigative domestic stories for the magazine in those years, believes the publication had forsaken its left-of-center past and become, bluntly put, "a propaganda organ for the U.S. government." Yet, its pro-contra articles carried extra weight because they could be cited by the conservative administration as evidence that even liberals now agreed with the White House policy.

"The real influence of *The New Republic* was that it was still considered a liberal voice," Waas told me in an interview. "For decades, it stood up to Joe McCarthy, the Vietnam War and Watergate. It had employed James Ridgeway and Walter Pincus. So it had a certain cachet when it said what it said about the Sandinistas for committing human-rights abuses or not being democratic. If the [conservative] *National Review* had published that kind of an article, people would have said, 'This is incredible. Look at the source.' But *The New Republic*, with a long liberal tradition, had a credibility in saying things about the Sandinistas."

For some years, after the magazine was purchased by Martin Peretz in the mid-1970's, *The New Republic* had shifted rightward, adopting a strongly pro-Israel stance and endorsing the Reagan Doctrine's rough-and-tumble interventionism. "The readership, the public wasn't aware of this change," Waas said. "The magazine tried to put on the appearance of being liberal [on domestic matters, but] the things that really mattered the most to Peretz and his crowd, they controlled: Israel and Central America."

Though Barnes's stock rose with his CW-defining articles on Nicaragua, his pro-contra flacking antagonized the remaining liberals writing for *The New Republic*. "Barnes was just another reporter following along wide-eyed," recalled ex–*New Republic* editor Jefferson Morley. "He was like what the conservatives say [*New York Times* correspondent] Herbert Matthews was with Castro. He was just taking down what was said uncritically."

Like Morton Kondracke, Barnes had parlayed a lackluster career as a journalist into Washington punditry stardom. After attending the patrician St. Alban's private school in Washington (where he was a classmate of ABC's Brit Hume), Barnes graduated from the University of Virginia. He covered the White House and Supreme Court for the now-defunct *Washington Star* and was national political correspondent for the *Baltimore Sun*, but could be recalled for nothing exceptional. When he joined *The New Republic* in 1985, however, his career took off. Before long, Barnes, now in his late forties, was a regular panelist on *The McLaughlin Group*, appeared frequently on CNN's *Crossfire*, offered political commentary on CBS's *This Morning* show and was the moderator of a weekly government-funded Voice of America show called *Issues in the News*.

"Fred Barnes is a mediocre writer, a mediocre reporter," Waas maintained. "You look at the body of his work. There's not much substance. He's gotten where he is because he took the line of the publisher [Peretz]. When he attacks Americas Watch or these other groups, I don't think he understands his own role. He just gets patted on the head for this."

But with its irreverent writing style—and its inside track with the White House and State Department—*The New Republic* had become the magazine that Washington insiders *had* to read. The political journal carried great influence at setting the editorial tone at much larger-circulation magazines, like *Newsweek*. But *The New Republic*'s greatest reach into setting public opinion came when its columnists amplified their and the government's views through redundant appearances on the television chat shows and by placing their syndicated writings in the ever-influential *Washington Post*.

In early 1986, Barnes traveled to the scene of the contra action to gaze firsthand on the object of his long admiration. As new contra-aid votes approached, Barnes went south to play the unlikely role of "Contra for a Day," the title of an April 7, 1986, article he wrote about "roughing it with the freedom-fighters." He used the dateline "on the Nicaraguan border" and offered his readers "some of the flavor" of his adventure: "My companion and I had to ford five streams. Yes, we had a four-wheel vehicle, but it didn't take the bumps in what passed for roads too smoothly. Some bumps were so bad I hit my head on the roof."[10]

Like a twelve-year-old out on a camping trip with teenagers, Barnes caught on to the tough-talking style of the guerrilla. "I had to settle for standard contra food," Barnes wrote in a manly sort of way. "It wasn't too bad if you like rice, beans and mystery meat for breakfast, lunch and dinner.* I ate hearty. The coffee wasn't hot enough, but it was sweet and strong. And the chow was better than the overnight accommodations at a training camp fifteen miles inside Nicaragua. I was told to bring a sleeping bag, heavy boots, water, bug spray, malaria pills, flashlight, toilet paper. I needed all of them. My bed in the *Hospedaje Visita*, the place for visitors, consisted of a plywood slab on legs. I've slept better."

As one might expect, it was worth the contras' public-relations team's while to ferry Fred Barnes into "contraland," as he called it. For three days, Barnes got to talk like John Wayne and, naturally, buy whatever stories the natives were selling. But he didn't have time, he said, to check out those nagging human-rights allegations. He did, however, find time to record former Somozista officer Enrique Bermudez lamenting the unfair charges leveled against his army: "The stories of continuing atrocities by his troops are untrue, he said. To prove it, he presented a commander named Tigrillo, who he said was blamed in a recent report for murder. The man was in the hospital at the time, Bermudez said." While critical of the human-rights groups for going soft on the Sandinistas, Barnes absorbed the contra tales like a sponge.

A year later, Tigrillo would be convicted by the contras themselves of murder, the slaying of one of his own men who allegedly left base without permission. The *Los Angeles Times* reported that Tigrillo was suspected of killing sixteen more contras under his command and of murdering an unknown number of unarmed pris-

---

*"Mystery meat" is one of those phrases like waking up at "oh-dark-thirty" that goes with a visit to contra camps.

oners of war.[11] Tigrillo was the same contra commander who had
been accused by the two hysterical woman contras of raping them
at knife point, according to Edgar Chamorro. But to Barnes, the
word of Bermudez and Tigrillo had been proof enough that these
human-rights concerns were hokum.

Although Barnes cited Bermudez as a credible source, the
contra commander had lied before, even to the CIA, to protect
another one of his subordinates from being purged over human-
rights violations. His chief intelligence deputy, Ricardo "Chino"
Lau, had fallen into disfavor with the agency in September 1982
when it linked him to "death squad" activities in Honduras where
contras were paid by the army to kill fifteen to eighteen local
dissidents. A former top Salvadoran intelligence official, ex-colonel
Roberto Santivanez, has also alleged that Lau was paid $120,000
for helping in the 1980 assassination of El Salvador's Roman Catholic archbishop Oscar Romero.[12]

Reagan administration officials told me that Bermudez and
other FDN leaders had assured them that Lau had been expelled
from the contra movement as punishment. "If Lau was there after
January 1983, it was clearly deceptive," one U.S. official said. But
it turned out that Bermudez simply had moved Lau to a more
secret position as head of counterintelligence. Two years later, after
the sleight of hand was discovered, the administration official said
the FDN apparently had decided to "fool the gringos."[13]

By 1986, Barnes and *The New Republic* were vital cogs in the
administration's propaganda machinery, all the more important because of the magazine's long history as a thoughtful liberal publication. Like a once fine restaurant that had been taken over by
contra cooks serving "mystery meat," *The New Republic* was no
longer dishing out honest journalism in the face of a hostile government. It was enjoying a privileged, insider status that elevated
the magazine and its prized pundits to prominence in spelling out
Washington's conventional wisdom. They also made loads of
money and got flattering invites from the White House.

The key moment in this magazine-administration bonding,
Jefferson Morley believed, came when Bernard Aronson, who had
been writing pro-contra articles for *The New Republic*, drafted a major
Central American address for President Reagan before a key vote

in 1986.* "By 1986, the aims of the magazine and the aims of the policymakers were identical," Morley said. "Nothing would get in their way—not international law, not any notion of journalist distance or independence."

Overall, Waas argued that *The New Republic*'s role in today's Washington "is to define the mainstream, to take people out of it or put people back into it. They're like the membership committee of the country club." Now part of the administration's Mighty Wurlitzer, compensated with access and influence, the once-liberal *New Republic* had taken the job of defining the CW.

---

*In 1989, Aronson was appointed assistant secretary of state for inter-American affairs, replacing Elliott Abrams.

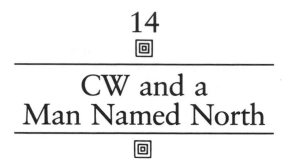

14

CW and a
Man Named North

The clubby, dark-wood Hay Room restaurant at
the Hay-Adams Hotel belonged to an earlier time, a time of cigar
smoke and men-only conversations. In the 1980's, its stone hearths,
medieval tapestries and quiet alcoves seemed almost quaint. Yet
it still attracted a bustling lunchtime power crowd, since the hotel
is just a stroll across Lafayette Park from the White House and the
Old Executive Office Building.

The younger power set preferred the Adams Room, the hotel's
other main-floor restaurant, with its light, yellow, airy look, matching better the trendy nouvelle cuisine of the eighties. But even
the men who still chose the dark recesses of the Hay Room would
often eat from the menu's lighter fare and sip iced tea or possibly
a white wine. Their forebears would have devoured blood-red
steaks and downed scotches and manhattans.

On a warm midsummer day in 1983, I was waiting at a table
in the Hay Room for my first meeting with a National Security
Council aide, a young Marine major named Oliver North. With me
was a conservative acquaintance who had been touting the virtues
of this brash, new, behind-the-scenes activist in the president's
national security establishment. North arrived only a few minutes
late for the lunchtime appointment. He was dressed in a dark suit,
but his crisp appearance and straight bearing had the air of a military
man even at first sight. He and I both ordered salads.

North told me that he had done some checking on my work
for the Associated Press before coming to lunch and had heard bad
things about me. He was frank at least. I imagined he meant my

articles on the continuing human-rights abuses in El Salvador, but I had also written about the Reagan administration's expansion of intelligence powers and William Casey's tangled finances.* I had never tried to be popular.

Although leery of me, North was not hostile. Over lunch, he talked expansively about his hopes for President Reagan's reelection in 1984. North said his feelings were not partisan—Republican or Democrat—just a strong belief that the country needed the continuity of a two-term presidency. And President Reagan had some important business to finish.

When a comment was made about the recent assassination of Lieutenant Commander Albert Schaufelberger in El Salvador, North launched into a personal recollection of the navy officer who had been second in command of the U.S. military group in that Central American war zone. In the calm, matter-of-fact tones of a military officer who has seen it all, North recounted how he and Schaufelberger had, just months before, flown over a battle between the Salvadoran army and a band of guerrillas. Immediately after the firing stopped, North said, they landed their light, propeller-driven plane on a dirt road, near the army's positions.

Like many North stories, this one would change later in its retelling by friends after Oliver North's name became a household word in 1986. Those versions would have North on a daring mercy mission to rescue wounded Salvadoran soldiers. But that is not what North said that day over lunch in the Hay Room restaurant. Between bites of his salad, North said he and Schaufelberger had wanted a fast after-action report on the fighting to assess how well

---

*Though North wouldn't be specific in his complaint, some of my AP stories in the months preceding our meeting had included one on January 26, 1983, which opened: "The Reagan administration, while claiming human rights progress in El Salvador, admits that evidence points to the involvement of Salvadoran security forces in two mass murders." Another, on February 11, 1983, read, "The body of Michael Kline, a 21-year-old American shot by Salvadoran soldiers last fall, showed bruises inflicted by 'blunt force' before his death, according to an autopsy report." A third, a March 11, 1983, analysis of White House policy on Central America, stated, "President Reagan's toughly worded speech declaring U.S. determination to defeat leftist insurgents in El Salvador has put his administration on the road to a larger military commitment in Central America. In near apocalyptic terms favored by some of his most conservative advisers, Reagan warned that a rebel victory in El Salvador would jeopardize U.S. security interests not just in Latin America, but throughout the world." And a fourth, on May 31, 1983, that would have angered North's mentor: "CIA Director William J. Casey, who has access to the government's most secret economic data, traded heavily in the stock market last year, buying and selling several million dollars' worth of stocks and other securities, according to his financial disclosure form."

the government soldiers had fared. He said they had waited for the shooting to stop before landing, but he winked as if I really wasn't supposed to believe that.

After the plane rolled to a halt on the dirt road, North said, he and Schaufelberger hopped out and soon found themselves pinned down under renewed firing by the guerrillas. The Americans also spotted two Salvadoran soldiers lying on the ground bleeding profusely from their wounds. North said he and Schaufelberger carried the wounded men back onto the plane. Schaufelberger administered CPR to one.

North climbed in behind the controls, turning the plane onto the dirt road for takeoff. Just then, North continued, a Salvadoran guerrilla jumped out from behind a bush and opened fire with an automatic rifle. Bullets blew out the windshield, North said with no special excitement in his voice. But the plane kept rolling down the dirt road, reaching takeoff speed and lifting off into the sky. The damaged plane fluttered back to El Salvador's Ilopango military airbase and landed.

Once on the ground, North said, he and Schaufelberger pulled the two soldiers from the plane. One was already dead and the other died soon afterward on a desk at the airfield. North told us that after he recounted this incident at the White House, President Reagan decided to waive the fifty-five-man trainer limit imposed on U.S. military personnel in El Salvador. A special medical training team was dispatched along with evacuation helicopters. Indeed, it was true that the president had made that decision at about that time, claiming that the brave Salvadoran soldiers had inadequate medical care on the battlefield.

But the calmly told tale revealed more about this man North than about conditions on the ground in El Salvador. His many admirers would see in it—and other action stories—North's courage, commitment, his flair for adventure and gift for spinning the dramatic anecdote that elevated dirty, brutal jungle wars into the stuff of heroism. But his detractors would point to his tendency toward recklessness and bravado that could do more to destroy a policy than make it work. Some would simply call him a liar.

The Salvadorans' need for medical-evacuation helicopters aside, North's flight into a battle zone could have meant disaster for U.S. policy objectives in El Salvador. At the time, U.S. military personnel were under strict orders to avoid combat situations, although it was an open secret that many of the fifty-five advisers skirted that rule. But North was not just some Green Beret sergeant who could—if caught—be disciplined for ignoring orders. North was a rising star on President Reagan's National Security Council staff, and Schaufelberger was second in command of the U.S. military group in the country.*

North's Salvadoran adventure story, which reached public attention only after his firing on November 25, 1986, also explains much about how Oliver North, an obscure Marine major when he started at the NSC in September 1981, could vault to power inside the Reagan White House. To Reagan, who only played soldiers in movies, North was a real-life decorated war hero who seemed to have stepped right out of the celluloid. He became the personal embodiment of the Reagan Doctrine's burning desire to roll back Soviet expansionism. As North would boast to friends about his relationship with Reagan: "The old man loves my ass."

But my journalistic problem with the El Salvador story was simpler: I had no idea whether to believe it or not. On its face, it seemed utterly implausible, though from what North would do later in his NSC career, it might not have been quite as ludicrous in retrospect. But in any case, with Schaufelberger dead, I could see no reasonable way to confirm it. What I had learned from the luncheon, however, was that here was a government official to keep an eye on—he was either going to do great things or make some horrendous mistakes.

As the focus of U.S. attention in Central America shifted from El Salvador to Nicaragua, I would hear bits and pieces about Oliver North's continuing adventures. One intelligence source claimed that North was at Ilopango airfield again when a contra plane took off for a foolhardy assault on Managua airport on September 8, 1983. The plane, with two five-hundred-pound bombs strapped under the wings, was shot down by defenders and crashed into the control tower, killing the plane's pilot and copilot as well as an airport worker on the ground. The attack also damaged the airport's terminal and sent dozens of waiting passengers scurrying for safety.

---

*Several weeks after the plane incident described by North, Lieutenant Albert Schaufelberger was shot to death by leftist guerrillas in San Salvador. Ignoring normal security guidelines, Schaufelberger was sitting in a parked car waiting for his girlfriend when the assassins struck.

And the incident antagonized two influential senators, Gary Hart and William Cohen, whose plane had been scheduled to land just minutes after the bombing raid. If they had arrived a few minutes early, they could have been casualties of an attack carried out by one of the CIA's own airplanes. Later, CIA director Casey would insist that the spy agency had not authorized the attack, but other intelligence sources said the bizarre raid fit the pattern of daring CIA operations mounted from mid-1983 through spring 1984. But as for North's alleged role, I could never corroborate the CIA man's account.

There were, however, other recurring allegations about North. Through late 1984 and early 1985, I heard reports that he was filling the breach left by the congressional decision to cut off CIA aid to the contras in October 1984. Somehow he was helping to raise money and was giving the contras political and military advice, but it wasn't clear exactly how he was doing it.

My first hard information came in two terse phone conversations with retired major general Jack Singlaub, whose World Anti-Communist League and its U.S. affiliate were scratching around raising money to help the "freedom fighters." Singlaub was an unwilling interviewee, but he is also a man who doesn't like lying. He acknowledged reporting to North about the fund-raising activities and receiving indirect guidance about what to do. But he insisted that those arrangements had been put in place prior to the flat congressional ban in October 1984 and that afterwards North had kept the Singlaub fund-raising at arm's length. Singlaub told me that he had an arrangement worked out with North so the lack of an objection was read as affirmation. "I say, 'This is what I'm going to do,' " Singlaub told me. " 'If it's a dumb idea, send me a signal.' Nobody has called me and told me, 'You're screwing up.' "

I also tracked down an administration official who had sat in on some of the White House meetings where ideas had been debated about how to keep the contras afloat as Congress first capped the CIA's money in 1983 and then chopped it off altogether a year later. This source described how in late 1983 or early 1984, NSC adviser Robert McFarlane brought to President Reagan a memo that North had written about recruiting private individuals and third countries to sustain financial support for the contras. The source said the memo carried at the top the word "non-paper." Officially, it didn't exist. McFarlane returned to the next day's meeting, the source said, and told the small group that the word back from Reagan was to go ahead. The White House began secretly to solicit funds and arrange other assistance for the contras.

Later, I located a third source who had been inside the NSC staff and who confirmed much about the comings and goings in North's office, a pattern of visits that clearly suggested that North was meeting with key figures in the contra support operation. That, along with anecdotal comments from sources inside the contra movement, including Edgar Chamorro, provided the basis for my first story about the North network which I began to write in late May 1985.

On May 31, 1985, I contacted the NSC press officer Karna Small and asked her to put a question to McFarlane. She wrote down my query as "it's my understanding that some day at the end of 1983 or the beginning of 1984, Reagan instructed McFarlane orally to arrange for private and other outside, non-USG funding for contras. Is that true? And what comment does McFarlane have about it?" Small also sketched my journalistic background for McFarlane, a description that I sometimes slip into job applications. "Bob Parry, AP (who can be tough"—underlined, no less—"but has awfully good sources) is working on a big piece on 'the national security council involvement in Nicaragua with respect to funding by private, outside groups.' "

McFarlane's scrawled answer at the bottom of the page said, "It is absolutely untrue—in fact, the guidance was firmly to the contrary, that there would be no solicitation by any USG official." In the meantime, North had gotten hold of Small's report to McFarlane, and in an internal memo to deputy NSC adviser John Poindexter, North railed against me. "For several weeks now there have been rumors of stories being prepared which allege an NSC connection to private funding and other support to the Nicaraguan resistance," North wrote. "The rumors originally surfaced with a reporter Alfonso Chardi [sic] from the Miami Herald and now seem to focus more [on] an Associated Press reporter named Robert Parry. Parry is the reporter who 'broke the story' on the so-called CIA 'murder manual.' "

North then claimed that Chardy had been threatened with a cutoff of access to contra base camps if he printed such a story and that "Chardi [sic] promised to drop the story"—a claim Chardy has since flatly denied. "The attached note from Karna is, however, more disturbing," North continued. "Parry is an avowed liberal with very close connections in the Democratic party." And if that accusation weren't vilifying enough, North added that "it is also reported that he has a personal relationship with one of the NSC staff."

I have since been asked by reporters to respond to these charges, and although they are false—I am not an avowed anything and have never slept with anyone on the NSC staff or elsewhere to get a story—denying such calumny always seemed silly or, even worse, made me feel like Michael Dukakis. But oddly, these are the kinds of remarks that when circulated around Washington can seriously damage a reporter's career by painting him as biased, even when his stories prove out to be true.

While North fumed to his boss, Small called back to steer me away from the NSC-contra article. She would give me no on-the-record response. A State Department spokesman continued the administration's flat denial. Still somewhat naive about how dishonest the government had gotten, I softened the lead slightly, so as not to directly challenge the administration's account.

The story, which ran on the AP wires on June 10, 1985, began: "The White House gave advice—at least initially—to individuals involved in private fund-raising for Nicaraguan rebels despite a public stance that it doesn't encourage or discourage those efforts, according to sources." The story quoted one of the sources as saying, "The National Security Council staff handled contacts with private groups, including the World Anti-Communist League, a conservative organization headed by retired Maj. Gen. John K. Singlaub." Singlaub is then quoted saying his contact point was Lieutenant Colonel Oliver North.* It was the first time North's name had surfaced publicly. But the story, getting no reaction from the administration spin-controllers, made only a small dent in the Washington CW.

While this scandal story of the decade was taking shape behind closed doors at the White House, the CW's hostility toward critical reporting on U.S. policy in Central America kept most of the Wash-

---

*By this time, North had been promoted from major to lieutenant colonel. At his lower rank, he was often called by his detractors "the military's only four-star major" because of his abrasive style in using his NSC powers to give orders to higher-ranking military officers.

ington news media at bay. Talk of secret White House operations to keep the contras going struck many in Washington as a ludicrous "conspiracy theory." By late 1985, few national news organizations were devoting any significant resources to investigate the secret contra support network. The aggressive "public diplomacy" bureaucracy had succeeded in exacting high costs from individual reporters and news organizations that did get too nosy. Some were frozen out of administration briefings, while their compliant competitors were rewarded with newsy administration leaks. In addition, many senior news executives had bought into Ronald Reagan's ideological goal of stopping communism, even when that meant brushing aside the fine points of U.S. or international law.*

Surprisingly, it fell to the Associated Press, a news organization with little interest and less success in investigative reporting, to do most of the digging. The impetus for this unlikely role was AP's second-place showing for the Pulitzer Prize for national reporting in 1984. My articles on the CIA's activities in Nicaragua, particularly the "murder manual," had reached that level, but the selection board had opted for a safer series of articles on the dangers of farm equipment.

AP executive editor Walter Mears, a crusty political writer and past Pulitzer winner himself, had pushed the AP entry in the jockeying that goes on among the top national news organizations for these honors. When the Pulitzer board extended the award to the farm safety series, Mears grumbled that all those stories had proven

---

*At the Associated Press, for instance, AP's general manager Keith Fuller welcomed Reagan's election in 1980 as a national turning point. "As we look back on the turbulent 60s, we shudder with the memory of a time that seemed to tear at the very sinews of this country," Fuller said in a speech on January 28, 1982, in Worcester, Massachusetts. "While our soldiers were dying in old Indochina, our young people, at least some of them, were chanting familiar communist slogans on the campuses around this nation. . . . Popular entertainers of that day were openly supporting a communist regime, denouncing the American position and a propaganda barrage against America was loosed in places like France and Britain and Scandinavia, Italy, Greece, all carefully financed and orchestrated by the USSR." According to Fuller, then the AP's top news executive, America continued to decline through the 1970's. "I think it changed at the ballot box in November. And I'm not speaking here of Democrats or Republicans at all. Totally apolitical. I think a nation is crying, 'Enough,' A nation is saying: 'We don't really believe that criminal rights should take precedence over the rights of victims. We don't believe that the union of Adam and Bruce is really the same as Adam and Eve in the eyes of creation. We don't believe that people should cash welfare checks and spend them on booze and narcotics. We don't really believe that a simple prayer or a pledge of allegiance is against the national interest in the classroom. We're sick of your social engineering. We're fed up with your tolerance of crime, drugs and pornography. But most of all, we're sick of your self-perpetuating, burdening bureaucracy weighing ever more heavily on our backs.' "

was that "it's dangerous to fall off a tractor." He encouraged me to keep on the CIA-Nicaragua story so he could "shove it back down their throats" next year.

My proposal back to Mears was to establish conclusively that an NSC aide named Oliver North was running a secret operation to sustain the contras in defiance of Congress and the law. I recommended that the AP temporarily hire Brian Barger, who had worked as an editorial assistant for *The Washington Post* but was then free-lancing. Barger spoke fluent Spanish, which I did not, and had developed excellent contacts among the disreputable lowlifes who were staffing the administration's Nicaragua policy in the field.

In a pattern that would repeat itself over the next year, the AP executives suddenly turned hesitant. Mears agreed to take Barger on as a "maternity leave" fill-in but with the bureaucratic proviso that he would be treated as a general-assignment reporter and not allowed to concentrate on the Nicaragua project. This edict would become a frustration to the investigation at key moments. But Mears's agreement to add Barger and his prodigious skills to the staff brought new depth to our reporting.

Tall and rangy, the son of a State Department foreign service officer, Barger was self-confident, sometimes to the point of arrogance. But his strong will and dogged interviewing techniques proved invaluable to the investigation. He understood the value of detailed interviews and could master mind-numbing details in a way more common to reporters at the leading newspapers, like *The Washington Post* and *The New York Times*, than to those at the AP. For AP staffers, who are required to handle the constant flow of fast-breaking news, speed and versatility were the most prized qualities.

In September 1985, shortly after teaming up, Barger and I proposed advancing the story on Oliver North. The memo to AP Washington bureau chief Charles Lewis said, "We have a story about National Security Council aide North's involvement in assisting, indirectly, with the shipment of weapons, ammunition and other military supplies from . . . the United States to Nicaraguan rebels." The memo detailed the roles of North, his courier Robert Owen and the governments of Israel and other U.S. allies. "We have evidence of the active involvement of officials from the National Security Council, the CIA, State Department and DOD [Department of Defense] in the not-so-private effort."

We traced the operation's origins to early 1984. "Concerned early last year that Congress would ban contra aid, even before revelations that the CIA was mining Nicaraguan ports, White House officials began looking for ways to continue the contra operations, even if that meant bypassing Congress," the memo said. "One former top NSC official has told us the order came directly from President Reagan through Bud McFarlane. Contra leaders have described to us in detail, meetings with senior CIA and NSC officials where creation of this operation was discussed. . . . Building an 'old boys' network of former military colleagues, North encouraged and oversaw creation of a sophisticated 'private aid' network. It involved money laundering through offshore banks, public fund-raising events, shipping military supplies from the United States to Honduras and Costa Rica in apparent violation of the Arms Export Control Act and the Neutrality Act, enlisting third-country support for the contra pipeline and using American 'volunteers' to replace CIA trainers in the field."

That same September, as we were writing our memo, NSC adviser Robert McFarlane had assured Congress that nothing like that was happening. "I can state with deep personal conviction that at no time did I or any member of the National Security Council staff violate the letter or spirit" of the congressional contra-aid ban, McFarlane wrote. "I am most concerned . . . there be no misgivings as to the existence of any parallel efforts to provide, directly or indirectly, support for military or paramilitary activities in Nicaragua. There has not been, nor will there be, any such activities by the NSC staff."

After the Iran-contra scandal broke, McFarlane would plead guilty to misleading Congress and acknowledge that his assurances had been "too categorical," one of the affair's many euphemisms for lying. But as the NSC staff branched out into illegal activities, the nature of the "public diplomacy" campaign also changed. Instead of simply working to shape the CW's perception of reality, the propaganda team became, in effect, part of a government cover-up. Almost naturally, the administration's image-shapers shifted from gluing black hats on the Sandinistas to stonewalling press and congressional investigators looking into the North network.

For its part, the White House press office would not even release North's photo or his NSC bio. In justifying the secrecy, North tended toward the melodramatic. When his children's dog died shortly after he was publicly identified in mid-1985 as a White House–contra link, he told friends that it had been poisoned by Sandinista agents. But one associate said the dog was known to have had cancer. Believing he was targeted for assassination by a Libyan hit team, North briefly moved his family onto a military base and would go to movies only at secure base facilities.

But the waters around North had kept steadily rising. *The New York Times* and *The Washington Post* weighed in with stories in August 1985 alleging that the White House operation had included military advice for the contras. The *Times* had discreetly left out North's name at the White House's request, but the *Post* included it, citing the earlier AP story. But going against the CW, which was aligning itself with the administration on Central America, the stories blipped onto the public radar screen and disappeared. After the summer of 1985, the two premier American newspapers, the *Post* and *Times*, dropped the story.* But the AP didn't.

On October 8, 1985, the AP ran another one of my stories about the secret White House network, and this one placed responsibility for its creation squarely on President Reagan himself. "Facing loss of congressional support for Nicaraguan rebels early last year [1984], President Reagan approved a secret plan to use assistance from American citizens and U.S. allies to replace CIA funds, current and former administration officials say," the story read. "Government sources, including one senior administration official, described the behind-the-scenes White House role in organizing and advising the aid network as much more extensive than has been acknowledged. The network has allowed the rebels to continue military operations during the 15-month cutoff of direct U.S. assistance and circumvent congressional efforts to shut down the CIA-supported war."[1] Never before had the president been so directly connected to the operation, but still the CW paid little heed.

House Democrats seized on the AP story to attack Reagan and demand release of documents about White House contacts with

---

*In 1986, the nation's two most venerated newspapers, *The New York Times* and *The Washington Post*, both did major takeouts about the inner workings of the NSC staff and somehow failed to mention the peripatetic North even once. When I asked a friend at the *Post* about the oversight, he told me that the newspaper's White House sources had assured the paper that North was an inconsequential figure.

the contras. "The president of the United States apparently authorized nothing less than an international plumbers group," charged Congressman Norman Y. Mineta of California. "With a wink and a nod, [Reagan] turned over United States' Central America policy to a group of extremist right-wing organizations and apparently encouraged U.S. allies to become their arms merchants."[2] The White House, however, continued to stonewall—and there was no sustained pressure from the press or Congress to break through for answers.

When Barger was not busy with his mandated "general assignment" stories—that is, anything the AP needed a warm body to go cover—we would team up on Central America. Toward the end of 1985, we were following some of Barger's leads on contra drug trafficking.

We got clearance for a trip to Miami, which had become for many in the contra hierarchy their home away from the home front. Since the AP management discouraged our traveling outside the United States, for bureaucratic turf reasons, Miami also became our chief window into the contra movement. For that reason, I will always have a fondness for the contras. The city was a far more pleasant site to run a war—or cover one—than dusty Tegucigalpa, Honduras or slimy San José, Costa Rica. One of the few pleasures of the contra investigation had been returning late at night from an interview with a contra leader on Key Biscayne—driving windows down, sea breezes all around, stereo on—back across the causeway toward Miami. Ahead would be the city's pastel-lit skyline, one of the most striking urban vistas in America.

Culturally, the city's Latin vibrancy and status as an international crossroads did create a feeling of an American Casablanca. And although the city is notorious for its political extremism, there was a far more honest debate within the Nicaraguan exile community about the contras' pros and cons than existed in the marble halls of CW-dominated Washington. Barger and I found a refreshing integrity among the Nicaraguans who had fled Sandinista rule. While hostile to the Sandinistas' socialist experimenting, many exiles felt degraded by the corruption they saw among the U.S.-groomed contra leaders. Disillusioned Nicaraguan exiles in Miami would be among our most valuable sources of honest information.

One of those Miami leads brought us to a disturbing discovery about the contras—that some of their troops had begun moonlighting as guards and transporters for cocaine shipments headed north. But to nail the story down, Barger and I needed to fly to Costa Rica, a trip the AP management did not want us to take. From my Miami hotel room, I argued over the phone with Washington bureau chief Lewis, who had found himself caught in the middle of AP's ambivalence about our investigative work. Finally, Lewis and AP's New York hierarchy relented and cleared the additional leg of our trip.

We arrived in San José, a city of old Spanish architecture and mountainous surroundings, as the city's residents were celebrating a pre-Christmas holiday. The narrow streets resounded with the crackling of fireworks and young men walked through the crowds throwing confetti in everyone's face. There was something festive but unnerving about the custom.

More unsettling had been the impact of the nearby contra war on Costa Rica's political and social fabric. Police complained that robbers were now armed with AK-47s. As American money and embassy personnel had poured in, open prostitution spread. So did an overall sense of decadence and sleaze. Though it lacked the palpable fear of San Salvador or the beggarly poverty of Tegucigalpa, San José was becoming the most licentious city in the region.

One night during our stay in Costa Rica, Barger took me to see some of the seamy sights of San José. One was the Key Largo bar, where Humphrey Bogart posters adorn the walls and prostitutes openly negotiate with their customers under slowly rotating ceiling fans. On the way back to our hotel, we were accosted by three street hookers. One propositioned me, *"Quiere amor, señor?"* Another asked Barger, *"Tiene cigarrillos, señor?"* The ever-hospitable Barger politely pulled out a pack of cigarettes as the ladies swarmed over him. After dispensing the cigarettes and watching the women quickly leave, Barger realized that the cash in his pocket was missing. Barger, more protective of AP expense money than I would have been, gave chase, confronting the women with charges of pickpocketing. One of the women promptly lifted up her blouse and told Barger to search her. Barger gave up. The money was gone.

When we got down to work, San José turned out to be a gold mine of information. Even from a short stay, it was clear, Costa Rica was a country in political turmoil. Key officials, particularly in the security and narcotics fields, seemed under intense pressure to overlook what the powerful U.S. embassy was overseeing at the northern border with Nicaragua. One senior internal security official with close ties to the CIA, Benjamin Piza, simply misinformed us, claiming that there were no contras at all in Costa Rica. The Iran-contra investigations would show much later that Piza had collaborated with CIA station chief Joe Fernandez. Piza's cooperation with the CIA was rewarded with a special trip for himself and his wife to the White House for a photo opportunity with President Reagan.

But we located other more forthcoming officials from the Costa Rican government and the U.S. embassy. One American official agreed to meet us in a bar near our hotel. Over several beers, he confirmed much of the information we already had. He described contra soldiers guarding clandestine air strips while drug planes refueled. Some contras, he said, even transported loads of cocaine into San José for transshipment by freighter to the United States.

The evidence implicated virtually all the contra groups, including the Honduran-based FDN, which had opened its own second front in Costa Rica. In addition, interviews with two more mercenaries whose work with the contras had landed them in Costa Rican prison added more pieces to the puzzle about how the contras were continuing their operations without official U.S. support. These out-of-luck mercenaries—British Peter Glibbery and American Steven Carr—described weapons flights from Miami and claimed one contra operation was getting $10,000 a month from the National Security Council.

When we boarded the plane back to the United States, Barger was euphoric. "We got it," he exulted. But my experience with AP's bureaucracy had been longer and more painful than his. "The trouble's only just begun," I responded.

Back in Washington, the contra drug story received a decidedly mixed reaction. Bureau chief Lewis liked it, but objections poured down from AP's headquarters in New York. To bolster the reporting, I got a senior White House official on the phone who tried to steer me away from implicating the FDN and CIA operative John Hull. But the official admitted that a recent National Intelligence Estimate, a secret CIA-prepared analysis on narcotics trafficking, had found that a top commander of a rival contra group, called ARDE, had used cocaine profits to pay for a $250,000 arms shipment and a helicopter.

Lewis felt the additional confirmation was enough to go with and instructed me to send the story to the Washington General Desk for final editing. Putting Lewis's initials at the top so the story would go to his personal attention, I transmitted the story by computer. The paper copy was torn off the printer and taken into him, but New York's concerns were not over. Later that afternoon, Lewis summoned me to his office and dejectedly told me that New York was insisting that we obtain an on-the-record confirmation from a government official. The trouble was that any government official insane enough to attach his name to an allegation against the contras could count on losing his job. Lewis felt the story was dead.

Over the next two days, Barger and I interviewed officials at the Drug Enforcement Administration and elsewhere, hoping to overcome New York's worries. DEA officials would confirm that northern Costa Rica had grown into a large-scale transit point for cocaine, but they said they had no idea of the political connections of the smugglers.

After returning from one interview, Barger received a call from an old acquaintance who wanted to compliment us for our story about contra drug trafficking. Barger exploded, demanding how the person knew about the article. The perplexed caller responded that it had been in newspapers all over Latin America. Barger, ashen faced, came to my desk with the shocking news that somehow the story had gone to AP subscribers in Spanish-speaking countries.

Checking back through the computer records, we discovered that the story I had sent to Lewis's attention had also popped up in another computer for AP's world services. It was routinely translated and sent out, again by computer, to newspapers throughout the Western Hemisphere that take AP's Spanish-language wire. The story that New York had been sitting on and that Lewis feared was dead had been sent out by accident.

AP editors in Washington and New York now hurried to complete work on the English-language version, which moved the next day, December 20, 1985. It read: "Nicaraguan rebels operating in northern Costa Rica have engaged in cocaine smuggling, using some of the profits to finance their war against Nicaragua's leftist government, according to U.S. investigators and American volunteers who work with the rebels. The smuggling activity has involved refueling planes at clandestine airstrips and sometimes helping transport cocaine to other Costa Rican points for shipment to the United States, said U.S. law enforcement officials." It carried official denials from the Reagan administration and the contras.[3] A week after the story moved on the AP wires, it was published in *The Washington Post*, with fresh denials.

Although months later the State Department would quietly release a report confirming the accuracy of the AP story, the short-term response was to heat up the "public diplomacy" attacks on Barger and me—and our suspected "agenda." Again, there was little interest from other news organizations, leaving AP management to worry that maybe it was climbing farther and farther out onto a dangerous limb. Early in 1986, when I approached Lewis with ideas about following up the contra-cocaine connection, he lowered his voice and said, "New York doesn't want to hear any more about the drug story."

But Barger and I pressed on with our broader contra investigation, looking always ahead to a definitive story on North's operation. Lewis's responses to our frequent story-idea memos and updates on the investigation turned cooler and cooler. Mostly our memos were simply ignored. I started slugging the stories in the computer file "deepsix1," "deepsix2," etc. Whenever we thought we had enough, Lewis would insist on more and more corroboration. Barger likened the process to always having the field goals moved.

While working on the North network, we wrote other stories, questioning the cheery public relations around the contra movement. One in January 1986 gave voice to anti-Sandinista Nicaraguans who felt their dream of retaking their homeland had been sullied by clumsy interference from Washington. It recounted how the United Nicaraguan Opposition, a contra coalition resulting from yet another White House shotgun marriage, had failed to unify the rebel forces.

Another story in March examined how congressional investigators could not account for how most of the contras' "humanitarian" aid had been spent.[4] In April, we disclosed the existence of a federal criminal investigation in Miami into contra gunrunning.[5] The stories, however, flew directly into the face of a powerful Washington CW, which wanted to believe the contras were the necessary means to a democratic end in Nicaragua.

During this period, one of the few members of Congress with

the courage to demand answers from the White House was fresh-man Democratic senator John Kerry of Massachusetts. When those answers were not satisfactory, Kerry assigned members of his own staff to examine the contra drug trafficking and reports about North's secret role in aiding the contras. That staff investigation— headed by Dick McCall, Ron Rosenblith and Jonathan Winer— would be a thorn in the administration's side as the Kerry team followed much the same trail that Barger and I were on. They encountered many of the same obstacles as well. But their authority to press for answers compelled the White House grudgingly to admit some of the problems, including the fact that the Miami criminal probe that the administration insisted had cleared the con-tras had, in fact, found substantial evidence to support the charges.

Kerry's reward for his political courage and tenacity was to be targeted by the "public diplomacy" apparatus. The battering he would endure for his pursuit of contra corruption would earn him a reputation as a conspiracy theorist. He also was briefly put under a Senate ethics committee investigation over the expenses for his probe. The right-wing *Washington Times* complained stridently about Kerry's interference with the president's foreign policy. The Moonie-owned newspaper published leaked information that pur-portedly debunked his investigations.

Even afer his suspicions were confirmed with the outbreak of the Iran-contra scandal in November 1986, the CW against him was so strong that no one bothered to go back and correct Kerry's image as a flake. As Kaus would say about the CW, "There's no honor in being right too soon. People just remember that you were out of step and crazy."

Kerry's own party shunned him. Kerry was blackballed by Senate Democratic leaders picking members for the Iran-contra investigating committee. His sin was that he had taken an early position asserting that the North network did exist and that some contra units had helped the drug trade. Although he was right, his CW as a conspiracy theorist would continue to dog his Senate career. One of the best-read political reference books, the *Almanac of American Politics*, states in its 1992 edition: "In search of right-wing villains and complicit Americans, [Kerry] tried to link Nicara-guan contras to the drug trade, without turning up much credible evidence."[6] In reality, Kerry's subcommittee on narcotics and terrorism had issued a massive report on its findings. The two-volume report contained detailed and documented accounts of contra drug trafficking, a problem that the Reagan administration had belatedly acknowledged. But those facts never penetrated the CW.

When Kerry's persistent investigation into wrongdoing at the Bank of Credit and Commerce International also proved right, *Newsweek*'s *CW Watch* finally offered some backhanded praise—but combined it with a gibe at his reputation for dating starlets. "Randy conspiracy buff prescient this time, but will it get him dates?" smirked the *Watch*.[7] When Kerry's aide, Jonathan Winer, protested that capsule comment, *CW Watch* writer Jonathan Alter defended the put-down. Alter argued that it had been an accurate description of how the Washington in-crowd viewed Kerry, even though Alter acknowledged that the CW assessment was changing and was not supported by the facts. The CW, of course, has little interest in fairness.

In the late winter and early spring of 1986, the AP's interest in pushing out front on such a controversial story also was on the wane. During one of the periodic lulls in the contra debate, Lewis advised me that I should move on to other stories, that AP management had never intended me to focus so much on one issue. "Nicaragua isn't a story anymore," he added. I didn't argue the point. I knew that whatever AP's executives might think, the contra issue would again dominate Washington news. The White House would make sure of that when it demanded resumption of CIA contra aid in May and June.

By spring, Barger and I felt that we had an abundance of sourcing to report in detail how North had run the contra support operation through a variety of cut-outs. But AP's top editors kept demanding more. While we dug for additional sources, Barger and I prepared two other stories for late May 1986. One revealed the CIA role in forcing independent contra leader Eden Pastora to quit the war and the other disclosed how the contras had exchanged their "humanitarian" aid dollars at "black market" rates and sank the profits into their weapons accounts.

Both were expected to run around the Memorial Day weekend when a hiatus in official government business gives investigative stories a better chance for wide usage among newspapers that take the AP wire. After these stories, we planned to push again for publication of the major North story. Word was spreading that the *Miami Herald*'s Al Chardy was onto the same story and our reporting lead was shrinking.

The Pastora and black-market money stories, however, were encountering inexplicable delays with AP senior editors. Early one evening after most of the AP staff had left the office, which is in a nondescript office building in the K Street business district, I confronted Lewis about the story holdups. Lewis, a tall, gangly man, then in his early forties, looked exhausted. His face was drained of color and his eyes were bloodshot. He had worries on his mind other than my concern about the Nicaragua stories.

Lewis told me he had just come from talking with Oliver North not about the contra story but about the fate of Terry Anderson, the AP's Middle East bureau chief who had been kidnapped by Islamic extremists in Beirut, Lebanon, on March 16, 1985. Anderson had been held hostage for more than a year, and AP executives were pained by their inability to win his release. North, it turned out, was the administration's point man assigned to gain the freedom of Anderson and several other American hostages.

Lewis began describing the inside of North's NSC office on the third floor of the Old Executive Office Building. The AP bureau chief marveled about North's bank of telephones, which rang with distinctly different sounds. The ever-active North would grab one receiver and then the next, fielding calls from the nation's most sensitive intelligence agencies. North would also tell visitors that his windows were specially coated to block enemy electronic spying.*

I came away from the strange encounter with Lewis, wondering if North might be playing a double game. That somehow Terry Anderson's freedom had become entwined with the AP's investigation of North's contra-aid network. Lewis has insisted since then—and assured me personally—that North's activism on the hostage issue did not interfere with the AP's investigative work on his contra network. The bureau chief has argued that the stories

---

*Walter Mears, AP's hard-bitten executive editor who also met with North about Anderson, would later compare the tightly wound Marine officer to the fictional TV character, *M*A*S*H*'s Colonel Flagg. Flagg, a superpatriotic CIA officer, frowned on the irreverent behavior of the TV show's medical staff and once even hid in a garbage can to overhear potentially subversive conversations.

were delayed to strengthen their sourcing, not to appease the White House.

But the delays did correspond to one of the most active periods of North's intervention to buy freedom for the hostages by selling weapons to Iran. Over the Memorial Day weekend of 1986—just when the two contra stories were being delayed—North headed to Teheran with HAWK missile parts and a chocolate cake. Certainly, the AP executives must have known that if North were exposed, his work on Anderson would be disrupted.*

Not until the end of the week—after the Teheran meetings had collapsed on May 27—was the Pastora story released by the AP, running on May 29 for newspapers published the next day, Friday, May 30.[8] The heavily edited story read clumsily: "Nicaraguan rebel leader Eden Pastora quit the contra war effort after six of his top lieutenants left his command to join a rival U.S.-backed umbrella group at the urging of a man known to them as a CIA officer, according to officials of rival contra factions." The next week, the "black-market money" story was put out after more arguments. But Lewis released the story at 8:15 P.M., a time so late that few morning papers would use it.

The comprehensive North story was also still on hold, even though we knew that the *Miami Herald* was about to beat us on a story that we had seen as the crown jewel of our investigation. Finally, exhausted by the internal battles and the external pressure, I wrote Lewis a memo, agreeing to drop the Nicaragua investigation: "It is now clear to me that I cannot persuade an unwilling news organization to pursue a story that it feels, at its highest levels, is not significant or not worthy of the risk entailed in writing it." Lewis and Mears both asked me to reconsider, which I did. But the damage from the interminable delays had been done. The *Miami Herald*, with far fewer sources, published its story ahead of us. It was that day that I knew our quest for the Pulitzer that Mears had envisioned a year earlier was lost.[†]

Finally, on June 10, 1986, Barger and I were allowed to put

---

*One of Lewis's secretaries said that during this period, Lewis got so many calls from North that she suspected that he was having an affair with a woman named Fawn. North's secretary, Fawn Hall, would place many of North's calls.
†The *Miami Herald* would win the 1986 Pulitzer Prize for its coverage of U.S. activities in Nicaragua.

out our story on North's network. The story cited two dozen sources, a number of them on the record. It read: "The White House, working through outside intermediaries, managed a private aid network that provided military assistance to Nicaraguan rebels during last year's congressional aid ban, according to government officials, rebel leaders and American supporters. The American intermediaries helped the rebels with arms purchases, fund raising and enlistment of military trainers after Congress, in October 1984, barred U.S. officials from 'directly or indirectly' aiding the contra war against Nicaragua's leftist government. . . . Lt. Col. Oliver L. North, deputy director for political-military affairs at the National Security Council, oversaw the work of the intermediaries, including conservative activist Robert W. Owen and retired Army Maj. Gen. John K. Singlaub."[9]

The AP story, with its multitude of sources, prompted members of the House Intelligence Committee to arrange a meeting with North in the White House situation room on August 11, 1986. In the polite give-and-take of the meeting, North insisted that "he did not in any way, nor at any time violate the spirit, principles or legal requirements of the Boland Amendment" barring aid to the contras, according to minutes of the meeting. At the end, Congressman Lee Hamilton, intelligence committee chairman, "indicated his satisfaction in the responses received." Hamilton later said publicly that he had no choice but to take the word of the president's national security advisers. The pro-contra CW was so strong that even senior congressmen would not challenge the White House cover stories. Only after the scandal erupted in fall 1986 and North was compelled to testify at the Iran-contra hearings the next year would he admit "that I misled the Congress. I misled . . . at that meeting . . . face to face."

North possessed few scruples when it came to protecting the secrecy of the contra operation, a kind of White-House-of-cards built from lies. He felt passionately about the Nicaragua issue. In a May 31, 1986, speech to the conservative Council for National Policy, North called Nicaragua "a national security threat of the first order." He denounced criticism of the contra forces as "the most sophisticated disinformation and active-measures campaign that we have seen in this country since Adolf Hitler." Unless Congress backs the contras, North declared, "this country, which last year had twenty-three of its citizens killed by terrorism around the world, will very soon find its citizens being gunned down on its own streets."[10]

While a single-minded North lied to keep a timid Congress at bay, the situation at the AP got worse. Lewis agreed to make Barger's job permanent but insisted that he spend the summer working the overnight desk, an assignment that moved Barger completely out of the contra story. When Lewis extended Barger's stay on the overnight into the fall, Barger resigned from the AP.

Still hoping to win Terry Anderson's release, the AP brass continued working with North. On September 8, 1986, North reported to Poindexter by computer message that AP executives understood the value of secrecy in the delicate hostage negotiations. AP general manager Louis D. Boccardi "is supportive of our policy on terroprism [*sic*] and on the hostage issue," North wrote. "He made a cogent observation that I think is relevant: 'I sure hope that you are dealing with someone regarding Terry and the others in Lebanon—and that you can keep it quiet—that's the only way that any of this will work.' "[11]*

By later summer 1986, I had concluded that North, protected by a wall of White House deceptions and the CW, had won. Between the aggressive "public diplomacy" campaign to manipulate the press and the administration's unblushing readiness to lie, the secrecy of an illegal intelligence operation—run out of the White House in direct defiance of Congress—had prevailed. It seemed the administration would go to any lengths to keep its secrets.

---

*Terry Anderson remained a captive for five more years. He was freed on December 4, 1991.

15

CW and
the Cover-up

Jack Terrell was exactly the type of guy the Washington CW couldn't stand. He had grown up in youth reformatories. He wore his blond hair cropped close to his head, a style that some thought "looked gay." He spoke in a soft Southern drawl. And when he pulled up his pants leg, he would show off a nasty-looking, black .380 Walther pistol strapped to his calf. He was also the sort of fellow who might just use it.

In 1986, as Oliver North scrambled to protect his contra supply apparatus, Terrell was one of North's biggest headaches. Terrell* had served briefly as a military trainer for the Nicaraguan contras. He had joined up with a paramilitary outfit called Civilian-Military Assistance (CMA) to help the contras after Congress cut off CIA support. Though CMA cultivated an image of redneck good ole boys, some of its volunteers were experienced in fighting and training for jungle wars. It drew some of its training experts from the ranks of the Alabama National Guard's reserve special forces units.

Terrell, tall and trim, went by the code name El Flaco, "the thin man," and worked with the Honduran-based contras drawn from the Miskito Indian tribes that had fled Nicaragua's Atlantic coast. The Miskitos had fought a merciless war with the Sandinistas. From the start, Terrell was more bluster than a bona fide trainer, and his team would soon be barred from the region. But

---

*Terrell's last name is pronounced with the accent on the first syllable. He corrected me once when I placed the accent on the second syllable, saying that the pronunciation made him sound like he was black.

during a trip to Central America, Brian Barger had met Terrell, and when the mercenary was kicked out, he began talking to Barger about what was going on inside the contra movement. Terrell provided some valuable leads for our investigation, even though we never went with anything he told us without multiple corroboration.

Terrell's main gripes with the contras were the "class separation"—the social chasm between the poorly fed peasant fighters and the pampered commander corps—and the brutality. U.S. officials "were trying to portray the Sandinistas as killers when the contras were slaughtering people like hogs," Terrell told me. "It was like living in a slaughterhouse. They [the contras] would bring in the people who were 'fleeing from communism' sometimes in handcuffs. They would take away their shoes and beat them with canes. They would go through their clothing. One old man—they had found a newspaper article folded up in his pocket that mentioned the Sandinistas. They said these were his 'Sandinista credentials.' They made him dig his own grave and then they stuck him in the neck to kill him. They said, 'We have to find a way to stop infiltrators.' This sixty-eight-year-old man, they murdered him as an example. He was too old to fight."

Other times, Terrell said he witnessed killings by the contras that "were almost ritualistic." One method, he said, was called a "Colombian necktie," where the victim's throat is cut open and his tongue is pulled through the opening. To carry out these executions and save ammunition, Terrell said the *comandantes* were issued high-quality K/Bar knives.

Terrell even admitted taking part in one mass execution, the close-quarter shooting of a half-dozen captured Sandinista soldiers. "The oldest one couldn't have been eighteen years old," he said. "It sickened me. I still have nightmares about it. I'll never forget the gun going off, the bone chips and blood hitting me in the face. I ran to a creek and couldn't get the blood off of me." Terrell said he shot the soldiers on orders from the contras and felt he had no choice but to carry out this blood-initiation rite. "Either you did it or you got dead," he offered as an excuse. "It was an incredible stain on my memory."

Terrell also talked about the NSC's secret role, giving orders and arranging the flow of weapons and trainers. Terrell's accounts fit with other information that Barger and I had been receiving from sources inside the administration, other mercenaries, and contacts within the contra movement. But more dangerous to North, Terrell was passing on his information to federal prosecutors in Miami. One team of federal investigators traveled to Terrell's home in New Orleans's French Quarter in early 1986 on the same day we were there interviewing the disaffected mercenary.

To assess and neutralize the threat Terrell posed, North assigned a private operative from his Iran-contra–funded Project Democracy to investigate and entrap the ex–mercenary. The man who got the job was Glenn A. Robinette, an ex–CIA officer who specialized in surveillance techniques. According to North, Robinette was Project Democracy's "security officer." For $4,000 a month, the twenty-year CIA veteran had been working to dig up "dirt" on those causing trouble for the secret operations.

Robinette, who had served in the CIA's technical division, could have passed for a kindly schoolteacher. He had white, thinning hair, a gentle voice and watery eyes. Robinette was the perfect embodiment of one of Smiley's people, le Carré's fictional British spies, quiet intelligence professionals who blend with their surroundings and fade easily from one's memory. Iran-contra investigators accidentally stumbled upon his damage-control work for North when they were looking into other odd payments to the NSC aide. Robinette was called to testify in 1987 only because he was the electronics expert who installed a $13,800 security fence around North's private home. But more importantly to North's apparatus, Robinette ran a mini–Plumbers network to crank down on leaks that were endangering North's secrecy.

When Terrell came to Washington in the spring of 1986 to tell his story to Congress, Robinette contacted the disaffected mercenary, took him out for expensive dinners and proposed a lucrative business venture in Central America. The goal, according to a July 17, 1986, memo written by Robinette and found in North's files, was to mount a "sting" against Terrell that would get him "in hand and somewhat in our control." Through the phony business deals, Robinette hoped to persuade Terrell to keep quiet and stop being "dangerous to our objectives." Terrell, however, said he became suspicious when Robinette mostly pumped him for information about North and Owen. Terrell cut off all contact, but discovered who Robinette really was only when the ex–CIA officer testified in the Iran-contra hearings.

While Robinette may have failed to lure Terrell into the phony business deal, the ex–CIA man still fed derogatory information about Terrell to the FBI, which briefly placed the former mercenary under investigation for a purported threat aginst President Reagan's life. Terrell had allegedly made an ambiguous remark in an intercepted phone conversation that he could "get the president." But even though Terrell and Reagan were both in Miami on July 23, 1986, the FBI found Terrell simply going about his own business. That, however, did not end the probe, which continued into August.

At the White House, North, too, escalated the anti-Terrell activities. In a July 17, 1986, memo to then NSC adviser John Poindexter, North reported that a special unit set up to counter international terrorism was assisting in the Terrell investigation. North said the high-powered Terrorist Incident Working Group (TIWG) had turned over "all information" on Terrell to the FBI. Further, North said the TIWG "operations sub-group" would review an FBI "counter-intelligence, counter-terrorism operations plan" aimed at Terrell. North added that "the FBI now believes that Terrell may well be a paid asset of the Nicaraguan Intelligence Services (DGSE) or another hostile intelligence service. . . . It is interesting to note that Terrell has been part of what appears to be a much larger operation being conducted against our support for the Nicaraguan resistance."

Eleven days later, North wrote a dramatically titled memo "Terrorist Threat: Terrell," which was initialed as read by President Reagan. In that July 28, 1986, memo, North suggested that Terrell was being targeted for his extraordinary treatment not because of any criminal violation, but because he had publicly criticized the contras and North's network.

The memo cited Terrell's "anti-contra and anti-U.S. activities," accusing him of becoming "an active participant in the disinformation/active measures campaign against the Nicaraguan Democratic Resistance. Terrell has appeared on various television 'documentaries' alleging corruption, human rights abuses, drug running, arms smuggling and assassination attempts by the resistance and their supporters. Terrell is also believed to be involved with various congressional staffs in preparing for hearings and inquiries regarding the role of U.S. government officials in illegally supporting the Nicaraguan resistance."

Of course, much of what Terrell had alleged about contra

abuses turned out to be true. North, in fact, had been receiving similar reports from his own field operative, Robert Owen, who privately told North about contra participation in drug trafficking, torture and other abuses. Owen summed up the contra leadership as "liars and greed and power motivated." But the administration's goal with Terrell was to discredit his information—and then use that positive CW bounce to roll over the few North-related inquiries still standing.

After being placed under federal surveillance, Terrell submitted to two days of polygraph examinations by the FBI and Secret Service in August 1986. Finding no evidence to support North's dark suspicions of a presidential assassination or espionage work, the FBI dropped its investigation. But Terrell told me later that his treatment at the hands of U.S. law-enforcement personnel convinced him to lower his profile. "It burned me up," he said. "The pressure was always there."

North's alarm over Terrell was wildly exaggerated in another way, too. The Washington press corps had already decided not to take the strange ex-mercenary and his charges seriously. Although a few reporters examined Terrell's allegations, most joined in ridiculing him. Around Washington, administration officials and their reporter friends would enjoy mispronouncing his nickname. Instead of "El Flaco" for "the thin man," it became "El Flako" for "the flake." By 1986, the CW in Washington had little patience for oddball characters like Terrell, even when their information was right.

The Terrell case was just one example of administration paranoia, however. For years, the Reagan administration had been hovering on the edge of outright abuse of its police powers, mounting intrusive criminal investigations of foreign-policy critics. Starting in 1981, the FBI launched a major probe of the Committee in Solidarity with the People of El Salvador and other advocacy groups that were challenging U.S. intervention in Central America. Before ending in 1985, the investigation had tasked fifty-two FBI field offices to probe CISPES and 138 related organizations. Generating thousands of pages of reports, the probe examined hazy allegations that CISPES was an illegal foreign agent or had supported international terrorism.*

---

*The Reagan administration deemed the Salvadoran guerrillas a terrorist group and thus any Americans who sympathized with the rebels came under suspicion of aiding and abetting

But some overly enthusiastic FBI agents saw their job more broadly as undercutting political dissidents. One FBI report from Cincinnati, Ohio, on December 14, 1984, made a point of identifying individuals and groups "involved in activities contrary to the foreign policy of the United States in Central America." On March 6, 1984, the Philadelphia FBI office cited twelve organizations "actively involved in demonstrations . . . regarding U.S. intervention in Central America." These groups included the Friends Peace Committee and a hospital workers union.

Another memo from the FBI's New Orleans office, dated November 10, 1983, said, "It is imperative at this time to formulate some plan of attack against CISPES and specifically, against individuals who defiantly display their contempt for the U.S. government by making speeches and propagandizing their cause." Many CISPES members complained that FBI agents would interview their employers or neighbors, creating suspicion around them. Despite five years of investigation, no charges were brought against CISPES or the other organizations.*

U.S. law enforcement targeted anti-contra activists, too. Tasked by the NSC staff, FBI agents subjected more than a hundred Americans to counterintelligence interrogation when they returned from visits to Nicaragua. According to documents released under the Freedom of Information Act, the FBI investigated groups, such as TecNica, which assisted Nicaragua on small development projects.[1]

One former member of North's private network, a far-right security consultant named Philip Mabry, of Fort Worth, Texas, said North advocated a strategy of covertly instigating FBI probes of dissidents. Mabry said that in 1984, North urged him and others to submit requests for FBI investigations of contra opponents.

---

international terrorism. Of course, the White House did not regard the Nicaraguan contras as terrorists, even though they targeted civilians for violent attacks far more often than the Salvadoran guerrillas did. The reason the contras were spared was obvious: if the contras were terrorists, that would make the U.S. government a sponsor of international terrorism.
*The CISPES investigation might have ended differently if the Reagan administration had succeeded in pushing through a new counterterrorism law that it proposed in April 1984. That bill would have given the government the power to jail Americans who assist or "act in concert with" groups or the militaries of governments labeled terrorist by the secretary of state. Although facing up to ten years in prison, American defendants would not have been allowed to challenge the administration's judgment about whether a designated group should have been deemed terrorist. The bill also did not spell out what was meant to "act in concert with." The overreaching legislation died in Congress.

"Ollie told me that if the FBI received letters from five or six unrelated sources all requesting an investigation of the same groups, that would give the Bureau a mandate to go ahead and investigate," Mabry told *The Boston Globe*.[2]

While stirring up trouble for contra critics, North got tips from law-enforcement authorities when investigations started peeking under the edges of his secret network. In a 1987 report to Congress, the FBI acknowledged sending three investigative documents to the NSC for dissemination to North in 1985. The reports dealt with FBI probes of possible Neutrality Act violations by contra supporters who were secretly associated with North.*

The congressional Iran-contra report cited seven cases in which the National Security Council staff succeeded in stopping or delaying probes that threatened to expose North's illegal activities. "These seven episodes collectively show how the NSC staff, and North in particular, tried to prevent exposure of the Enterprise by law enforcement agencies," the report said. "The fault lies with the members of the NSC staff who tried to compromise the independence of law enforcement agencies by misusing claims of national security."[3]

But the evidence actually suggests that senior members of the Justice Department were eager accomplices in the obstruction of these politically embarrassing investigations. Senior Justice Department officials tipped off the NSC when a federal gunrunning probe in Miami began closing in on the White House.

"Please get on top of this," came the worried message from Stephen Trott, then head of the criminal division. "DLJ [Deputy Attorney General D. Lowell Jensen] is giving a heads-up to the NSC." The Justice Department later confirmed that on March 24, 1986, Jensen did brief NSC adviser John Poindexter about the progress on a Miami investigation into gunrunning and other allegations about the contras. Then–department spokesman Terry Eastland insisted, however, that despite the language of the note— about "giving a heads-up"—it was Poindexter who requested "an update on the case."

By the time of the March 24 "heads-up," federal investigators

---

*The Neutrality Act forbids Americans from participating in violent acts against governments with which the United States is not at war.

in Miami had received corroborated allegations of an NSC role in the contra resupply operation. Not only had Terrell spoken with the investigators, but a defense attorney, named John Mattes, had relayed similar charges from one of his clients and from two other mercenaries, Steven Carr and Peter Glibbery, jailed in Costa Rica. Carr and Glibbery had claimed their operation was receiving $10,000 a month from the NSC. Mattes said he was told by the FBI that his account and a six-page telex on Terrell's allegations had been forwarded to Washington.

Later in March, Jeffrey Feldman, the assistant U.S. attorney assigned to the case, flew to Costa Rica to interview participants in North's network himself—and he quickly put together the pieces. His discussions with U.S. ambassador Lewis Tambs and CIA station chief Joe Fernandez, who was secretly advising the contra resupply operation, were promptly reported back to North. Iran-contra investigators would later learn that Fernandez was communicating regularly with North over a top secret KL-43 encoding device that can send secure messages over regular telephone lines.*

One message went via North's private courier, Robert Owen, who in an April 7, 1986, memo told North that Feldman had outlined a contra support network headed by North. "Feldman looks to be wanting to build a career on this case," Owen told North. "He even showed . . . the Ambassador a diagram with your name underneath and John [Hull]'s underneath mine, then a line connecting the various resistance groups in C.R. [Costa Rica]. Feldman stated they were looking at the 'big picture' and not only looking at a possible violation of the neutrality act, but a possible unauthorized use of government funds."

Remarkably, eight months before the official Iran-contra disclosures, Feldman had outlined the actual line of authority from the White House to the field. But his investigation never went much further. On April 4, after Feldman returned from Costa Rica, another assistant U.S. attorney, David Leiwant, claimed to overhear Miami's U.S. attorney Leon Kellner saying he had been told to "go slow" on the probe because of upcoming congressional votes—an assertion that Kellner and other of his aides denied.

---

*Fernandez's federal indictment for lying to official investigators about his contra role was dismissed in 1990 after the Bush administration refused to declassify documents that Fernandez's lawyers had demanded for his defense.

Attorney General Edwin Meese III also discussed the case with Kellner during a trip to Miami, but Kellner denied that Meese pressured him to drop the investigation.

In mid-April, on the AP wire, Barger and I reported the existence of the Miami probe. Kellner angrily attacked the accuracy of our article, as did the Justice Department. Meese spokesman Patrick Korten dismissed the investigation story, claiming to *The New York Times* that "various bits of information got referred to us. We ran them all down and didn't find anything. It comes to nothing."[4]

Amid these public knockdowns, prosecutor Feldman and local FBI investigators continued to plod ahead with their probe. On May 14, 1986, Feldman recommended to his superiors that the evidence of gunrunning and mercenary training was strong enough to take the case to a grand jury. Kellner scribbled on the memo, "I concur that we have sufficient evidence to ask for a grand jury investigation."

However, on May 20, a meeting of senior officials of the U.S. attorney's office in Miami reversed the memo's findings. Its conclusion was rewritten to say that "a grand jury investigation at this point would represent a fishing expedition with little prospect that it would bear fruit." On June 3, still bearing the May 14 date and initialed by Kellner for Feldman, the memo was sent to the Justice Department. Feldman told me later that he had not concurred in the changes. The revised prosecutorial memo was slipped to congressional Republicans, who used it to discredit Senator John Kerry and the few questioners still inquiring about North's network.

In Miami, the case languished over the summer. Feldman was reassigned to a case that took him to Thailand and the promised follow-up work made little headway. A grand jury was not convened until after North's operations came crashing down in October when one of the supply planes was shot down over the jungles of Nicaragua. When indictments were finally brought for Neutrality Act violations, those charged included Jack Terrell and other whistleblowers who had pointed out the bigger scandal years earlier. Eventually, a federal judge threw out even those charges, observing, understandably, that the U.S. government did, indeed, seem to be at war with Nicaragua. The case against Terrell was dismissed.

It was to be one of the last flights of Oliver North's little air force of broken-down planes and burnt-out pilots. After skirting

Nicaragua's west coast, the C-123 cargo plane, laden with assault rifles and ammunition, sliced inland over Costa Rica's rugged jungles and up into Nicaragua.

There, on October 5, 1986, a sleepy Sunday morning, a teenage Sandinista draftee aimed a surface-to-air missile at the plane. He fired and watched mesmerized as the missile soared into the sky, right at its target. The missile struck near an engine below the wing, spinning the doomed plane wildly out of control. On board, an unemployed Wisconsin construction worker and onetime CIA cargo handler named Eugene Hasenfus struggled to the open cargo door. Somehow he pulled his way through the opening, pushed himself clear of the plane and parachuted safely to earth. He was the only survivor of the four-person crew.

One of the first names out of Hasenfus's mouth when he was brought before the international press in Managua three days later was "Max Gomez," who, Hasenfus said, was a CIA man running the air resupply operation out of Ilopango air base in El Salvador. Gomez had often boasted of his close ties to the office of Vice-President George Bush, Hasenfus said.

The Reagan administration scrambled to put together a public response to the story. North was traveling in Europe on the Iran project, and one source at a White House meeting told me there was confusion about how categorical to make the cover story. But still cocky after all these years with the CW on its side, the administration chose to flatly deny Hasenfus's allegation. President Reagan, Vice-President Bush and a host of subordinates insisted that there was "no U.S. government connection" to the downed flight.

In a classic display of the administration's CW arrogance, Assistant Secretary of State Elliott Abrams even went on television to dispute the existence of "Max Gomez." Appearing on a CNN show, Abrams told hosts/columnists Rowland Evans and Robert Novak that "I can say first of all there's no Max Gomez."[5] It was one of those narrowly constructed deceptions that must have thrilled Abrams.

But as a measure of how the pro-contra CW had gulled the press, the two battle-tested columnists swallowed Abrams's story whole. "I've seen a lot of cover-ups in this town, Rowland," Novak noted sagely, "but this doesn't look like a cover-up, and it doesn't because there's no equivocation. . . . The so-called Max Gomez, the CIA operative, supposedly hired by the CIA or Vice-President

Bush, doesn't even exist." But Max Gomez did exist, as Abrams knew full well. Only his real name was Felix Rodriguez, a CIA veteran who had, in fact, been placed in Central America by the office of Vice-President George Bush.

The crash of Hasenfus's plane and the documents found on board would end, finally, the secrecy around Ollie North's network. The explosive event would shock the CW into considering the possibility that the whacko stories about North that had been officially dismissed and ridiculed for more than a year might not have been so crazy after all. Abrams and associates worked overtime to save the old CW, but Washington was shaking itself awake after a long sleep of self-delusion.

Even *The New Republic*, the bastion of the administration's pro-contra CW, had begun to open its eyes to the reality that had been passing by all around it. At the urging of *New Republic* editor Jefferson Morley and reporter Murray Waas, the magazine even accepted a cover story from Brian Barger and me. The cover drawing showed a long shadow from the White House stretching down to Nicaragua. The title read: "The Secret Contra War: How the White House Planned It, Ran It and Hid It."

The article began, "The crash of an arms-laden cargo plane in southern Nicaragua on October 5 exposed more than an operation mounted by private American mercenaries or, as one critic put it, by ex–CIA men with 'a wink and a nod' from the U.S. government. It brought into sudden focus a highly covert paramilitary network of former intelligence operatives working for the White House. The secret organization was set up by Reagan administration officials in early 1984 and enabled the White House to circumvent a congressional ban against 'directly or indirectly' aiding the contra rebels fighting to overthrow the government of Nicaragua. It was a shadow CIA—hidden from Congress, unaccountable to the American public, and answering only to the White House."[6]

The *New Republic* story threw Abrams into a frenzy. He had been betrayed by the publication that he may have trusted most, and he wrote an angry "Dear Marty" letter on November 10, 1986, to *The New Republic*'s publisher, Martin Peretz. "The cover story in your issue of November 24* is astonishing. First, it violates the

---

*Magazines always date their issues a week or more ahead so they will not seem too stale on the newsstands.

elementary rules of journalism. 'A U.S. official confirmed.' 'One prominent rebel official said.' 'One U.S. official also said.' 'One American arms dealer said.' Whatever happened to the idea of corroboration? Second, the article is filled with innuendo."

After citing several specific criticisms, Abrams berated Peretz for the magazine's inconsistency. "Your [pro-contra] editorials on Central America must shock your readers, for they are totally contradicted by numerous articles on the subject printed in *The New Republic*. Like the one in the Nov. 24 issue, these articles misinform, employ innuendo, and cite no sources or facts which can be verified. I do not subscribe to *The Nation* because I cannot abide this kind of journalism. While you are permitting it in your pages, and indeed promoting it in cover stories, please delete my name from your subscriber list."

Abrams's rearguard attack to protect the secrecy of the North network was a textbook example of CW defensive strategy. Finding that some Washington reporters would no longer accept assurances like "there's no Max Gomez," Abrams mixed outrage with arm-waving tirades against minor points in the story. He apparently hoped Peretz, already on board ideologically, would simply side with him, rather than examine the details of the article, which takes time and energy.

The assistant secretary of state's first complaint, for instance, hammered us for this indiscretion: "The GAO [congressional General Accounting Office] did not say half the $27 million [in nonlethal assistance in 1985] could not be tracked but rather that they could not track it—a rather large distinction and the result of the fact that they have no access to covert operations." Abrams's semantical distinction was neither large nor significant, but it also begged another question: why would an openly approved, "humanitarian" aid package need to be financed in secret? The answer was that the package was never intended to be covert, there was no reason for it to be secret, and the "covert operations" dodge was simply an excuse for a program that had experienced widespread, embarrassing abuse, including contras submitting false receipts and using the money to buy weapons.

His second point showed off another CW-tested technique for discrediting unfriendly news stories: pretend they say something they never said. Abrams wrote: "The GAO did not discover the diversion of $15,000 [of nonlethal aid to buy weapons]—we did."

But again, this tactic trusts that the publisher or editor will be too lazy to reread the story. If Peretz had, he would have seen that the offending sentence read: "A draft GAO audit has also concluded that $15,000 earmarked for the purchase of clothes for Indian rebels based in Costa Rica was diverted to buy ammunition." We didn't say who originally discovered the misuse of funds.

Thirdly, Abrams insisted that the administration had been honest with the American people about the contra drug charges. "As to drug charges against Pastora's forces, this is hardly something we have been unaware of or covering up," the assistant secretary wrote. "We made those charges." Abrams may have momentarily forgotten who had written the *New Republic* story. Barger and I had been the first ones to disclose publicly the problem of contra drug trafficking—and we were initially trashed by the State Department and others in the administration. On the day our story moved on the AP wires in December 1985, State Department spokesman Charles Redman said the department was "not aware of any evidence to support those charges."

But Abrams's letter and his long cozy relationship with the *New Republic*'s management would still have an impact at the magazine. His complaint soured Peretz's relations with Waas and Morley. Waas would almost immediately be dropped as a writer for the magazine, a move he blames on his role brokering the North article. Morley would leave as an editor in the months ahead, taking an editing job at the still-liberal *Nation* magazine.

But while Waas and Morley saw their careers suffer for getting at the truth, those writers and columnists who had missed a historic story that happened almost literally under their noses—Morton Kondracke, Fred Barnes and Charles Krauthammer—would go on to fame and fortune as respected Washington pundits. And *The New Republic* would resume its CW-setting role on behalf of American interventionism.

The Reagan propaganda team had long ago learned that reality and logic were superfluous to a successful CW campaign. But as Abrams fought to keep the secrets in fall 1986, for once his bullying tactics would not be enough. Despite Abrams's valiant efforts, the conventional wisdom was in for an even bigger shake-up.

16

□

CW, Breakthrough and Cover-up Redux

□

One of the AP's office assistants, a pained expression on his face, approached my desk. I had been on the phone and a slightly abusive caller was demanding that the switchboard let him through to my line. The caller's name was Andy Messing, the office assistant said. By that fall day in 1986, I had known Messing for four years. A conservative activist and expert on insurgent wars, Messing had made a point of getting to know the press despite his deep ideological suspicions. Over time, we had become friendly.

Messing struck many in CW-dominated Washington as a showboat who raised money for his conservative foundation by hyping tales about his adventures in Third World war zones. To me, however, the solidly built Vietnam War veteran seemed sincere, almost boyish, about his goal of winning the hearts and minds of Salvadorans, Filipinos or other unhappy residents of nations in conflict. He possessed an infectious enthusiasm for his mission of delivering food and medicines to citizens being tempted by the utopian promises of communist guerrillas.

While often loud and sometimes crude, Messing was a fun-loving, beer-drinking soul, a refreshing contrast to the chablis-sipping, gray-suited ranks of Washington insider-wannabes. In Messing's lexicon, those people were, simply put, "dickheads." Messing had another edge over those nouvelle power brokers who would pontificate at fancy dinner parties or on TV chat shows about the latest theories on counterinsurgency warfare: Messing was truly an insider in the decade's most dramatic foreign-policy action.

Messing was an initiate in Oliver North's closed cloister of activist anticommunists. North, Messing would tell me, "was at the cutting edge of the Reagan Doctrine. Reagan talked about anticommunism, but . . . it was Ollie North who put meat on the bones of rhetoric." Through Messing, I found that I could keep track of North's thinking on Central America and a variety of other international hot spots. Although careful about keeping secrets, Messing was such a devoted North apostle that he could be trusted to spread the master's policy gospel about what needed to be done without adulteration.*

Messing's voice that fall morning conveyed an urgency bordering on panic. "They've hosed Ollie," Messing said. National Security Council adviser John Poindexter was also out. For a moment, I lost my breath at the news. It had been clear for weeks that a crisis had been building in the White House after the October 5 shootdown of a contra supply plane and the November 3 disclosure in a Beirut weekly newspaper of President Reagan's secret trading of arms for hostages. But Messing's urgent message meant that the White House bloodletting had begun. I peppered Messing with questions about how and why, but Messing insisted he knew little more and advised simply, "Call Fawn."

The names Ollie and Fawn had yet to become household words across America, but to those of us who had followed the White House intrigue in Central America, the names had the familiarity that police investigators might feel toward the subjects of a long, frustrating investigation. Indeed, Messing once told me that North would compare my pursuit of his secret network to the old-time TV series *The Fugitive,* in which a plodding police detective single-mindedly chases a wrongly accused man week in and week out. In the show's last episode, the fugitive, played by the handsome David Janssen, is vindicated. He had been innocent all along. In North's mind, of course, I was the detective and he was David Janssen.

After hanging up with Messing, I called the direct line to Oliver

---

*North also shared a mutual admiration with air force major general Edward G. Lansdale, the legendary "Ugly American" who pioneered psy-war tactics while working for the CIA in the Philippines and Vietnam in the 1950's and 1960's. In an interview with me before his death, Lansdale praised North for "trying to help in different places." The two met in 1985, at a lunch arranged by Messing. North brought a copy of Lansdale's autobiography, *In the Midst of War,* and asked the renowned covert-ops man to sign it. Messing said it was like watching "Lansdale Sr. and Lansdale Jr."

North's NSC office. North's secretary, Fawn Hall, answered. Her voice was quavering. She seemed to have lost her normal composure. I had met Fawn only once, several months earlier, while visiting a bar called Portner's in Old Town Alexandria with Messing. She had been sitting with a woman friend at one of those high tables that are common in up-scale bars. She seemed startled when Messing introduced me to her, but was coolly polite, agreeing to let Messing and me join her for a drink.

A long-legged, pretty blonde, Fawn Hall would step forward as the sex symbol for the Iran-contra affair. Her romance with a handsome contra leader would be the talk of the tabloids, but she would be best remembered for blurting out the arrogant leitmotiv of the scandal: "Sometimes you have to go above the written law." After a half hour of small talk at the bar, she and her friend left and climbed into a red Fiero sports car. The vanity plate read, simply, "FAWN." But when I reached Fawn that morning of November 25, 1986, she was not the haughty young woman I had met in Portner's. She was hesitant, flustered. Haltingly she confirmed Messing's account.

It was mornings like this one that made work at the Associated Press almost worth the many frustrations. The nation's largest wire service sent out a steady stream of stories to thousands of newspapers and broadcast outlets around the country and the world. It dealt best with urgency, putting out bits and pieces of a breaking story as the overall picture came mosaiclike into view. AP careers are often made or broken by how a staffer handles an emergency like a plane crash or a natural disaster. In Washington, the AP bureau's last resident hero was Walter Mears, who won the Pulitzer Prize in 1976 for speed-typing leads on the major stories of that presidential election campaign.* Modestly, Mears would liken his skill to a "parlor trick," but admiration for his work among AP reporters was like the respect test pilots in the late 1950's felt for the peerless Chuck Yeager. What is most important in filing an AP bulletin series, as it is in keeping an experimental jet under control, is never to panic. The consequences of screwing up, of course, are different. At AP, only your career would go down in flames.

---

*Mears was famous for getting the key new elements of a political event into the lead, or top paragraph. Reporters for other news outlets would often check on Mears's lead before filing their own stories, out of fear that they would get callbacks from their editors for going with an opening paragraph different than the one Mears had.

With the few pieces we had about the White House firings, the AP moved out a series of urgent stories. They focused on the reported departure of NSC adviser John Poindexter, the pipe-smoking admiral who was the top-ranked casualty of the morning. The firing of the then-little-known North was a secondary angle. There was also the presumption that the dismissals were tied to the still-emerging furor over the secret sale of weapons to the radical Islamic government of Iran.

In a brief argument at the AP desk, I insisted that we include North's role as White House point man for private assistance to the Nicaraguan contras. The discussion seemed like a minor point at the time, but I had long bristled at the Washington CW, which dismissed North's contra activities as of little consequence. I had also begun to suspect over the previous weekend that money generated from the Iranian arms sales might have gone to the contras—a suspicion that arose from the odd crossover relationships between the principal figures in the Iran deal and those in the contra resupply operation. My suspicion had prompted me to call two well-placed intelligence sources. Both treated my query as if it were evidence that I had finally gone over the edge.

As the day's events unfolded, the Poindexter-North story was repeatedly "written-thru"—AP talk for substantially redoing a story after more facts become known and a new lead or top is put on the article. President Reagan was expected to make an announcement around noon, requiring even more new leads. By then, some of the fog over what was happening should have lifted.

When Reagan did finally appear in the White House press room, he looked stricken and suddenly old, as if some terrible event had finally pierced his actor's detachment. At the AP General Desk, knots of reporters and editors stopped the constant tapping of computer keys to watch the television sets positioned around the office, like monitors on the outside world. It might not have been immediately apparent, but Ronald Reagan's dominance of the Washington CW, which he had ruled like a personal feifdom for six years, was about to end.

As expected, Reagan announced the departures of Poindexter and North. He then abruptly turned the news conference over to his longtime confidant, Attorney General Edwin Meese III. The two men crossed as Reagan left the press room and Meese stepped to the podium. Meese looked oddly jovial. The president looked in pain. The attorney general got quickly to the point. He described a brief investigation that he and some of his top aides had conducted into the Iranian arms sales. They had discovered, he said, that some of the proceeds from the clandestine weapons deals had been diverted to Central America. Meese said the only officials who knew about the diversion were North and Poindexter.

Though Washington prides itself as a city where historic events are taken in stride, there are only a few genuinely exciting news moments, events that are not choreographed and stage-managed. Meese's announcement qualified as one of them. Involuntarily, I slapped my hand to my forehead and exclaimed, "Holy shit, these people are crazier than I ever thought." In that dizzying moment, I felt what investigative reporters perhaps cherish most: that rush of adrenaline, the exhilaration when a story checks out. A story that I had pursued for what seemed like an eternity, in the face of widespread skepticism and disturbing internal resistance from AP editors, had checked out.

But one of the healthy sides of wire-service journalism is that it never gives you time to gloat. There are always new demands for compiling a new set of facts, packaging it into story form and rushing it out onto the wire. Meese's news conference had come as such a shock that even the normally unflappable AP desk editors were flustered. But a new write-thru was quickly cobbled together and sent out over the wires to the nation's newspapers.

There are few journalistic pleasures greater in today's Washington than pushing around the CW. As much as the White House and the PR specialists have learned about manipulating the CW to mesmerize the Washington press corps and, through it, the American public, journalists can still change the CW by determinedly exposing the truth. The great journalists, like Seymour Hersh, have built their careers around their ability to change the way the rest of us look at a historic event. Hersh's ground-breaking exposés, from the My Lai massacre to Noriega's drug taint, have forced the CW to shift perceptibly closer to the truth.

But just as Elliott Abrams covered the administration's hasty retreat after the Hasenfus plane was shot down, the White House sought to contain and limit the damage from the Iran-contra diversion disclosure. North would later describe that cover-up strategy as the "fall-guy plan." He would testify to Congress that CIA

director William Casey had decided that North and his boss, Poindexter, would have to be tossed overboard to save the rest of the
crew. They, along with ex–NSC chief Robert McFarlane, were
the preordained candidates to take the blame. As it would turn out,
Casey, who collapsed in December 1986 suffering from terminal
brain cancer, would also serve as a convenient scapegoat as he lay
on his deathbed.

But rarely has a cover story been so openly discussed by the
participants—and still been believed. "There was always a need
for cover to explain that which people could see," North's NSC
assistant Robert Earl told Iran-contra investigators, "so that the
covert operation would not be blown by the press or somebody else
stumbling onto something and not having a plausible explanation
to make it go away."[1] In other words, CW-shaping needed to take
into account what would happen if reality got in the way.

"You have to have an explanation for what you're doing that
does not give away that which you are attempting to keep secret,"
Earl continued. Some compartments of an operation might have
to be sacrificed to save other compartments.

Earl described three phases of a "damage control operation."
The first two phases went from "no comment" to "where possible,
some sort of cryptic, artful truth" to "deny it if there's no other
way." But the overriding responsibility was "to protect the compartment" at all costs. Besides denials to the press, Earl said these
tactics led to preparation of an early Iran-contra chronology and
testimony to Congress, both of which were later found to be false
and misleading.

"Phase three is what I believe we were now in [when the Iran-
contra scandal exploded in November 1986], which was termination
of the compartment," the Marine lieutenant colonel said. That
phase included shredding documents so the compartment's inner
boxes could still be protected. Earl said the clean-up required
destroying "all the sensitive, all the inner boxes, not the total box
that had already been briefed to Congress, but the sensitive material
within the box within the box within the box, however far it went."[2]
As the Iran-contra scandal unraveled in mid-November 1986, Earl
recalls North shredding secret documents and steeling himself to
take the fall. "It's time for North to be the scapegoat," Earl recalled
North saying. "Ollie has been designated the scapegoat."[3]

But how successful the White House damage control would

be was still in question. At first, the strategy even sought to protect the existence of the long-running secret White House network to resupply the contras. At his news conference, Attorney General Meese tried to pin the blame for transferring Iran profits to the contras on the Israelis. And even then, the Iran-contra diversion was to be sold as an anomaly, one desperate grab for money, not part of a larger fund-raising apparatus. A senior investigator on the presidentially appointed Tower Commission told me that the three-member board had tentatively decided that there had been no contra support network run out of the White House. But in January 1987, the surprise discovery of hundreds of PROFS computer messages spread the scandal further. The pouring forth of the computer give-and-take established the existence of North's network beyond a doubt and forced the commission to ask for a month's delay to graft the new evidence onto its final report.

In those early months of the scandal, the Washington press corps, awakened from its long CW-induced sleep, arose to demonstrate more aggressiveness than it had for years. North's shredding of documents was uncovered by *The Los Angeles Times*. *The Washington Post* devoted major space to the scandal. So did *The New York Times*.

Two of my stories also pushed the edges of the story along. On January 7, 1987, even as the Tower board was doubting the existence of the contra support operation, the AP wire moved this lead: "Lt. Col. Oliver L. North, while overseeing a network to assist Nicarguan rebels the past two years, managed cash and other funds out of his National Security Council office to pay for contra expenses, according to sources in the administration and the aid network. One well-placed administration official said that around 'Christmastime 1984,' North even used his office safe to store cash which North said was 'for the contras.' "[4]

Another of my AP stories jumped the firebreak that was being built around the CIA. "The Central Intelligence Agency, acknowledging that one of its officers helped funnel weapons to the Nicaraguan rebels despite a congressional ban, is forcing the station chief in Costa Rica to accept early retirement, intelligence sources said," a February 1, 1987 story reported. "The sources, insisting on anonymity, also said the station chief sent secret messages to then White House aide Oliver L. North and to the aid network over sophisticated encoding devices that North obtained from the National Security Agency, the U.S. government's top-secret communications arm."[5] The facts, spilling out from the administration's chaotic finger-pointing, were inching the CW closer to reality.

But the story about the CIA's Costa Rican station chief Joe Fernandez helping the North operation would be my last at the AP. Still disturbed by the events of the spring and summer, I accepted a job as correspondent for *Newsweek* magazine, which was beefing up its coverage of what would likely be a hot story for some months to come. At *Newsweek*, though, I would discover that the CW supporting the Reagan intervention in Central America was more deeply rooted than I had understood. Too many important figures in the upper echelons of American politics and journalism had committed themselves to the rightness of the cause. These were not men and women who readily admitted error.

The asparagus was cooked just right. I would come to expect as much from these delightfully catered dinners where *Newsweek* executives and correspondents engaged in friendly sparring with news makers. The nonadversarial tone matched the light and delicate dinner fare. Dinner might start with an artichoke salad, then a main course of fish or chicken covered by a fine white sauce. Dessert would be appealing to the eye but have an understated flavor suggesting no excess calories. Throughout the meal, a tuxedoed waiter would move starchily around the dinner table, serving food and tending to empty wineglasses.

This dinner on March 10, 1987, was only my second at *Newsweek*, so this social hobnobbing with Washington's powerful was alien and rather curious to me. I had joined the magazine a month earlier after almost thirteen years at the AP. While both important news outlets, *Newsweek* and AP are stark contrasts. *Newsweek* has glitz and glamour; the AP doesn't.

The AP is an everyman's news company, staffed by overworked and underpaid reporters and editors who, by and large, missed out on the name colleges. Most dress unfashionably and live in the less expensive Washington suburbs. There's always something downtrodden and unappreciated about AP staffers, possibly from the long hours, rotten night shifts, constantly ringing telephones and the incredible pressure of filing bulletin series when a fast-breaking news story hits.

Newsweek, particularly at its upper reaches, has a dilettantish air. Ivy League educations are preferable, pleated pants the norm, and long years in the trenches of tough daily journalism not required. *Newsweek*'s top executives tend to be tall, patrician, socially agile. Some inside the magazine contend that the small oligarchy of most senior editors—known as the Wallendas—are most adept at traversing the magazine's high wire without falling from the favored graces of the matriarch of the *Newsweek–Washington Post* family, Katharine Graham. Stylistically, too, *Newsweek* and AP are polar opposites. *Newsweek* prizes clever writing, sometimes even over substance, while AP's prose is careful and workmanlike.

So when I settled into my chair at a crowded dinner table at the elegant home of *Newsweek*'s Washington bureau chief, I was still getting to know my new professional surroundings. Around the table were *Newsweek*'s well-bred top brass, a few reporters and two guests of honor: General Brent Scowcroft (ret.), who had been one of three members of the Tower Commission, and Congressman Dick Cheney, who was to be the ranking House Republican on the congressional Iran-contra committee. Both had served in Gerald Ford's White House—Scowcroft as NSC adviser and Cheney as chief of staff. The CW on the pair was that these were two men of the Establishment who could be counted on for intelligence and integrity.

The Tower Commission had just completed its work and was receiving hosannas around Washington for meting out what was considered surprisingly tough criticism of President Reagan. The scandal had been a "failure of responsibility," the three-member panel had found. "The NSC system will not work unless the President makes it work."[6] The board even made a pointed reference to Reagan's laissez-faire approach to governance: "The President's management style is to put the principal responsibility for policy review and implementation on the shoulders of his advisers."

After gently biting the hand that had appointed it, the board laid the primary blame for the Iran-contra disaster at the feet of the president's subordinates: the zealous Oliver North, the enigmatic John Poindexter, the Valium-swallowing Robert McFarlane, the near-dead William Casey, and the president's bombastic chief of staff, Donald Regan.

While chastising Reagan for failing to "have ensured that the NSC system did not fail him," the Tower board accepted Reagan's assurances that he knew nothing about North's efforts to direct military aid to the contra rebels and that he had no hand in the clumsy White House cover-up. "The Board found evidence that immediately following the public disclosure, the President wanted to avoid providing too much specificity or detail out of concern for the hostages still held in Lebanon and those Iranians who had supported the initiative," the report said, understandingly. "In doing so, he did not, we believe, intend to mislead the American public or cover-up unlawful conduct. . . . The Board is convinced that the President does indeed want the full story to be told."[7]

Many of the board's conclusions would later be shown to be woefully off target. Reagan himself would acknowledge several months later that the contra-aid scheme was "my idea to begin with" and North's trial in 1989 would demonstrate clearly that the president was an active player in arranging the contras' money and ensuring the delivery of supplies. Instead of wanting "the full story to be told," Reagan would resist demands for his testimony from his subordinates, North and Poindexter, when they were tried on criminal charges. Finally, in 1990, compelled to testify in the Poindexter case, the aging president affably fended off questions about his knowledge and even returned to out-of-date cover stories that he had already admitted were false.*

The Tower board's findings also meshed neatly with an original draft for Chief of Staff Regan's "plan of action" to contain the scandal's damage. Even before the diversion was disclosed, the plan's first draft recommended that "tough as it seems, blame must be put at NSC's door—rogue operation, going on without President's knowledge or sanction. When suspicions arose he took charge, ordered investigation, had meeting with top advisers to get at facts, and find out who knew what. Try to make the best of a sensational story. Anticipate charges of 'out of control,' 'President doesn't know what's going on,' 'Who's in charge,' . . . Try to get answers to such charges in advance." Although the proposal for putting blame "at NSC door" was crossed out of a later version, the draft plan was essentially implemented.

---

*Reagan insisted, for instance, that the deal with Iran was not "arms for hostages," although he had admitted three years earlier, on March 4, 1987, that "what began as a strategic opening to Iran deteriorated in its implementation into trading arms for hostages." In his Poindexter testimony, Reagan also disputed the existence of a diversion. "I still have never been given one iota of evidence" on the diversion, Reagan said. Prosecutor Dan Webb put the Tower report before the ex-president and cited the board's finding that "there was considerable evidence before the Board of a diversion to support the contras."

But as the main course was served that evening of March 10, the Tower report's shortcomings and how closely they fit with the White House damage-control strategy were on nobody's mind. The Tower board and Brent Scowcroft were the toast of the town. They had come up with a solution to the nasty Iran-contra problem that could please nearly everyone. Reagan, his lazy management style and some overzealous subordinates could take the blame— and official Washington could be spared an ugly constitutional crisis.

The Tower Commission saw the scandal as a failure of individuals, not a case of institutional corruption or a fundamental abuse of power by the executive branch. Even before the congressional hearings had begun, Washington's men of substance were eager to get the unfortunate episode behind them. One could hear the beginning of a new CW: "The country can't stand another Watergate." And after all, respectable men—Scowcroft, former senator John Tower and Jimmy Carter's secretary of state, Edmund Muskie—had sought the truth and reached what appeared to be wise and judicious conclusions.

Scowcroft, a slight, studious-looking man, sat across from me at dinner, and my ears picked up as the retired general began to talk. "Maybe I shouldn't say this, but . . ." started Scowcroft. I paused with my fork partly through cutting a piece of asparagus and looked up. Scowcroft continued, "If I were advising Admiral Poindexter and he *had* told the president about the diversion, I would advise him to say that he hadn't." Now, that was an odd remark from a man who only two weeks earlier had been scouring for the truth about this scandal.

I quietly put down my fork and, not fully cognizant of the etiquette of these affairs, asked with undisguised amazement in my voice: "General, you're not suggesting that the admiral should commit perjury, are you?" But before Scowcroft could answer, *Newsweek* editor Maynard Parker, who had been sitting to my left, tut-tutted my impertinence. "Sometimes," Parker reminded me, "you have to do what's good for the country."

Though presumably a lighthearted way to steer clear of a socially awkward moment, Parker's remark left me speechless. As surprising as I had found Scowcroft's wish that Poindexter should do the right thing and lie, Parker's admonition was even more disturbing, that somehow obscuring the truth and sweeping a major national security scandal under the rug might be "good for the country."

However, the evening was young yet, and I would learn more about my new surroundings before it was over. By the time we had reached dessert, I had been struck by Cheney's partisan hostility toward Democratic plans for pressing the Iran-contra investigation. I was perplexed by Cheney's hard-line attitude, since I had known him for several years and had covered him during a congressional fact-finding trip to Grenada after the U.S. invasion. He had always struck me as a responsible public official who would put the national interests ahead of Republican partisan concerns.

But now there seemed to be developing around the table a CW consensus among these two Republican stalwarts and the *Newsweek* executives that unraveling the scandal further would be irresponsible. As we ventured through a delectable dessert and fresh-brewed coffee, I wanted to know if Cheney would press the White House to come clean despite the political costs. At one point, during a give-and-take on Republican strategy, I asked Cheney, "What will you advise your president to do?" Again, Parker intervened. "It's not 'your president,' " he scolded. "It's 'our president.' " For a new employee at *Newsweek*, this evening surely wasn't going very well. I had not mastered the requisite patriotic togetherness that bonded these journalistic and government movers and shakers.

To many observers, the Iran-contra investigation died with Ollie North's boffo testimony in July 1987—or a week later, when Poindexter actually did say he never told Reagan about the diversion of Iranian arms profits to the contras. Without question, North's compelling personality and no-apologies style threw the committee's bland and boring Democrats into full-scale retreat.

But in my view, the drive to get at the truth ended months earlier, when official Washington reached a consensus—possibly over the clicking of plates and polite dinner conversations like the one on March 10—that the truth was too costly. The Wise Men of the Washington CW judged that the country's self-confidence would be shaken, that pressing ahead would generate acrimony and partisanship—and that, possibly worst of all, their stewardship of the nation's fate might be questioned.

The congressional Iran-contra investigation, like the Tower board, got to the bottom of almost nothing, while quickly boring the public because it set such limited goals. Once the Democrats had accepted the premises for the contra war and once the conflict's dark underbelly was excluded from examination, the American people were certain to tire of the scandal and, indeed, sympathize with the zealous patriots who put their commitment to freedom fighters ahead of their government careers.

The Democrats marched their forces into the Waterloo of North's impassioned testimony by focusing the investigation on such bloodless issues as whether it's ever right to lie to Congress or whether the NSC staff was covered by the Boland Amendment barring military aid to the contras. Looking back, Iran-contra staff investigators contend that Congress deliberately chose to ignore the bigger question of President Reagan's role authorizing an illlegal and extraconstitutional intelligence operation to supply the contras. The reason was fear the investigation would have provoked a governmental crisis. It might not be, in the *Newsweek* dinner formulation, "good for the country."

"We were never given a green light to go at the White House," said Tom Polgar, a former CIA officer who worked on the congressional probe. "The committees had no heart to take action that would lead to impeachment or even talk of impeachment." There was a determination, Polgar told me, that the "*I*-word" never be spoken.

The new CW soon took shape: the Iran-contra scandal was too boring, too complicated, no Watergate. As *Newsweek*'s *CW Watch* cofounder Jonathan Alter would say in 1991, "For some years now, the CW [on Iran-contra] has been, 'Hey, give it a rest, that's history.' Every story about Iran-contra has had trouble making its way in the world because that's a very powerful conventional wisdom."

When *Newsweek* hosted new CIA director William Webster at another dinner in late September 1987, one concern expressed by the *Newsweek* executives was that the lingering scandal should not force major changes in the intelligence community. One senior editor told Webster that the CIA's obligations to inform Congress about its covert actions had gone far enough. "These procedures seem so elaborate and isn't one of the dangers after something like the Iran-contra business that there'll be all sorts of pressures, particularly from Congress but perhaps from the executive himself, to set up new procedures?" the editor asked the CIA chief. But the editor then answered his own question: "These things are self-correcting to a great degree. The publicity, the appointment of someone like yourself." Webster, not surprisingly, agreed.

In October 1987, when the congressional Iran-contra report was issued, Washington bureau chief Evan Thomas said *Newsweek*'s New York editors were not interested in doing much on it. "We don't want more than two sentences on the report," Thomas told me as we walked to the elevators outside the office. A story would be done only if we could find something new that the report had missed, he said. As it turned out, *Newsweek* devoted three columns—or one page—to a piece on the report, but the focus was on new pressures building for Attorney General Meese's resignation.

A strong anti–Iran-contra CW had taken shape even earlier in 1987, ruling out a thorough examination into the contra war's brutality, its criminality and the president's responsibility. The Scowcroft-Cheney dinner disabused me of a belief I had once held while pursuing the North story for the AP—that once the official investigations started, the truth would be told. It was suddenly clear to me that the Republicans' chief goal would still be manipulating the CW to limit the damage to the Reagan presidency. It was equally clear that influential sectors of the news media, including the magazine I worked at, would go along.

The dinner seemed like a way for Scowcroft and Cheney to test-market a damage-control strategy with an important media group. The new cover story, blaming North and his zealous friends, would be transformed into the new CW. If that was the Scowcroft-Cheney goal, they must have finished sipping their coffee and headed out the door into the late-winter air believing that their job would be much easier than they had any right to expect.

Although the Iran-contra scandal was a shock to the CW system, it failed to change Washington's overriding attitudes toward Central America. The Sandinistas remained the CW's hated enemies, and the contras were seen as bumbling and brutal but still America's boys. The "public diplomacy" apparatus survived the Iran-contra hearings, battered but unbroken. And the restyled Reagan administration continued to push for contra aid.

When Congress again considered contra money in December 1987, the State Department "public diplomacy" team pulled another defector out of the hat. This time, the defector was a former major, Roger Miranda, and his story was that the Sandinistas were building an offensive military force to dominate the region and were importing those famous MiG-21's from Moscow. Although the Washington press had seen the trick before, it still fell for it.

Like earlier defectors, Miranda was unveiled before a select group of journalists, key documents were withheld until the media frenzy had built, and the few dissenting press voices then were shouted down. Front-page headlines accepted the administration's information and let the State Department control the spin. Congress, too, panicked, denouncing the Sandinistas in a stampede of outrage. The White House got the $8.1 million for the contras that it had wanted. It was as if the press and Congress had learned nothing from the Iran-contra affair and the administration's long record of media manipulation.

This time, administration hard-liners concentrated press attention on Miranda's claim that the Sandinistas planned to build an "army" of 500,000 to 600,000 men. That would have enlisted virtually every able-bodied man in the country of about two million. The Sandinistas responded that their aim indeed was to give rudimentary training to the country's male population, but the purpose of handing out rifles to Nicaraguan citizens was to deter a feared American invasion, not roam up and down the isthmus.

When Miranda's supporting documents were finally released, they showed that nearly 90 percent of the Nicaraguan force would, in fact, be civilian militia. The active-duty armed forces might actually decline under the military plans, going from 80,000 at the time to between 70,000 to 80,000 by the mid-1990's. Miranda also could not explain why, if the Sandinistas were so unpopular, they would want to give every able-bodied man a rifle.

Also widely overlooked in the Miranda scare was the defensive nature of the Nicaraguan military force. The defector's secret documents stated that the reason for the preparations was to "more convincingly avert the possibility of a direct invasion by American troops." Even Miranda acknowledged the defensive nature of the militia force, but that did not stop a Pentagon official, while briefing the press, to warn that if contra aid were killed, the Sandinista army could rumble unchecked down the Pan American Highway all the way to the Panama Canal. I asked the briefer if he thought, maybe, "the 82nd Airborne might not show up."*

But Miranda was the last gasp for the administration's hard-liners, who still wanted to fight the contra war. Regional peace negotiations had continued to stumble forward, getting past one obstacle after another, many laid down by the White House. But by spring 1988, all sides in the Nicaragua struggle in Washington and Central America were exhausted—and the contras were coming apart at the seams.

Contra field commanders were demanding the ouster of long-time strategic commander Enrique Bermudez, whom they called "the Noriega" of the contra movement. Other leaders were squabbling over what was left of the money and power. The contra directorate seemed to be writing a bizarre subrule to Machiavelli's law of political power: the less likely a movement's chances for winning, the more intense the struggle to be in charge. The contras were no closer to capturing Managua than they were seven bloody years earlier.

By the summer of 1988, the administration's interest had shifted to Nicaragua's internal political opposition, which was seen as the U.S. ace in the hole. As the Sandinistas announced increased political freedoms, Washington used its influence over the opposition to spur greater challenges to the nation's political system. That way, if the Sandinistas did nothing, disorder would spread, and if they cracked down, the administration could use that argument to renew contra military aid. Putting the Sandinistas in this vise had always been part of Casey's CIA strategy, but now with a crumbling economy and more U.S. money pouring into the opposition groups, the gambit was beginning to work.

Yet again, it was crucial to the plan that the CIA's covert relationship with Nicaragua's internal opposition be secret, not so much from the Sandinistas, who had detailed intelligence about this thoroughly penetrated operation, but from the American people. The U.S. public would get outraged at Sandinista reprisals against these "independent" groups only if the CIA's hand were kept hidden. Again, the CW and the nation's leading publications cooperated.

The greatest furor erupted in the summer of 1988, when a

---

*Oh yes, by the way, the MiG-21's never did make it to Managua.

spasm of contra ambushes left seventeen Nicaraguans dead. Those attacks were followed by a violent demonstration in the town of Nandaime, a protest rally that the Sandinista police dispersed with tear gas. The government then closed the opposition newspaper *La Prensa* and a Roman Catholic Church radio station, and expelled the American ambassador, Richard Melton, and seven other embassy officials for allegedly coordinating the disorders. The U.S. press and Congress were outraged. The Senate condemned the Sandinista actions, 91–4, and the House did the same, 385–18.

Melton testified before the Senate Intelligence Committee first in secret and then in public session. He found it hard to hide the open secret of Washington—that Nicaragua's internal opposition, like the contras, was getting covert as well as overt help from the U.S. government. When asked by a senator in public session about covert American funding to the opposition, Melton dissembled awkwardly: "As to other activities that might be conducted, that's—they were discussed—that would be discussed yesterday in the closed hearing." When pressed by Senator Howard Metzenbaum on whether the embassy provided "encouragement—financial or otherwise—of dissident elements," Melton responded stiffly: "The ambassador in any post is the principal representative of the U.S. government. And in that capacity, fulfills those functions." He then declined to discuss "activities of an intelligence nature" in open session.

According to more than a dozen sources I have interviewed inside the contra movement or close to U.S. intelligence, the Reagan administration funneled CIA money to virtually every segment of the internal opposition, from the Roman Catholic Church to the newspaper *La Prensa* to business and labor groups to political parties. "We've always had the internal opposition on the CIA payroll," one U.S. government official acknowledged. But the sources said the issue of CIA control is more complicated. Some elements of the opposition will follow U.S. orders, the sources said, but others are funded only to help them carry out anti-Sandinista activities already under way. The CIA's budget line for Nicaraguan political action, separate from contra military operations, was about $10 million a year, the sources said.

For instance, the CIA's support for Cardinal Miguel Obando y Bravo and the Roman Catholic Church was funneled through a maze of cut-outs in Europe, so even Obando would not know precisely where the money had originated, U.S. intelligence sources said. One Nicaraguan exile, however, told me that he had spoken with Obando about the money and the cardinal had expressed the fear that his past receipt of CIA funding would be revealed.

Obando was also skittish about answering *Newsweek*'s questions in June 1987 on his alleged receipt of U.S. money. *Newsweek*'s Central American correspondent Joseph Contreras outlined the queries to the cardinal's aides and then prepared a list of questions based on my information about the payments. When Contreras went to Obando's home in a posh suburb of Managua to deliver the letter, the cardinal literally evaded the issue.

As Contreras waited at the gate, it suddenly swung open and the cardinal, sitting in the front seat of his burgundy Toyota Land Cruiser, blew past the reporter. As Contreras made eye contact with the cleric and waved the letter, Obando's driver gunned the engine. Contreras jumped into his car and hastily followed. Though he had lost sight of the Land Cruiser, Contreras guessed correctly that Obando had turned left at one intersection and headed north toward Managua.

Contreras caught up to the cardinal's vehicle at the first stoplight. The driver apparently spotted the reporter and, as the light changed, sped away, veering from lane to lane. The Land Cruiser again disappeared from view, but at the next intersection, Contreras turned right and spotted the car pulled over, with its occupants presumably hoping that Contreras had turned left. Quickly, the cardinal's vehicle pulled back onto the road and now sped back toward Obando's house. Contreras gave up the chase, fearing that any further pursuit might appear to be harassment.

Several days later, having regained his composure, the cardinal finally met with Contreras. Obando denied receiving any CIA money. But Contreras told me that he had found Obando's denial unconvincing.

The facts, as I had put them together, showed the following: in 1985, congressional oversight committees discovered that the CIA had been covertly sending the church hundreds of thousands of dollars and insisted that the aid be cut off to avoid compromising Obando. But Oliver North picked up where Casey's CIA had been forced to stop. In fall 1985, North earmarked $100,000 of his privately raised money to go to Obando for anti-Sandinista activities.

The *Newsweek* story,[8] though true, was heatedly denounced by pro-contra organizations and the administration's "public diplomacy" team. The story and its ugly aftermath also put me deeper into the *Newsweek* doghouse, even though an internal review reconfirmed the truth of the story. Later, the congressional Iran-contra report referred to $80,000 of a $100,000 payment going to a "humanitarian organization" in Nicaragua in fall 1985.[9] An internal document I obtained from the committee identifies that organization as the Roman Catholic Church.

Similarly, the CIA financed the opposition newspaper, *La Prensa*, during the early years of the contra war, according to a half-dozen U.S. government sources. The CIA paid for printing supplies and even paid salaries. Indeed, the paper and its hostile, anti-Sandinista writings continued for most of the decade, with many of *La Prensa*'s bills picked up by the U.S. government. After creation of the U.S-funded National Endowment for Democracy, *La Prensa* began to receive overt U.S. assistance totaling $250,000 for 1985–86. However, when the Sandinistas closed the paper down after Congress renewed contra military aid in 1986, the CIA again stepped in to pick up salaries during the one-year shutdown, intelligence sources said.

One well-placed source said the CIA-paid salaries included payments to publisher Violeta Chamorro, but Mrs. Chamorro's aides have denied that she received CIA money and, considering the CIA's ability to launder its funds through cut-outs, many recipients have no clear idea who is their original benefactor.

While the CIA's manipulation of Chile's internal politics had been a major story in the 1970's, the CW was disinterested in the far more aggressive use of intelligence powers against Nicaragua in the 1980's. The Sandinistas, after all, wore black hats, and if the contras' hats looked a little soiled, the Washington CW agreed that the internal opposition, as embodied in Violeta Chamorro, was swathed in white from head to toe.

On the morning of February 25, 1990, even Willard Scott, the NBC *Today* show weatherman, was ecstatic about the "wonderful news" down in Nicaragua. The American-supported candidate, *La Prensa*'s publisher Violeta Chamorro, had handily defeated incumbent Nicaraguan president Daniel Ortega. A decade after taking power, when they were cheered by thousands in Managua's central

plaza, the Sandinistas stood defeated, not at the point of contra
guns, but through the ballot box. In Washington, the CW breathed
a contented sigh of relief. Not only was this a happy ending, but
the CW was thoroughly sick and tired of Nicaragua as an issue.

In the days after Violeta Chamorro's stunning victory, Reagan-
Bush administration officials could not resist stepping forward to
take bows for their help in devising the winning game plan. Some
of these strategists told me the Sandinistas' defeat traced back to
an age-old truism that "people vote their pocketbooks." And for
Nicaragua—reduced to near-starvation levels through a combination of American sanctions, the contra war and Sandinista mismanagement—voters had opted for a change. They also apparently
hoped that the United States would replace a decade of hostility
with a friendlier day of generous aid programs.

One of the architects of the economic war against Nicaragua,
former NSC officer Roger Robinson, said the success against the
Sandinistas "will serve as a positive, instructive example of the role
that carefully crafted economic and financial sanctions can play in
the 1990's and the twenty-first century." When President Reagan
imposed maximum economic sanctions against Nicaragua in June
1985, Robinson told me that the hope was that "downgrading Nicaragua's economy could help in bringing a better day for that country."

Another key component of Chamorro's victory, Bush administration officials declared, was their success in pressuring other
countries to curtail economic support of the Sandinistas. A senior
State Department official told me that Secretary of State James
Baker had "burned up the telephone wires" trying to thwart
Ortega's request to European countries in April 1989 for $250 mil-
lion in aid. Ortega returned home with only $20 million in assis-
tance.

Besides undercutting the Sandinistas, the administration had
built up the UNO political coalition* around Mrs. Chamorro. Some
UNO conservatives, especially close to business leader Enrique
Bolanos, even complained that Mrs. Chamorro and her running

*Mrs. Chamorro's UNO coalition, standing for Unión Nacional Opositora—or National
Opposition Union—should not be confused with the contras' UNO, though both used the
acronym matching the Spanish word for "one." Some cynics in the Nicaraguan exile community joked that UNO was possibly the only Spanish word many policy makers in Washington knew.

mate, Virgilio Godoy, were foisted on them by American pressure. Some anti-Sandinista Nicaraguans charged that the U.S. money was the only cement holding the UNO coalition together.

One aide to Alfredo César, a top Chamorro adviser and former contra leader, said César had promised that if UNO followed his lead, "we're going to be swimming in money." According to U.S. and UNO sources, César's faction and the Chamorro campaign received hundreds of thousands of dollars in cash funneled through the Venezuelan government, sometimes arriving in embassy pouches. The money reportedly arrived in at least two tranches, the first totaling about $200,000 delivered to César's supporters in late spring 1989. The second load of $500,000 went through a senior foreign-policy official to the UNO campaign. In an interview with *Newsweek*, César denied receiving any of this money.

American and Venezuelan sources told me that President Bush personally coordinated Venezuelan cooperation through private telephone calls to President Carlos Andres Pérez, who was looking for U.S. help on his country's debt problem. U.S. and Venezuelan government officials confirmed that money was sent to César's group through Venezuela, but they offered different opinions about the funding sources.

Nicaraguan exile sources asserted that the Venezuelan money originated with the CIA, but one senior Bush administration official denied that the agency provided the money. "I have to believe that CAP [Carlos Andres Pérez] has his own resources," the official said. "Alfredo [César] went to Caracas and Madrid and was pleading for money." Andres Pérez also supplied a Venezuelan military plane and crew to fly Mrs. Chamorro to the United States and elsewhere during the campaign.

Whatever the original source of the Venezuelan money, the U.S. government poured in its own millions to influence the outcome of the election. As part of an agreement with Congress to forgo a CIA covert operation inside Nicaragua, the administration settled on a $9 million open fund, disbursed through the National Endowment for Democracy and other channels, to pay for election monitoring and to back the UNO coalition. "The playing field had to be leveled," explained one senior State Department official. "Therefore, UNO at least had to have the minimum resources to compete and be visible and get their message out."

However, the administration also exploited a loophole in its deal with Congress and let the CIA spend another $6 million for a "regional" program, based outside Nicaragua, to support the UNO campaign, according to U.S. intelligence sources. That money financed training of UNO activists in Costa Rica, paid to fly foreign journalists to Nicaragua to write critical stories against the Sandinistas and supported a radio station in Costa Rica that beamed propaganda into Nicaragua in the months before the election. The sources said the CIA had run another five-million-to-six-million-dollar program in 1989 that paid for building the opposition's political "infrastructure."

A senior administration official said the congressional intelligence committees only restricted the CIA from interfering directly in the campaign. "You could support the election," the official said. "But you could not use any money for campaigning."

But the CW had little interest in how the U.S. policy prevailed. What was important was that the American side finally had won.*

---

*At *Newsweek*, my constant disagreements with the top editors over their unwillingness to peruse the still-secret corners of the Iran-contra scandal and their hostility to reporting evenhandedly the Nicaragua story led to my departure from the magazine in June 1990. The CW had proved too powerful.

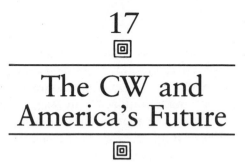

The CW and America's Future

As America nears the twenty-first century, the nation's honest CW might be written as "Good news is we're No. 1. Bad news is it's the wrong No. 1." The globe's unchallenged military superpower, the United States finds itself in a world where that armed might can be reasonably used only against miscreant Third World countries. Where it counts, where the strength of developed nations will be measured in the years to come, the United States suffers glaring weaknesses. Conservative national security expert Edward Luttwak put it well: "The threat is no longer geopolitical, it is geoeconomic."

Compared to its foremost competitors, the United States ranks far from the top in education, transportation, modern industrial production, banking, health care for its citizens, and a variety of other key domestic indicators. Unemployment and underemployment remain stubbornly high; the national debt is spiraling out of control; racial tensions tear at the social fabric; and the stock market could collapse anytime the Japanese bankers fail to show up for a Treasury auction. Even as the United States celebrates its Cold War victory over the Soviet Union, it is a nation in crisis.

Yet, from Washington, awash in foreign interest money and drowning in the trivialized CW, there are few ideas about what can be done. The foreign money has turned many of Washington's power elite into citizens with dual loyalties, one its pocket and the other its countrymen. These insiders insist, of course, that their actions for their clients/pocketbooks are also in the best interests of America.

The lawyers/lobbyists/PR specialists argue that foreign investment is good even if the new factory managers come from overseas; that the world is now in a postindustrial age, in which manufacturing is no longer important anyway; and that it really doesn't matter who holds the money, since we are entering a one-world economy. These arguments would be laughed out of town—if the town were Tokyo, Frankfurt, Seoul or Brussels. Only amid the Washington CW are these rationalizations for the American decline taken seriously.

However comforting to say otherwise, it does matter who makes the products and controls the money. Ask any Third World country that has only sugar or coffee to sell. Bluntly put, a nation that has lost control of its financial institutions and its industrial base is a nation that can be coerced by foreign powers. In time, the United States could become like those developing nations, deeply in hock, who are ordered by the world banking consortia to make massive spending cuts.

The day might not be far off when Japan or another creditor nation could dictate an American action that is in its own interest, not that of the United States. The $3.7 trillion total of red ink, amassed mostly over the past decade, is not just a drag on America's economic recovery. It is a threat to the nation's sovereignty. The punishment for an American refusal could be a boycott of U.S. government securities, which would throw the nation into an economic crisis as the nation's debt would suddenly come due.

But the prevailing CW in Washington sees little of this danger. Isolated from the hard times sweeping the rest of the country, many of Washington's elite live well as handsomely paid consultants and lobbyists to hundreds of foreign companies and governments. Naturally, these power brokers throw great parties, bringing together journalists and government officials for social chats about what's good for the country. While Americans—in cities, suburbs and rural communities—worry about how they will make ends meet, the inhabitants of official Washington are looking toward the next black-tie shindig to honor a conquering general or a catered dinner for a confidential talk with an assistant secretary of state. The CW is insulated from the severity of the nation's fears.

As the nation has sold off its productive capacity to foreigners, the conventional wisdom has kept Washington endlessly entertained, with tidbits about politicians' personal lives, with the excitement over foreign adventures in Latin America or the Middle East, with campaign coverage that cares more about a candidate's polls than his policies. While the CW may grudgingly agree that there must be a better way to elect the nation's leaders, it can't wait to be distracted by the next titillating trivia: the sex scandal, the personality flaw, the financial peccadillo. News companies insist that their test marketing shows that whatever the American people might say, they, too, have more prurient than public interest when it comes to politics.

Even the selection of Supreme Court justices is now governed by the immutable laws of conventional wisdom. When sex-harassment charges exploded against President Bush's Court nominee, Clarence Thomas, on the eve of his scheduled Senate confirmation in October 1991, the nation was transfixed by the sordid spectacle of the televised hearings. The charges by Oklahoma University law professor Anita Hill were, in effect, that Thomas had talked dirty and asked her for dates while she worked for him at the Education Department's civil-rights division, and later at the Equal Employment Opportunities Commission.

Hill, a poised and articulate woman, claimed that Thomas's comments about pornographic movies, boasts about his sexual prowess and a bizarre remark about finding a pubic hair on his Coke can were part of a clumsy come-on. Hill's depiction of Thomas as a man who made inappropriate remarks to pretty female staffers was buttressed by a second woman employee, Angela Wright, who told the Senate that Thomas had inquired about her breast size. Thomas, not surprisingly, denied everything.

One of my longtime sources with close ties to the Thomas crowd at EEOC said that even some of Thomas's friends believed the allegations were true. Yet, the Bush administration, remembering its impressive record for molding the CW, devised a strategy for winning Thomas's confirmation, regardless of the truth. First, Thomas stonewalled the senators' questions. He defiantly rejected "roving questions" that pried into "the sanctity of my bedroom." Although the allegations dealt with conversations in his government office and the employees' cafeteria, not his bedroom, the endlessly polite Democrats agreed not to press the point. Thomas also shifted the discussion from his personal behavior to alleged racism on the part of his accusers. Even though Hill, too, was black, Thomas termed the investigation into her charges "a high-tech lynching for

uppity blacks who in any way deign to think for themselves."
Meanwhile, with the explicit approval of President Bush, the Re-
publicans set out, in the language of political campaigns, "to raise
Anita Hill's negatives."

Republican senators—Alan Simpson, Orrin Hatch and Arlen
Specter—subjected Thomas's accuser to a merciless cross-exami-
nation, zeroing in on minor inconsistencies in her testimony. These
modern-day Clarence Darrows, eyebrows arched suspiciously, wondered why she had accepted a second job under Thomas after his
initial advances. Her explanation that she feared that her young
legal career might end if she stayed at the Education Department,
which President Reagan had vowed to abolish, didn't persuade the
GOP senators. They thought it made more sense that this seem-
ingly sane woman was really a *Fatal Attraction* sicko who wanted
to destroy a good man who had spurned her romantic interest in
him. They, of course, had no evidence to support this supposition,
but it struck a responsive chord with millions of Americans who
had seen the movie.

As the Republicans pulled out their sharp knives, the Democrats on the Senate Judiciary Committee did a creditable imitation
of Michael Dukakis. Instead of carrying the fight to the Republicans, they tried pathetically to appear impartial, giving Thomas an
absurdly generous benefit of the doubt. One of their cleverest
tactics was to ask repeatedly, "What did Anita Hill have to gain
by making these charges?" While the Democrats meant to imply
that her apparent lack of gain should argue for her honesty, the
Republicans stepped forward to fill the void left by the rhetorical
question.

Aided by the Bush Justice Department, the GOP senators
unearthed an obscure legal case that had mentioned "Long Dong
Silver," the porno star allegedly cited by Thomas in his talk with
Hill. The odd point seemed to be that Hill may have read the
ruling and then used it to concoct her conversation with Thomas.
Upping the ante even more, Senator Hatch waved a copy of *The
Exorcist* which contained a reference to a pubic hair in a glass of
gin. Again, the suggestion was that Hill had lifted the pubic-hair-
on-the-Coke-can reference from a book that conveniently also
raised the subliminal issue of a young woman possessed by Satan.

These irrational arguments caused the Republican senators no
visible embarrassment. They had a job to do: discredit Anita Hill

by creating for her a highly negative CW as a vengeful woman who had come forward at the eleventh hour to invent stories about Judge Thomas. The fact that four of Hill's acquaintances testified that she had told them about her troubles with her boss years ago didn't shake the Republicans. They were determined to win Thomas's confirmation at all costs, even if that meant installing a perjurer on the Supreme Court for life.

The Democrats proved again to be either cowardly or politically inept, if not both. They could have asked the corollary to their query about Hill's motive for fabricating her tale: What did Clarence Thomas have to gain by falsely denying that he had behaved improperly toward Hill? The answer, of course, was the Supreme Court, a lifetime job, a high salary, fame, his name in the history books, and the power to change the course of the nation. Not exactly insignificant motives. But the Democrats, proving that sometimes discretion has nothing to do with valor, failed to ask. As the Democrats fumbled, the Bush strategy of tearing down Anita Hill worked.

The *New Republic* trio—Fred Barnes, Morton Kondracke and Charles Krauthammer—were quick to pick up the new conventional wisdom that Anita Hill was a psycho and that Clarence Thomas had gotten a raw deal. On Saturday night, October 12, 1991, as the hearings continued, *The McLaughlin Group* word-wrestled over the meaning of it all. Barnes sounded like a parapsychologist who had been recruited by a desperate police department to analyze the personality of a serial killer.

BARNES: There is emerging here, I think, the growing evidence and I think you couldn't prove it now, but I think it will be credible by the end of these hearings that her motives are these: frustration, revenge and shame. And what has happened, this is my theory anyway, as to the frustration, she comes to Washington, she's not—her plans and hopes and ambitions of working under Clarence Thomas are frustrated. She leaves to a lesser law school in 1983, embarrassed by all that. Along the way, she invents a tale of sexual harassment and tells a couple of friends to hide her embarrassment about not doing well. Okay. Jump to 1991. Her friends remember when Thomas is on the Supreme Court, call her and say, "You

have to tell this to the Senate Judiciary Committee." She
doesn't do it. They tell the committee. The committee
calls her. She knows it's a lie, so she doesn't even tell
them at first. Finally, she tells them. Then she talks to
them more and says, "I want this charge to remain anonymous." Of course, she does. . . .

Finally, *Newsweek*'s Eleanor Clift interrupted Barnes's ram-
blings: "I've heard enough. This is fantasy that you couldn't even
find in *The Exorcist*. To imagine that this woman sits and makes
records to herself concerning sexual harassment is totally absurd,
especially before 1982 when you need an eyewitness in order to
file a suit. And then to go into her head like this and concoct a
fantasy, undermining her, and acting as though you have some
evidence to go on as Clarence Thomas's defense attorney."[1] But
the far-fetched fantasizing of Barnes and others badly damaged
Hill's credibility.

While Barnes played pop psychologist, Kondracke staked out
less fanciful CW territory. Kondracke argued that absent conclusive
evidence against Thomas, he should be confirmed. "There is no
definitive corroborating evidence on either side," Kondracke argued. "So it seems to me . . . if you can't tell on the basis of what
you've heard which one's lying, then you really have to say that
the charges are not proved because he's innocent till proven guilty
and, therefore, senators will have to go back to what they would
have done before these charges came up."[2] That is, confirm
Thomas. Kondracke, of course, was laying a safe bet, since there
is almost never 100 percent certainty of guilt in sex-harassment
cases, short of an outright admission by the culprit. By stonewalling,
Thomas would win, regardless of who was telling the truth.

In his influential column on the *Post*'s opinion page, Krauthammer also rallied to the defense of President Bush's judicial
nominee. He compared Anita Hill's allegation to a scene from a
Perry Mason melodrama where a last-minute witness fingers the
guilty man. Krauthammer's arguments, however, were illogical.
The columnist agreed that Thomas should be disqualified if the
charges were true—and Krauthammer offered little to refute the
allegations, other than the predictably lame questions about Hill.
"Why not raise the complaint when Thomas was a little-known
Reagan administration official?" Krauthammer wondered.[3] "Why

wait until he becomes the most famous man in America and she
has to lay her charges on national television?" The answer should
have been obvious: Thomas was about to be confirmed as a justice
to the United States Supreme Court and Hill, a law professor, had
been asked about her former boss as part of the congressional
investigation into his fitness. Even by Krauthammer's own admission, the Thomas nomination was important to the nation's future
and the charges, if true, would require his rejection.

But Krauthammer pressed on, turning his attack against Congress for discovering the allegations in the first place. "Hill, after
all, says that she was not prepared to come forward with her charges
until Democratic Senate staffers, canvassing for dirt, solicited her
story in early September," he wrote.[4] This played to a popular CW
theme that the "process" was to blame for the disturbing Thomas
hearings. But how could Krauthammer argue simultaneously that
Thomas should be disqualified if the allegations were true and
denounce a Senate staffer for uncovering them? Krauthammer
seemed to favor a comforting know-nothingism for the public: What
the people don't know won't hurt them. As a member of the CW
elite, Krauthammer apparently preferred keeping evidence relevant to the fitness of a Supreme Court judge limited to a small
cadre of insiders.

The hard-hitting White House campaign against Hill and the
bumbling Democratic questioning of Thomas contributed to public-opinion polls that were solidly sympathetic to the Supreme
Court nominee. Krauthammer seized on the poll results to insist
that the case of Clarence Thomas was settled once and for all.
Adopting the ever-popular courtroom trial metaphor, the columnist
contended that "a civilized society needs such conventions [as jury
verdicts] to resolve the unresolvable." For Krauthammer, the opinion polls became the equivalent of a finding by a jury after it had
weighed all the evidence in a criminal trial. But a chink in this
logic was that at the Thomas hearings, there had been no prose-
cution, only aggressive Republican "defense attorneys" and mea-
lymouthed Democrats who cringed at the very thought of
confronting the nominee.

Then, drawing on his past training as a psychiatrist, Krauthammer spun out his own theory about what really happened. "I
have doubts about both stories," Krauthammer wrote. "I find it
hard to believe Hill because sexual abusers tend to be abusive

generally, not just to one person." He conveniently ignored the second woman who had come forward with a similar account of Thomas's crude advances. "But I find it hard to believe Thomas that nothing ever passed between them," he continued. "My theory . . . is that the truth lies not between the two versions but outside them. My guess is that something did indeed happen between Clarence Thomas and Anita Hill, something neither will admit to, something quite licit, perhaps—they were, after all, single adults—that ended very badly."[5] The only trouble with Krauthammer's theory, besides its glaring lack of evidentiary support, is that it would make perjurers out of *both* Hill and Thomas—and one is sitting on the Supreme Court. But the CW never cared much for facts or truth; it is, by definition, Washington's approved version of reality, which of course is nothing like real reality.

With the White House exploiting the messy confusion of the affair and the Democrats afraid to offend anybody, Thomas got a nearly limitless benefit of the doubt—and won confirmation, 52 to 48. Despite all the lingering questions about his competence and honesty, Clarence Thomas took his seat as the ninth justice on the highest court in the land.

Newsweek's *CW Watch* quickly sized up the affair's winners and losers. Among the winners, naturally, was Clarence Thomas, who earned an up arrow and the comment: "Played the race card and it came up aces. Maybe he lied, but, hey, it worked." The Republicans, too, had their arrow pointing skyward: "As Nasty as They Want to Be. But at least these gunslingers know what it takes to win." Although a "loser," Anita Hill won the consolation of an up arrow: "Victim of a high-tech lynching. The CW thinks she's classy and should be a judge." The *CW Watch*'s strongest loathing was for the Democrats, who had so wanted to be liked. With an arrow down, the Democrats' incompetence was disdained as "more mush from the wimps. They can't play hardball even when they own the field."

As the Thomas case had demonstrated, the mechanisms of CW fabricating continued to dominate Washington as the nation entered a new presidential-election cycle in 1992. Manipulation of public opinion, even when done to obscure the truth, still rated highly. Winners got respect; losers contempt. Clucking over unethical means did not outweigh admiration for successful ends. The strategically placed CW masters, pontificating on the talk shows and dominating *The Washington Post*'s influential opinion page, could shape the capital debate by validating the most absurd arguments or repudiating the most obvious facts. Though the country had turned cynical about Washington, it remained vulnerable to cleverly fashioned public-relations campaigns that succeeded in exploiting the nation's cynicism. Personal ridicule was still the most effective way to turn the public against an individual who found himself or herself standing in the way of the White House public-relations steamroller.

But as the United States stumbled toward the new century, there had been a change in the game. Years of trivial government had hamstrung America's ability to keep pace with the rest of the developed world. The country's limping economy was now obvious to everyone—and the U.S. electorate had begun to realize that Washington had sold the country short, trillions of dollars short. Burdened by that debt, much of it owed to foreign competitors, the government had no easy options left to reverse America's steady economic decline, a dropoff that was hurting households nationwide. To Americans, the price for the past decade's pleasant fantasies was suddenly very high and very real. Hourly income was dropping precipitously, steady jobs were disappearing, decent living standards depended on two-earner incomes that stretched families to the breaking point. The ugly reality of the 1990's had shaken many Americans awake, but it was a cold, gray dawn.

Despite America's economic fears, the CW elite of Washington was showing neither the desire nor the ability to confront the nation's problems. The politicians and pundits have neither the right answers nor, it seems, the right questions. They are quite self-satisfied enough to keep on pontificating while the nation's future burns.

But what can be done?

First and foremost, the American people must demand some seriousness from Washington, both from its politicians and its permanent elite of high-paid journalists, bureaucrats and pundits. Politicians must be forced to focus on the nation's fundamental problems and not get away with sleight-of-hand tricks that shift the voters' gaze to trivial issues or opponents' personal traits. If the voters want more issues-oriented campaigns, they should punish those who offer them something else. Politicians live by survival instincts and will continue to run silly, negative campaigns as long as they win. As for Washington's opinion elite, they should not be immune from public criticism when they fall short of the principles of good journalism. Yet, the public should remember that honest reporting sometimes means giving the nation unpleasant information.

Second, beware "symbolic issues," a favorite of the conventional wisdom. The CW loves nothing more than working itself into a condemnatory fury over insignificant personal foibles of politicians, such as the furor about the congressional bank's practice of not charging a penalty when a congressman overdraws his account. While this offense may fall short of cardinal sin, it ranks high with the CW because this indiscretion is deemed "symbolic" of some larger issue: pampered government. So, as punishment, some decent members of Congress have been pilloried and pounded at the polls. But the larger problem of government failing to confront the structural weaknesses of the national economy is obscured by periodic outrage over such petty issues.

Third, the voters should demand that their representatives and presidential candidates offer coherent ideas to confront the daunting challenges to the country's economy. Should more money be spent for highways, railroads, port facilities, schools, research centers—programs that could help American industry compete better with Japan and a unified Europe? Does the military need to remain so large and costly? How can the nation's huge debt to foreign interests be brought back under American control? A demand for straightforward thinking about bread-and-butter issues will make diversionary campaigns more obvious and harder to justify.

Fourth, avoid simplistic solutions. In the early 1980's, the United States rolled the dice and gambled the national treasury on a high-risk policy called supply-side economics. Besides slashing taxes, this policy embraced sweeping deregulation of key industries and financial institutions. The country dreamed of a get-rich-quick solution to sluggish economic growth. The program also promised elimination of the federal deficit which was running at about $35 billion a year and restoration of American military might. The public awoke a decade later to an economy with a devastated productive capacity, a 1,000 percent increase in the annual federal debt, a near-bankrupt banking system and greater insecurity about personal incomes. The military undeniably is stronger but lacks an enemy worthy of its awesome firepower.

Fifth, journalists must return to their profession's principles of objectivity and evenhandedness—and basic reporting. Instead of simply conveying what Washington's in-crowd thinks and says, journalists must find ways to tell the reader or viewer what's actually happening. If that puts the nation's press in an adversarial relationship with the nation's power brokers, so be it. That would be far healthier than today's cozy contacts.

Sixth, to the degree punditry is necessary, the television stations should demand a much broader spectrum of commentators. That would make the debate livelier and more thought-provoking. The current first team of talkers should spend more time on the bench, if not in the showers. Let some fresh thinkers run the offense for a while; they certainly could do no worse. And so what if there's an occasional oddball comment? It's not like the current debate is that uplifting.

Seventh, on foreign-policy issues, simply taking the "American side" is not good enough. Journalists are the eyes and ears of all the American people, those who agree and those who disagree with what the government is doing. The press, therefore, has a profound responsibility to report all the relevant facts, whether many Americans want to hear them or not. The press should not forget that its patriotic role in a constitutional democracy is to tell the truth, as best it can. Editors and reporters must be tougher, even ready to withstand accusations of disloyalty in defense of this principle.

Eighth, when the press does catch the government lying, it should exact a high price. Officials like Elliott Abrams, who willfully misled the American people, should not be allowed on to news programs without a clear warning about their past duplicity. Lies should not be laughed off as a boys-will-be-boys reaction just because it was one of the credentialed elite who deceived the American people. As impolite as it might seem, news shows should ask each "talking head" who's paying his salary. The public has a right to know that.

Ninth, the press must recognize the danger of too much "access." While a reporter obviously wants to know what high-level government officials are planning, he must never forget that his

constitutional allegiance is to the readers, not the politicians. Too
many reporters have allowed the self-serving pursuit of insiderdom
to become an end in itself. That they party, jog, dine and even
vacation with the great and powerful is often the measure of their
journalistic skills. It shouldn't be.

Tenth, reporters and editors should be less interested in the
government-leaked scoop than in the tough story that the government wants to keep hidden. There are, after all, two kinds of stories
in Washington: those the government wants you to get and those
the government doesn't want you to get. By lavishing praise on
the reporters who are first with the stories that the government
wants out, the editors make doubly difficult the already tough task
of uncovering the secrets the government doesn't want the public
to know.

Eleventh, beyond the obvious need to revive the watchdog
role of the press, the nation must find a way to rebuild its pluralism.
Pluralism—the competition of different ideas and values—is the
lifeblood of democracy and the most effective antidote to phony
CWs. Even unpopular ideas must be given space and respect if a
democratic society is to flourish. To silence those points of view
that run counter to the prevailing wisdom is not only anti-intellec-
tual, it's antidemocratic. The public as well as the pundits should
give a fair hearing to the fresh idea or unusual argument.

Twelfth, secret government programs for punishing dissenters
have no place in America or any other democratic country. The
president has more than adequate means of making his case to the
people, without spending taxpayers' money to wage propaganda
campaigns, intimidate whistle-blowers or browbeat journalists into
adopting the administration's point of view.

Thirteenth, Congress must overcome its fear of thirty-second
campaign spots. Only by reestablishing an aggressive watchdog role
vis-à-vis the executive branch can Congress make the constitutional
balance of powers work. Over the past decade, a timid Congress
has readily bought the administration's quack remedies for the
nation's ills. Mindless deregulation did not solve the problem of
excessive red tape: It only unlocked the vaults of American banks.
Indiscriminate tax cuts did not reinvigorate the economy: They
turned over the nation's mortgage paper to foreign competitors.
And use of aggressive military force to solve international problems
did not make the nation more secure: It simply showed off Amer-

ican armed might abroad while U.S. economic muscle withered at home.

Fourteenth, Americans should follow Jonathan Alter's advice about the CW: "Be skeptical about the high and mighty." Rather than punditry, the public must insist on the facts, pure and simple. Only with straightforward information—not carefully crafted public-relations themes—can a nation understand the dangers of the moment and anticipate the challenges ahead. While the institutions of Washington should do a much better job than they have for more than a decade, only an aroused public can counter the careerism and financial self-interest that have made the CW the capital's dominant institution.

As even the citizens of the old Soviet bloc take control of their national destinies by standing up to tanks and constructing barricades, the American people must demand an end to Washington's antidemocratic elitism. They must show the determination to force their elected representatives to change the course of the nation, to refocus the government onto the pressing national priorities—or to get out of the way and let someone else do it. They must insist that the constitutionally protected news media earn its constitutional protection by digging for the truth even if that means fewer invites to Georgetown cocktail parties.

In short, the American people must insist that Washington take the actions needed to restore U.S. competitiveness in the world. Americans must show that they can make democracy work. They must make clear that they will tolerate nothing less. They must demonstrate that they will not be fooled again.

Notes

INTRODUCTION

1. Ellen Hume, "Why the Press Blew the S&L Scandal," *The New York Times*, May 24, 1990, A25.
2. Guy Gugliotta and Michael Isikoff, "U.S. Let BCCI Probe Languish, Hill Told," *The Washington Post*, August 2, 1991, A1.
3. Chuck Conconi, "Personalities," *The Washington Post*, September 24, 1990, B3.
4. Dan Balz, "Report Finds Americans Angry at Political System," *The Washington Post*, June 5, 1991, A4.
5. Kevin Goldman, "Test for TV: Dodging Gulf Propaganda," *The Wall Street Journal*, August 28, 1990, B1.
6. Pat Choate, *Agents of Influence* (New York: Alfred A. Knopf, 1990), p. 15.

CHAPTER 1 THE CW RUNS FOR PRESIDENT

1. Jonathan Alter and Mickey Kaus, "Reign of Errors," *Newsweek*, October 31, 1988, p. 22.
2. Alan Hirsch, *Talking Heads* (New York: St. Martin's Press, 1991), p. 194.
3. Eric Alterman, "Washington's Loudest Mouth," *The Washington Post Magazine*, March 18, 1990, p. 14.

4. Don Kowet, "MOR-TONE! Kondracke Stumbles into the Truth," *The Washington Times*, May 20, 1991, E1.
5. Timothy Crouse, *The Boys on the Bus* (New York: Ballantine Books, 1974), p. 46.
6. Howard Fineman, "Gary Hart: A Candidate in Search of Himself," *Newsweek*, April 13, 1987, p. 25.
7. Excerpts from Senate Foreign Relations Committee confirmation hearing, "The Interrogation of Justice Clark," *The Washington Post*, February 15, 1981, C3.
8. Alter and Kaus, op. cit., p. 22.
9. Roger Simon, *Road Show* (New York: Farrar, Straus & Giroux, 1990), p. 213.

CHAPTER 2 THE CW TAKES THE WHITE HOUSE

1. "The Great TV Shout-Out," *Newsweek*, February 8, 1988, p. 20.
2. Ibid., p. 24.
3. "Bush Battles the 'Wimp Factor,' " *Newsweek*, October 19, 1987, p. 28.
4. Roger Simon, op. cit., p. 4.
5. "Guns for Drugs?" *Newsweek*, May 23, 1988, p. 22.
6. Tom Wicker, "Bush and Noriega," *The New York Times*, April 29, 1988, A39.
7. John Dinges and Saul Landau, *Assassination on Embassy Row* (New York: Pantheon Books, 1980), p. 246.
8. "How the Media Blew It," *Newsweek*, November 21, 1988, p. 24.

CHAPTER 3 THE GOVERNING CW

1. Helen Thomas, "Bush Shares His Limo with Reporters Who Go Jogging First," UP International, *Chattanooga News-Free Press*, April 7, 1991, B6.
2. "Bush Tells 'Slovenly' Press to Shape Up," *The Washington Post*, May 13, 1990, A25.
3. Jude Wanniski, *1989 Media Guide* (Morristown, N.J.: Polyconomics Inc., 1989), p. 118.

4. Ann Devroy, "Quayle Buys a (Blush) Souvenir," *The Washington Post*, March 12, 1990, C1.
5. Joel Achenbach, "Quayle, Par for the Course," *The Washington Post*, May 7, 1991, B1.
6. Charles Krauthammer, "Dan Quayle's Bum Rap," *The Washington Post*, May 10, 1991, A23.

CHAPTER 4 THE CW GOES TO WAR

1. William Branigan, "Noriega Appointed 'Maximum Leader,' " *The Washington Post*, December 16, 1989, A21.
2. "Opposition Leader in Panama Rejects a Peace Offer from Noriega," Reuters dispatch, *The New York Times*, December 17, 1989, p. 5.
3. Michael Isikoff, "U.S. 'Power' on Abductions Detailed," *The Washington Post*, August 14, 1991, A14.
4. "Objective Journalists or State Propagandists?" *Extra!*, a publication of Fairness and Accuracy in Reporting, January–February 1990, p. 6.
5. Bob Woodward, *The Commanders* (New York: Simon & Schuster, 1991), p. 157.
6. Sara Fritz and James Gerstenzang, "Force 'Never Ruled Out' in Panama," *The Los Angeles Times*, October 5, 1989, p. 20.
7. *The McLaughlin Group*, taped on October 6, 1989.
8. *The McLaughlin Group*, taped on October 13, 1989.
9. Woodward, op. cit., p. 129.
10. Cynthia J. Arnson, *Crossroads* (New York: Pantheon, 1989), p. 61.
11. Edward Walsh, "Kin of Slain Nuns Denounce Haig for 'Smear Campaign,' " *The Washington Post*, March 20, 1981, A17.
12. Lee Hockstader, "In Panama, Civilian Deaths Remain an Issue," *The Washington Post*, October 6, 1990, A23.
13. Michael R. Gordon with Andrew Rosenthal, "U.S. Invasion: Many Weeks of Rehearsals," *The New York Times*, December 24, 1989, A1.
14. *Extra!*, op. cit., p. 6.
15. *MacNeil/Lehrer Newshour*, December 22, 1989.
16. CBS News, *60 Minutes*, September 30, 1990.

17. Don Oberdorfer, "U.S. Officials Defend Panama's Democracy as 'on Track.'" *The Washington Post*, July 31, 1991, A6.
18. William Branigan, "50 Kilos of Cocaine Turn Out to Be Tamales," *The Washington Post*, January 23, 1990, A22.
19. Lee Hockstader, "In Year Since U.S. Invasion, Panama's Problems Mount," *The Washington Post*, December 16, 1990, A51.
20. James S. Henry, "Panama: Dirty Business as Usual," *The Washington Post Outlook*, July 28, 1991, C1.
21. Ibid.
22. Michael Isikoff, "Drug Activity in Panama Has Increased, GAO Says," *The Washington Post*, July 23, 1991, A3.
23. Congressman John Conyers, Jr., "Whatever Happened to Panama?" *The Washington Post*, July 29, 1991, A11.

CHAPTER 5 CW, NORIEGA, CONTRAS AND DRUGS

1. Seymour M. Hersh, "Panama Strongman Said to Trade in Drugs, Arms and Illicit Money," *The New York Times*, June 12, 1986, A1.
2. Frederick Kempe, "The Noriega Files," *Newsweek*, January 15, 1990, p. 19.
3. Mark Cook and Jeff Cohen, in *Extra!*, op. cit., p. 5.
4. Dan Raviv and Yossi Melman, *Every Spy a Prince* (Boston: Houghton-Mifflin Company, 1990), p. 189.
5. Senate Foreign Relations Subcommittee on Terrorism, Narcotics and International Operations, "Drugs, Law Enforcement and Foreign Policy," December, 1988, p. 84.
6. Ibid., p. 85.
7. Ibid., p. 97.
8. Ibid., p. 92.
9. Ibid.
10. Ibid., p. 94.
11. Ibid.
12. Public Prosecutors' Investigation of La Penca Case, San José, Costa Rica, December 26, 1989.
13. Ibid.

CHAPTER 6 THE CW FIGHTS A MIDDLE EAST BAD GUY

1. Anthony Sampson, *The Seven Sisters*, revised 4th ed. (New York: Bantam, 1991), p. 5.
2. Caryle Murphy, "Iraq Accuses Kuwait of Plot to Steal Oil, Depress Prices," *The Washington Post*, July 19, 1990, A25.
3. Pierre Salinger and Eric Laurent, *Secret Dossier: The Hidden Agenda Behind the Gulf War* (New York: Penguin, 1991), p. 67.
4. Ibid., p. 83.
5. Ibid.
6. Christopher Dickey, "Kuwait, Inc." *Vanity Fair*, November 1990, p. 156.
7. Sampson, op. cit., p. 1.
8. Ibid., pp. 2–3.
9. William Safire, "Iraq's U.S. Support," *The New York Times*, May 4, 1990, A35.
10. Charles Krauthammer, "Nightmare from the '30s," *The Washington Post*, July 27, 1990, A27.
11. Ibid.
12. Carla Hall, "Don't Call It Courage," *The Washington Post*, August 17, 1984, B1.
13. Ibid.
14. Charles Krauthammer, "Eyeless in the Gulf," *The Washington Post*, August 7, 1987, A23.
15. Stephen S. Rosenfeld, "Indonesia 1965: Year of Living Cynically?" *The Washington Post*, July 13, 1990, A21.
16. *The McLaughlin Group*, taped on July 27, 1990.
17. "Excerpts from Iraqi Transcript of Meeting with U.S. Envoy," *The New York Times*, September 23, 1990, p. 19.
18. Ibid.
19. Don Oberdorfer, "Glaspie Says Saddam Is Guilty of Deception," *The Washington Post*, March 21, 1991, A23.
20. David Hoffman, "U.S. Envoy Conciliatory to Saddam," *The Washington Post*, July 12, 1991, A1.
21. *The McLaughlin Group*, taped on August 3, 1990.
22. Ibid.
23. Ibid.
24. *The McLaughlin Group*, taped on August 10, 1990.

25. Jim Hoagland, "A Real Arab Awakening," *The Washington Post*, August 16, 1990, A23.

26. Sharif S. Elmusa, "Take Saddam Seriously," *The Washington Post*, August 23, 1990, A25.

27. E. J. Dionne, Jr., "Conservatives Are Leading Murmurs of Dissent to Bush Actions in Mideast," *The Washington Post*, August 24, 1990, A29; Luttwak was speaking on ABC's *Nightline*, August 21, 1990.

28. Rowland Evans and Robert Novak, "The Arab Solution," *The Washington Post*, August 29, 1990, A25.

29. Eleanor Randolph and Howard Kurtz, "Rosenthal Attacks Buchanan," *The Washington Post*, September 15, 1990, D1.

30. A. M. Rosenthal, "Forgive Them Not," *The New York Times*, September 14, 1990, A33.

31. Howard Kurtz, "Pat Buchanan & the Jewish Question," *The Washington Post*, September 20, 1990, D1.

32. Ibid.

33. *The McLaughlin Group*, taped on September 14, 1990.

34. *The McLaughlin Group*, taped on November 9, 1990.

35. Ibid.

36. Charles Krauthammer, "Bush's March Through Washington," *The Washington Post*, March 1, 1991, A15.

37. Ibid.

CHAPTER 7 THE CW, THE AL-SABAHS AND THE CIA

1. Thomas L. Friedman, "Among War's Problems: It Would Be a Hard Sell," *The New York Times*, November 11, 1990, E3.

2. Christopher Dickey, op. cit., p. 156.

3. Ibid., p. 158.

4. Deposition of Robert M. Sensi, October 10–11, 1987, U.S. District Court for the District of Columbia, Civil Action 86-2542, p. 96.

5. Ibid., p. 91.

6. Ibid., pp. 97–98.

7. Ibid., p. 98.

8. Ibid., p. 163.

9. Ibid., p. 334.

10. Ibid., pp. 475–476.

11. Ibid., p. 499.
12. Ibid., p. 201.
13. Ibid., p. 196.
14. Ibid.
15. Ibid., pp. 198–199.
16. Ibid., p. 470.
17. *The McLaughlin Group*, taped on January 18, 1991.

CHAPTER 8 CW AND PEACE

1. "Was It Worth It?" *Time* cover, August 5, 1991.
2. Michael Kramer, "Kuwait: Back to the Past," *Time*, August 5, 1991, p. 33.
3. Susan Okie, "Iraqi Children Face Postwar Disease Threat," *The Washington Post*, May 22, 1991, A23.
4. Salinger and Laurent, op. cit., p. 96.
5. Woodward, op. cit., p. 234.
6. Salinger and Laurent, op. cit., p. 106.
7. Ibid., p. 113.
8. Ibid., p. 45.
9. Ibid., p. 127.
10. Knut Royce, *Newsday*, August 29, 1990.
11. Knut Royce, "U.S. Ignored Secret Offer," *Newsday*, August 30, 1990.
12. Thomas L. Friedman, "No Compromise on Kuwait, Bush Says," *The New York Times*, October 24, 1990, A10.
13. John M. Goshko, "U.S. Rejects Idea of Iraq Land Deal," *The Washington Post*, October 17, 1990, A1.

CHAPTER 9 CW VERSUS THE VIETNAM SYNDROME

1. Rick Atkinson and Ann Devroy, "Bush: Iraq Won't Decide Timing of Ground War," *The Washington Post*, February 2, 1991, A1.
2. Jim Hoagland, "America's Mettle," *The Washington Post*, September 2, 1990, B7.
3. Rowland Evans and Robert Novak, "No Vietnam Syndrome," *The Washington Post*, February 25, 1991, A9.

4. William Claiborne and Caryle Murphy, "Retreat Down Highway of Doom," *The Washington Post*, March 2, 1991, A1.
5. E. J. Dionne, Jr., "Kicking the Vietnam Syndrome," *The Washington Post*, March 4, 1991, A1.
6. *The McLaughlin Group*, taped on March 1, 1991.
7. Rowland Evans and Robert Novak, "On Being Wrong," *The Washington Post*, March 8, 1991, A21.
8. "Conventional Wisdom," *Newsweek*, March 11, 1991, p. 8.
9. *Extra!*, May 1991, p. 5.
10. Linda Wheeler and Patricia Davis, "Love Affair on the Mall: People and War Machines," *The Washington Post*, June 9, 1991, A26.
11. Phil McCombs and Dana Thomas, "Sharp Barbs & Witty Ditties," *The Washington Post*, March 25, 1991, C1.
12. Ibid., C10.
13. Dana Thomas, "The Boys' Night Out," *The Washington Post*, March 22, 1991, C1.
14. Charles Krauthammer, "Bless Our Pax Americana," *The Washington Post*, March 22, 1991, A25.
15. Charles Krauthammer, "In Praise of Parades," *The Washington Post*, May 24, 1991, A23.

CHAPTER 10 CW AND THE CIA DIRECTOR

1. Memo from Walter Raymond to NSC adviser William Clark, August 9, 1983.
2. Michael T. Klare and Peter Kornbluh, *Low-Intensity Warfare* (New York: Pantheon Books, 1988), pp. 14–15.
3. Alfonso Chardy, *The Miami Herald*, July 19, 1987.

CHAPTER 11 CW, THE SANDINISTAS AND BUZZ WORDS

1. Karen DeYoung, "Nicaraguan Junta Assumes Rule in Jubilant Managua," *The Washington Post*, July 21, 1979, A1.
2. Roy Gutman, *Banana Diplomacy* (New York: Simon & Schuster, 1988), p. 86.
3. Ian Black, "OAS Press Official Who Disputed Reagan Put on Special Leave," *The Washington Post*, July 23, 1983, A14.

4. Robert Parry, "CIA Officers Reportedly Plotted Ouster of Nicaraguan Regime," AP wire, February 23, 1985.
5. Robert Parry, "CIA Reportedly Attacked Nicaraguan Ports," AP wire, April 18, 1984.
6. Robert Parry, AP wire, December 20, 1984.
7. Text of an address by the president on Central America, May 9, 1984.
8. Text of an address by the president to the nation, March 16, 1986.
9. Robert Parry, "Refugee Fear Key to Policy," AP wire, August 12, 1983.
10. Ibid.
11. Ibid.
12. "The Case for the Contras," *The New Republic*, March 24, 1986, p. 7.
13. Ibid., pp. 8–9.
14. Paul Lewis, "World Court Supports Nicaragua After U.S. Rejected Judges' Role," *The New York Times*, June 28, 1986, A1.

CHAPTER 12 CW AND THE MIGHTY WURLITZER

1. Mark Hertsgaard, *On Bended Knee* (New York: Farrar, Straus & Giroux, 1988), p. 191.
2. Ibid.
3. Jefferson Morley and Tina Rosenberg, "The Real Heroes of Contragate," *Rolling Stone*, September 10, 1987, p. 48.
4. Buzenberg's speech was given on September 9, 1985.
5. Staff Report: State Department and Intelligence Community Involvement in Domestic Activities Related to the Iran/Contra Affair. House Committee on Foreign Affairs, September 7, 1988, p. 25.

CHAPTER 13 CW AND CONTRA-DICTIONS

1. Christopher Dickey, *With the Contras* (New York: Touchstone Books, 1987), p. 219.
2. Ibid., p. 248.
3. Brian Barger, "CIA Manual Said Aimed at Contra Abuses," *The Washington Post*, October 31, 1984, A1.

4. Robert Parry, AP wire, December 2, 1984.

5. Robert Parry, AP wire, October 14, 1984.

6. Robert Parry, AP wire, October 17, 1984.

7. Robert Parry, AP wire, October 20, 1984.

8. Dan Noyes and Ellen Morris, "The Trouble with Father Tom," *San Francisco Examiner, Image* magazine, November 8, 1987, p. 14.

9. Fred Barnes, "The Sandinista Lobby," *The New Republic,* January 20, 1986, p. 11.

10. Fred Barnes, "Contra for a Day," *The New Republic,* April 7, 1986, p. 13.

11. Marjorie Miller and Doyle McManus, "Rebels Jail Top Officer for Murder," *The Los Angeles Times,* January 24, 1987, p. 1.

12. Robert Parry, "Contra Link Charged in Archbishop Slaying," AP wire, March 21, 1985.

13. Robert Parry, "Was CIA Fooled by Nicaraguan Rebels?" AP wire, January 28, 1985.

CHAPTER 14 CW AND A MAN NAMED NORTH

1. Robert Parry, "Reagan Reportedly Cleared Secret Contra Aid Plan," AP wire, October 8, 1985.

2. Robert Parry, "Democrats Demand Documents on White House–Contra Ties," AP wire, October 9, 1985.

3. Brian Barger and Robert Parry, "Reports Link Nicaraguan Rebels to Cocaine Trafficking," AP wire, December 20, 1985.

4. Robert Parry, "GAO Says US Cannot Account for Most of Contra Aid," AP wire, March 4, 1986.

5. Brian Barger and Robert Parry, "FBI Reportedly Probes Contras on Drugs, Guns," AP wire, April 10, 1986.

6. Michael Barone and Grant Ujifusa, *Almanac of American Politics–1992* (Washington, D.C. National Journal, 1991), p. 569.

7. "Conventional Wisdom Watch," *Newsweek,* August 5, 1991.

8. Brian Barger and Robert Parry, "CIA Officer Said to Play Role in Pastora's Downfall," AP wire, May 29, 1986.

9. Robert Parry and Brian Barger, "White House Said to Manage Private Contra Aid," AP wire, June 10, 1986.

10. "The World According to Oliver North," *The Washington Post*, December 21, 1986.
11. Report of the President's Special Review Board, February 26, 1987, B-151.

CHAPTER 15 CW AND THE COVER-UP

1. Ross Gelbspan, *Boston Globe*, June 18, 1988.
2. Ross Gelbspan, "Texan Says North Set FBI on Foes of Administration," *Boston Globe*, February 29, 1988, p. 3.
3. Report of the Congressional Committees Investigating the Iran-Contra Affair, November 1987, p. 113.
4. *The New York Times*, May 6, 1986, A6. Patrick Korten was not identified in the *Times* article, but he confirmed to me later that he was the unnamed spokesman.
5. *Evans and Novak*, CNN, October 11, 1986.
6. Robert Parry and Brian Barger, "Reagan's Shadow CIA," *The New Republic*, November 24, 1986, p. 23.

CHAPTER 16 CW, BREAKTHROUGH AND COVER-UP REDUX

1. Robert Earl Deposition, May 2, 1987, Report of the Congressional Committees Investigating the Iran-Contra Affair, Appendix B, Vol. 9, p. 732.
2. Ibid., p. 627.
3. Ibid., p. 624.
4. Robert Parry, "North Reportedly Managed Money for Contras," AP wire, January 7, 1987.
5. Robert Parry, AP wire, February 1, 1987.
6. Report of the President's Special Review Board, op. cit., p. IV-10.
7. Ibid, p. IV-12.
8. "Covert Aid and the Church," *Newsweek*, June 15, 1987, p. 27.
9. Report of the Congressional Committees Investigating the Iran-Contra Affair, op. cit., p. 97.

CHAPTER 17 THE CW AND AMERICA'S FUTURE

1. *The McLaughlin Group*, October 12, 1991.
2. Ibid.
3. Charles Krauthammer, "Clarence Thomas and the Decline of Congress," *The Washington Post*, October 11, 1991, A27.
4. Charles Krauthammer, "The Case of Hill v. Thomas," *The Washington Post*, October 18, 1991, A21.
5. Ibid.

INDEX